MARKETING RESEARCH AND MODELING: PROGRESS AND PROSPECTS

A Tribute to Paul E. Green

INTERNATIONAL SERIES
IN QUANTITATIVE MARKETING

Series Editor:
Jehoshua Eliashberg
The Wharton School
University of Pennsylvania
Philadelphia, Pennsylvania USA

MARKETING RESEARCH AND MODELING: PROGRESS AND PROSPECTS
A Tribute to Paul E. Green

edited by

Yoram (Jerry) Wind
The Wharton School, University of Pennsylvania

Paul E. Green
The Wharton School, University of Pennsylvania

KLUWER ACADEMIC PUBLISHERS
Boston / Dordrecht / New York / London

Distributors for North, Central and South America:
Kluwer Academic Publishers
101 Philip Drive
Assinippi Park
Norwell, Massachusetts 02061 USA
Telephone (781) 871-6600
Fax (781) 681-9045
E-Mail <kluwer@wkap.com>
Distributors for all other countries:
Kluwer Academic Publishers Group
Post Office Box 17
3300 AH Dordrecht, THE NETHERLANDS
Tel: +31 (0) 78 657 60 00
Fax: +31 (0) 78 657 64 74

E-Mail <services@wkap.nl>

  Electronic Services <http://www.wkap.nl>

Marketing research and modeling : progress and prospects : a tribute to Paul E. Green/
   edited by Yoram (Jerry) Wind, Paul E. Green.
       p.cm.—(International series in quantitative marketing ; 14)
    Book stemming from a conference held in May 2002.
    Includes bibliographical references and index.
    ISBN 1-4020-7596-0 (alk.paper)
       1.   Marketing research—Methodology. 2. Marketing—Mathematical models. 3. Green,
    Paul E. 4. Conjoint analysis (Marketing) I. Green, Paul E. II. Wind, Yoram. III. Series.

HF5415.2.M35557 2004
658.8'3—dc22   2003061984

Permission for books published in Europe: permissions@wkap.nl -
Permissions for books published in the United States of America: permissions@wkap.com
Printed on acid-free paper.
Printed in the United States of America

The Publisher offers discounts on this book for course use and bulk purchases.
For further information, send email to <kluwer@wkap.com> .

Paul E. Green

Dedication

This book is dedicated to three groups:

- *the innovators from a wide variety of disciplines who have contributed powerful new methods and techniques,*

- *the academics and industry consultants who have adapted and extended these tools to marketing research and modeling, and*

- *the courageous business leaders who have been willing to apply these new tools in responding to business challenges.*

Contents

Acknowledgements

We would like to thank all who participated – in person or by video or letter – in the tribute dinner and conference in honor of Paul Green in May 2002 that led to the creation of this book.

Among these participants were many of Paul's protégés and collaborators over the years. These include former Ph.D. students Pradeep Bansal, Max Bosch, Frank J. Carmone, Wayne DeSarbo, Susan Douglas, Chaim Ehrman, James Emshoff, Marcia Flicker, Bari Harlam, Kris Helsen, Michael Hess, Arun Jain, John Keon, Jinho Kim, Vicki Morwitz, Les Neidell, Ambar Rao, Robert Rothberg, William Rudelius, and Joel Steckel. There were other university co-authors, including Manoj Agarwal, Gerald Albaum, Phipps Arabie, Douglas Carroll, Martin Christopher, Peter FitzRoy, Ron Frank, Irv Gross, Richard Harshman, Pardeep K. Kedia, James Lattin, Peter Lenk, Jay Minas, Rishiyur R. Nikhil, Vithala Rao, Cathy Schaffer, Stan Shapiro, Judy Shea, Scott Smith, U.N. Umesh, James Wiley, and Mark R. Young. There were industry co-authors, including Shahrzad Amirani, Anil Chaturvedi, Leo Fox, Marshall Greenberg, John McMennamin, Mila Montemayor, Karen Patterson, Patrick Robinson, Jeffry Savitz, Bruce Shandler, Terry Vavra, and Bill Neal.

We also were joined by many colleagues from the University of Pennsylvania. Participants from the Wharton Marketing Department included Scott Armstrong, David Bell, Lisa Bolton, Eric Bradlow, George Day, Jehoshua Eliashberg, Peter Fader, Gavan Fitzsimons, Teck Ho, Steve Hoch, Wesley Hutchinson, Barbara Kahn, Len Lodish, Marcia Longworth, Mary Frances Luce, Robert Meyer, Amy Myers, Terry Oliva, Jagmohan Raju, Americus Reed II, Dave Reibstein, Dave Schmittlein, Paul Schoemaker, Christophe Van den Bulte, Scott Ward, Patti Williams, and Z. John Zhang. In addition to Dean Patrick Harker, other participants from Wharton included Tony Adams, Elizabeth Bailey, Stanley Baiman, Marshall Blume, Morris Cohen, Stew DeBruicker, Marshall Fisher, Michael Gibbons, Joseph Gyourko, Paul Kleindorfer, Jean Lemaire, Mark

Pauly, Paul Shaman, Kenneth Shrophire, and Harbir Singh. Several distinguished emeritus professors also welcomed Paul to their ranks, including Russ Ackoff, Charles Goodman, Morris Hamburg, and Bill Kelly.·

We were joined by faculty from institutions around the globe, an indication of the extent of Paul's impact and reputation, including Greg Allenby, Frank Bass, Randy Batsell, Bob Blattberg, Ray Burke, John Farley, Wolfgang Gaul, John Hauser, Joel Huber, Wagner Kamakura, Philip Kotler, Don Lehmann, John Little, Jordan Louviere, Vijay Mahajan, Ajay Manrai, Alan Montgomery, Don Morrison, Rich Oliver, Arvind Rangaswamy, Tom Roberton, Bill Ross, Peter Rossi, Roland Rust, Seenu Srinivasan, Glen Urban, John Walsh, Brian Wansink, Michel Wedel, Russ Winer, Gordon Wyner, and Andy Zoltner

We were also pleased to be joined by industry and other participants including Lynd D. Bacon, Nana Banerjee, Steve Cohen, Bruce Cowgill, Stacey Cowgill, Liz Dunn, Joe Goldstein, Juliet Goodfriend, Michael Halpert, Rich Johnson, Irene Lange, Len Laufer, Howard Moskowitz, William Moult, Donna Peters, Paul Saatsoglou, Harprit Singh, and Timothy Sprik.

Finally, we were joined by current Ph.D. students Eric Eisenstein, Anita Elberse, Ye Hu, Narayan Janakiraman, George Knox, Noah Lim, Jane Machin, Elizabeth Miller, Andrea Morales, Andres Musalem, Ritesh Saini, Orkun Sak, Sangyoung Song, David Schweidel, Yusong Wang, and Shengui Zhao.

We are grateful to the Wharton Marketing Department and the SEI Center for Advanced Studies in Management for their support of this project. Finally, we would like to acknowledge the writing assistance of Robert Gunther, the many contributions of John Carstens in scanning, editing and formatting the book, and the skilled editing of Nancy Bouldin. This project would not have made it into print but for their untiring efforts. We also appreciate the administrative support of Michele Faulls, Marcia Longworth, and Patricia Adelman in addressing many and various details of organizing the conference and developing the book.

INTRODUCTION

Paul Green and a Brief History
of Marketing Research

Unraveling the tradeoffs between personal memoir and intellectual history in telling Paul Green's story is perhaps a problem worthy of the sophisticated research tools that he pioneered. He has been so directly involved in the development of the field of marketing research over more than four decades that it is difficult to separate the life of Paul Green from the story of the field. A retrospective on marketing research and the man who shaped it must go hand in hand. A conference to celebrate Green's intellectual contributions and the development of the field, such as the one to celebrate his 40th anniversary at Wharton in May of 2002 – an event that launched this book – inevitably turns into a personal celebration of Paul Green himself. He is a pioneer in marketing research, a prolific scholar, and a mentor to the next generation of scholars, not to mention an accomplished pianist.

In weighing the "partworths" of these two aspects of the book – personal biography and intellectual history – we give a bit more emphasis to his contributions to the progress of marketing research than to his personal story. But to set the stage in this introduction, we take a "full profile" approach, exploring the man, his work, and the evolution of the discipline simultaneously. This "multidimensional" portrait is admittedly idiosyncratic and incomplete, although there are number of excellent histories of the field, many written by Green himself, as noted in the following chapters and the appendix of this book. Through this sketch, we hope to trace the interwoven paths of Green's career and the evolution of marketing research.

The field of marketing research has grown considerably in rigor and stature during Green's more than four decades of involvement. The emeritus professor at the Wharton School has played a central role in the development and evolution of powerful tools such as conjoint analysis, multivariate data analysis, multidimensional scaling, and the application of Bayesian statistics.

Called "the father of conjoint analysis," Green is one of the most published and widely cited researchers in the field of marketing, with more than 200 books and articles. He has also made many direct contributions to marketing practice that have proven the business value of the theoretical concepts and tools he developed and refined. He has used conjoint analysis to help Marriott create the original concept for its Courtyard hotels for business travelers, AT&T's first cellular phone system, the E-Z Pass automated toll collection system, and the design and pricing for IBM's Risc 6000 and AS400 computer systems. Green also has used cluster analysis to help develop AT&T's "Reach out and touch someone" campaign and applied multidimensional scaling to issues such as Life cereal's "Mikey" ad campaign and Coca-Cola's "It's the real thing" slogan. His projects have ranged from technology to drugs to ladies panties (to assess the importance of DuPont brands). Green's students have applied his work even more broadly in their own corporations and in developing commercial software for conjoint analysis.

But at the heart of this work is the life story of a talented and persistent researcher. Paul Green arrives early and keeps a steady stream of new research flowing out of his Wharton office, most often with long-time collaborator Abba Krieger, professor of statistics at Wharton, who has described himself as "Paul Green's sidekick." Green draws upon his own varied background in statistics, operations research, and other disciplines to develop innovative solutions to marketing research challenges.

In this book, leaders in marketing research explore key concepts and current challenges in the field. But we begin with the story of the man whose life is inextricably bound to the progress of marketing research during its formative years in the last half of the 20th century. We first meet Paul Green.

"That's Paul Green"

To meet the soft-spoken and thoughtful Paul Green in the hallway at the Wharton School, you probably would not be immediately aware of his quiet power, prominence, and profound influence on the field of marketing research.

In remarks shared at the anniversary conference (included in Chapter 12 with the personal reflections of other colleagues), David Schmittlein, professor of marketing and deputy dean at Wharton, describes the experience of bumping into Green in the hallway and listening to him discuss his current research:

> This scene is one of contrast, Paul calmly, logically, smoothly articulating a point of algebra, or data manipulation, or probability models – me in near panic, holding on by my fingernails to

the ideas that are flying by with the speed – and yes, the elegance – of the Concorde. Scary – but exhilarating.

Years earlier, Schmittlein, then a newly minted Ph.D. graduate from Columbia, first met Green and was "struck by the force of Paul's intellect and graced by the warmth of his humanity." Around that same time, Schmittlein also was exposed to another side of the multi-faceted Green at a doctoral consortium in Madison, Wisconsin. Standing with friends, Schmittlein remarked upon the wonderful piano player in the corner.

"You don't know who that is?" remarked a colleague. "That's Paul Green."

A Random Walk into Academia

Paul Green came into marketing by what he describes as a "random walk." This walk led from chemistry to mathematics to operations research to statistics and across a dozen years in business practice before finally joining the marketing faculty at the University of Pennsylvania's Wharton School.

Returning from World War II in the fall of 1946, Green entered the University of Pennsylvania's School of Arts and Sciences on the GI Bill. He seemed destined to be a chemist, which had been his passion since fifth grade, punctuated by a near-death experience in his parents' attic involving a Tesla high-voltage coil when he accidentally brushed against a water pipe.

To Green's dismay, Penn's chemistry courses were reserved for GI's in pre-med, so by this chance his career veered away from chemistry to the less perilous study of mathematics and economics. In college, he was already pursuing his lifelong musical interest. He helped to pay his way through college by performing a few nights a week at local bars and bistros, among the few venues of his illustrious career that he could accurately describe as being "of dubious reputation."

Green did not go directly into academia. When he graduated in 1950, he went to work for Sun Oil Company in Philadelphia as a statistical research analyst. At the same time, he earned his master's degree at Penn in statistics, working with Simon Kuznets, who was later to win the Nobel Prize in economics. Three years later, Green switched from petroleum to steel, joining Lukens Steel Company in its marketing research department. While there, he began working in the fledgling field of operations research, studying with West Churchman and Russ Ackoff, and using the insights to tackle scheduling, inventory control, and simulation problems for the steel manufacturer. With an ever-curious mind, he entered Penn's doctoral program in statistics, a pursuit that he continued after he moved from Lukens to DuPont. In 1961, eight years after completing his master's degree, he received his Ph.D. in statistics from Penn.

A Test of Bayesian Analysis

His doctoral dissertation advisor Morris Hamburg recalls that he was intrigued when Green came to him with a proposal to apply a relatively new approach in statistics, Bayesian analysis, to real-world marketing challenges at DuPont. Hamburg describes one application of the work:

> DuPont, at that time, produced an industrial end-use fiber for which top management was considering a price decrease. The decision problem was quite complex. Three other firms produced this fiber at identical prices to DuPont, and product quality and service among all four producers were comparable. There were four interrelated market segments. Furthermore, there was a competitive fiber produced by six other firms in the four market segments. Paul designed and carried out a complex Bayesian decision analysis of four pricing alternatives. Most of the data consisted of informed judgments by sales management personnel. One of the price decreases emerged from the analysis as the recommended best course of action.

The work on Green's dissertation, "Some Intra-firm Applications of Bayesian Decision Theory to Problems in Business Planning," reflected key interests that would shape Green's future work. As Hamburg notes:

> After completion of his thesis, Paul had a phenomenally prolific run of publications in a variety of fields using Bayesian decision theory and analysis. His work was extremely widely cited, and he developed a well-deserved reputation as an outstanding researcher.

> However, with his fertile and creative mind, Paul went on to make seminal contributions to the other areas of modeling and applications ... such as multivariate data analysis, multi-dimensional scaling and clustering, and conjoint and related analyses. Nevertheless, I believe that it is fair to say that Paul carried over, throughout the succeeding decades, concepts and techniques that he dealt with in his doctoral dissertation, such as the multiplicity of goals in decision making under uncertainty, alternative concepts of optimization, and the intellectual wrestling match that takes place in the application of normative theories to real-world problems, Von Neumann-Morgenstern utility functions, tradeoffs and sensitivity analysis.

In his doctoral research, Green also demonstrated his lifelong interest in applied theory, which he continued even after he left DuPont to start a new career in academia.

Meeting Wroe Alderson and the Origins of Marketing Research

During his last years in Penn's doctoral program, Green sat in on lectures by Wroe Alderson of the Marketing Department, who was *the* leading figure in marketing theory from the early 1950s until his death in 1965. Alderson started the annual Marketing Theory seminars that defined the frontiers of the field and authored the influential book *Marketing Behavior and Executive Action* in 1957. Alderson set an example of combining theory and practice through his own consulting work – with university presidents, corporate chief executives, and government leaders – that Green was to follow.

In 1962, Alderson invited Green to join Wharton's Marketing Department, an invitation that Green willingly accepted, leaving DuPont for the university. Together, Green and Alderson authored *Planning and Problem Solving in Marketing*, published in 1964, showing how some relatively new tools such as Bayesian analysis could be used to address marketing problems. Two years later, Green and Don Tull – who worked through the mails and never met one another until after their book was published – co-authored the textbook *Research for Marketing Decisions,* which has shaped education in marketing research.

In their book, they defined marketing research as: "The systematic and objective search for, and analysis of, information relevant to the identification and solution of any problem in the field of marketing."[1] Explaining the importance of marketing research, they note that colonial silversmith Paul Revere personally knew the customers who bought his tankards, platters, and teapots, while the modern president of Revere Copper and Brass, Inc., is isolated from the thousands of customers of his products. Advertising and personal selling represent communication to the market, while marketing research is a formally organized "feedback loop" from the market to the company.[2]

As Green found in his research at DuPont, the complexity and uncertainty of large modern businesses required more sophisticated tools. Drawing on his experience in statistics and other disciplines, Green helped to create and refine these tools for marketing and put them into practice. He pursued this research with a passion and prolific output that in large part defined the field.

Defining Marketing Research

The chapters of this book explore some of these streams of scholarship in marketing research that were initiated or strengthened through Green's work.

Current leaders in these research areas examine the history of research and future directions in four key streams of knowledge:

Bayesian Decision Theory (BDT)

As noted, Green's thesis represented an early application of the Bayesian approach to marketing research. Bayes theorem is named for eighteenth-century clergyman, Thomas Bayes. The theorem is the cornerstone of what has become known as the Bayesian approach, or Bayesian Decision Theory (BDT). In contrast to traditional statistics, based on determining the limit of a relative frequency over the long run, the Bayesian approach to making decisions under partial ignorance makes use of the confidence that the decision maker has in the truth of specific propositions. It allows marketing executives, who rarely have enough solid information to determine the relative frequency of outside events, to consider both objective probabilities and subjective probabilities based on judgment. It also allows researchers to update their probabilities, based on new information, and to determine whether it is worthwhile to seek that information through marketing research. As Eric Bradlow, Peter Lenk, Greg Allenby, and Peter Rossi consider in Chapter 1, even with the emergence of richer data sets, marketing remains a "decision-oriented discipline," and, as such, Bayesian approaches continue to make important contributions to these decisions.

Multivariate Data Analysis

Paul Green was one of the first to introduce latent variable models in marketing research, using latent class analysis and logit models. As Wayne DeSarbo, Wagner Kamakura, and Michel Wedel note in Chapter 2, "a multivariate statistical model specifies the joint distributions of a set of random variables and it becomes a latent variable model when some of these variables – the latent variables – are unobservable." These models can be used to help marketing managers and researchers in "depicting market structure, market segmentation, product design and positioning, competitive influences and patterns, and relationships between consumer perceptions and choice." They discuss the development of a large variety of models and approaches – including unrestricted latent class, latent class regression, latent class multidimensional scaling, generalized factor analysis, and factor regression models – in the three decades since Paul Green introduced multivariate data analysis to marketing. They also examine applications to problems such as new product development in personal computers and customer satisfaction in financial services.

Multidimensional Scaling and Clustering

While multidimensional scaling was developed in the late 1930s by Gale Young and Alton Householder, followed quickly by Marion Richardson, it was not until the development of computing technology in the 1950s and 1960s that the field took off, including applications to marketing. Multidimensional scaling (MDS), which transforms Euclidian distances into a set of point coordinates, offers a powerful tool for addressing problems of consumer perceptions and evaluation through perceptual and preference mapping. Applications in marketing research rapidly expanded after 1962, when Roger Shepard published the first operational procedure for the multidimensional scaling of rank order (nonmetric) input data. Paul Green and Frank Carmone, writing the first marketing-oriented book on the subject in 1970, extended its applications to problems such as market segmentation, product life cycle analysis, and product/service evaluation. As Douglas Carroll, Phipps Arabie, Anil Chaturvedi, and Lawrence Hubert write in Chapter 3, Green has continued to play a role in the evolution of research in this area. They note in the chapter that MDS modeling has become increasingly complex and sophisticated, incorporating "all the best features associated with new models and methods applied to marketing."

In Chapter 4, Wolfgang Gaul explores the implications of enabling technologies such as the Internet for extending and applying these marketing research approaches.

Conjoint Analysis and Related Modeling

Green's interest in applying conjoint analysis to marketing research grew out of frustration with the limits of multidimensional scaling as a way to define consumer perceptions and preferences. MDS users might plot a pair of cars based on two or three dimensions, such as expense and performance, to create a brand-positioning map that allows one to separate the lower-cost, lower-performance Ford Focus from the high-cost, high-performance Porsche. But the product might really need 10 or 20 dimensions or more to provide a rich picture of customer perceptions and desires. (Courtyard by Marriott, for example, looked at 50 different attributes before developing its new hotel format for business travelers.)

"The earlier methodology was not powerful enough," Green said in an interview with the Marketing Science Institute (MSI).[3] "It becomes a many-to-one function. Do we change the paint job, engine, or transmission? Which one do we choose? There was a feeling that we could only go so far. Multidimensional scaling is good in showing product positioning in current markets that are out there, but it is not good from a dynamic point of view in helping you design a new item or change the character of an old item."

As he wrestled with the limits of multidimensional scaling in the 1960s, Green found the beginnings of an answer. "Fortunately, I was reading a lot of the literature that was outside the field of marketing," he said. He came across a 1964 study in the *Journal of Mathematical Psychology* by mathematical psychologist R. Duncan Luce and statistician John Tukey that pointed him in a new direction. The research dealt with making tradeoffs among different attributes to develop scales and rankings. Green realized these principles could be applied to marketing research and, along with Vithala Rao, introduced conjoint analysis to the marketing research community in 1971. Since then, conjoint has become one of the most documented methods in marketing research and one of the most popular multi-attribute choice models in marketing, with thousands of applications.

Conjoint analysis is both a tradeoff measurement technique for analyzing preferences and intentions-to-buy responses and a method for simulating how consumers might react to changes in current product/services or the introduction of new products as well as not-for-profit offerings.

Conjoint offers an extremely efficient process for weighing diverse attributes of a product or service offering. For example, in one study a financial services company designing a new credit card offering needed to make decisions about setting annual fees, cash rebates, an 800 number, different types of insurance, and other features. To consider 12 attributes, each of which had two to five options, the total number of possible combinations is an overwhelming 186,624. Conjoint combines options into profiles using orthogonal arrays, reducing these thousands of combinations to just 64 different profiles.

"It was a very exciting time," Green said of the birth of conjoint analysis. "We knew we were on to some new stuff. The students at that time, even some of our master's students, were doing very top-notch work in this area. It was like a little club, and that was very exciting."

In Chapter 5, Green and colleague Abba Krieger reflect on three decades of conjoint analysis. In Chapter 6, John Hauser and Vithala Rao explore some recent developments in conjoint analysis and related modeling. In Chapter 7, Green, Krieger, and Wind examine buyer choice models, optimizers and dynamic models. In Chapter 8, Jordan Louviere, Deborah Street, and Leonie Burgess offer a broad perspective on conjoint-based choice experiments. Finally, in Chapter 9, Howard Moskowitz offers insights on applications, particularly through conjoint analysis software.

As noted in the discussion of the four research streams above, Paul Green's impact on colleagues, students and the field cannot be completely assessed in academic tributes and retrospectives. Part Six offers some of these more personal and biographical perspectives from Paul and the many colleagues who have been influenced by his work and benefited from his personal presence.

Finally, the concluding chapter examines strategies for bridging research and practice, one of the key concerns of Paul's work, and an ongoing challenge for the field.

The Parlin Award

In May 1977, just 15 years after embarking on his career in marketing research, Green followed in Alderson's footsteps to receive the Charles Coolidge Parlin Award for outstanding contributions to marketing research. In making the award, the Parlin Board of Governors called Green "one of the major architects of modern marketing science and practice. The marketing discipline's familiarity with the utilization of Bayesian statistics, multidimensional scaling, conjoint measurement, and more recently, the analysis of qualitative data are all due to the pioneering work of Paul Green." At that time, he had already written more than 12 books and 100 articles, and had spoken to audiences at more than 50 universities around the world. As a reviewer and editor, he helped to "structure the current marketing literature." As an educator, he helped to "mold a new generation of marketing researchers."

Any professor might hope to win such praise as a capstone to a successful career. But Green was just warming up. For a quarter century after the award, he has continued to broaden and deepen his contributions to the field. His students and collaborators – more than 50 different co-authors – read like a *Who's Who* of marketing research. (Green, with typical attention to statistics, actually analyzed and ranked his top seven collaborators, noting that while these individuals account for just 13 percent of the names, they worked with him on half of all his joint publications, roughly reflecting his own "80/20" rule of scholarship.)

Not only has Green won virtually every major award in the field of marketing, he even has an award named in his honor. Established by the AMA's *Journal of Marketing Research,* the Paul Green Award is given to the *JMR* paper that "shows or demonstrates the most potential to contribute significantly to the practice of marketing research and research in marketing."

Some of his admirers are still not satisfied. As Morris Hamburg comments, referring to the Nobel Prize: "If there was such an award in the field of marketing research, I think you would agree that a prime candidate to be the first recipient of that prize would be Paul Green."

Future Generations

Green continues to actively participate in scholarship and applications in business. He also helps to shape the next generation of marketing professors. Among the personal reflections of Chapter 12, Raymond Burke, a former Wharton faculty member and professor at Indiana University, recalls:

When I joined the Wharton faculty, I had the good fortune to be assigned to an office next door to Paul Green. Fresh out of school from the University of Florida's Ph.D. program, my mind was focused on theoretical issues in consumer psychology. Given Paul's reputation in marketing research and modeling, I did not think we would have much to talk about. In fact, our conversations were some of the most stimulating and enriching experiences that I had during my years at Wharton. Paul valued interdisciplinary research, and his innovations in the field of marketing reflected a deep understanding of consumer behavior, psychometrics, and statistics. He was continually exploring ways in which the science of consumer psychology could be used to improve management decisions, including product design, pricing, advertising, promotion, and assortment planning. Paul also recognized the importance of working with practitioners on real world problems, and developing software to make his analytic techniques broadly accessible. His work set an example for the Wharton faculty and profoundly affected my view of the discipline and future research.

Green, himself, looks back on his career with typical humility. "Big ideas in market research methodology are rare, and any researcher is fortunate to be associated with one, let alone several, over the course of a career," he wrote in a retrospective on his career for the *Journal of Marketing,* reprinted in Chapter 10. "I have tried to develop the methodological skills needed to tackle various substantive problems, be they research questions on segmentation, pricing, competition, product positioning, or whatever."

Asked in an interview by MSI to offer advice for people starting out in the field, Green recommended that students to pick an area in which they can make contributions to theory to establish themselves. As they progress in their careers, they will very likely move to more applied challenges. While not stated explicitly, additional insights can be drawn from Green's own experience:

- *Find a strong mentor:* Green's relationship with Wroe Alderson was what attracted him to the university and shaped his early work.

- *Read widely:* Green's background in mathematics and statistics, and interests in other areas, gave him fresh perspectives on his marketing work. The most interesting new ideas and approaches may come from outside the field.

- *Tackle applied challenges:* While there is much fruitful work to be done in theory, Green's focus has been on "marketing engineering." His 12 years in industry before entering academia helped to sharpen this focus, and his continued interaction with the challenges of practice helped him develop solutions that have immediate application.

Paul Green has a passion for research, a spark that remains undimmed by four decades of achievements. Colleague Abba Krieger notes that even after hundreds of papers and more than a dozen books, Green is still "delighted to have a paper accepted or a program running that makes an idea accessible."

While he is officially an emeritus professor, there are still many questions to be answered in the field of marketing research, as noted in this book and particularly in the closing chapter by the editors. And, while he may have a little more time for piano playing, skiing or his grandchildren, Green will continue to play a role in answering these questions.

Over the course of his career, Paul Green has traded off corporate and consulting careers to enter academia. He has passed by the allures and titles of academic administration to focus on research and teaching. But for someone with a passion for discovery and devotion to offering new insights and tools to practitioners, it is a career that undoubtedly has been optimized.

One theme you will hear echoed throughout this book is the deep respect and personal appreciation so many leaders of marketing research hold for Paul. I share that sentiment. I hope through this volume, in a small way, we can do justice to the far-reaching contributions Paul has already made to the field and to his professional and personal impact on so many of us.

Yoram (Jerry) Wind
The Wharton School, University of Pennsylvania

NOTES

[1] Paul E. Green and Donald S. Tull, *Research for Marketing Decisions, Third Edition,* Englewood Cliffs, NJ: Prentice-Hall, Inc., 1975, p. 4.
[2] Green and Tull, p. 5.
[3] "Paul Green: Mastering Tradeoffs," *MSI Featured Academic,* http://www.msi.org/msi/facad-pg.cfm.

The Multi-Faceted Paul Green

Green in high school (left) and during the Navy years (right).

Green with Ph.D. students (above), lecturing in Israel in 1996 (left) and visiting China in the 1990s (right).

A Life of Partworths Optimized

Green, who took up skiing in his 40s heads down a slope in Chile (left).

He could often be found at a piano keyboard (above right), although in the 1940s, he played guitar with the group "Three Lads and a Lass" (below, second from left).

Green with the loves of his life (from left to right): Betty Green, Donna Peters, and three granddaughters.

PART ONE: BAYESIAN APPROACH

Beginning with his doctoral dissertation, Paul Green was a pioneer in the application of Bayesian Decision Theory (BDT) to marketing decisions. In Chapter 1, Eric Bradlow, Peter Lenk, Greg Allenby, and Peter Rossi examine some of Green's early work in this area – focusing on key marketing challenges such as product development, advertising, and weighing the cost of gathering additional information. They then consider the impact of the emerging data-rich environment and more complex models on the application of BDT to marketing challenges. While the context has changed in an environment of burgeoning scanner and panel data, many of the same questions and approaches Green identified in his early work remain relevant today.

Chapter 1

When BDT in Marketing Meant Bayesian Decision Theory: The Influence of Paul Green's Research

Eric T. Bradlow, *The Wharton School*
Peter J. Lenk, *University of Michigan*
Greg M. Allenby, *Ohio State University*
Peter E. Rossi, *University of Chicago*

Paul Green had it right, and we are seeing evidence of it again 40 years later. Advances in Bayesian computation, the collection of new and unique data, and the development of complex models has been the focus of much research in Bayesian modeling over the last 20 years. Now, armed with these tools, researchers and managers again have the ability to emphasize, as Green did in the early 1960s, the application of Bayesian theory to making improved decisions – Bayesian Decision Theory (BDT).

Bayesian Decision Theory provides an integrative approach to both rational economic behavior and inference. Paul's early work in this area can be summarized as, "Just do the right thing," where "right thing" is selecting the course of action that leads to the greatest benefit. The "Bayesian" part of BDT describes the updating of the probabilities of uncertain states after obtaining additional information. BDT generalized decision theory to inference by expanding the state space to include unknown parameters.

Savage (1961) nicely summarizes BDT for inference: "For us, a problem in analysis, as opposed to one in design, can conveniently and properly be separated into two phases. First, compute the new distribution induced by the original distribution and the data. Second, use the new distribution and the economic facts about terminal actions to pick one of the terminal actions that now has the highest expected utility." This use of decision theory for inference extends back at least to Wald (1950) and Blackwell and Girshick

(1954), arguably reaching its apogee with Savage (1954) and De Finetti (1937).

Bayesian inference, as commonly practiced in academics, has historically concentrated on this first step. Statisticians tend to be more comfortable in reporting what we have found in the data than in being prescriptive to managers about rational behavior. However, marketing is an applied field with a clear decision orientation, and empirical researchers in marketing have always sought to guide managerial decisions. Bayesian decision theory offers a framework for distinguishing the data generating process, as reflected in the prior distribution and likelihood function, from economic aspects of the decision that are modeled in the utility or loss function. This distinction preserves the descriptive orientation of statistical inference while facilitating decision-oriented analyses relevant to marketing.

In honoring Paul Green and his early research in BDT, this chapter begins with a summary of his work on decisions with limited data. We then consider the subsequent dramatic increase in the use and availability of survey data, including the use of demand data from a variety of sources, and the impact of these data sources on the nature of Bayesian work. Both survey and demand data have stimulated Bayesian developments that account for subject-level heterogeneity. In addition, the new data have spurred the development of new models. We review how Bayesian approaches are well suited to the analysis and development of new data structures. Armed with more powerful methods of inference and a toolkit of flexible models, we return with renewed interest to the decision orientation of Green's early work. We conclude with some summary comments and thanks to Paul.

DECISIONS WITH LIMITED DATA

Paul Green is widely hailed as a pioneer of conjoint analysis, multi-dimensional scaling and clustering methods. Unbeknownst to many researchers in marketing today, Green was also a pioneer in the use of Bayesian Decision Theory (BDT). From an historical perspective, his dissertation, "Some Intra-Firm Applications of Bayesian Decision Theory to Problems in Business Planning," completed in 1958-1961 while working at the DuPont Corporation in Wilmington, Delaware, places Green's work as contemporary to that of Savage (1954), Chernoff and Moses (1959), Schlaifer (1959), Raiffa and Schlaiffer (1961), and Hirshleifer (1961), other well-known early researchers in BDT. We start with a review of Paul Green's early work in BDT, as contained in Green (1961, 1962a, 1962b, 1963a, 1964a, 1964b) and Frank (1966).[1] The hope is that this summary will provide the "hub" for the next sections on the recent advances in Bayesian methods, and an ability to define the "spokes" – how all of this fits into Green's view of BDT.

One thing that characterizes the early BDT work of Green is the centrality to marketing thought in his choices of problems. His dissertation work began with a practical application of Bayesian Decision Trees and the mathematics of BDT to the problems of whether DuPont should add textile fiber capacity through plant construction and how to design the company's long-range pricing strategy. Green went on to use BDT to address other key challenges in the practice of marketing, including product decisions (Green 1962a), advertising (Green 1962b), using computers in business planning (Green 1963a), uncertainty and information in marketing decisions (Green 1964b), analyzing customer characteristics (Green 1964b), marketing research (Frank and Green 1966a), and decisions related to the economics of information (Green 1967).

In addition to his focus on practical marketing applications, Green's dissertation also is characterized by three other aspects central to the application of BDT: elicitation of subjective probabilities, construction of a firm-level utility function, and the decision rule of the firm (expected value and minimax are described in detail). The completeness of the work – that is, the fact that his research describes *all* the necessary BDT steps from start to finish – provides the roadmap that practitioners require, and the roadmap for this chapter. Furthermore, as is typical of Green's BDT work, he carefully lays out the central aspects of implementation: (a) the prior distribution over the states of nature, (b) the conditional distribution of outcomes given the states of nature, (c) the temporal choices of the firm to "decide now" or "collect information at a cost" (what Green calls the pre-posterior analysis), (d) the computation of marginal and posterior probabilities using Bayes' rule, and (e) the payoffs (potentially computed as the net present value of future cash flows). Green's focus on the cost of collecting information (pre-posterior analysis) provides a decision tool to managers as to whether to spend time, money, and resources on marketing data when the information sources are perfectly accurate or only partially accurate (the Expected Value of Perfect/Imperfect Information, respectively). This work is continued in Green and Tull (1966), *Research for Marketing Decisions*.

For example, in his consideration of product decisions (Green 1962a), Green addresses a question central to the new product development process: Should support for a new offering be terminated, passed onto the next stage of development, or have its status decision delayed waiting for more information to be collected? The practicality of Green's work is demonstrated here in that he considers details unto minutia such as the necessary discounting of payoffs due to the time value of money, the greater uncertainty in competitive reaction given that rivals have more time to react, and the possible increase in the number of competitors in future time periods.

In Green's application of BDT to advertising decisions (Green 1962b), he addresses a question weighing heavily on a hypothetical manager of a soft-drink company, "As they are losing market share, should they spend advertising dollars to upscale the vending machine exterior (packaging) as well as give a fortune cookie (in-product giveaways) with each purchase?" In this work, the focus is two-fold: the introduction of Bayes' rule as a method of computing posterior probabilities, and secondly the use of a parametric probability distribution (in this case Gaussian) to describe the conditional probability of events (sales outcomes) over pre-defined discrete ranges.[2]

To illustrate the use of BDT in marketing research and the role of computers in business planning (Green 1963a), he uses a device that he employs in later papers: storytelling. In this article, Green invents the characters "Market Research Man," who by the way is inept because of his lack of use of BDT and the fact that he can't give the answers requested immediately (hence the need for computers), "Chart-Flipper Man," "Vu-Graph Man," and Executives 1, 2, and 3. As Green states in summarizing this article, the computer can be used for screening courses of action, exploring relevant states of nature, facilitating Bayesian computation, and implementing sensitivity analyses (always emphasized in Green's work).

In his paper on uncertainty in marketing decision making (Green 1964a), he recognizes the link between BDT and other information techniques from signaling theory (e.g., Shannon Entropy, channel signal-to-noise). Specifi-cally, in this work Green decomposes the "error" in the marketer's "system" into that due to the accuracy of the marketing report (noise in the channel), and the amount of error in the data (the accuracy of the salesman). Green then links the amount of information (using classic measures) to the amount of economic benefit that can be gained by buying information or not. Notice in all these works the focus on "information" and the question, "Is the data worth it?" – one of the major issues facing Bayesian thinking in the 1960s.

Green's paper on analyzing customer characteristics (Green 1964b), which discusses the use of Bayesian classification methods as an alternative to classic discriminant analysis, may have started him down the road to the development of multivariate statistical procedures. In this manuscript, Green considers the following marketing challenge and variables:

(a) Assume that there are two classification groups (C_1 = high sales, C_2=low sales) where the goal of the procedure is to take act A_1 = assign person to C_1 or act A_2 = assign person to C_2.

(b) Assume that there are three binary indicators X_1, X_2, X_3 that inform about C.

(c) Let $Z_1,\ldots, Z_8$ denote the $2^3=8$ possible states of X_1, X_2, X_3 with known conditional probability distribution $P(Z_i|C_i)$.

(d) Let $P(C_1)$, $P(C_2)$ denote the prior probability of group membership.

(e) Let $OL(C_1)$ and $OL(C_2)$ denote the opportunity loss of mis-classification from each group.

(f) Let V denote the cost of Z, the "market" information about C.

Green makes the following observations: First, with strong priors, the value of Z is less and hence the cost one is willing to pay (V) should go down. Secondly the optimal number of Z you should buy increases and then decreases as a function of $P(Z_i|C_i)$. While this may be counter-intuitive, Green describes this simply: "If the information is poor, then the information is not valuable, if the information in Z is very accurate, you don't need to buy them all." Three other findings listed in the paper include the critical posterior probability for selecting A_1 or A_2 as a function of $OL(C_1)$ and $OL(C_2)$,[3] the fact that the amount of information that should be bought is increasing with OL, and finally that an increase in V, decreases the amount of information that should be purchased. Again, Green could have stopped at simply demonstrating the classification procedure via Bayes rule, but he goes on to provide useful advice to managers as to when to purchase, when the information will be more or less valuable, etc. Such extra-mileage is the link between academic and practitioner work.

Green has not only contributed directly to the development of BDT in marketing, but also provides a service to academic colleagues and practitioners by summarizing the progress of the field. Frank and Green (1966) provide a "state-of-the-union" address on the first eight to ten years of Bayesian work in marketing. Frank and Green not only help the reader understand where the field has come but also what problems still need to be solved. It is interesting to note that this work was published in *Applied Statistics*, an indication of Green's ability to publish cross-over work as well as his vision that other fields can contribute to the practice of marketing.

Finally, Green (1967) examined the way that actual decision makers deviate from "optimal Bayesian rational decision making," testing his earlier work on normative models against the complex empirical evidence of a behavioral experiment. In this paper, Green manipulates three things – an additive constant, a shift in odds, and a multiplicative constant – and looks at the effect that each has on the choices between two competing options. What is interesting is that in both the case of the additive constant and the shift in odds, the difference in expected value is 0, and hence no change in behavior should occur. In the multiplicative case, there is a shift in expected value difference of varying degrees. The study, using students and managers, found that students are more biased than managers, the additive constant and the odds manipulation fooled the students but not the managers, subjects still picked the right outcome, and personality scales were not useful predictors of non-normative behavior.

BAYESIAN INFERENCE AND MARKETING DATA

The explosion of data has been one of the biggest changes in the environment since Green's early work on BDT, which was carried out in a relatively data-poor environment. By the mid 1960s, survey methods provided a rich new class of data on consumer and buyer preferences. In the 1980s, actual behavior data on consumers became available for an increased set of products. These new data sources stimulated research on new data structures and models. In the subsequent sections, we will discuss how the Bayesian modeling and inference approaches used by Green in his early work can be applied to this new data.

The analysis of marketing data, either from conjoint experiments or large, observational databases, gives rise to three challenges: (1) substantial hetero-geneity in preferences, tastes, and responses to marketing mix by subjects; (2) short subject histories relative to the number of parameters; and (3) an interest in making decisions (e.g., offering price promotions) at a lowest possible level of aggregation. Thus, the statistical model and inference methods must accommodate heterogeneity across panelists and provide panelist-level inferences necessary for customization.

If there were a large number of observations on each subject, then it would be possible to fit models at the individual level and to describe how these estimated parameters vary across individuals. The problem with this scheme for most marketing data is that it does not account for errors in individual-level estimates, which may be poorly estimated or nonexistent. The estimation uncertainty at the individual level can and often does distort the true distribution of heterogeneity and masks important relationships among subjects.

BDT and one of its operational arms, Hierarchical Bayes (HB) methods, provide a unified approach to both the marketing decision problem and individual-level statistical inference. HB models estimate individual-level parameters from the within-subjects model, even when the maximum likelihood (ML) or least-squares (OLS) estimates do not exist, by using information about parameter heterogeneity from the between-subjects model. HB analysis can be conceptualized as a compromise between two extremes: estimates from an aggregate model using pooled data and individual-level ML estimates that do not account for the between-subjects model. HB analyses automatically combine these two approaches where the relative weight for the two extremes is optimally selected according to the precision of the individual-level and aggregate estimates. The resulting estimators are biased but tend to be more accurate than either of the two extremes.

General Panel Structure and Hierarchical Bayes Models

The model for the general panel data setting or, more generally, multiple observations on each sample unit can be expressed with a random coefficient as follows:

$$\prod_{i=1}^{n} f(Y_i \mid \Omega_i, \xi)g(\Omega_i \mid \Phi) \quad \text{or} \quad \prod_{i=1}^{n} l(\Omega_i, \xi \mid Y_i)g(\Omega_i \mid \Phi)$$

where Y_i are the observations for the ith panelist, and there are n panelists. The conditional distribution f of Y_i depends on individual-level parameters Ω_i and population-level parameters ξ. Here, l is the conditional likelihood for the ith panelist, and $g(\Omega_i \mid \Phi)$ is the random coefficient model that describes the variation in individual-level parameters across the population. In a fully Bayesian treatment of this problem, an additional layer – a second stage prior $p(\xi, \Phi \mid H)$ – is imposed which describes the prior uncertainty in ξ and Φ. The hyper-parameters H are assumed to be known. The complete model, or joint distribution for the data and unknown parameters, becomes:

$$\prod_{i=1}^{n} f(Y_i \mid \Omega_i, \xi)g(\Omega_i \mid \Phi)p(\xi, \Phi \mid H)$$

The model above is often called a Hierarchical Bayes (HB) Model. One of the principal benefits of the Bayesian approach is the exact sampling distribution of both the common and individual parameters, summarized by the posterior distribution of the parameters:

$$p(\Omega_1, ..., \Omega_m, \xi, \Phi \mid Y_1, ..., Y_n, H)$$

where the list of individual-level parameters Ω_1, ..., Ω_m may include ones for individuals outside the panel. From this posterior distribution, we can obtain inferences at the appropriate level of aggregation. Since the amount of information available for any one panelist is apt to be small, we also desire methods of estimation that are free from large sample approximations.

An Example of Linear Hierarchical Bayes Models

Lenk, DeSarbo, Green, and Young (1996) propose a HB model for full-profile, metric conjoint data (see also Allenby and Ginter 1995). Specifically, imagine that subject i evaluates n_i profiles on a metric scale. The within-subjects model (the conditional likelihood) is a standard linear regression model:

$$Y_i = X_i \beta_i + \varepsilon_i \quad \text{for} \quad i = 1, \ldots, n$$

where Y_i is a n_i-vector of evaluations for subject i, X_i is the n_i x p design matrix for subject i that describes the profiles attributes and levels, β_i are subject-specific regression coefficients (partworths), and the error term ε_i has a n_i-dimensional, independent, normal distribution with mean 0 and variance σ_i^2. The between-subjects model captures the heterogeneity in the regression coefficients and error variances:

$$\beta_i = \Theta z_i + \delta_i \text{ and } \sigma_i^2 \approx IG\left(\frac{\alpha}{2}, \frac{\psi}{2}\right) \text{ for } i = 1, \ldots, n$$

where z_i is a q-vector of subject-specific covariates; Θ is a p x q matrix of regression coefficients; the error term δ_i has a p-dimensional normal distribution with mean 0 and covariance matrix Λ; and "IG(r,s)" is the inverted gamma distribution with shape parameters r and scale parameter s. Prior distributions are specified for Θ, Λ, α, and ψ. In terms of the HB model of the previous section, $\Omega_i = (\beta_i, \sigma_i^2)$; $\Phi = (\Theta, \Lambda, \alpha, \psi)$; and ξ, the population-level parameters, are absent.

Hierarchical linear models have a long history in the Bayesian statistics literature. Hill (1965) was one of the earliest papers to provide a HB analysis of random effects (in the conjoint case the partworths) in a one-way ANOVA. Lindley and Smith (1972) and Smith (1973) consider HB linear models as well. However, the analysis of these models was limited to special cases or approximate Bayes solutions until the reintroduction of Markov Chain Monte Carlo (MCMC) methods for these models by Gelfand and Smith (1990) (see also the comment by Morris on Tanner and Wong 1987 and Hastings 1970).

Much of the work on heterogeneity in marketing uses a multivariate normal distribution. The very clear message from this work is that heterogeneity is very pronounced in all types of marketing data and that extremes are important. While the normal distribution is flexible, its thin tails and lack of multi-modality may be restrictive for some situations in marketing, although a multivariate regression model can accommodate non-normal heterogeneity if the appropriate covariates can be identified. Other forms of heterogeneity have been proposed; the most popular alternative is finite mixture models (Kamakura and Russell 1989). There are two interpretations of this model. The first is that there are K subpopulations, and members of the subpopulations are homogeneous. That is, they share common parameters in the within-subjects model. The second interpretation is that if one uses enough support points, then it can approximate any distribution. The question of which one of non-nested models of heterogeneity is best is an empirical issue and context dependent. A natural extension of the normal model and finite mixture model is a mixture of normal components (Allenby, Arora, and Ginter 1998 and Lenk and DeSarbo 2000). Another flexible model is the mixture of Dirichlet processes (Antoniac 1974, Ferguson 1973 and 1974, Escobar 1994, and Escobar and West 1995).

Lenk et. al (1996) use HB models to reduce task demands in conjoint experiments and still recover parameter heterogeneity. They do this empirically by deleting profiles and demonstrating that the HB analysis can fairly accurately estimate individual-level parameters and the distribution of heterogeneity with limited information. The paper then investigates survey design. Bayesian experimental design is conceptually simple, though often daunting in practice. As Savage (1961) writes:

> Of course, a full statistical problem typically involves design as well as analysis. The Bayesian method for such a problem is, in principle, to survey all designs, each followed by optimal terminal decision, and to select one of those with the highest expected income, taking into account the expected cost of experimentation as well as the overall over-all expected income of the terminal act.

In their 1996 paper, Lenk and colleagues investigate the tradeoff between the number of subjects and the number of profiles per subject on estimation accuracy and experimental cost. They generalize the pre-posterior analysis of Green's early work on the cost of perfect and imperfect information to linear HB models. The paper derives economic designs for fractional factorial surveys where different subjects receive different fractions. It proves that one can recover partworth heterogeneity in a highly fractionated experiment by using many subjects. This implies that very complex products or services with many attributes and levels can be designed without requiring unreasonable task demands. Sandor and Wedel (2001) consider the much more complex problem of specifying the attribute levels in pick-one-of-k conjoint experiments.

Thus we see the influence of Green's early work on BDT for optimal marketing strategy in that individual-level data flows quite naturally into Bayesian inference for large and complex databases, when it is available. Individual-level data on consumer behavior in the marketplace also raises some challenges in the specification of the conditional likelihood for the data. The next section explores these challenges.

CHALLENGES IN ANALYZING MARKETPLACE DATA

The introduction of scanning technology and bar codes in the mid-1980s provided marketing researchers with access to large volumes of sales data at a level of detail and accuracy that was previously not available. Weekly sales of individual stock keeping units (SKUs), and causal data that included the shelf price and merchandising activity (e.g., displays, feature advertising, coupon activity) became available for analysis and explanation. Panels were also created in which the purchases of households were recorded and tracked over time.

In the 1980s, most of the work on panel data models in marketing was severely constrained by computational concerns. For example, the availability of IRI panel data stimulated a great deal of interest in the multinomial logit model (MNL), but the standard i.i.d. MNL model is not very well suited for application to panel data in marketing due to the pronounced heterogeneity of brand tastes and the restrictive nature of the logit model elasticity or market structure. Guadagni and Little (1983) made use of a constructed loyalty measure to capture both heterogeneity in brand preferences across subjects and dependence between purchase occasions. The loyalty measure, which is an exponentially weighted moving average of past purchases at the individual level, adjusts the brand intercepts at the individual level and introduces state dependence into the model.

The development of Markov Chain Monte Carlo (MCMC) methods (Gelfand and Smith 1990) facilitated the estimation of vastly more complex models. Allenby and Lenk (1994 and 1995) extend Guadagni and Little by directly modeling the heterogeneity in brand preferences and sensitivity to the marketing mix and serial correlation with a logistic-normal model. McCulloch and Rossi (1994) develop exact Bayesian inference for multinomial probit models, which do not have the IIA property, typically undesirable, of logit models.

High-Dimensional Analysis

The emergence of marketplace data created opportunities for Bayesian researchers in marketing to explore and develop specifications of the likelihood function and the prior distribution. One of the challenges present in the analysis of weekly scanner data is dealing with high-dimensional models that result from the competitive effects of one brand on another. For example, a study of price responsiveness of 10 brands leads to 100 different own and cross-elasticities. Accurate estimation of model parameters was problematic in the analysis of even a small number of offerings because of the large number of parameters. Many cross-elasticities are estimated with large standard errors, and the algebraic sign of parameter point estimates often had incorrect algebraic signs. Since marketing is an applied field with a decision orientation (as championed by Green in his early work), the presence of incorrect algebraic signs is problematic for deriving optimal pricing policies. Traditional approaches to dealing with this problem include directly specifying a particular parameter's values (e.g., zeroing out some of the cross-elasticities), or re-parameterizing the model specification in a lower dimension by imposing deterministic constraints in the likelihood.

Increased raw computational power and the MCMC methods have created less restrictive alternatives to traditional, deterministic approaches. In a Bayesian model, restrictions can be imposed stochastically through the prior distribution. The prior distribution can reflect the form and precision of the restrictions, with a tightly specified prior leading to posterior distributions that reflect the restrictions more than diffuse priors. Estimates derived from the posterior distribution can therefore be viewed as maximum likelihood estimates that have been shrunk toward estimates based on the prior, with the degree of shrinkage dependent on two factors – the precision of the prior specification and the amount of information contained in the likelihood. Montgomery and Rossi (1999) develop alternative prior specifications based on economic theory, and illustrate their usefulness in improving estimates of cross-elasticities. Their Bayesian approach produces estimates that outperform standard estimates produced by unrestricted or restricted least squares. Lenk and Rao (1990) illustrate the benefit of shrinkage models for studying new product adoption. The HB approach allows early forecasts of the new product adoption process by using previous product launches, which have nearly complete data histories, to develop the prior distribution for the new one. In the early stages when data are lacking, the HB methodology provides forecasts that are similar to a pooled forecast from past products. As sales data for the new product become available, these priors are updated, and the reliance on previous products diminishes. The Bayes analysis automatically adjusts the tradeoff between past product launches and data for the current one based on their relative impact on parameter uncertainty. The value of these methods is tied to the decision problem, a theme found in Green's work on decision theory and discussed in more detail below.

Non-Standard Data

The analysis of household panel data presents additional challenges to empirical modelers. Disaggregate demand data often takes on a mixture of integer and real values, including zero, which rules out the use of standard regression models. In addition, economic models of these data involve assumptions about utility maximization and budgetary restrictions that are not well represented by standard statistical distributions (e.g., binomial and Poisson). Household purchases among brands in a product category, for example, are often discrete with just one alternative having non-zero demand. In other categories, such as yogurt and soup, multiple items are purchased, and data take on more than just 0-1 values.

The presence of zeroes in the disaggregate data or the importance of choice between products has received a great deal of attention in the recent marketing literature. Mutually exclusive choice between products is often modeled using a linear utility model which gives rise to corner solutions. To develop the statistical model or likelihood a random utility approach is often taken. The basic linear utility model behind standard logit or probit choice models can be written as:

$$U(x) = \sum_j \psi_j x_j$$

where ψ is the vector of marginal utilities for the offerings under investigation, and x is the vector of quantity. This utility structure corresponds to indifference curves that are linear and parallel, leading to a utility maximizing solution that is discrete – i.e., only one of the choice alternatives is selected. In particular, it can be shown that the maximum value of utility obtainable, subject to a budgetary restriction:

$$\sum_j p_j x_j \leq y$$

where p is the vector of prices and y is the budget, corresponds to selecting the alternative with the greatest "bang-for-the-buck," ψ_i/p_i, where "i" is used to index the choice alternatives. Log marginal utility, ln ψ_i, is typically modeled with stochastic error, leading to choice probabilities of the form:

$$Pr(i) = Pr(\psi_i/p_i > \psi_j/p_j \text{ for all } j) = Pr(V_i + \varepsilon_i > V_j + \varepsilon_j \text{ for all } j)$$

where $V_i = \ln \overline{\psi}_i - \ln p_i$ can be considered as the deterministic portion of indirect utility. An assumption of normally distributed errors leads to the probit model, and an assumption of extreme value errors leads to the logit model.

As useful as the linear utility model is for deriving standard choice models, there is empirical evidence that utility is not linear in product attributes. In the conjoint literature pioneered by Green, it is typical to use a dummy-variable or non-parametric approach to enter product attribute levels. While the assumption of linear utility does not necessarily create problems in economic models of demand (x) that take on values of only zero and one, these assumptions become restrictive when considering demand across a greater range of values. For example, the utility maximizing solution for the linear utility model does not involve the budgetary allotment, y. As consumers allocate greater expenditure to a product class, the linear utility model would predict that more of the same good would be demanded. This property of the model is not empirically supported in product categories in which larger expenditures are associated with a shift toward purchasing higher quality goods (see Allenby and Rossi 1991), consistent with a non-constant price effect.

New developments in model estimation have facilitated the departure from a linear latent model structure. Simulation-based approaches to evaluating integrals, such as the simulated likelihood method of Geweke (1991), and new approaches to generating simulates from non-standard densities such as the Metropolis-Hastings algorithm (cf. Smith and Roberts 1993 and Chib and Greenberg 1995), griddy Gibbs methods (Tanner 1993), and slice sampling (Polson 1996 and Damien, Wakefield, and Walker 1999) has freed analysts from the restrictive requirement of employing conjugate densities. These developments allow analysts to investigate model specifications that more closely reflect the previous empirical findings while maintaining a tight theoretically structure.

Consider, for example, a non-linear utility specification with diminishing marginal returns that reflect consumer satiation (see Kim, Allenby, and Rossi 2002):

$$U(x) = \sum_j \psi_j (x_j + \gamma_j)^{\alpha_j}$$

where $0 < \alpha_j \leq 1$ and $\gamma_j > 0$. The indifference curves associated with this utility specification are convex to the origin and have finite, non-zero slopes at the axes, which create the possibility of corner and interior solutions. The model can therefore reflect sales data comprised of both discrete and continuous components. The discrete component of the likelihood functions corresponds to a point mass similar to that found in a discrete choice model. The continuous component corresponds to a density contribution evaluated at a point of tangency between the budgetary restriction and an indifference curve. Markov Chain Monte Carlo (MCMC) methods can be employed to estimate the model with heterogeneous model parameters, despite the complexity of a mass/density likelihood specification.

MCMC methods are ideally suited for estimating hierarchical models because they exploit the conditional independence assumption made between levels of the hierarchy. In a random-effects model, the hyper-parameters of the random-effect distributions are conditionally independent of the data and other model parameters given the current realizations of the individual parameters. The assumption of conditional independence greatly simplifies the computations needed to estimate the model parameters, helping to avoid compromises and short-cuts in model specification made so that the model is estimable.

The conditional independence assumption can also be employed to investigate various explanations of model parameters. For example, the satiation parameter, α_j, can be related to product attributes through a variety of specifications, including a simple additive model:

$$\alpha_j = \sum_k \beta_k c_{jk}$$

where c_{jk} represents the level of attribute k in offering j, and β_k is the partworth of the attribute-level. Alternatively, an ideal point model could be employed:

$$\alpha_j = \sum_k | c_{jk} - \theta_k |$$

where θ_k is the ideal level of attribute k. The empirical performance of these attribute-level specifications has been previously studied by Green and others using survey data. The extension of this work to models of sales data is straightforward with modern Bayesian methods.

The challenge of modeling large datasets with a mixture of continuous and discrete data can be addressed by employing theory-based specifications of the prior distribution and likelihood function. Much of the underlying theory is based on the notion that product offerings are comprised of attributes and levels that are differentially valued by individuals, and these attributes provide a basis upon which theories of preference are derived. The availability of marketplace demand data and Bayesian estimation tools facilitate the development of new marketing theories that build on the attribute-based approach championed by Green in his early work.

A RETURN TO DECISION THEORY

In Green's early papers on Bayesian decision theory, the model or likelihood was specified as a small number of discrete states of nature and associated probabilities. The decision maker directly assesses the model form and probabilities. Much of the work of the 1990s can be regarded as elaborating a very rich class of models for panel data of many forms. These models have the basic form of a set of input or marketing mix variables, which translate into output in the form of sales response. The ultimate purpose of this extensive modeling effort is to inform decisions about the optimal values of the marketing mix variables. We now turn to a more modern version of the BDT problem.

Most standard treatments of BDT (cf. Ferguson 1967, DeGroot 1970, and Berger 1985) frame the decision problem in terms of a loss function. A loss function associates a loss with a state of nature and an action, $\ell(a,\theta)$ where a is the action and θ is the state of nature. Some classic examples of loss functions are the squared-error loss used in estimation problems and the 0/1 loss function used in classification problems. Many decision problems in marketing involve a loss function that is the negative of a profit function. The "actions" in marketing consist of value of an input variable such as the level of price or advertising. The states of nature are summarized by the response coefficients. Profit is derived from a demand or sales response equation. The goal is to maximize expected profits through choice of the values of the marketing variables. BDT provides a unified approach to both the marketing decision problem and statistical inference. For example, Green, Carroll, and Goldberg (1981) use these ideas for product design optimization. Blattberg and George (1992) synthesize the marketing decision and parameter estimation problem by basing the loss function for parameter estimation on economic considerations from the marketing problem instead of using an ad hoc criterion, such as squared-error loss.

We begin with a probability model that specifies how the outcome variable is driven by the inputs and covariates, conditional on parameter θ.

$$p\left(y|x,\theta\right)$$

The decision maker has some control over a subset of the x vector, $x' = \left[x'_d, x'_{cov}\right]$. x_d represents the variables under the decision maker's control and x_{cov} are the covariates. The goal of the decision maker is to choose x_d so as to maximize the expected value of profits (π). In a fully Bayesian Decision Theoretic treatment, this expectation is taken with respect to the relevant posterior distribution as well as the predictive conditional distribution $p(y|x_d, x_{cov})$.

$$\pi^*\left(x_d|x_{cov}\right) = E_\theta\left[E_{y|\theta}\left[\pi\left(y|x_d\right)\right]\right]$$
$$= E_\theta\left[\int\pi\left(y|x_d\right)p\left(y|x_d, x_{cov},\theta\right)dy\right]$$
$$= E_\theta\left[\bar{\pi}\left(x_d|x_{cov},\theta\right)\right]$$

The expectation $= E_\theta[\ ]$ is taken with respect to the posterior distribution of θ and the decision maker chooses x_d to maximize profits π^*.

Plug-in vs. Full Bayes Approaches

The use of expected profits, where the expectation is taken with respect to the posterior distribution of the parameters is an important contribution of the Bayesian approach. In an approximate or conditional Bayes approach, the full integration of the profit function with respect to the posterior distribution of θ is replaced by an evaluation of the function as the posterior mean of the parameters (often the Bayes estimate). This approximate approach is often called the "plug-in" approach, or according to Morris (1983), Bayes Empirical Bayes.

$$\pi^*\left(x_d\right) = E_\theta\left[\bar{\pi}\left(x_d|\theta\right)\right] \neq \bar{\pi}\left(x_d|\hat{\theta} = E[\theta]\right)$$

In decision-theoretic applications to disaggregate data, it is quite likely that the uncertainty in θ is very large. Coupled with a nonlinear $\pi(\ )$, this implies that errors from the use of the "plug-in" approach could be very substantial. In general, failure to account properly for parameter uncertainty will overstate the potential profit opportunities. This is a sort of "overconfidence" that will result in an overstatement of the value of information.

Use of Alternative Information Sets

One of the most appealing aspects of the Bayesian approach is the ability to incorporate a variety of different sources of information. All adaptive shrinkage methods utilize the similarity between cross-sectional units to improve inference at the unit level. This is often termed "borrowing strength." The amount of "borrowing" is determined by the dependence in the first stage prior or random coefficient model. Since this is typically determined by the data, the "shrinkage" aspects of Bayesian estimates adapt to the data. An application of this concept is the paper by Neelamegham and Chintagunta (1999), where similarities between countries are used to predict sales patterns following the introduction of new products.

In general, the role of a given information set is to specify the posterior of θ. For example, consider two information sets A and B along with corresponding posteriors, $p_A(\theta), p_B(\theta)$. We value these information sets by solving the decision problem using these two posterior distributions.

$$\Pi_l = \max_{x_d} \pi_l^*\left(x_d | x_{\text{cov}}\right) = \max_{x_d} \int \overline{\pi}\left(x_d | x_{\text{cov}}, \theta\right) p_l(\theta) d\theta$$

$$l = A, B$$

Rossi, McCulloch, and Allenby (1996) emphasize the use of Bayesian Decision problems to value various information sets available on individual households. A targeting couponing problem, which anticipated the now popular Catalina Marketing Inc. products, was used to value a sequence of expanding individual-level information sets. We now turn to the problem of valuing disaggregate information.

Valuation of Disaggregate Information

Once a fully decision-theoretic approach has been laid out, we can use the profit metric to value the information in disaggregate data. That is, we must compare profits that can be obtained via our disaggregate inferences about $\{\theta_i\}$ with profits that could be obtained using only aggregate information.

The profit opportunities afforded by disaggregate data will depend on both the amount of heterogeneity across the units in the panel data as well as the level of information at the disaggregate level. For example, if there is a very small amount of information at the panelists level, the optimal solutions to the

Bayesian Decision problems will vary little from panelist to panelist and will approximate the uniform decision that would be obtained using only aggregate data.

To make these notions explicit, we will lay out the disaggregate and aggregate decision problems. To do so, we must fix some notation for the disaggregate data. We will use a general panel structure of the form:

$$p(y_i|\theta_i)p(\theta_i|\tau)$$

Here $p(\theta_i|\tau)$ is the random effect or first stage prior. As emphasized earlier, Bayesian methods are ideally suited for inference about the individual or disaggregate parameters as well as the common parameters.

Recall the profit function for the disaggregate decision problem.

$$\pi_i^*\left(x_{d,i}|x_{cov,i}\right) = \int \tilde{\pi}\left(x_{d,i}|x_{cov,i},\theta_i\right)p\left(\theta_i|Data\right)d\theta_i$$

That is, we must maximize expected profits where the expectation is taken with respect to the posterior distribution of θ_i. Total profits from the disaggregate data are simply the sum of the maximized values of the profit function above.

$$\Pi_{disagg} = \sum \pi_i^*\left(\tilde{x}_{d,i}|x_{cov,i}\right) \text{ where } \tilde{x}_{d,i} \text{ is the optimal choice of } x_{d,i}$$

Aggregate profits can be computed by maximizing the expectation of the sum of the disaggregate profit functions with respect to the predictive distribution of θ_i

$$\pi_{agg}\left(x_d\right) = E_\theta\left[\sum \tilde{\pi}\left(x_d|x_{cov,i},\theta\right)\right] = \int \sum \tilde{\pi}\left(x_d|x_{cov,i},\theta\right)\bar{p}(\theta)d\theta$$
$$\Pi_{agg} = \pi_{agg}(\tilde{x}_d)$$

The appropriate predictive distribution of θ, $\bar{p}(\theta)$, is formed from the marginal of the first stage prior with respect to the posterior distribution of the model parameters.

$$\bar{p}(\theta) = \int p(\theta|\tau)p(\tau|Data)d\tau$$

Comparison of Π_{agg} with Π_{disagg} provides a metric for the achievable value of the disaggregate information. Such calculations mimic those in Green in which he computes a pre-posterior analysis by integrating the potential profits over the predictive distribution.

SUMMARY

In an information-rich environment, much of the recent emphasis in the marketing literature is on enlarging the class of likelihood functions and priors to accommodate the wide variety of new sources of marketing data. In particular, much of the newer data comes from a panel setting. Analysis of these new models provides new insights into consumer behavior and the nature of marketing data that can aid marketing decision making. New sources of disaggregate data hold out the promise of customized marketing actions such as micro-pricing at the zone or store level, targeted couponing at the customer level, and customized trade promotions at the key account level. Green's early work reminds us that we need a Bayesian treatment of these decisions to take into account parameter uncertainty when we devise customized strategies. Finally, the value of any set of information (including disaggregate information) can only be determined in a decision context. We expect a renewed emphasis on decision problems and profit metrics of valuation of information in the future of research in marketing.

In closing, we would be remiss if we did not take this opportunity to share some personal thoughts and give thanks to Paul Green, who has been an inspiration to each of us in our careers. His early work on Bayesian Decision Theory is a prime example of this. In a time when business schools eschewed formal analysis of any sort, Paul Green put forth a logically compelling argument for the Bayesian approach to making marketing decisions. This argument is no less compelling today, and he has been joined by a large group of "descendents" in the Bayesian tradition.

We refuse to talk about Paul Green in the past tense, for those of us who know him well know that the only thing that will change is that he will no longer be in the classroom. As much admiration as Paul Green should generate from his body of work, he should generate even greater admiration for the quality of person he is. We give him our deepest thanks.

NOTES

[1] One relevant article that we did not review was Green 1963b, "Bayesian Decision Theory in Pricing Strategy," winner of the *Journal of Marketing*'s Alpha Kappa Psi Award.

[2] One clear indicator that this is an early paper in the use of BDT is Green's inclusion of the classic Bertrand Box problem to clarify the key ideas and demonstrate computation. In the Bertrand Box problem, there are three boxes – one with two gold coins, one with one silver and one gold coin, and one with two silver coins. The experimenter opens one of the boxes and pulls out a gold coin: What is the probability that it is the box with two gold coins?

[3] Note that the equation for the critical value $w^*=OL(C_1)/(OL(C_1)+OL(C_2))$ is now "common" knowledge, however was certainly not at the time.

REFERENCES

Allenby, G. M., and Lenk, P. (1994), "Modeling household purchase behavior with logistic normal regression," *Journal of the American Statistical Association,* 83 (428), 1218-1231.

Allenby, G. M., and Ginter, J. L. (1995), "Using extremes to design products and segment markets," *Journal of Marketing Research,* (November), 392-403.

Allenby, G. M., and Lenk, P. (1995), "Reassessing brand loyalty, price sensitivity, and merchandising effects on consumer brand choice," *Journal of Business and Economic Statistics,* 13 (3), 281-290.

Allenby, G. M., Arora, N., and Ginter, J. L. (1998), "On the heterogeneity of demand," *Journal of Marketing Research,* 35 (August), 384-389.

Antoniac, C. E. (1974), "Mixtures of Dirichlet processes with applications to Bayesian nonparametric problems," *The Annals of Statistics,* 2, 1152-1174.

Berger, J. O. (1985), *Statistical Decision Theory,* New York: Springer Verlag.

Blackwell, D., and Ben-Amos, P. G. (1954), *Theory of Games and Statistical Decisions*, New York: John Wiley & Sons.

Blattberg, R. C., and George, E. I. (1992), "Estimation under profit-drive loss functions," *Journal of Business and Economic Statistics,* 10 (4), 437-444.

Chernoff, H., and Moses, L. E. (1959), *Elementary Decision Theory*, New York: Wiley; London: Chapman & Hall.

Chib, S., and Greenberg, E. (1995), "Understanding the Metropolis-Hastings algorithm," *The American Statistician*, 49, 327-335.

Chintagunta, P., and Neelamegham, R. (1999), "A Bayesian model to forecast new product performance in domestic and international markets," *Marketing Science,* 18, 2, 115-136.

Damien, P., Wakefield, J. C., and Walker, S. (1999) "Gibbs sampling for Bayesian nonconjugate and hierarchical models using auxiliary variables," *Journal of the Royal Statistical Society, Series B,* 61, 331-344.

De Finetti, B. (1937), "La previsions: ses lois logiques, ses sources subjectives," *Ann. Inst. H. Poincare*, 7, 1-68.

DeGroot, M. (1970), *Optimal Statistical Decisions,* McGraw-Hill, New York.

Escobar, M. D. (1994), "Estimating normal means with a Dirichlet process prior," *Journal of the American Statistical Association,* 89 (425), 268-277.

Escobar, M. D., and West, M. (1995), "Bayesian density-estimation and inference using mixtures," *Journal of the American Statistical Association,* 90 (430), 577-588.

Ferguson, T. S. (1967), *Mathematical Statistics, A Decision Theoretic Approach,* New York: Academic Press.

Ferguson, T. S. (1973), "A Bayesian analysis of some nonparametric problems," *The Annals of Statistics,* 1, 209-230.

Ferguson, T. S. (1974), "Prior distributions on the space of probability measures," *The Annals of Statistics,* 2, 615-629.

Frank, R. E., and Green, P. E. (1966). "Bayesian statistics in marketing research," *Applied Statistics,* 173-190.

Gelfand, A., and Smith, A. F. M. (1990), "Sampling-based approaches to calculating marginal densities," *Journal of the American Statistical Association,* 85, 398-409.

Geweke, J. (1991), "Efficient simulation from the multivariate normal and student-t distributions subject to linear constraints," in E.M. Keramidas (ed.), *Computating Science and Statistics: Proceedings of the Twenty-Third Symposium on the Interface,* Fairfax: Interface Foundation of North American, Inc., pp. 571-578.

Green, P. E. (1961), "Some intra-firm applications of Bayesian Decision Theory to problems in business planning," Doctoral Dissertation, The Wharton School of the University of Pennsylvania.

Green, P. E. (1962a), "Bayesian statistics and product decisions," *Business Horizons,* (Fall).

Green, P. E. (1962b), "Bayesian Decision Theory in advertising," *Journal of Advertising Research,* (December).

Green, P. E. (1963a), "The computer's place in business planning: A Bayesian approach," in Alderson and Shapiro (eds.), *Marketing and the Computer,* Prentice-Hall.

Green, P. E. (1963b), "Bayesian Decision Theory in pricing strategy," *Journal of Marketing,* (January).

Green, P. E. (1964a), "Uncertainty, information and marketing decisions," in Cox, Alderson, and Shapiro (eds.), *Theory in Marketing,* Richard D. Irwin.

Green, P. E. (1964b), "Bayesian classification procedures in analyzing customer characteristics," *Journal of Marketing Research,* (September).

Green, P. E. (1967), "A behavioral experiment in the economics of information," in G. Fisk (ed.), *The Psychology of Management Decisions,* Sweden: C.W.K. Gleerup.

Green, P. E., Carroll, J. D., and Goldberg, S. M., (1981) "A general approach to product design optimization via conjoint analysis", *Journal of Marketing,* Summer.

Green and Tull (1966), *Research for Marketing Decisions,* Prentice-Hall.

Guadagni, P., and Little, J. (1983), "A logit model of brand choice calibrated on scanner data," *Marketing Science*, 2(3), 203--238.

Hastings, W. K. (1970), "Monte Carlo sampling methods using Markov chains and their application," *Biometrika*, 57, 97-109.

Hill, B. (1965), "Inference about variance components in the one-way model," *Journal of the American Statistical Association*, 60, 806-825.

Hirshleifer, J. (1961), "The Bayesian approach to statistical decisions: An exposition," *Journal of Business*, 34, 471-489.

Kamakura, W. A., and Russell, G. J. (1989), "A probabilistic choice model for market segmentation and elasticity structure," *Journal of Marketing Research*, 26, 4, (November), 379-390.

Kim, J., Allenby, G. M., and Rossi, P. E. (2002), "Modeling consumer demand for variety," *Marketing Science*, 21, 229-250.

Lenk, P. J., and Rao, A. (1990), "New models from old: Forecasting product adoption by hierarchical Bayes procedures," *Marketing Science*, 9, 42-53.

Lenk, P. J., DeSarbo, W. S., Green, P. E., and Young, M. R. (1996), "Hierarchical Bayes conjoint analysis: Recovery of partworth heterogeneity from reduced experimental designs," *Marketing Science*, 15 (3), 173-191.

Lenk, P. J., and DeSarbo, W. S. (2000), "Bayesian inference for finite mixtures of generalized linear models with random effects," *Psychometrika*, 65 (1), 93-119.

Lindley, D. V., and Smith, A. F. M. (1972), "Bayes estimates for the linear model," *Journal of the Royal Statistical Society, Series B,* 34, 1-41.

McCulloch, R., and Rossi, P. E. (1994), "An exact likelihood analysis of the multinomial probit model," *Journal of Econometrics*, 64, 207-240.

Montgomery, A. L., and Rossi, P. E. (1999) "Estimating price elasticities with theory-based priors," *Journal of Marketing Research*, 36, 413-423.

Morris, C. N. (1983), "Parametric empirical Bayes inference: Theory and applications," *Journal of the American Statistical Association*, 78, 47-55.

Polson, N. G. (1996), "Convergence of Markov Chain Monte Carlo algorithms," in J. M. Bernardo, J. O. Berger, A. P. Dawid, and A. M. F. Smith (eds.), Bayesian Statistics, 5, Oxford University Press, 297-312.

Raiffa, H., and Schlaifer, R. (1961), *Applied Statistical Decision Theory*, Boston: Division of Research, Graduate School of Business Administration, Harvard University.

Rossi, P. E., McCulloch, R., and Allenby, G. (1996) "On the value of household information in target marketing," *Marketing Science,* 15, 321-340.

Sandor, Z., and Wedel, M. (2001), "Designing conjoint choice experiments using manager's prior beliefs," *Journal of Marketing Research*, 38, 4, (November), 430-444.

Savage, L. J. (1954), *The Foundations of Statistical Inference*, New York: Wiley.

Savage, L. J. (1961), "The foundations of statistics reconsidered," in J. Neyman (ed.), *Proceedings of the Fourth Berkeley Symposium on Mathematical Statistics and Probability,* Vol. I, University of California Press, pp. 575-586.

Schlaifer, R. (1959), *Probability and Statistics for Business Decisions*, New York: McGraw-Hill.

Smith, A. F. M. (1973), "A general Bayesian linear model," *Journal of the Royal Statistical Society, Series B,* 35, 67-75.

Smith, A., and Roberts, G. O. (1993), "Bayesian computation via the Gibbs sampler and related Markov Chain Monte Carlo methods," *Journal of the Royal Statistical Society, Series B,* 55, 3-23.

Tanner, M. (1993), *Tools for Statistical Inference,* New York: Springer-Verlag.

Tanner, M., and Wong, W. (1987), "The calculation of posterior distributions by data augmentation," *Journal of the American Statistical Society* 82, 82-86.

Wald, A. (1950), *Statistical Decision Functions*, New York: John Wiley & Sons.

PART TWO: MULTIVARIATE ANALYSIS

Paul Green was among the first to introduce latent variable models to the field of marketing via latent class analysis and logit models. Building on his pioneering work, Chapter 2 highlights several more recent applications of latent variable models in marketing, including unrestricted latent class, latent class regression, latent class multidimensional scaling, generalized factor analysis, and factor regression. Wayne DeSarbo, Wagner Kamakura, and Michel Wedel offer a description of the technical aspects of these models, estimation procedures, identification issues, and applications for each of the associated models.

Chapter 2

Applications of Multivariate Latent Variable Models in Marketing

Wayne S. DeSarbo, *Pennsylvania State University*
Wagner A. Kamakura, *Duke University*
Michel Wedel, *University of Groningen and University of Michigan*

Paul Green, writing with Carmone and Wachpress (1976), was among the first scholars to introduce latent variable models to marketing by utilizing the CANDECOMP procedure (Carroll 1980) on contingency tables. A year later, Green, Carmone, and Wachpress (1977) introduced logit and log-linear multivariate models to the field of marketing. Green went on to write several key books in the area of multivariate analysis, including *Analyzing Multivariate Data* (Green 1978), which describes many of these techniques in depth. Latent variable models have since become important tools for the analysis of multivariate data in marketing. In this chapter, we consider some more recent marketing applications of latent variable models based on Green's pioneering work.

A multivariate statistical model specifies the joint distribution of a set of random variables, and it becomes a latent variable model when some of these variables – the latent variables – are unobservable. One can treat both manifest (observed) and latent variables as either continuous or discrete in this context. Bartholomew and Knott (1999) provide a framework for latent variable models, which we extend. The classification is based on the metrics of the manifest and latent variables. Both are considered to be either discrete or continuous or a combination of these, leading to the classification shown in Table 2-1. We will use this classification below to review multivariate latent variable models in marketing.

Von Eye and Clogg (1994) examine latent variable models in several formats. One format arises when latent variables are regarded as causal variables, or, more generally, as predictors in some regression type model, or as moderators of a regression among manifest variables. Another format can be described as an attempt at measurement, when latent variable models serve to define the measurement process. For example, one might be interested in examining how well a given set of manifest variables actually measures an underlying construct. Or, a pertinent research question might be to determine the relationship between manifest variables and latent variables in some model in order to infer essential properties of both sets, such as "dimensionality" (see also Loehlin 1998). These formats will be reflected in our review of models below.

Table 2-1. **Classification of Latent Variable Models**
Adapted from Bartholomew and Knott (1999)

Latent Variables	Manifest Variables		
	Continuous	**Discrete**	**Continuous/Discrete**
Continuous	Factor Models, Factor Regression Models, MDS	Generalized Factor Models, Factor Regression Models MDS, Latent Trait Analysis	Generalized (Mixed outcome) Factor Models
Discrete	Finite Mixture Models, Mixture Regression Models, Latent Profile Analysis	Latent Class Models, Mixture Logit Regression Models	Mixed Outcome Finite Mixture Models
Continuous / Discrete	Mixture MDS Models	Mixture MDS Models	

Von Eye and Clogg (1994) examine latent variable models in several formats. One format arises when latent variables are regarded as causal variables, or, more generally, as predictors in some regression type model, or as moderators of a regression among manifest variables. Another format can be described as an attempt at measurement, when latent variable models serve to define the measurement process. For example, one might be interested in examining how well a given set of manifest variables actually measures an underlying construct. Or, a pertinent research question might be to determine the relationship between manifest variables and latent variables in some model in order to infer essential properties of both sets, such as "dimensionality" (see also Loehlin 1998). These formats will be reflected in our review of models below.

All of the types of latent models we will discuss are based on assumptions on the distributions of the measured variables. Most of the more commonly used distributions represent specific members of the exponential family of distributions. This family is a general set that encompasses both discrete and continuous distributions. The common properties of these distributions enable them to be studied simultaneously, rather than as a collection of unrelated cases. Table 2-2 presents several characteristics of a number of the most well known distributions in the exponential family. The table lists a short notation for each distribution, the form of the distribution as a function of the parameters, and the canonical link function.

Table 2-2. **Some Distributions in the Univariate Exponential Family**
Adapted from Wedel and DeSarbo (1996)

Distribution	Notation	$f(y)$	Domain	Link-function
Discrete				
Binomial	$B(K,\pi)$	$\binom{K}{y}\pi^y(1-\pi)^{K-y}$	$[0,K]$	$\theta = \ln\left(\dfrac{\pi}{1-\pi}\right)$
Poisson	$P(\mu)$	$\dfrac{e^{-\mu}\mu^y}{y!}$	$(0,\infty)$	$\theta = \ln(\mu)$
Continuous				
Normal	$N(\mu,\sigma)$	$\dfrac{1}{\sqrt{2\pi}\sigma}\exp\left[\dfrac{-(y-\mu)^2}{2\sigma^2}\right]$	$(-\infty,\infty)$	$\theta = \mu$
Exponential	$G1(\mu)$	$\left(\dfrac{1}{\mu}\right)\exp\left[-\dfrac{y}{\mu}\right]$	$(0,\infty)$	$\theta = \mu^{-1}$
Erlang-2	$G2(\mu)$	$\dfrac{1}{2y}\left(\dfrac{2y}{\mu}\right)^2\exp\left[-\dfrac{2y}{\mu}\right]$	$(0,\infty)$	$\theta = \mu^{-1}$
Gamma	$G(\mu,\nu)$	$\dfrac{1}{y\Gamma(\nu)}\left(\dfrac{y\nu}{\mu}\right)^\nu\exp\left[-\dfrac{\nu y}{\mu}\right]$	$(0,\infty)$	$\theta = \mu^{-1}$

We review three important types of multivariate latent variable models, according to the metric of the latent variable (Table 2-1). We first discuss Unrestricted Finite Mixture Models and Mixture Regression Models, in which the latent variable moderates the regression equation. Next, we describe Latent Class MDS Models that have both discrete and continuous latent variables. Note that, when applied in a marketing context, the discrete classes uncovered by such finite mixture models are often interpreted as derived market segments. We then examine Generalized Factor Models and Factor

Regression Models before turning our attention to Software for estimating many of the latent variable models discussed. We conclude by discussing some areas for future research and investigation.

UNRESTRICTED FINITE MIXTURE MODELS

To formulate the finite mixture model, assume that a sample of N subjects is collected. For each subject, K variables $y_n = (y_{nk}, n = 1,..., N; k = 1,..., K)$ are measured/observed. These subjects are assumed to arise from a population that is a mixture of T unobserved classes, in (unknown) proportions $\pi_1,...,\pi_T$. It is not known in advance from which class a particular subject arises. Given that y_{nk} comes from class t, the distribution function of the vector of observed measurements y_n, is represented by the general form $f_t(y_n | \theta_t)$. Here θ_t denotes the vector of unknown parameters for class t. For example, in the case that the y_{nk} within each class are independent normally distributed, θ_t contains the means, μ_{kt}, and variances, σ_t^2, of the normal distribution within each of the T classes. The unconditional distribution is obtained as:

$$f(y_n | \phi) = \sum_{t=1}^{T} \pi_t f_t(y_n | \theta_t), \tag{1}$$

where $\phi = (\pi, \theta)$ denotes all parameters of the model.

The conditional density function, $f_t(y_n | \theta_t)$, can take many forms including the normal, Poisson, and binomial distribution functions (as well as other distribution functions in the exponential family). Often, the K repeated measurements (or K variables) for each subject are assumed independent. This implies that the joint distribution function for the K observations factors into the product of the respective marginal distributions: $f_t(y_n | \theta_t) = \prod_{k=1}^{K} f_{tk}(y_{nk} | \theta_{tk})$. Note that the distribution functions are subscripted by k so that each observed outcome variable k may have its own distribution, i.e., some normal, others binomial, Poisson, etc.

The posterior probability, p_{nt}, that subject n comes from class t can be obtained from Bayes' Theorem:

$$p_{nt} = \frac{\pi_t f_t(y_n | \theta_t)}{\sum_{t=1}^{T} \pi_t f_t(y_n | \theta_t)}, \tag{2}$$

given estimates of the parameters θ_t.

Identification and Estimation

A potential problem associated with mixture models is that of under identification. Titterington, Smith, and Makov (1985) show that in general mixtures involving members of the exponential family, including the univariate binomial, normal, Poisson, exponential, and gamma distributions, are identified.

The parameters are usually estimated by maximizing the log-likelihood:

$$l(\phi \mid y_1, ..., y_N) = \sum_{n=1}^{N} \ln \left(\sum_{t=1}^{T} \pi_t f_t(y_n \mid \theta_t) \right). \tag{3}$$

This can be done by direct numerical maximization, but the E-M algorithm is a convenient algorithm often applied for that purpose (cf. Dempster, Laird, and Rubin 1977). The value of T (the number of classes) is that which minimizes: $CAIC_T = -2 \ln L + N_T (\ln N + 1)$, where N_T is the effective number of parameters estimated and N is the number of independent data observations (Bozdogan 1987). Several other model selection heuristics also exist (see Wedel and Kamakura 2001).

Application: Audio Equipment Buyers

Dillon and Kumar (1994) offer an example of the application of mixture models to examine shopping behavior, using data from Dash, Schiffman, and Berenson (1975) on the shopping behavior of 412 audio equipment buyers, categorized by five descriptors:

1. *Store in which the merchandise was purchased:* full-line department store (DEPT = 1) or specialty merchandiser (SPEC = 2).
2. *Catalog experience:* individual had sought information from manufacturers catalogs (YES=1); else (NO = 2).
3. *Prior shopping experience:* individual had shopped for audio equipment prior to making final decision (YES = 1); individual had not shopped for audio equipment prior to making final decision (NO = 2).
4. *Information seeking:* individual had sought information from friends and/or neighbors prior to purchase (YES = 1); individual had not sought information from friends and/or neighbors prior to purchase (NO = 2).
5. *Information transmitting:* individual had recently been asked for an opinion about buying any audio-related product

(YES = 1); individual had not been asked for an opinion about buying any audio-related product (NO = 2).

These five categorical variables have two levels each, generating 32 unique response patterns.

For illustrative purposes, Dillon and Kumar (1994) compute the parameter estimates and corresponding standard deviations for the latent two- and three-class models shown in Table 2-3.

Table 2-3. **Store Choice Data: Parameter Estimates**
Standard deviations parameters assure boundary value – treated as if fixed, and degrees of freedom adjusted accordingly. Adapted from Dillon and Kumar (1994)

	2-class model		3-class model		
	1	2	1	2	3
Class size θ_s	0.4617	0.583	0.3110	0.1293	0.5597
	(0.055)	(fixed)	(0.053)	(0.045)	(fixed)
Conditional probabilities	0.0295	0.6690	0.000	1.000	0.4368
ϕ_{jrs} store dept.	(0.037)	(0.053)	(bounded)	(bounded)	(0.076)
Specialty	0.4706	0.3310	1.000	0.0000	0.5032
	(fixed)	(fixed)	(bounded)	(bounded)	(fixed)
Catalog experience					
Yes	0.7969	0.6466	0.8282	0.6414	0.6709
	(0.034)	(0.036)	(0.043)	(0.089)	(0.041)
No	0.2031	0.3534	0.1718	0.3580	0.3291
	(fixed)	(fixed)	(fixed)	(fixed)	(fixed)
Prior shopping					
Yes	0.7826	0.2667	0.8678	0.0000	0.4198
	(0.047)	(0.042)	(0.063)	(bounded)	(0.061)
No	0.2174	0.7533	0.1372	1.0000	0.5802
	(fixed)	(fixed)	(fixed)	(bounded)	(fixed)
Information seeking					
Yes	0.7463	0.2437	0.8410	0.0553	0.3699
	(0.049)	(0.039)	(0.071)	(0.101)	(0.047)
No	0.2537	0.7563	0.1590	0.9447	0.6301
	(fixed)	(fixed)	(fixed)	(fixed)	(fixed)
Information transmitting					
Yes	0.9517	0.5455	1.000	0.2528	0.6956
	(0.030)	(0.045)	(bounded)	(0.142)	(0.049)
No	0.0483	0.4545	0.000	0.7472	0.3044
	(fixed)	(fixed)	(bounded)	(fixed)	(bounded)

In the latent two-class model, Class 1, representing a little over 46 percent of the population, contains almost exclusively specialty store shoppers. These shoppers, compared to Class 2, exhibit more catalogue experience, shop in stores prior to purchase, and both seek and transmit information prior to purchase. In the latent three-class model, the classes have an interesting structure with respect to department and specialty store shoppers. Notice that

Class 1 is exclusively made up of specialty store shoppers, whereas Class 2 is exclusively made up of department store shoppers. Class 3 is made up of both types of shoppers, with the odds favouring specialty store shoppers slightly.

Note that whenever a latent class parameter assumes a value of 0.0 or 1.0, a *boundary solution* has been obtained. Here, four parameters in the latent three-class model hit boundary values. When boundary values are encountered, the sampling distribution of X^2 and G^2 are not known. The convention in such cases, according to these authors, is to act as if these parameters had been set *a priori* to 0.0 or 1.0, in which case the large sampling theory underlying the X^2 and G^2 would apply. Thus, in the case of the latent three-class model, the degrees of freedom reported in the table are 18 instead of 14, reflecting the fact that four fewer parameters were estimated. The contrast between Class 1 and Class 2 is apparent. Class 1 specialty store shoppers initiate and engage in all of the pre-purchase activities with greater probability than their Class 2 department store shopper counterparts.

MIXTURE REGRESSION MODELS

The mixture regression framework extends the unconditional mixture approach described in the previous section. As above, we assume that the vector of observations (on the dependent variable) of subject n, y_n, arises from a population which is a mixture of T unknown classes in unknown proportions. The distribution of y_n, given that y_n comes from class t, $f_t(y_n | \theta_t)$, is assumed to be one of the distributions in the exponential family. In addition to the dependent variables, a set of P non-stochastic explanatory variables $X_1, ..., X_P$ ($X_p = (X_{np})$; $p = 1, ..., P$) is specified.

The development of the class of mixture regression models is very similar to that of the mixture models described above. However, the means of the observations in each class here are to be predicted from a set of explanatory variables. To this end, the mean of the distribution is written as $\eta_{nkt} = g(\mu_{nkt})$, where $g(\cdot)$ is the link-function, and η_{nkt} is the linear predictor. Convenient link-functions, called canonical links, are respectively the identity, log, logit, inverse, and squared inverse functions for the normal, Poisson, binomial, gamma, and inverse Gaussian distributions (see Table 2-2). The linear predictor in class t is a linear combination of the P explanatory variables:

$$\eta_{nkt} = \sum_{p=1}^{P} X_{nkp} \beta_{tp},\tag{4}$$

where $\beta_t = (\beta_{tp})$ is a set of regression parameters to be estimated for each class.

Identification and Estimation

The same remarks on identification made above apply to mixture regression models. However, for the mixture regression model, an additional identification problem presents itself concerning the conditioning of the X-matrix and the size of P. Collinearity of the predictors within classes may lead to instable estimates of the regression coefficients and large standard errors. In mixture regression models, this situation is compounded by the fact that there are fewer observations for estimating the regression model in each class than at the aggregate level. Therefore, the condition of the X-variables is an important issue in applications mixture regression models.

The parameters are again estimated by maximizing the log-likelihood:

$$l(\phi \mid y_1,...,y_N) = \sum_{n=1}^{N} \ln\left(\sum_{t=1}^{T} \pi_t f_t(y_n \mid \beta_t)\right),\tag{5}$$

through direct numerical maximization. The E-M algorithm can also be used (cf. Dempster, Laird, and Rubin 1977), where the M-step in this case involves numerical optimization. Again, the number of mixture components is determined as that value which minimizes CAIC.

Application: Trade Show Performance

DeSarbo and Cron (1988) designed a mixture regression model that enables the estimation of separate regression functions (and corresponding object memberships) in a number of classes using maximum likelihood. They used the model to analyze the factors that influence perceptions of trade show performance, and to investigate the presence of classes that differ in the importance attributes to these factors in evaluating trade show performance. The model is a finite mixture of univariate normal densities. The expectations of these densities are specified as linear functions of a pre-specified set of explanatory variables.

In their study, DeSarbo and Cron asked 129 marketing executives to rate their firm's trade show performance on eight performance factors, as well as on overall trade show performance. The performance factors included: 1) Identifying new prospects, 2) Servicing current customers, 3) Introducing new products, 4) Selling at the trade show, 5) Enhancing corporate image, 6) Testing of new products, 7) Enhancing corporate morale, and 8) Gathering competitive information.

An aggregate-level regression analysis of overall performance on the eight performance factors, the results of which are depicted in Table 2-4, revealed that identifying new prospects and new product testing were significantly related to trade show performance. These results were derived by a standard OLS regression of the overall performance ratings on the ratings of the eight factors. However, a mixture regression model revealed two classes (on the basis of the AIC criterion), composed of 59 and 70 marketing executives respectively. The effects of the performance factors in the two classes are markedly different from those at the aggregate level, as shown in Table 2-4.

Table 2-4. **Aggregate and Segment-level Results of the Trade Show Performance Study**
Adapted from DeSarbo and Cron (1988)

	Aggregate	Class 1	Class 2
Intercept	3.03*	4.093*	2.218*
1. New prospects	0.15*	0.126	0.242*
2. Current customers	-0.02	0.287*	-0.164*
3. Product introduction	0.09	-0.157*	0.204*
4. Selling	-0.04	-0.133*	0.074*
5. Enhancing image	0.09	0.128*	0.072
6. New product testing	0.18*	0.107	0.282*
7. Enhancing morale	0.07	0.155*	-0.026
8. Competitive information	0.04	-0.124	0.023
Size (%)	1	0.489	0.511

* $p< 0.05$.

Managers in Class 1 primarily evaluate trade shows in terms of non-selling factors, including servicing current customers and enhancing corporate image and morale. Managers in Class 2 evaluate trade shows primarily on selling factors, including identifying new prospects, introducing new products, selling at the shows, and new product testing. Neither of the two classes considers gathering competitive information important. Whereas the percentage of variance explained by the aggregate regression was 37%, the percentages of explained variance in overall trade show performance in Classes 1 and 2 were respectively 73% and 76%.

LATENT CLASS MULTIDIMENSIONAL SCALING MODELS

Multidimensional Scaling (MDS) can be defined as a set of spatial models and associated estimation procedures utilized to obtain a multidimensional spatial representation of the structure in various types of data including proximity (similarity or dissimilarity), dominance (preferences, ratings), or discrete choice (e.g., "pick any") data. Multidimensional scaling can assist marketing managers and researchers in depicting market structure, market segmentation, product design and positioning, competitive influences and patterns, and relationships between consumer perceptions and choice. Carroll and Arabie (1981) provide an excellent taxonomy of the various MDS methods based on the types of data collected and the associated form of the spatial display of the structure derived from such data. For example, simple unfolding and vector MDS models typically provide a joint space representation of both subjects (e.g., consumers) and stimuli (e.g., brands) in a common dimensional representation for dominance data (e.g., consumers rating their preference for various brands in a specified product class).

One of the obvious limitations of such traditional MDS procedures stems from their inability to represent the structure in such data collected from a representative sample of consumers in a particular market. Marketing research suppliers often collect samples from thousands of consumers, and the ability of MDS procedures to fully portray the structure in such volumes of data is indeed limited. The resulting joint spaces or individual weight spaces become saturated with points/vectors, often rendering interpretation impossible. Yet, marketers are rarely interested in the particular responses of consumers at the individual level because of the impracticality of developing marketing strategy for each consumer. Given the traditional role of market segmentation in marketing strategy, marketers are more concerned with identifying and targeting market segments – homogeneous groups of consumers who share some designated set of characteristics (e.g., demographics, psychographics, consumption patterns, etc.) – that are relevant to the purchase of the brand under study. And this interest in market segmentation is the fundamental motivation for using Latent Class Multidimensional Scaling (LCMDS) methods in marketing. LCMDS performs MDS and segmentation/cluster analysis simultaneously. That is, in a marketing context, LCMDS can portray the structure in the same types of data as traditional MDS procedures, with the difference being that market segments are represented in the resulting maps in place of the individual consumers. Furthermore, a classification of each consumer into the derived market segments is simultaneously estimated (cf. DeSarbo, Manrai, and Manrai 1994; Wedel and DeSarbo 1996).

Let:

$i = 1,\ldots,$ N consumers;

$j = 1,\ldots,$ J brands;

$s = 1,\ldots,$ S dimensions;

$t = 1,\ldots,$ T latent classes;

Δ_i = a one or two-way data array collected from consumer i, where

$$\Delta = ((\Delta_i));$$

θ_{ts} = a concatenated vector of LCMDS parameters where

$$\theta = ((\theta_{ts}));$$

π_t = the latent class mixing parameter where $\pi = ((\pi_t))$.

In the general case, it is assumed that:

$$\Delta_i \sim G_i(\Delta_i^*; \pi, \theta) = \sum_{t=1}^{T} \pi_t f_{it}(\Delta_i \mid \theta_{ts}), \tag{6}$$

where $f_{it}(\Delta_i \mid \theta_{ts})$ is specified depending upon the type of data collected and LCMDS model to be fitted, and the T-1 independent mixing proportions are defined as before.

The specification in (6) implies that if a consumer belongs to segment t, then the structure in the data can be represented by θ_{st} for $s = 1,...,S$ dimensions. The mixing proportions, π_t, can be construed as the prior probability that any consumer belongs to segment t. Once estimates of θ_{st}, for $t = 1,...,T$ and $s=1,...,S$ are obtained, the posterior probability of membership for consumer i in segment t can be computed using Bayes' rule as in equation (2).

Identification and Estimation

Since the number of dimensions and latent classes or groups is rarely known in practice, the E-M estimation algorithm must be run for a varying number of latent classes (T) and number of dimensions (S). (For most LCMDS models, solutions with $S > T$ are not identifiable.) Further issues of identification exist (e.g., origin, rotation) depending upon the specific spatial model estimated. Note that the regularity conditions for the likelihood ratio test typically do not hold for this class of models (see McLachlan and Basford 1988). Accordingly, the "optimum" values of S and T are those for the solution which minimizes CAIC.

Application: Personal Computers

DeSarbo, Howard, and Jedidi (1991) present the results of their latent class vector MDS model, MULTICLUS, on survey data about personal computers. They surveyed 69 graduate and undergraduate students enrolled in the business school of a large southwestern university to measure their evaluations of the importance of various attributes/features of microcomputers. Based on the prior responses of a team of microcomputer experts (owners and heavy users) and novices (non-owners and nonusers), a list of 15 microcomputer product attributes was utilized summarizing the most important aspects of a microcomputer. Researchers also asked this pretest group for judgments about whether the attributes were easy to understand and utilize as simple inferential cues concerning product quality, or whether they were characteristics one would come to appreciate or understand through extensive usage and the experiences associated with purchase or leasing decision-making.

Seven attributes were judged to be best described by the first classification and were expected to be weighted higher in importance by persons with low prior knowledge: (1) ease of use; (2) total package purchase/lease price; (3) length of warranty; (4) compatibility with IBM products/software; (5) the particular brand name or manufacturer; (6) physical styling of the computer; and (7) portability. Hereafter, these seven attributes will be referred to as "heuristic" product attributes. Eight additional attributes were judged to be best described by the alternative criterion noted above: (1) the type (PC, XT, AT) of computer; (2) the amount of internal RAM; (3) whether there is a hard disk; (4) size of the hard disk; (5) type of monitor/screen (e.g., monochrome, color, EGA); (6) number of floppy disk drives; (7) processing speed; and (8) software availability. Hereafter, these eight attributes will be referred to as "focal" product attributes. All 15 attributes were presented to the respondents in this study who were asked "regardless of whether you currently own/lease a microcomputer, indicate the relative importance of the below listed features to you in your purchasing a microcomputer." Items were scored on seven-point scales (not at all important – very important).

MULTICLUS was performed for $S = T = 1,..., 4$, assuming a normal distribution for the observed variables. The CAIC heuristic pointed to the $T = S = 2$ solution as most parsimonious. Figure 2-1 presents the MULTICLUS results for this solution ($\lambda_1 = 0.52$, $\lambda_2 = 0.48$) where the 15 attributes/features are designated by the letters A-O according to the key provided in the Figure, and the two class vectors by "1" and "2". The first dimension appears to separate attributes that relate specifically to user operating convenience, where software availability (E), IBM compatibility (N), and ease of use (A) lie on the extreme left end of the dimension, from those attributes that can be easily inferred through visual observation, where brand name (B), styling (O), and portability (J) lie on the extreme right side. The second dimension clearly distinguishes the "focal" attributes such as hard disk (F), its size (G), and internal RAM (D) from the "heuristic" attributes such as price (K), warranty length (I), ease of use (A), and portability (J). Of interest is the positioning of the two vectors for the two classes. In particular, the focal characteristics such as hard disk and size, internal RAM, software availability, and processing speed project higher on the vector for Class 1, while ease of use, package price, and warranty length (heuristic characteristics) project higher on Class 2's vector. Thus, Class 1 evaluates the more functional and technical (focal) features of microcomputers as most important, while Class 2 appears to weigh the financial and ease of use (heuristic) aspects more heavily.

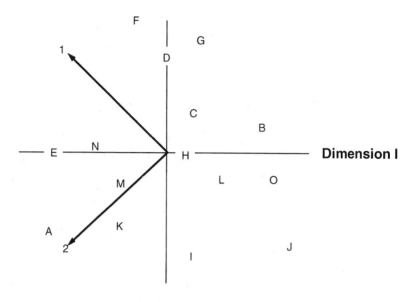

Figure 2-1. **MULTICLUS Configuration of Attributes and Class Vectors for the Microcomputer Data** *(Adapted from DeSarbo, Howard, and Jedidi 1990)*

A: ease of use
B: brand name/manufacturer
C: type of computer
D: amount of internal RAM
E: software availability
F: whether there is a hard disk
G: size of hard disk

H: type of monitor
I: length of warranty
J: portability
K: total package purchase/lease price
L: number of floppy drives
M: processing speed
N: compatibility with IBM products/system
O: styling

FACTOR MODELS

The models discussed so far classify subjects into discrete latent classes based on observed relationships among manifest variables. This is equivalent to measuring these subjects on a discrete latent variable representing their membership to each of the latent classes. In these finite-mixture models, unobserved heterogeneity on the canonical parameter is assumed to be discrete. We now discuss models where the canonical parameter is assumed to be continuously distributed over the population of subjects. Let $n = 1,\ldots, N$ denote subjects, $k = 1,\ldots,K$ variables and $p = 1,\ldots,P$ factors. We assume to have a two-way data matrix Y classified by subjects, n, and variables k. The observations, y_{nk}, are realizations of random variables that have a distribution in the exponential family, $f_k(y_{nk} | \theta_{nk})$. Here, θ_{nk} denotes the canonical parameter.

We specify $f_k(y_{nk} | \theta_{nk})$ to depend upon k; i.e., we allow each observed variable to have its own distribution. For example, we can model a set of variables, where some are described by a normal and others by a binomial distribution. For each of those distributions, we use the canonical link function, $g(\cdot)$, to relate the canonical parameter to the expectation of the random variable. We now specify the canonical parameter as a factor model:

$$\Theta = \lambda_0' + Z\Lambda', \tag{7}$$

with $\Theta = (\theta_{nk})$, Z the $(N \times P)$ matrix representing the scores on the latent variables, Λ a $(K \times P)$ matrix of fixed parameters and λ_0 a $(K \times 1)$ vector with an intercept for each observed variable. The number of latent variables, P, is unknown in most applications and needs to be identified from the data.

We assume that the latent variables, contained in the $(N \times P)$ matrix Z, are independent and follow a distribution in the exponential family. To remain within the factor analysis framework, we consider only continuous distributions in the exponential family. Discrete distributions such as the binomial lead to latent class models discussed above. Note that, conditional upon Z, $f_k(\cdot)$ is a member of the exponential family; the marginal distribution of y_{nk} might not be tractable.

Identification and Estimation

The standard factor model suffers from location, scale, and rotation indeterminacy. Location indeterminacy is typically handled by constraining the mean of the factor scores to zero. With the exception of those cases where the factor scores are normally distributed, the model is not rotation invariant. Rotation invariance may or may not be considered a useful property of exploratory factor models, but can be easily handled by imposing $P(P-1)/2$ constraints to the weights in Λ.

Estimation is again accomplished by maximizing the log-likelihood function, which is obtained by integrating over the distribution of the unobserved factor scores:

$$l(\phi | y_1,..., y_N) = \sum_{n=1}^{N} \ln\left(\iint f(y_n | Z, \Lambda) f(Z | \varphi) dZ\right), \tag{8}$$

The estimation of ϕ is often not feasible, given the high-dimensional integration involved in the likelihood, since that in general cannot be evaluated numerically. However, advances in simulated likelihood (SML) estimation have made the approximation of such integrals possible (Gouriéroux and Monfort 1997). One of the advantages of estimating factor models via simulated maximum likelihood as opposed to traditional least squares approach, even when this latter approach is feasible, is that the former tends to perform better in the presence of missing data. This feature makes the generalized factor model useful for purposes of missing data imputation (Kamakura and Wedel 2000).

Application: The Challenge of Missing Data

Kamakura and Wedel (2000) used a factor model to examine data from a commercial customer-satisfaction survey among 1,375 bank customers. This application illustrates the flexibility of the generalized factor model described above, combining: (a) customer perceptions on twelve satisfaction attributes, assessed with 3-point rating scales and binary items, (b) overall satisfaction, assessed on a 4-point rating scale, and (c) ten customer characteristics, assessed on binary, interval, and ratio scales.

The main purpose of this particular application was to test and demonstrate the usefulness of the factor model for imputing missing data. For this purpose, the authors created a scenario in which the researcher is interested in linking customer satisfaction to service perceptions. Due to concerns about data collection costs or about potential common-methods biases, however, the researcher in the scenario decides to collect the satisfaction and service perception data from two separate, randomly split samples. To simulate this scenario, Kamakura and Wedel randomly split the sample, and held out the data on satisfaction or service perceptions in either half, so that the only the data on customer characteristics are common across the two samples.

Application of the factor model with mixed outcome variables and normally distributed factor scores to these highly incomplete data led to the factor solution shown in Table 2-5. Since the factor model is only used to capture the covariances among the observed variables as a vehicle for data fusion, interpretation of the factor loadings (λ) is not of direct interest in this case.

The main purposes of this experiment were twofold. The first was to test the quality of the imputations of the missing (holdout) data using the actual holdouts. The quality of missing data imputations is reported in Table 2-6 (from Kamakura and Wedel 2000) under the heading R_{OI}, which shows the correlations between imputations and actual holdout values. These correlations are quite high, around 0.7 or higher in all cases. Thus, the generalized factor model recovers the two blocks of data missing by design quite well.

Table 2-5. **Factor Solution for the Customer Satisfaction Study Based on Incomplete Data**
Adapted from Kamakura and Wedel (2000)

Item	λ_0	ϕ	λ_1	λ_2
Transactions/mo	0.01	0.97	-0.07	0.17
Contribution	0.00	0.66	0.39	0.61
Volume of Deposits	0.01	0.83	0.38	0.68
Education (1-5)	2.84		-1.46	0.77
Age (10s, 20, 30, 40, 50, 60+)	0.81		0.47	0.33
Female/Male	1.26		0.17	0.13
Own/Not Car	-3.66		1.56	-0.06
Own/Not Phone	-4.26		0.66	-1.50
Own/Not Fax	2.36		1.44	-0.94
Own/Not PC	0.38		1.59	-1.08
Clerks are competent (1-3)	1.97		1.19	1.53
Clerks are polite (1-3)	2.36		1.20	1.66
Clerks willing to answer questions (1-3)	1.50		1.01	1.44
Too much time wasted on lines (1-2)	-0.12		-1.26	-1.61
No consideration to loyal customers (1-2)	-0.90		-1.43	-1.67
Difficult to pay bills at the branch (1-2)	-1.98		-1.33	-1.83
Bank made mistakes on my account (1-2)	-3.18		-1.15	-1.42
Electronic equip always out of order (1-2)	-0.92		-1.06	-1.72
Electronic equip always short of paper (1-2)	-1.65		-1.34	-1.98
Electronic equip always short of cash (1-2)	-3.24		-1.27	-2.62
Bank is disorganized and bureaucratic (1-2)	-2.29		-1.57	-2.09
Bank commercials promise more than deliver (1-2)	-1.98		-1.60	-1.96
Would recommend the bank (1-4)	1.45		1.46	0.57

The second purpose of the experiment was to demonstrate that the generalized factor model can be used to estimate the relationship between overall satisfaction and service perceptions, even if predictors and dependent variable are collected from two separate samples. This feature can be seen in the other two columns of Table 2-6, which compare the correlation between service perceptions and overall satisfaction on the true (shown as R_O) and on the imputed data (shown as R_I). Note that in the second (data fusion) case, service perceptions and satisfaction ratings are never observed for the same consumers, and therefore cannot be computed directly on the observed data; these correlations can only be estimated through imputations of the missing data. Table 2-6 shows that the true and the recovered correlations are relatively close. However, the correlation coefficients computed from the imputed data seem to be somewhat biased upwards in an absolute sense, even though these correlations were averaged across 50 imputations.

Table 2-6. Comparisons between Imputed and Actual Data
Adapted from Kamakura and Wedel (2000)

Satisfaction Items	R_{OI}	R_O	R_1
Clerks are competent	0.766	0.579	0.630
Clerks are polite	0.794	0.543	0.538
Clerks willing to answer questions	0.756	0.524	0.532
Too much time wasted on lines	0.743	-0.385	-0.491
No consideration to loyal customers	0.761	-0.451	-0.535
Difficult to pay bills at the branch	0.727	-0.379	-0.481
Bank made mistakes on my account	0.722	-0.302	-0.295
Electronic equip always out of order	0.730	-0.351	-0.441
Electronic equip always short of paper	0.740	-0.287	-0.476
Electronic equip always short of cash	0.683	-0.240	-0.376
Bank is disorganized and bureaucratic	0.781	-0.522	-0.539
Commercials promise more than delivered	0.732	-0.470	-0.533
Would recommend the bank	0.816	-	-

FACTOR REGRESSION MODELS

Similar to their discrete counterpart (i.e., finite mixtures), factor models can be used for a parsimonious account of unobserved heterogeneity in regression models. Let the canonical parameter θ_{nk} for variable k and subject n be regressed on a ($R \times 1$) vector of predictors X_{nk}, with a ($1 \times R$) vector of regression coefficients β_{nk} :

$$\theta_{nk} = \beta_{nk} X_{nk} \tag{9}$$

However, instead of estimating one regression coefficient for each item k and subject n, we account for unobserved heterogeneity in response parameters across subjects via a factor model,

$$B = \lambda_0' + Z\Lambda', \tag{10}$$

with $B = (\beta_{nk})$, an ($N \times RK$) matrix, Z the ($N \times P$) matrix representing the scores on the latent variables, Λ a ($RK \times P$) matrix of fixed parameters and λ_0 a ($RK \times 1$) vector with the average response parameters for each item k and predictor r across all subjects. This formulation provides the average regression for each item (through the parameter vector λ_0), as well as insights into how each subject's response deviates from this average regression, through the factor scores $Z\Lambda'$. The formulation also provides a more parsimonious representation of unobserved heterogeneity than the usual random-coefficients model, reducing the number of parameters to be estimated by $(R*K)[(R*K-1)/2 -P+1)]$.

The factor solution in (10) may also provide valuable insights on the patterns of response to the R predictors for the K items across subjects. If subjects who are more responsive than average to predictor r for item k are also as responsive to predictor r' for item k', these predictor/item combinations will have similar weights in Λ, and will be represented as vectors pointing to the same direction in the factor space.

Identification and Estimation

The factor regression model suffers from location, scale, and rotation indeterminacy, similar to the standard factor model. Rotation invariance may or may not be considered a useful property of exploratory factor models, but can be easily handled by imposing $P(P-1)/2$ constraints to the weights in Λ. However, for the factor regression model an additional identification problem presents itself concerning the conditioning of the X-matrix and the size of P.

Estimation is again accomplished by maximizing the log-likelihood function, which is obtained by integrating over the distribution of the unobserved factor scores:

$$l(\phi \mid y_1,...,y_N) = \sum_{n=1}^{N} \ln\left(\iiint f(y_n \mid Z,\Lambda)f(Z \mid \varphi)dZ\right), \qquad (11)$$

The estimation is done using simulated likelihood (SML) estimation (Gouriéroux and Monfort 1997).

Application: Drug Prescriptions

To illustrate factor regression models, we summarize the Multivariate Tobit Factor model proposed by Kamakura and Wedel (2001), which they used to analyze the volume of drug prescriptions written by a group of physicians over the course of a year. This model is a multivariate extension of the well-known Tobit model, which allows for two types of partially observed variables $y_{nk}^{(1)}$ and $y_{nk}^{(2)}$ that drive the zero and non-zero observations, respectively. These partially observed variables differ in their mean values, η_k and μ_k, and are assumed to be explained by the same $(Rx1)$ vector of predictors X_{nk} through the same linear model, defined by the same $(Rx1)$ vector of regression coefficients β_{nk},

$$y_{nk}^{(1)} = \eta_k + \beta_{nk} X_{nk} + \varepsilon_{nk} ,$$
$$y_{nk}^{(2)} = \mu_k + \beta_{nk} X_{nk} + \varepsilon_{nk} ,$$
$$y_{nj} = y_{nj}^{(2)} \text{ if } y_{nj}^{(1)} > 0 ,$$

$$y_{nj} = 0 \quad \text{if} \quad y_{nj}^{(1)} \leq 0.$$

$$\varepsilon_{nk} \sim \text{i.i.d. } N(0,\sigma_k) . \tag{12}$$

The multivariate Tobit model described above involves a large number of parameters at the subject-item level (β_{nk}) and at the item level $(\eta_k$, μ_k and $\sigma_k)$, which make its estimation infeasible. For this reason, the factor structure in (10) is imposed on the distribution of the regression coefficients β_{nk} across subjects, leading to a much more parsimonious model that accounts for the unobserved heterogeneity in response across subjects. The model described above amounts to a random-coefficients multivariate Tobit regression model, with a factor decomposition of the covariance of the random-coefficients distribution. With the assumption of i.i.d. factor scores, the model requires the estimation of $(R*K*P)$ factor loadings, $(R*K)$ average response coefficients, and $(3K)$ item-specific intercepts, thresholds, and standard deviations. Details about the estimation of the multivariate Tobit factor model can be found in Kamakura and Wedel (2001, appendix).

The factor loadings can be visually represented as vector termini for each item k and for each predictor including the intercept, with the angles among these vectors representing the correlation among item coefficients across subjects. This mapping of intercepts and regression coefficients for all the items results in a simple and intuitive representation of cross-sectional heterogeneity in response.

Kamakura and Wedel (2001) used factor regression models to address the challenge of truncated data in analyzing the volume of prescriptions for 33 different pharmaceutical drugs written by 500 physicians during one year. These data are heavily truncated because each physician prescribes only a subset of these 33 drugs. Because there were no exogenous variables to predict the prescription levels for each drug, the authors apply a special case of the factor regression model with heterogeneity only in the regression intercept. Table 2-7 (adapted from Kamakura and Wedel 2001) shows the parameter estimates obtained with a 3-factor solution, chosen based on the BIC criterion.

The last two columns of Table 2-7 show two measures of fit for each of the 33 drugs, the correlation between observed and fitted volume of prescriptions among prescribing physicians (R), and the percentage of correct predictions of whether each data point is observed or censored (%C). While the performance of the model varies across drugs, in general it seems to fit well both in the discrete (censoring mechanism) and continuous portion of the data. Moreover, the factor solution seems to have face validity, as shown in Figure 2-2 (from Kamakura and Wedel 2001), which displays the factor loadings (λ_{i1}, λ_{i2}, and λ_{i3}) for the 33 drugs, identified by therapy. Based on the top panel of Figure 2-2, Factor 1 can be interpreted as the propensity to prescribe *neurological drugs,* while Factor 2 seems to indicate the propensity to prescribe *analgesics.* The bottom panel indicates that Factor 3 can be interpreted as the propensity to prescribe *psychiatric drugs.*

Table 2-7. **Parameter Estimates for the 3-Factor Tobit Factor Model**

DRUG	Therapy	σ_j	μ_j	η_j	λ_{j1}	λ_{j2}	λ_{j3}	R	%C
ADDERALL	convulsion	93.6	12.0	-87.9	-0.042	-0.030	<u>0.992</u>	0.53	86.4
AMBIEN	Psychoter	41.2	53.5	99.2	0.074	0.206	<u>1.144</u>	0.65	94.6
ARICEPT	alzheimer	14.8	13.9	2.0	0.505	0.202	0.526	0.51	42.8
CATAFLAM	arthritic	13.1	-0.2	-8.5	0.168	<u>0.791</u>	0.039	0.19	30.6
DAYPRO	arthritic	33.0	8.2	13.1	0.224	<u>0.847</u>	-0.073	0.50	64.0
DURACT	analgesic	14.3	-0.5	-9.4	0.168	<u>0.956</u>	-0.087	0.47	66.4
DURAGESIC	analgesic	18.4	8.4	-7.6	0.133	0.317	-0.104	0.16	65.2
EFFEXOR	antidepress	16.4	18.0	13.1	0.146	-0.058	<u>1.702</u>	0.56	59.0
EFFEXOR XR	antidepress	32.7	17.3	-7.7	0.025	0.032	<u>1.231</u>	0.33	29.0
IMITREX (INJ)	analgesic	4.7	1.2	-1.2	<u>4.255</u>	<u>1.902</u>	0.184	0.97	90.6
IMITREX (TAB)	analgesic	24.2	14.6	23.0	<u>1.153</u>	0.656	0.139	0.64	65.0
IMITREX NASL	analgesic	8.8	2.6	-2.7	<u>0.904</u>	0.530	0.148	0.57	73.6
LODINE	arthritic	7.8	3.0	-5.5	0.165	<u>0.757</u>	-0.078	0.36	70.2
LODINE XL	arthritic	24.3	0.8	-11.9	0.084	<u>0.800</u>	0.232	0.42	65.6
LUVOX	antidepress	19.3	8.6	-3.9	0.055	-0.121	<u>1.861</u>	0.63	73.8
NAPRELAN	arthritic	13.1	1.0	-8.0	0.243	<u>0.874</u>	0.066	0.33	68.2
NEURONTIN	convulsion	77.5	31.4	17.8	0.221	0.156	0.486	0.17	49.8
ORUVAIL	arthritic	9.4	2.0	-7.2	0.190	<u>0.848</u>	-0.073	0.43	71.0
PAXIL	antidepress	53.8	95.9	139.9	0.318	-0.159	<u>2.045</u>	0.80	88.8
PROSOM	Psychoter	6.3	5.7	-6.3	0.032	0.203	0.213	0.15	85.2
RELAFEN	arthritic	37.1	15.5	24.4	0.280	<u>0.823</u>	-0.090	0.52	70.0
REMERON	antidepress	56.6	21.0	-15.7	0.072	-0.141	<u>1.346</u>	0.71	74.0
RISPERDAL	Psychoter	34.6	28.5	22.4	0.157	-0.261	<u>2.219</u>	0.84	48.4
SERZONE	antidepress	23.0	25.7	23.9	0.298	-0.140	<u>2.215</u>	0.80	54.6
SINEMET CR	parkinson	19.8	10.5	-10.3	0.503	0.321	0.134	0.48	31.0
STADOL NS	analgesic	9.4	7.1	-4.7	0.431	0.440	0.392	0.28	73.8
TEGRETOL XR	convulsion	40.4	17.3	-39.5	0.507	0.053	0.572	0.49	87.8
TORADOL ORL	analgesic	2.1	2.0	-2.9	0.068	0.502	-0.303	0.17	87.2
ULTRAM	analgesic	29.9	21.8	32.0	0.236	<u>0.975</u>	0.065	0.64	77.4
VICOPROFEN	analgesic	14.7	5.1	-12.0	0.067	0.523	0.144	0.24	77.4
VOLTAREN-XR	arthritic	17.9	0.4	-9.5	0.150	<u>0.879</u>	-0.109	0.43	63.4
ZOLOFT	antidepress	77.5	110.0	205.2	0.246	-0.105	<u>1.829</u>	0.73	91.6
ZYPREXA	Psychoter	51.4	15.6	-8.2	0.093	-0.356	<u>1.910</u>	0.72	25.8

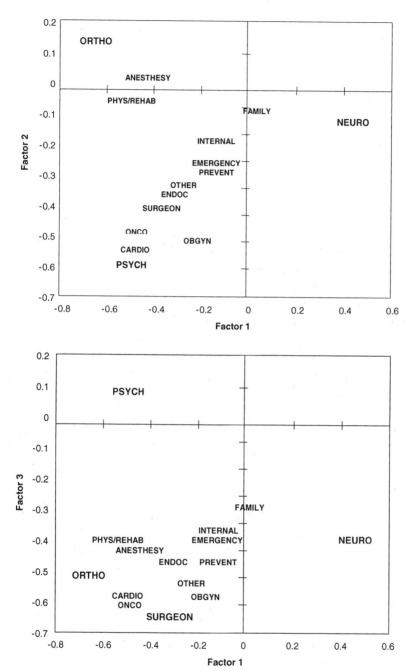

Figure 2-2. **Factor Loadings by Therapy**
Adapted from Kamakura and Wedel (2001)

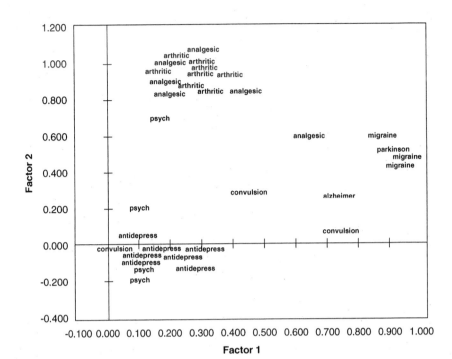

Figure 2-3. **Average Factor Scores by Physician Specialty**
Adapted from Kamakura and Wedel (2001)

Further evidence of face validity for the 3-factor solution can be found in Figure 2-3 (from Kamakura and Wedel 2001), which displays the average factor scores, based on the same factor solution shown in Table 2-6, for a larger sample of 4,361 physicians, classified by specialty. As one would expect, Figure 2-3 shows that neurologists have the highest average score on Factor 1, which was identified as the propensity to prescribe neurological drugs. Similarly, orthopedists have the highest score on Factor 2, identified as the propensity to prescribe analgesics and anti-arthritic drugs. Again as one might expect, physicians in family, internal, and preventive practice also have a high propensity to prescribe analgesics, according to the factor solution. Finally, a comparison of the factor loadings map in Figure 2-2 with the average scores in Figure 2-3 shows psychiatrists as having the highest average scores on Factor 3, the propensity to prescribe anti-depressants and other psychiatric drugs.

SOFTWARE

In addition to the developments in modeling since Paul Green began his pioneering applications of multivariate models to marketing, we have also seen the emergence of powerful new computer programs to support this work. As an example, we consider one of these software programs, GLIMMIX, which is the most widely dispersed software for the estimation of latent variable models involving finite mixtures. GLIMMIX is a statistical program for estimating exponential family mixture models and mixtures of generalized linear regression models. (GLIMMIX 3.0 executes under WINDOWS 95, NT, 2000 and XP.)

GLIMMIX operates in five major steps, which are activated from the five buttons on the toolbar: *Step 1*: Define the variables in the dataset; *Step 2*: Recode the variables in the dataset; *Step 3*: Make a selection of cases from the dataset; *Step 4*: Provide the specifications for the analysis; *Step 5*: View the results of the analysis.

GLIMMIX supports various types of input data. One may fit a standard mixture model, or a regression mixture model. It accommodates several specifications of the statistical distribution of the dependent variable, where the options normal and gamma are available for continuous variables, and binomial, multinomial, and Poisson for discrete variables. Documented applications of GLIMMIX include mixture model analysis of customer satisfaction data, direct marketing list segmentation problems, conjoint analysis and conjoint choice experiments, and so on. In addition, GLIMMIX 3.0 allows one to estimate specific forms of concomitant variable models, to add a random responder class to the model, to filter out subjects that do not show effects of the independent variable on the dependent variables and to do analyses specifically for (rank order) rating scales. GLIMMIX 3.0 deals with missing observations in the data and allows one to select a subset of subjects for analysis. The posterior probabilities are also computed for the missing subjects, which is useful for data-fusion, split questionnaire, and sub-sampling problems. For each distribution, a number of link functions can be chosen. Several output items are available, such as estimates of the posterior probabilities, coefficients and standard errors, the selection statistics AIC, CAIC, MAIC, BIC. Several graphics can be displayed, e.g., showing histograms of the coefficient estimates across classes, plots of the likelihood against the EM iterations, or plots of the information statistics against the number of classes. A demo-version of the software can be downloaded from the ProGAMMA homepage: http://www.gamma.rug.nl.

CONCLUSION AND AREAS FOR FUTURE RESEARCH

Extending the framework for latent variable models provided by Bartholomew and Knott (1999), we have illustrated some of the progress made in the development and application of multivariate latent variable models in marketing in the three decades since their introduction by Paul Green. Now, a large variety of models, in which either discrete or continuous latent variables, or a mix of both are assumed, can be estimated to marketing data, due to the availability of numerical methods such as the E-M algorithm and Simulated Maximum Likelihood. What method is most appropriate in a particular application depends on the extent to which the latent variable structure and the assumed metrics of manifest and latent variables in the model match the properties of the data and the intended purpose of the application.

There are several areas for future research in multivariate analysis. First, whereas rough indicators and guidelines are available for model selection, much more theoretical work is needed to guide the selection of the most appropriate model. Second, we need to see more efforts at combining discrete and continuous heterogeneity via random effects and finite mixtures to model marketing phenomena. Third, efforts to make the derived market segments in finite mixture approaches more managerially meaningful need to take front stage in future research efforts. The derived segments need to display the desired characteristics (e.g., identifiability, differentiability, reachability, actionability, substantiality, etc.) of all market segment results. Finally, more comparative research is needed that contrasts the results of such advanced methodology to more traditional methods by type of marketing problem area.

REFERENCES

Bartholomew, D. J., and Knott, M. (1999), *Latent Variable Models and Factor Analysis* (2nd ed.), Kendall's Library of Statistics 7, New York: Edward Arnold.

Bozdogan, H. (1987), "Model selection and Akaike's Information Criterion (AIC): The general theory and its analytical extensions," *Psychometrika*, 52, 345-370.

Carroll, J. D. (1980), "Models and methods for multidimensional analysis of preferential choice data," in E.D. Lantermann and H. Feger (eds.), *Similarity and Choice*, Bern: Hans Huber, 234-269.

Carroll, J. D., and Arabie, P. (1981), "Multidimensional scaling," *Annual Review of Psychology*, 31, 607-649.

Dash, J. F., Shiffman, L. G., and Berenson, C. (1975), "Information search and store choice," *Journal of Advertising Research*, 16, 35-40.

Dempster, A. P., Laird, N. M., and Rubin, R. B. (1977), "Maximum likelihood from incomplete data via the EM-algorithm," *Journal of the Royal Statistical Society,* B39, 1-38.

DeSarbo, W. S., and Cron, W. L. (1988), "A maximum likelihood methodology for clusterwise linear regression," *Journal of Classification*, 5, 249-282.

DeSarbo, W. S., Howard, D. J., and Jedidi, K. (1990), "MULTICLUS: A new method for simultaneously performing scaling and cluster analysis," *Psychometrika,* 56, 121-136.

DeSarbo, W. S., Manrai, A. K., and Manrai, L. A. (1994), "Latent class multidimensional scaling: A review of recent development in the marketing and psychometrika literature," in R. P. Bagozzi (ed.), *Advanced Methods of Marketing Research*, Cambridge, MA: Blackwell, pp. 190-222.

Dillon, W. R., and Kumar, A. (1994), "Latent structure and other mixture models in marketing: An integrative survey and review," in R. P. Bagozzi (ed.), *Advanced Methods of Marketing Research,* Cambridge, MA: Blackwell, pp. 295-351.

Gouriéroux, C., and Monfort, A. (1997), *Simulation Based Econometric Methods*, New York: Oxford University Press.

Green, P. E. (1978), *Analyzing Multivariate Behavior*, Hinsdale, IL: Dryden Press.

Green, P. E., Carmone, F. J., and Wachpress, D. P. (1976), "Consumer segmentation via latent class analysis," *Journal of Consumer Research*, 3, 170-174.

Green, P. E., Carmone, F. J., and Wachpress, D. P. (1977), "On the analysis of qualitative data in marketing research," *Journal of Marketing Research*, 14, 52-59.

Kamakura, W. A., and Wedel, M. (2000), "Factor analysis and missing data," *Journal of Marketing Research,* 37 (4), 490-98.

Kamakura, W. A., and Wedel, M. (2001), "Exploratory Tobit factor analysis for multivariate censored data," *Multivariate Behavioral Research,* 36 (1), 53-82.

Loehlin, J. C. (1998), *Latent Variable Models: An Introduction to Factor, Path, and Structural Analysis*, (3rd ed.), Mahwah, NJ: Lawrence Erlbaum.

McLachlan, G.J., and Basford, K.E. (1988), *Mixture Models*, New York: Marcel Dekker.

Titterington, D. M., Smith, A. F. M., and Makov, U. E. (1985), *Statistical Analysis of Finite Mixture Distributions,* New York: Wiley.

Von Eye, A., and Clogg, C. (1994), *Latent Variable Analysis: Applications for Developmental Research*, Thousand Oaks, CA: Sage.

Wedel, M., and DeSarbo, W. S. (1994), "A review of latent class regression models and their applications," in R. P. Bagozzi (ed.), *Advanced Methods for Marketing Research*, Cambridge, MA: Blackwell, pp. 353-388.

Wedel, M., and DeSarbo, W. S. (1996), "An exponential family multidimensional scaling mixture methodology," *Journal of Business and Economic Statistics*, 14, 447-459.

Wedel, M., and Kamakura, W. A. (2001), *Market Segmentation, Methodological and Conceptual Foundations* (2nd ed.), Dordrecht: Kluwer.

PART THREE: MULTIDIMENSIONAL SCALING

Paul Green helped to develop and refine Multidimensional Scaling (MDS) and clustering methodologies. In Chapter 3, Douglas Carroll, Phipps Arabie, Anil Chaturvedi, and Lawrence Hubert examine the development of MDS methodologies, with particular attention to Paul Green's contributions.

Chapter 3

Multidimensional Scaling and Clustering in Marketing: Paul Green's Role[1]

J. Douglas Carroll, *Rutgers University*
Phipps Arabie, *Rutgers University*
Anil Chaturvedi, *Capital One*
Lawrence Hubert, *University of Illinois-Champaign and University of Leiden*

This paper is divided into two main parts: The first concerns the history of Multidimensional Scaling (MDS), focusing especially on Paul Green's role in defining the role of MDS in marketing. The second concerns Clustering, again emphasizing Green's role in defining the theory and practice of clustering methodology applied to marketing, both in the form of market segmentation and various tools used in competitive market structure analysis.

INTRODUCTORY OVERVIEW: PAUL GREEN'S ROLE IN REDEFINING MARKETING DECISION MAKING

It would be an understatement to say that Paul Green is the most widely recognized name in marketing research, both nationally and internationally. Nearly all marketing researchers in industry and academia, both in the U.S. and internationally, have heard of Paul Green and have been influenced by his work in some aspects of their daily marketing activity. The breadth of impact of Green's work on the theory and practice of marketing can be gauged from the fact that he has (re)defined the following fundamental concepts found in nearly all undergraduate and graduate marketing texts: new product design, concept testing, concept evaluation, product positioning, market segmentation, product portfolio, profitability, product line extensions, perceptual mapping, and many others.

Without restating the many contributions that Green has made to marketing, we would like to bring to our readers' notice the following two facts about his work that are not (at least yet) as widely known among marketing academicians and practitioners. First, while both academicians and practitioners have successfully understood and applied Green's work in improving the quality of marketing decision making, another substantive application of Green's work on conjoint analysis has thus far been ignored. Although derived attribute importances from conjoint analysis applications have been used for designing products, a very important interpretation of the derived attribute importances from conjoint applications has gone virtually unnoticed – that attribute importances can be considered to be fundamental measures of consumers' needs for those attributes. This interpretation of attribute importances derived from conjoint analyses as "consumer needs" results in conjoint analysis being used as a technique for needs measurement in addition to being used for product design, at least in those cases and product categories where product attributes can be specified à priori. Further elaboration will be given later in this chapter.

MULTIDIMENSIONAL SCALING

The earliest development of multidimensional scaling (MDS) was the theoretical work published in *Psychometrika* by G. Young and Householder (1938), which showed how to produce a Euclidean MDS representation with the origin placed at any one of the n stimulus points, often representing products in marketing applications, and assuming, as input, ratio scale distance estimates. Richardson (1938) followed that work with the first paper applying this approach to MDS, a strictly one-dimensional application involving stimuli consisting of various shades of gray (a rather colorless application to the "color" domain).

The computational intractability of this methodology (no doubt complicated by the onset of WWII) resulted in the field's lying fallow until the early 1950s, when, expedited by the emergence of digital computer technology, Torgerson and various mentors and collaborators (Gulliksen, Tucker, Abelson, Messick, B. F. Green, and probably others) revived and improved this methodology, enabling use of interval as well as ratio scale data, making the method much more robust by devising a solution putting the origin at the centroid of all the stimuli instead of at some arbitrary stimulus point, and, probably most importantly, adapting it to use on digital computers. This development led to what is now usually called the "classical two-way metric MDS" method most typically associated with Torgerson (1952, 1958), and also later Gower (1966). As Paul Green has pointed out, the very first marketing application of MDS was an unpublished one by Torgerson, in which the stimuli/products were various silverware patterns.

Soon after Torgerson's work, Coombs (1964) and some of his students developed an approach to what they called "nonmetric MDS" (now sometimes called "completely nonmetric MDS"; see Holman, 1978, for a good exposition and an attempt to convert this into a computer algorithm). The Coombs school's approach was not so much a methodology as a set of somewhat vaguely expressed ideas and some "rules of thumb" that constituted more of a rough outline of a method than a precise algorithm, but it did provide a theoretical basis for the notion that well-defined MDS solutions could, in principle, be derived from even weaker, ordinal scale (or "nonmetric") data on similarities or dissimilarities (i.e., "proximities," to use the more general term first employed in this context by Coombs).

In 1962 Roger Shepard (1962a, 1962b) devised the first successful computer implemented algorithm, which he called "analysis of proximities," for nonmetric MDS in the modern sense. Shepard was (originally, at least) more interested in the theoretical problem of finding the nature and "shape" of the typically monotone distance function transforming observed proximities into recovered distances in an underlying Euclidean space than in the use of nonmetric MDS to infer the underlying dimensions inherent within a specific domain of stimuli. It soon became clear, however, that the power of MDS (metric *or* nonmetric) to find such underlying dimensional structure in proximity data was by far the most important potential application of this powerful new methodology. The fact that *nonmetric* MDS enabled use of a much wider variety of types of data than did the metric counterparts was perhaps the most exciting aspect of Shepard's seminal work.

In 1964, Joseph Kruskal (1964a, 1964b) developed a much more mathematically rigorous approach to what he now, following Coombs's earlier terminology, explicitly called "Nonmetric Multidimensional Scaling," devising an algorithm using in alternation *both* monotone regression *and* the method of steepest descent (or gradient method), the latter being a numerical procedure for optimizing a nonlinear function of many variables that was essentially unknown to most psychometricians and mathematical psychologists at that time (although now this, as well as much more sophisticated optimization techniques, are generally quite well known in these fields, as well as in marketing) to minimize a measure of "badness-of-fit" he called STRESS. (A different measure of STRESS, called STRESS2, was later introduced (Kruskal and Carroll 1969) primarily to handle the case of what Coombs had dubbed "off diagonal conditional proximity data," most often associated with unfolding analysis – or what we prefer to refer to as "fitting of an ideal point model" to individual difference preferential choice data.) Kruskal also introduced the idea of fitting MDS models assuming metrics *other than* Euclidean – specifically the "Minkowski-*p*" or L_p metrics, the best known and most widely used of which is the well-known L_1 or "city block" metric, in which distance is the sum over dimensions of absolute values of coordinate differences instead of the square root of the sum of squared coordinate differences (see review by Arabie 1991, and references therein to specialized algorithms and software for fitting city-block metrics).

The INDSCAL Model

In 1969 and 1970, Carroll and Chang introduced the INDSCAL model and method (Carroll and Chang, 1970), which assumes a generalized, weighted, Euclidean metric, with a different profile of weights for each subject (or other source of data), so that a very wide variety of different "private perceptual spaces" can be accommodated within the purview of this model, having a common "group stimulus space" containing dimensions common to all subjects/sources, and the profile of salience weights for these dimensions differing from subject/source to subject/source. The INDSCAL model assumes, as input, interval scale data, and has the additional very important property called "dimensional uniqueness," which means that, even though it is basically a Euclidian distance model, the dimensions or coordinate axes are uniquely identified, and *not* subject to rotational indeterminacy. This feature provides a tremendous advantage in interpreting MDS configurations (which may be almost impossible to interpret in higher than two or three dimensions because of the near intractability of finding a "right" or "interpretable" rotation of a high dimensional spatial representation). Much experience with the INDSCAL methodology demonstrates that this theoretical property in fact works very well in practice, given that INDSCAL representations are almost always interpretable without rotation.

The most user-friendly implementation of the INDSCAL method is provided by Pruzansky's (1975) SINDSCAL program, which is specialized to the case of the kind of three-way symmetric data matrices most often arising in application of individual differences MDS. The older INDSCAL program is still useful for more general analyses – called CANDECOMP (for *CANonical DECOMPosition* of *N*-way tables) of three-way or higher-way data – thus providing, among other options, an approach to three-way or higher-way factor or components analysis. CANDECOMP is closely related to Harshman and Lundy's (1984) PARAFAC approach. The INDSCAL program also allows certain other analyses of more general proximity structures; e.g., "four-way MDS," in which, say, different subjects (e.g., consumers) judge similarity or dissimilarity of pairs of stimuli (e.g., products) under different "scenarios" (e.g., before and after some promotional message has been delivered, or after different such promotional messages are delivered).

Other methods of both two-way and three-way (or individual differences) MDS have been devised since then; most notably Takane, Young, and de Leeuw's (1977) ALSCAL approach, Ramsay's (1977, 1983) maximum likelihood approach (called MULTISCALE), and Heiser and de Leeuw's (1979) SMACOF. The recently implemented version of SMACOF, now available as PROXSCAL in the CATEGORIES module for SPSS (Meulman, Heiser, and SPSS 1999), includes a three-way nonmetric option (fitting the INDSCAL weighted Euclidean model to ordinal – or nonmetric – data) as well as two-way nonmetric MDS, with various options for missing data, unfolding analysis, etc. This is perhaps the most flexible MDS method now widely available for nonmetric analysis.

For metric analyses of three-way MDS data, either SINDSCAL, PROXSCAL, or MULTISCALE are the preferred methods, while for strictly two-way analysis either the "classical" two-way MDS method or KYST are probably still the preferred methods for most purposes, provided that the user is familiar with FORTRAN formats, but the two-way option in MULTISCALE may be appropriate if a maximum likelihood solution is sought. Well-written software for fitting both two-way and three-way MDS models is included in SYSTAT, originally founded by Leland Wilkinson (SYSTAT 2002). Various theoretical and methodological problems make ALSCAL less appropriate for most MDS analyses (see, e.g., Weinberg and Menil 1993, or MacCallum 1977).

Unfolding Analysis and "Ideal Points"

Unfolding analysis, as mentioned, can be implemented by using KYST with appropriate options (see Kruskal and Carroll 1969, or Carroll 1972, 1980, 2002, for details), and is the preferred approach for multidimensional analysis of individual differences preference data (using an "ideal point" model). Unfolding is, *de facto*, subject to a very serious and seemingly intractable "degeneracy" or "quasi-degeneracy" problem (see Heiser 1981). In practice, probably the most effective MDS method for analysis of individual differences preferences is the MDPREF (Chang and Carroll 1969, 1989) method, or some other approach based on the much simpler linear model called the "vector model for preferences." Carroll (1972, 1980, 2002) discusses the theoretical basis for this model and the underpinnings of the MDPREF methodology in considerable detail. Suffice it to say that the vector model, which MDPREF fits via a straightforward procedure based on singular value decomposition, can be viewed as a special (limiting) case of the ideal point model underlying unfolding analysis, with ideal points "infinitely distant" from the stimuli.

Apparently, in practice, ideal points for individuals are, if not infinitely distant from the actual stimuli (e.g., products in a marketing application), so far from realistic stimuli (say, products) as to be, for all practical purposes, effectively "infinitely distant." In the case of "ideal automobiles," for example, many consumers would, if not otherwise constrained, describe their "ideal car" as a very spacious, luxurious, comfortable, exceedingly safe sports car, which gets as close as possible to an infinite number of miles per gallon and is extremely economical in terms of maintenance and other costs, while having a price equal or very nearly equal to zero. Thus, given no constraints at all, most people would have an "ideal product" that simply does not (and could not) exist, so that such ideal points are precisely or near infinitely distant from the actual products (or other stimuli). It is for this reason, we believe, that a vector model, which corresponds to the special case of an ideal point model with ideal points at infinity, may be so much more robust and useful in practice than the more theoretically elegant ideal point model of which it is a (very) special case.

The Bell Labs MDS Group

In 1966, Paul Green, reading the basic papers such as Shepard's and Kruskal's on MDS, called Doug Carroll at Bell Labs and was quite interested in learning more about this methodology, with a view to applying it to marketing analysis. While Roger Shepard had left by then for Harvard (and moved in 1968 to Stanford), the remainder of what might be called the "Bell Labs MDS group" at the time remained, and continued working on this class of problems. Bell Labs was then the center of activity in this area of methodological research, following the breakthrough papers on nonmetric MDS by Shepard and by Kruskal. Green began a series of visits to Bell Labs in Murray Hill, New Jersey, that would last for over 20 years, driving up from Philadelphia along with his longtime friend and colleague Frank Carmone, as well as, later, (a) numerous students, ranging from Les Neidell and Vithala Rao to Arun Jain and Wayne DeSarbo, with many others in between, and also (b) frequent collaborators like Vijay Mahajan.

With reciprocal visits to Wharton by a number of the Bell Labs group, this exchange comprised an informal ongoing seminar series on MDS and related methods of data analysis applied to marketing research that was beneficial for all involved. In addition to the work on nonmetric MDS done at Bell Labs, Green became quite interested in the research by Shepard and Carroll (1966) on "parametric representation of nonlinear data structures," especially the Parametric Mapping procedure and program developed by Carroll and Chang, the work on unfolding analysis by Kruskal and Carroll (1969), using an enhanced version of Kruskal's MDSCAL algorithm, and that of Carroll and Chang on the MDPREF model and method for multidimensional analysis of preference data. Green was especially supportive of and excited by the development of the INDSCAL approach to three-way MDS, and by the many other developments in MDS methodology occurring in those years of intense research in this area. He was also exceptionally fast and thorough in mastering and advancing this new methodology, and was superbly efficient and effective in disseminating these ideas and methods within the marketing community. This pedagogical skill has been especially manifest in a trilogy of books, beginning with Green and Carmone's (1970) *Multidimensional Scaling and Related Techniques in Marketing Analysis*, followed closely by Green and Rao's (1972a) *Applied Multidimensional Scaling,* and Green and Wind's (1972) *Multiattribute Decisions in Marketing* (to which Carroll contributed a technical appendix), with the last book including a composite of conjoint analysis and MDS methods for marketing.

In addition to these books, Green was author or coauthor of numerous expository and/or applications papers on MDS and related methods: Green and Robinson (1971); Green (1973, 1975a, 1975b, 1975c); Green and Carmone (1969, 1970, 1972); Green, Carmone, and Robinson (1968a, 1968b); Green and Carroll (1981); Green, Carroll, and Carmone (1976a, 1976b); Green and Greenberg (1970); Green, Halbert, and Robinson (1968); Green and Jain (1972); Green and Maheshwari (1969, 1970); Green, Maheshwari, and Rao (1969); and Green and Rao (1969a, 1969b, 1971, 1972b, 1977). Green went far beyond merely disseminating and applying MDS to marketing – he was often quite influential in stimulating the development of new methodology, most frequently by suggesting important unsolved problems he predicted would have considerable application in marketing or other social and behavioral sciences, for which such methodology was needed. An excellent example is provided by Green's suggestion to Doug Carroll (circa Summer 1975) that it would be very useful to produce a model for preference data combining the strengths of conjoint analysis with those of MDS (the vector model, à la MDPREF, in particular) by formulating a vector model in which the stimulus/product points *and* the subject/consumer vectors could be decomposed via a conjoint model. This suggestion led to development of the CANDELINC approach, first discussed in a paper presented at an international conference by Carroll, Green, and Carmone (1976) and including marketing applications. Later, Carroll, Pruzansky, and Kruskal (1980) generalized this approach to the three-way and multiway case, and provided a rigorous proof of the properties of CANDELINC.

Conjoint Analysis

Apropos conjoint analysis, as most marketers know, at some point in the sixties Green began to shift interest from MDS to conjoint analysis – the field of marketing methodology he invented, virtually single-handedly. In a sense, though, it was his interest in MDS (or in scaling and measurement more generally) that led to his focusing on what eventually evolved into the general approach now called "conjoint analysis." Like many others, he was first impressed by the seminal paper on "additive conjoint measurement" by Luce and Tukey (1964) – the lead article in the inaugural issue of the *Journal of Mathematical Psychology*. This paper laid out the theory of conjoint *measurement*, which should be distinguished from conjoint *analysis*, especially as the latter is now practiced in marketing. Kruskal (1965) was led by Luce and Tukey's work to produce a practical method for *fitting* a conjoint measurement model to *fallible* (or "noisy") data. Because the basic assumption Luce and Tukey made was that the observed data were related to an additive conjoint model via an arbitrary monotone transformation, the MONANOVA program (Kruskal and Carmone 1969) resulting from Kruskal's (1965) paper qualifies as a "nonmetric MDS method," although it could be viewed as an inherently unidimensional, *not* a multidimensional, scaling method. That is, conjoint measurement/analysis could still be viewed as a special case of MDS that just happens to be limited to the case of a single dimension. Green applied Kruskal's MONANOVA program to what would now be called "conjoint data" and obtained results that could be called "conjoint analysis of ordinal scale data," or "nonmetric conjoint analysis."

While Green was continuing to experiment both with MDS (in the "narrow sense") and additive conjoint measurement for marketing analysis, some of the Bell Labs group had experimented, in various contexts, with applying a metric MDS method when the proximity (or other) data were clearly defined merely on an ordinal scale (i.e., "nonmetric" data). It turned out that in almost all cases, both with proximity and with preferential choice data, the results were remarkably robust under this theoretically inappropriate analysis – from which it was concluded that, at least in many cases, it was probably acceptable to do a metric analysis even when a nonmetric approach was theoretically more appropriate. Based on these empirical results, it was not surprising that Green eventually tried "metric" conjoint measurement in the case of marketing stimuli generated via a conjoint design (i.e., a full or fractional factorial design). The results were extremely robust under this theoretically inappropriate analysis, with the fitted parameters nearly identical to those from nonmetric analyses in essentially all cases. He concluded from this experiment that – particularly when interest centers primarily on estimation of the parameters of the additive model – the metric approach was as good as, and in many cases, even superior to, the nonmetric approach to conjoint measurement/analysis. Of course *metric* (additive) conjoint measurement (optimizing an OLS loss function) is mathematically equivalent to main effects only ANOVA, so that Paul began using OLS ANOVA, often implemented as a special case of multiple linear regression with dummy variables encoding the particular factorial design used – which, of course, quickly led to including selected interaction terms, and fitting even more general members of the class of general linear models – thus evolving under Green's expert tutelage into the highly general approach known today as "conjoint analysis."

Categorical Conjoint Measurement (CCM)

One particular development in conjoint measurement and analysis that should be mentioned here was the introduction of an approach called "Categorical Conjoint Measurement" (CCM) by Carroll (1969, 1973). CCM can be viewed as one extreme of the continuum ranging from totally metric to totally nonmetric conjoint measurement and conjoint analysis; CCM corresponds, in fact, to the most radically nonmetric version of conjoint analysis, namely, that dealing with the weakest form of preference data, nominal scale.

Carroll (1969) showed that conjoint measurement/analysis could be applied to such categorical or nominal scale data via use of a special case of canonical correlation analysis, in which one set of variables corresponds to a design matrix for the factorial design representing the conjoint analysis structure of the experiment. That set of variables encodes the various levels of the m attributes defining the conjoint design via dummy variable encoding using binary variables, each indicating which of several levels of each of the m attributes is possessed by a particular stimulus. The second set of variables, the dependent or input data from the subjects, provides an analogous dummy variable encoding of the values of the categorical or nominal scale dependent variable, usually (but not always) a variable defining preference for the stimuli, in this case defined on a merely nominal scale.

Green and Wind (1973) used CCM in their seminal work on multiattribute decisions in marketing. As a result, the methodology was discussed extensively by Carroll (1973) in his comprehensive appendix describing the various models and methods of multidimensional scaling and related data analytic approaches that were used in Green and Wind's volume. This appendix, which provides perhaps the most comprehensive description of a large part of the "Bell Labs library" of programs for MDS analysis (as well as of other methodology not included in that particular library), offers the best description of CCM, in particular. (For a detailed description of much of this

Bell Labs software for MDS and related techniques, see Chang 1971.) Paul Green and Jerry Wind used CCM quite adeptly and with highly significant practical consequences in their very well known and prize-winning design (Wind, Green, Shifflet, and Scarbrough 1989) of "Courtyard by Marriott."

MDS, Clustering, and Their Interrelationship

Another class of models and methods Green became (or already was) interested in was clustering – hierarchical, non-hierarchical, and overlapping, as considered later in this chapter. Clustering, of course, is particularly applicable to market segmentation, but also provides an alternate (or, in many cases, a complementary) approach to MDS, in particular for competitive market structure analysis of the same proximity data. In many cases applying clustering and MDS (separately) to the same proximity data results in much greater insight into the structure underlying the data than either approach taken exclusively (see Kruskal 1977).

Some other papers on MDS, clustering, and the interrelations between them of which Green was author or coauthor include: Carroll and Green (1995, 1997); Carroll, Green, and Kim (1989); Carroll, Green, and Schaffer (1986, 1987, 1989); Chaturvedi, Carroll, Green, and Rotondo (1997); Chaturvedi and Green (1995); Chaturvedi, Green, and Carroll (2001); DeSarbo, Carroll, Clark, and Green (1984); Frank and Green (1968); Green (1970, 1977); Green and Carmone (1977); Green, Carmone, and Fox (1969); Green, Carmone, and Kim (1990); Green, Carmone, and Wachspress (1976); Green and Carroll (1988); Green, Frank, and Robinson (1967); Green and Kim (1993); Green and Krieger (1989, 1995, 2000); Green, Krieger, and Carroll (1987); Green and Rao (1972); Green and Schaffer (1999); Green, Schaffer, and Patterson (1988); Hinkle, Robinson, and Green (1969); and Krieger and Green (1999). Also, there was another book on MDS, an update of the earlier Green and Carmone (1970) book, now by Green, Carmone, and Smith (1989).

For a recent comprehensive overview of MDS literature through about 1997, see Carroll and Arabie (1998). Also, see Kruskal and Wish (1978) and/or Arabie, Carroll, and DeSarbo (1987) for general but fairly non-technical overviews of the fields of two-way and three-way MDS, as well as some topics in "three-way clustering." As for clustering in general applied to marketing, an expository overview is provided by Arabie and Hubert (1994).

Predictions and Recommendations for MDS and Conjoint Analysis

Carroll and Green (1995, 1997) discuss the history of and inter-relationships between conjoint analysis and MDS, making predictions and recommendations as to how these methodologies will and should evolve in the future, especially as applied to marketing research. One recommendation for future methodological research in these areas was to focus even more intensely on models and methods synthesizing the two approaches, taking up where the CANDELINC (Carroll, Pruzansky, and Kruskal 1980) approach left off, while devising more sophisticated methods for defining constrained MDS representations with constraints imposed on the dimensional structure by attributes of the stimuli/products and/or subjects/consumers, based on conjoint design. This strategy allows for the strengths of MDS – finding dimensions not necessarily known in advance – as well as that of conjoint analysis, leading to these dimensions being much more immediately interpretable and, especially, *actionable* – e.g., such that design of new stimuli/products filling observed or inferred "gaps" which, if filled, would command a sizable (or a particularly profitable) share of the market, or enabling prediction of where in the spatial representation a *hypothetical* stimulus (or product) will fall. Developments along these lines strongly advance solving the problems with MDS methodology that led Green to move from a strong emphasis on that methodology to one on conjoint analysis in his later methodological and applications oriented research – specifically, difficulty in interpreting dimensions (or deciding on the "correct" dimensionality) and, particularly, on using these dimensions for "actionable" marketing decisions.

A second recommendation was to put more emphasis on devising new approaches combining proximity and preference data in the same representation, so that the power of proximity data to determine dimensional structure of multidimensional representations could be usefully exploited while the resulting representations could optimally represent preference data using an ideal point, vector, or other models for individual differences preferential choice data. Such an approach, one could argue, is superior to either internal or external preference analyses (Carroll 1972, 1980), both of which have serious problems of degenerate or quasi-degenerate solutions for representing individual subjects' or consumers' preferences. There is reason to believe that solving for all the relevant parameters for representation of both the proximities and preferences simultaneously will tend to avoid such problems – especially if combined in a flexible manner with the recommendation mentioned earlier of incorporating conjoint design, as far as possible, into MDS representations (Green, Halbert, and Robinson 1968). Some or all of these capabilities are incorporated by Ramsay (1980) into later versions of his MULTISCALE program. Some attempts have been made to incorporate such ideas into MDS or related approaches for marketing analysis.

Another recommendation was to devise improved algorithms for fitting so-called "hybrid models" (in a very different sense than Green has used this term in the context of conjoint analysis, or Kruskal in the documentation for KYST-2A) incorporating both continuous spatial structure à la standard MDS representations and discrete non-spatial models incorporating cluster-like structure in the form of tree or network structure, partitions, or overlapping but non-hierarchically organized clusters, as a way simultaneously to glean the two types of structure from the same proximity (or other) data, rather than fitting these two different types of structures independently to the same data. Like models combining proximity and preferential choice data in the same analysis, this approach should enable fitting these two complementary types of structures independently to the data to optimize the account of the original data via these two different types of structure – continuous and discrete (recalling that discrete structure can generally be formulated as dimensions that happen to be binary or otherwise categorical in nature, rather than continuously valued). It should be pointed out that, given the work already done on analyzing preference data using tree structure(s) or other discrete models (see, e.g., De Soete, DeSarbo, Furnas, and Carroll 1984a, 1984b; Carroll, DeSarbo, and De Soete 1987, 1989; DeSarbo, De Soete, Carroll and Ramaswamy 1988; De Soete and Carroll 1992; Hubert and Arabie 1994, 1995a, 1995b; Hubert, Arabie, and Meulman 1997, 1998, 2001), such "hybrid" MDS and cluster, tree, or network structure models that are designed to fit proximity and preferential choice data simultaneously are also quite feasible, and should be pursued as well (while, if desired, utilizing information incorporated into a conjoint design).

The earliest approach we know of attempting to fit this particular type of "hybrid" MDS and clustering/network model to proximity data was by Carroll and Pruzansky (1975), as also described by Carroll (1976) and later expanded on by Carroll and Pruzansky (1980, 1986). After the ADCLUS/ MAPCLUS/INDCLUS class of overlapping clustering models was introduced (Shepard and Arabie 1979; Arabie and Carroll 1980; Carroll and Arabie 1980; Chaturvedi and Carroll 1994), a general formulation was introduced allowing a wide variety of options for such hybrid continuous and discrete MDS-like models, under the general rubric of what Carroll and Chaturvedi (1995) have called the CANDCLUS approach, which generalizes CANDECOMP to cases of multiway data analyses via multilinear models in which some parameters are continuously valued while others may be discretely valued, and includes a large number of special cases of considerable theoretical interest and potentially wide application to marketing. Some of these, already cited, are to purely discrete models, such as overlapping K-centroids clustering (Chaturvedi, Carroll, Green, and Rotondo 1997), K-midmeans (Carroll and Chaturvedi 1998), and K-modes (Chaturvedi, Green, and Carroll 2001) clustering. It is especially noteworthy that the first and the last of these three were stimulated in very large part by practical market segmentation problems raised by Green, his influence on this work manifested by his co-authorship on both papers. Chaturvedi and Carroll (2001) provided an approach that is genuinely "hybrid" in the sense described earlier.

Additionally, and very importantly, Carroll and Green (1997) argued for more sophisticated use of methods, whenever feasible, based on maximum likelihood, latent class models, and the like. Ideally, these methods will lead, among other things, to models in which inferential tests of hypotheses about number or nature of dimensions – more confirmatory rather than merely exploratory MDS (and related) models, in other words – can be dealt with, while at the same time making this methodology more legitimately a part of standard multivariate statistics, not just of multivariate data analysis. Although it may seem like simple exploitation of every new "fad" in modeling and analysis of marketing data, what we are suggesting here can be reduced to one conceptually simple, but methodologically extremely complicated, rule – namely, allow for incorporation of all the best features associated with new models and methods applied to marketing, being careful however to do so in as statistically sound and rigorous a manner as possible, lest one fall into the trap of simply fitting (or trying to fit different models with) enough parameters to enable accounting for any data whatever. While "data mining" may have its place in engineering and possibly even in marketing, we deplore the habit of mining veins of data that are distinctly lacking in number of observations, and so in degrees of freedom, thus falling into the proverbial trap of what used to be called "data snooping"– fitting so many different models that the one that finally seems to fit may be just the result of a hidden game of trying out different models until one is found, very likely capitalizing on error to a very large extent, that appears to fit the given data very well, but would not at all if the *real* number of degrees of freedom actually used were taken into account. As one commentator remarked, "We can be sure that if we torture the data long enough, they will confess."

Recent Work in MDS Methodology

In closing, we list some papers using MDS methodology specifically in a marketing context that have been published in recent years. It is noteworthy that many of these are authored or co-authored by one of Paul Green's most prolific students, Wayne DeSarbo – underscoring the sense in which Green's ultimate legacy consists of his students, and, already, some students of students – i.e., the "conceptual genetic chain" passed down in this form through generations yet to come of marketing researchers, academics, and practitioners. DeSarbo, in particular, is a very good example of this, since Carroll was also on his dissertation committee, and DeSarbo worked very closely with him at Bell Labs over a summer on the research on "three-way metric unfolding" that became DeSarbo's dissertation in 1979. (See DeSarbo and Carroll 1985, for a good overall account of some of this work.) Largely as a result, DeSarbo spent his first five years post-Ph.D. at Bell Labs, in one of the statistics departments, prior to his return to academia. Paul had thus succeeded in implanting one of his academic progeny as sort of an "intellectual mole" directly at Bell Labs for a time, which in actuality greatly enhanced all of these mutual interactions in those and later years.

A sampling of papers on MDS methodology in these later (post mid-nineties) years motivated by marketing and related concerns includes the following: DeSarbo, Lehmann, Carpenter, and Sinha (1996); Wedel and DeSarbo (1996); DeSarbo, M. R. Young, and Rangaswamy (1997); Bijmolt, DeSarbo, and Wedel (1998); Chaturvedi and Carroll (1998); DeSarbo, Kim, and Fong (1998); Sinha and DeSarbo (1998); Kim, Chatterjee, and DeSarbo (1999); Bijmolt and Wedel (1999); Kim, Rangaswamy, and DeSarbo (2000); and DeSarbo, Kim, Choi, and Spaulding (2002). One very general paper discusses a diverse array of techniques for market structure analysis, many closely related to MDS. Coauthored by Elrod, Russell, Shocker, Andrews, Bacon, Bayus, Carroll, Johnson, Kamakura, Leak, Mazanec, Rao, and Shankar (2002), this paper may help define the future direction of a large part of the marketing research community dedicated to MDS and other quantitative approaches to marketing measurement and data analysis. Most of these papers and the research on which they are based incorporate one or more of the features argued above as being important for a really mature "MDS and related models" based methodology optimally applicable to marketing analysis as well as to data analysis in other closely related social and behavioral sciences (e.g., Schaffer, Green, and Carmone 2000).

CLUSTERING

As was noted earlier for MDS, Paul was exceptionally fast and thorough in absorbing this new methodology, and was superbly efficient and effective in disseminating these ideas and methods within the marketing community. The same statement holds for clustering. By current standards, hierarchical clustering has a long history – going back at least five decades (see Gordon 1996, for a very scholarly review), but in 1967, three very influential papers appeared: (a) Jardine, Jardine, and Sibson, (b) Lance and Williams, and (c) S. C. Johnson. The last of these three had the greatest impact in the behavioral sciences in North America. A primary reason was that S. C. Johnson (1967) wrote a user-friendly FORTRAN program, distributed gratis by his then-employer, Bell Laboratories, for single- and complete-link clustering. In various areas of the behavioral sciences, Johnson's program was used by a pioneer in the substantive discipline, and then the methodology was adopted widely throughout the respective discipline. For marketing research, that pioneer, as with so many other multivariate techniques, was Paul Green. Moreover, Green was again demonstrating his uncanny sense of where that methodology was headed and how it should be tailored to marketing research. For example, in most of the behavioral sciences, the clustering software was often limited to a few hundred entities (e.g., customers in market segmentation); concretely, S C. Johnson's (1967) software was limited to $n = 100$. Green, however, was already advocating in 1969 (Hinkle, Robinson, and Green 1969, p. 56) software where the upper bound of n was 2,000. However, algorithm developers quickly afterward developed software capable of clustering (via hierarchical or partitioning methods but not for overlapping clustering) hundreds of thousands of consumers (e.g., Steve Herman's ProClus[2], Bretton-Clark 1993; SYSTAT 2002; see references in Arabie and Hubert 1996).

Beginning with his co-authored review papers on (a) relevance of applications of "numerical taxonomy" (a term used by some biologists to encompass several multivariate methods of data analysis, including clustering) to marketing research (Frank and Green 1968), (b) cluster analysis in industrial marketing (Hinkle, Robinson, and Green 1969; Doyle and Saunders 1985), and (c) test market selection (Green, Frank, and Robinson 1967), Green and his collaborator Frank Carmone, Jr. (Green and Carmone 1970) included lengthy tutorials on clustering in their textbook *Multidimensional Scaling and Related Techniques in Marketing Analysis.* Soon followed *Applied Multidimensional Scaling* (Green and Rao, 1972a), with illustrations of the use of both single- and complete-link clustering, applied to an input matrix of "direct measures" of dissimilarity (e.g., judgments of pairwise dissimilarities for pairs of entities, or brand switching data) or of derived measures (e.g., from raw data coded in a matrix of entities by attributes, converted into a proximity matrix of entities by entities; see Green and Rao 1969a). Both books had major influence in marketing research and other related behavioral sciences. The second book provided a classic data set on fifteen breakfast foods that has since been used in publications ranging from undergraduate textbooks (Dillon, Madden, and Firtle 1994) to academically oriented research articles (Arabie, Carroll, DeSarbo, and Wind 1981). Green and Rao (1972a, p.144) also pointed out the potential relevance of MDS (and, by implication, clustering) to data-based market segmentation.

Both academic researchers and practitioners in marketing were quick to follow Paul Green's lead and embrace various forms of clustering in addition to the hierarchical forms found in the trilogy of Green's co-authored books listed earlier. In addition to the obvious application to market segmentation (see Beane and Ennis 1987; Wind 1978a, 1975b; Green, Krieger, and Schaffer

1985), the variety of applicable methods of clustering and sophistication of their underlying assumptions has increased enormously (e.g., Mahajan and Jain 1978) in response to the problems chronicled by Wind (1978a). Among the more noteworthy advances are segmentation based on price sensitivity (Elrod and Winer 1982; Blozan and Prabhaker 1984), a simultaneous approach to segmentation and market structuring by Grover and Srinivasan (1987), and a simultaneous approach to segmentation and estimation in the framework of conjoint analysis (Ogawa, 1987). (Many more references are given in reviews by Beane and Ennis 1987; Punj and Stewart 1983; Arabie and Hubert 1994.)

Mixture Models, Optimal Weighting, and Tandem Clustering

Just as Green had heralded the use of clustering for market segmentation, he has defined major emphases in the further development of clustering, tailored for marketing research application. Among the directions he set for such advances are (a) mixture models, (b) optimal weighting and selection of variables when partitioning is employed and consensus representation of structures, and (c) demonstrating the drawbacks of the commonly used "tandem clustering."

Concerning the first of these three, Green, Carmone, and Wachspress (1976) provided the first application of mixture models in marketing (Wedel and Kamakura 2000, pp. 76-77), and Green and Carmone (1977, p. 221) called for further developments of this approach to segmentation. Since then, the marketing literature on this methodology has greatly expanded. See DeSarbo and Cron (1988), Wedel and DeSarbo (1994), Wedel, Kamakura, and DeSarbo (1995), and Wedel and Kamakura (2002, chapter 6) for a comprehensive overview as well as an interesting list of applications (2002, p. 97).

Many of these developments seek simultaneously to provide both segmentation that was initially based on extant mixture models (McLachlan and Basford 1988; see review in Wedel and DeSarbo 1995, pp. 21-24) and also the attribute importances yielded by traditional approaches to conjoint analysis. Noteworthy contributions to this and closely related areas of marketing research include: Zenor and Srivastava (1993), Wedel and DeSarbo (1993, 1995), and Böckenholt, de Borrero, Bozdogan, DeSarbo, Dillon, Gupta, Kamakura, Kumar, Ramaswamy, and Zenor (1994).

We noted earlier that for a two-mode two-way matrix of the type traditionally used in market segmentation (e.g., partitioning of n customers according to m attributes), the number of customers can be extremely large in practical applications. While algorithmists have helped marketers overcome increasingly large values of n, Green has shrewdly considered *both* modes of such a database. Deciding just which of the *m* variables are relevant underlies many practical problems, such as "collaborative filtering" in predicting e-purchases by individual consumers (cf. Iacobucci, Arabie, and Bodapati 2000). The variables of such a matrix cannot be expected to be uncorrelated, leading to the usual red herring of whether Euclidean distances can legitimately be computed between pairs of consumers who are thus not represented on orthogonal axes, and usually, the original value of *m* is too large to be managerially useful. Green and his colleagues (e.g., DeSarbo, Carroll, Clark, and Green 1984) were among the first researchers to seek iteratively and differentially weighted variables as the emergent partitioning structure arises. To date there is no general agreement on how well the various strategies for weighting variables actually work (e.g., Green, Carmone, and Kim 1990; Milligan 1989), but promising work continues (Carmone, Kara, and Maxwell 1999; Brusco and Cradit 2001).

A related approach to managing the abundance of both input data and the resulting structures often fitted to them consists of seeking a *consensus* representation (see Day 1986) over the various structures that can be fitted to the same market segmentation data (and consumers). Characteristically, Green had already led the way in seeking such representations in marketing research (e.g., Green and Carmone 1977; Green and Carroll 1988; Green and Krieger 1999) using continuous multivariate techniques to obtain the basic structures. Using the same consensus approach for partitioning (most methods of which are variants of MacQueen 1967) is risky because most such approaches are notoriously dependent on the "seeds," or initial clusters, variously generated to begin the iterative partitioning (Milligan 1996, p. 359), as demonstrated in marketing research by Helsen and Green (1991). Research problems as complex as partitioning often call for Monte Carlo analyses for evaluating the validity of the ensuing partition (when the underlying structure is known) and even for measures for gauging the success of such approaches to partitioning (especially in marketing research; see Helsen and Green 1991) and other forms of clustering (see Leclerc 1998, for a review, and other references in Arabie and Hubert 1996, p. 16). Krieger and Green (1999) developed a method for consensus clustering of various partitions, based on optimizing the Hubert-Arabie (1985) measure for comparing partitions (as recommended by Milligan and Cooper 1986). Krieger and Green (1999, p.80) also compared the results of their new approach to that from the traditional, canonical example of mixture models, the "traditional latent class analysis," as applied to categorical variables and found that the newer strategy gave superior results.

We noted earlier that the number of consumers, *n*, can often be very large. For decades this computational problem was often finessed in the behavioral sciences by first submitting the two-mode, two-way input matrix to principal components analysis (PCA, where the computational effort is largely a function of the number of variables rather than the number of consumers) and then running various clustering methods on the output of the PCA rather than on the original data matrix. In marketing, this quaint practice is known as "tandem clustering" and has been heavily criticized by some of us on both theoretical and empirical grounds (Arabie, Carroll, and DeSarbo 1987, p. 54, and Arabie and Hubert 1994, p. 165, give summaries and supporting references). Nonetheless, the (mis)use of the tandem approach continues both in advertised practitioners' workshops and textbooks. Green and Krieger (1995, p. 223) summarized our criticisms as

> " ... unequivocal: 'tandem clustering is an outmoded and statistically unsupportable practice.' The importance of this problem in marketing research and, particularly, in post hoc [data-based] segmentation methods is unquestioned."

Using both empirical and synthetic data (Green and Krieger 1995) in this research program, Schaffer and Green (1998, p. 162) concluded that "[u]ntil subsequent research is undertaken, preliminary results indicate that researchers desirous of reducing dimensionality of the variables space, prior to clustering, might consider an alternative to the tandem approach." Thus, Green and his collaborators continue to pinpoint and seek to resolve both theoretical and practical matters in the use of clustering in marketing research.

CONCLUDING NOTE

As we have seen, Paul Green had been centrally involved, in more than one way, in the evolution of this field over the years – beginning in the early 1960s and already extending well into the 2000s. We all fully expect his contributions – both direct and indirect – to this field, and to marketing research and methodology in general, to continue for uncounted years to come.

NOTES

[1] We are most grateful to Mrs. Kathleen Power for her expert editorial, administrative, and other assistance in preparing this manuscript and to Mr. Ulas Akkacuk for his invaluable bibliographic support.

[2] Available from Bretton-Clark, 89 Headquarters Plaza, North Tower, 14th Floor, Morristown, New Jersey 07960.

REFERENCES

Arabie, P. (1991), "Was Euclid an unnecessarily sophisticated psychologist?" *Psychometrika*, 56, 567-587.

Arabie, P., and Carroll, J. D. (1980), "MAPCLUS: A mathematical programming approach to fitting the ADCLUS model," *Psychometrika*, 45, 211-235.

Arabie, P., Carroll, J. D., and DeSarbo, W. S. (1987), *Three-way Scaling and Clustering*. Newbury Park, CA: Sage. Translated into Japanese by A. Okada and T. Imaizumi (1990), Tokyo: Kyoritsu Shuppan.

Arabie, P., Carroll, J. D., DeSarbo, W., and Wind, J. (1981), "Overlapping clustering: A new method for product positioning," *Journal of Marketing Research*, 18, 310-317. Republished in Green, P. E., Carmone, F. J., Jr., and Smith, S. M. (1989), *Multidimensional Scaling,* Boston: Allyn and Bacon, pp. 235-246.

Arabie, P., and Hubert, L. J. (1994), "Cluster analysis in marketing research," in R. P. Bagozzi (ed.), *Advanced Methods in Marketing Research*, Oxford: Blackwell, pp. 160-189.

Arabie, P., and Hubert, L. J. (1996), "An overview of combinatorial data analysis," in P. Arabie, L. J. Hubert, and G. De Soete (eds.), *Clustering and Classification*, River Edge, NJ: World Scientific, pp. 5-63.

Beane, T. P., and Ennis, D. M. (1987), "Market segmentation: A review," *European Journal of Marketing*, 21, 20-42.

Bijmolt, T. H. A., DeSarbo, W. S., and Wedel, M. (1998), "A multidimensional scaling model accommodating differential stimulus familiarity," *Multivariate Behavioral Research*, 33, 41-63.

Bijmolt, T. H. A., and Wedel, M. (1999), "A comparison of multidimensional scaling methods for perceptual mapping," *Journal of Marketing Research*, 36, 277- 285.

Blozan, W., and Prabhaker, P. (1984), "Notes on aggregation criteria in market segmentation," *Journal of Marketing Research*, 21, 332-335.

Böckenholt, I., de Berroro, M. S., Bozdogan, H., DeSarbo, W. S., Dillon, W., Gupta, S., Kamakura, W., Kumar, S., Ramaswamy, V., and Zenor, M. (1994), "Issues in the specification and application of latent structure models of choice," *Marketing Letters*, 5, 323-334.

Bretton-Clark Inc. (1993), *ProClus*, Morristown, NJ: Bretton-Clark.

Brusco, M. J., and Cradit, J. D. (2001), "A variable selection heuristic for K-means clustering," *Psychometrika*, 66, 249-270.

Carmone F. J., Jr., Kara, A., and Maxwell, S. (1999), "HINoV: A new model to improve market segmentation by identifying noisy variables," *Journal of Marketing Research,* 3, 501-509.

Carroll, J. D. (1969), *Categorical Conjoint Measurement*, Technical Report, Murray Hill, NJ: AT&T Bell Laboratories.

Carroll, J. D. (1972), "Individual differences and multidimensional scaling," in R. N. Shepard, A. K. Romney, and S. B. Nerlove (eds.), *Multidimensional Scaling: Theory and Applications in the Behavioral Sciences.* Vol.1: *Theory*, New York: Seminar Press, pp. 105-155. Reprinted (1984) in P. Davies and A. P. M. Coxon (eds.), *Key Texts on Multidimensional Scaling*. Portsmouth, NH: Heinemann.

Carroll, J. D. (1973), "Models and algorithms for multidimensional scaling, conjoint measurement, and related techniques (Appendix B)," in P. E. Green and Y. Wind (eds.), *Multiattribute Decisions in Marketing*, Hindsdale, IL: Dryden Press, pp. 299-387. Partially reprinted (1989) in P. E. Green, F. J. Carmone, Jr., and S. M. Smith, *Multidimensional Scaling: Concepts and Applications*, Boston, MA: Allyn and Bacon.

Carroll, J. D. (1976), "Spatial, non-spatial and hybrid models for scaling," Presidential Address for Psychometric Society, *Psychometrika*, 41, 439-463.

Carroll, J. D. (1980), "Models and methods for multidimensional analysis of preferential choice (or other dominance) data," in E. D. Lantermann and H. Feger (eds.), *Similarity and Choice*, Bern: Hans Huber, pp. 234-289.

Carroll, J. D. (2002), "Psychometrics: Multidimensional scaling in psychology," in N. J. Smelsor and P. B. Baltes (eds.), *2001 International Encyclopedia of Social and Behavioral Sciences*, Oxford, England: Pergamon, pp. 10189-10193.

Carroll J. D., and Arabie, P. (1980), "Multidimensional scaling," in M. R. Rosenzweig and L. W. Porter (eds.), *Annual Review of Psychology*, Vol. 31, Palo Alto, CA, pp. 607-649. Also in (August, 1979) *Harvard-Yale Preprints in Mathematical Sociology*, Vol. 14. Reprinted (1989) in P. E. Green, F. J. Carmone, Jr., and S. M. Smith, *Multidimensional Scaling: Concepts and Applications*, Boston, MA: Allyn and Bacon, pp. 168-204.

Carroll, J. D., and Arabie, P. (1998), "Multidimensional scaling," in M. H. Birnbaum (ed.), *Handbook of Perception and Cognition. Volume 3: Measurement, Judgment and Decision Making*, San Diego, CA: Academic Press, pp. 179-250.

Carroll, J. D., and Chang, S. J. (1970), "Analysis of individual differences in multidimensional scaling via an N-way generalization of 'Eckart-Young' decomposition," *Psychometrika*, 35, 283-319. Reprinted (1984) in P. Davies and A. P. M. Coxon (eds.), *Key Texts in Multidimensional Scaling*, Portsmouth, NH: Heinemann.

Carroll, J. D., and Chaturvedi, A. (1995), "A general approach to clustering and multidimensional scaling of two-way, three-way, or higher-way data," in R. D. Luce, M. D'Zmura, D. D. Hoffman, G. Iverson, and A. K. Romney (eds.), *Geometric Representations of Perceptual Phenomena*, Mahwah, NJ: Erlbaum, pp. 295-318.

Carroll, J. D., and Chaturvedi A. (1998), "K-midranges clustering," in A. Rizzi, M. Vichi, and H.-H. Bock (eds.), *Data Science, Classification and Related Methods*, Berlin: Springer, pp. 3-14.

Carroll, J. D., DeSarbo, W., and De Soete, G. (1987), "Stochastic Tree UNfolding (STUN) models," *Communication and Cognition*, 20, 63-76.

Carroll, J. D., DeSarbo, W., and De Soete, G. (1989), "Two classes of stochastic tree unfolding models," in G. De Soete, H. Feger and K. C. Klauer (eds.), *New Developments in Psychological Choice Modeling*, Amsterdam: North-Holland, pp. 161-176.

Carroll, J. D., and Green, P. E. (1995), "Psychometric methods in marketing research: Part I, Conjoint analysis," A guest editorial for the *Journal of Marketing Research*, 32, 385-391.

Carroll, J. D., and Green, P. E. (1997), "Psychometric methods in marketing research: Part II, Multidimensional scaling," A guest editorial for the *Journal of Marketing Research*, 34, 193-204.

Carroll, J. D., Green, P. E., and Carmone, F. J., Jr. (1976), "CANDELINC (CANonical DEcomposition with LINear Constraints): A new method for multidimensional analysis with constrained solutions (Abstract)," *Proceedings of the 21st International Congress of Psychology*, Paris: Presses Universitaires de France.

Carroll, J. D., Green, P. E., and Kim, J. (1989), "Preference mapping of conjoint-based profiles: An INDSCAL approach," *Journal of the Academy of Marketing Science*, 17, 273-281.

Carroll, J. D., Green, P. E., and Schaffer, C. M. (1987), "Comparing interpoint distance comparisons in correspondence analysis," *Journal of Marketing Research*, 23, 271-280. Reprinted (1989) in P. E. Green, F. J. Carmone, Jr., and S. M. Smith, *Multidimensional Scaling: Concepts and Applications,* Boston, MA: Allyn and Bacon, pp. 338-346.

Carroll, J. D., Green, P. E., and Schaffer, C. M. (1989), "Reply to Greenacre's commentary on the Carroll-Green-Schaffer scaling of two-way correspondence analysis solutions," *Journal of Marketing Research*, 26, 366-368.

Carroll, J. D., and Pruzansky, S. (1975), "Fitting of hierarchical tree structure (HTS) models, mixtures of HTS modes and hybrid models, via mathematical programming and alternating least squares," *Proceedings of the US.-Japan Seminar on Multidimensional Scaling and Related Techniques*, 9-19.

Carroll, J. D., and Pruzansky, S. (1980), "Discrete and hybrid scaling models," in F. D. Lantermann and H. Feger (eds.), *Similarity and Choice*, Bern: Hans Huber, pp. 108-139.

Carroll, J. D., and Pruzansky, S. (1986), "Discrete and hybrid models for proximity data," in W. Gaul and M. Schader (eds.), *Classification as a Tool of Research*, Amsterdam: North-Holland, pp. 47-59.

Carroll, J. D., Pruzansky, S., and Kniskal, J. B. (1980), "CANDELINC: A general approach to multidimensional analysis of many-way arrays with linear constraints on parameters," *Psychometrika*, 45, 3-24.

Chang, J. J. (1971), *Multidimensional Scaling Program Library*, unpublished paper, Murray Hill, NJ: AT&T Bell Laboratories.

Chang, J. J., and Carroll, J. D. (1969), *How to Use MDPREF, a Computer Program for Multidimensional Analysis of Preference Data*, Murray Hill, NJ: AT&T Bell Laboratories.

Chang, J. J., and Carroll, J. D. (1989), "A short-guide to MDPREF: Multidimensional analysis of preference data," in P. E. Green, F. J. Carmone, Jr., and S. M. Smith, *Multidimensional Scaling: Concepts and Applications*, Boston, MA: Allyn and Bacon, pp. 279-286.

Chaturvedi, A., and Carroll, J. D. (1994), "An alternating combinatorial optimization approach to fitting the INDCLUS and generalized INDCLUS models," *Journal of Classification*, 11, 155-170.

Chaturvedi, A., and Carroll, J. D. (1998), "A perceptual mapping procedure for analysis of proximity data to determine common and unique product-market structures," *European Journal of Operational Research*, 111, 268-284.

Chaturvedi, A., and Carroll, J. D. (submitted), "CLUSCALE (CLUStering and multidimensional SCAL[E]ing: Application of a three-way hybrid model incorporating clustering and multidimensional scaling structure."

Chaturvedi, A., Carroll, J. D., Green, P. E., and Rotondo, S. A. (1997), "A feature based approach to market segmentation via overlapping K-centroids clustering," *Journal of Marketing Research*, 34, 370-377.

Chaturvedi, A., and Green, P. E. (1995), "Book Review: *SPSS for Windows, CHAID 6.0*," *Journal of Marketing Research*, 32, 245-254.

Chaturvedi A., Green, P. E., and Carroll, J. D. (2001), "K-modes clustering," *Journal of Classification*, 18, 35-56.

Coombs, C. H. (1964), *A Theory of Data*, New York: Wiley.

Day, W. H. E., ed. (1986), "Consensus classification," Special Issue of *Journal of Classification*, 3 (2).

De Soete, G., and Carroll, J. D. (1992), "Probabilistic multidimensional models of pairwise choice data," in F. G. Ashby (ed.), *Multidimensional Models of Perception and Cognition*, Hillsdale, NJ: Erlbaum, pp. 61-88.

De Soete, G., DeSarbo, W. S., Furnas, G. W., and Carroll, J. D. (1984a), "The estimation of ultrametric and path length trees from rectangular proximity data," *Psychometrika*, 49, 289-310.

De Soete, G., DeSarbo, W. S., Furnas, G. W,, and Carroll, J. D. (1984b), "Tree representations of rectangular proximity matrices," in E. Degreef and S. van Buggerhaut (eds.), *Trends in Mathematical Psychology*, Amsterdam: North-Holland, pp. 377-392.

DeSarbo, W. S., and Carroll, J. D. (1985), "Three-way metric unfolding via alternating weighted least squares," *Psychometrika*, 50, 275-300.

DeSarbo, W. S., Carroll, J. D., Clark, L. A., and Green, P. E. (1984), "Synthesized clustering: A method for amalgamating alternative clustering bases with differential weighting of variables," *Psychometrika*, 49, 57-78.

DeSarbo, W. S., and Cron, W. L. (1988), "A conditional mixture maximum likelihood methodology for clusterwise linear regression," *Journal of Classification*, 5, 249-289.

DeSarbo, W. S., De Soete, G., Carroll, J. D., and Ramaswamy, V. (1988), "A new stochastic ultrametric tree unfolding methodology for assessing competitive market structure and deriving market segments," *Applied Stochastic Models and Data Analysis*, 4, 185-204.

DeSarbo, W. S., Kim J., Choi, S., and Spaulding, M. (submitted), "A gravity-based multidimensional scaling model for deriving spatial structures underlying consumer preference/choice judgments."

DeSarbo, W. S., Kim J., and Fong, D. (1998), "A Bayesian multidimensional scaling procedure for the spatial analysis of revealed choice data," *Journal of Econometrics*, 89, 79-108.

DeSarbo, W. S., Lehmann, D. R., Carpenter, G., and Sinha, I. (1996), "A stochastic multidimensional unfolding approach for representing phased decision outcomes," *Psychometrika*, 61, 485-508.

DeSarbo, W. S., Young M. R., and Rangaswamy, A. (1997), "A parametric unfolding procedure for incomplete, non-metric preference/choice set data in marketing research," *Journal of Marketing Research*, 34, 499-516.

Dillon, W. R., Madden, T. J., and Firtle, N. H. (1994), *Marketing Research in a Marketing Environment* (3rd ed.), Burr Ridge, IL: Irwin.

Doyle, P., and Saunders, J. (1984), "Market segmentation and positioning in specialized industrial markets," *Journal of Marketing*, 49, 24-32.

Elrod, T., Russell, G. J., Shocker, A. D., Andrews, R. L., Bacon, L., Bayus, B. L., Carroll, J. D., Johnson, R. M., Kamakura, W. A., Lenk, P., Mazanec, S. A., Rao, V. R., and Shankar, V. (2002), "Inferring market structure from customer response to competing and complementary products," *Marketing Letters*, 13, 219-230.

Elrod, T., and Winer, R. S. (1982), "An empirical evaluation of aggregation approaches for developing market segments," *Journal of Marketing* 46, 65-74.

Frank, R. E., and Green, P. E. (1968), "Numerical taxonomy in marketing analysis: A review article," *Journal of Marketing Research*, 5, 83-94.

Gordon, A. D. (1996), "Hierarchical classification," in P. Arabie, L. Hubert, and G. De Soete (eds.), *Clustering and Classification*, River Edge, NJ: World Scientific, pp. 65-121.

Gower, J. C. (1966), "Some distance properties of latent root and vector methods used in multivariate analysis," *Biometrika*, 53, 325-338.

Green, P. E. (1970), "Measurement and data analysis," *Journal of Marketing*, 34 (1), 15-17.

Green, P. E. (1973), "Multidimensional scaling and conjoint measurement in the study of choice among multiattribute alternatives," *Studies in Multiple Criterion Decision Making*, University of South Carolina Press.

Green, P. E. (1975a), "On the robustness of multidimensional scaling techniques," *Journal of Marketing Research*, 12, 73-81.

Green, P. E. (1975b), "Marketing applications of MDS: Assessment and outlook," *Journal of Marketing*, 39, 24-31.

Green, P. E. (1975c), "MDS applications in marketing: The art of the states," *Proceedings of the U.S.-Japan Seminar on Multidimensional Scaling and Related Techniques*, 21-26.

Green, P. E. (1977), "A new approach to market segmentation," *Business Horizons*, 20 (February), 61-73.

Green, P. E., and Carmone, F. J., Jr. (1969), "Multidimensional scaling: An introduction and comparison of nonmetric unfolding techniques," *Journal of Marketing Research*, 6, 330-341.

Green, P. E., and Carmone, F. J., Jr. (1970), *Multidimensional Scaling and Related Techniques in Marketing Analysis,* Newton, MA: Allyn and Bacon.

Green, P. E., and Carmone, F. J., Jr. (1972), "Marketing research applications of nonmetric scaling methods," in A. K. Romney, R. N. Shephard, and S. B. Nerlove (eds.), *Multidimensional Scaling: Theory and Applications in the Behavioral Sciences*, Vol. II, New York: Seminar Press, pp. 183-210.

Green, P. E., and Carmone, F. J., Jr. (1977), "Segment congruence analysis: A method for analyzing associations among alternative bases of market segmentation," *Journal of Consumer Research*, 3, 217-222.

Green, P. E., Carmone F. J., Jr., and Fox, L. B. (1969), "Television program similarities: An application of subjective clustering," *Journal of the Market Research Society*, 11, 70-90.

Green, P. E., Carmone, F. J., Jr., and Kim, S. (1990), "A preliminary study of optimal variable weighting in K-means clustering," *Journal of Classification*, 7, 271-285.

Green, P. E., Carmone, F. J., Jr., and Robinson, P. J. (1968a), "A comparison of perceptual mapping via confusions data and direct similarities judgments," in R. L. King (ed.), *Proceedings of the Denver Conference of the American Marketing Association*, Chicago: American Marketing Association, pp. 323-334.

Green, P. E., Carmone, F. J., Jr., and Robinson, P. S. (1968b), "Nonmetric scaling methods – An exposition and overview," *Wharton Quarterly*, 2 (Spring-Winter), 27-41.

Green, P. E., Carmone, F. J., Jr., and Smith, S. (1989), *Multidimensional Scaling: Concepts and Applications,* Boston: Allyn and Bacon.

Green, P. E., Carmone, F. J., Jr., and Wachspress, D. P. (1976), "Consumer segmentation via latent class analysis," *Journal of Consumer Research*, 3, 170-174.

Green, P. E., and Carroll, J. D. (1981), "New computer tools for product strategy," in Y. Wind, V. Mahajan, and R. Cardozo (eds.), *New Product Forecasting: Models and Applications*, Lexington, MA: Lexington, pp. 109-154.

Green, P. E., and Carroll, J. D. (1988), "A simple procedure for finding a composite of several multidimensional scaling solutions," *Journal of the Academy of Marketing Science*, 16, 25-35.

Green, P. E., Carroll, J. D., and Carmone, F. J., Jr. (1976a), "Superordinate factorial designs in the analysis of consumer judgments," *Journal of Business Research*, 4, 281-295.

Green, P. E., Carroll, J. D., and Carmone, F. J., Jr. (1976b), *A Stagewise Approach to Estimating Interactions in Conjoint Analysis*, unpublished manuscript, AT&T Bell Laboratories, Murray Hill, NJ.

Green, P. E., Frank, R. E., and Robinson, P. J. (1967), "Cluster analysis in test market selection," *Management Science*, 13, B387-B400.

Green, P. E., and Greenberg, M. (1970), "Ordinal methods in multidimensional scaling," in R. Ferber (ed.), *Handbook of Marketing Research,* McGraw-Hill, Section 3, pp. 62-84.

Green, P. E., Halbert, M. H., and Robinson, P. J. (1968), "Perception and preference mapping in the analysis of marketing behavior," in I. Crespi (ed.), *Attitude Research on the Rocks*, I, Chicago: American Marketing Association, pp. 172-201.

Green, P. E., and Jain, A. K. (1972), "A note on the robustness of INDSCAL to departures from linearity," *Proceedings of the AMA National Conference*, Chicago: American Marketing Association.

Green, P. E., and Kim, J. (1993), "Replicated weights determined in the SYNCLUS optimal variable weights clustering program," *Proceedings of the Academy of Marketing Science Annual Meeting*, December.

Green, P. E., and Krieger, A. M. (1989), "Recent contributions to optimal product positioning and buyer segmentation," *European Journal of Operational Research*, 41, 127-141.

Green, P. E., and Krieger, A. M. (1995), "Alternative approaches to cluster-based market segmentation," *Journal of Marketing Research Society*, 37, 221-239.

Green, P. E., and Krieger, A. M. (1999), "A generalized Rand-Index method for consensus clustering of separate partitions of the same data base," *Journal of Classification*, 16, 63-89.

Green, P. E., and Krieger, A. M. (2000), "Market segmentation involving mixtures of quantitative and qualitative variables," *Journal of Segmentation in Marketing*, 4, 85-106.

Green, P. E., Krieger, A. M., and Carroll, J. D. (1987), "Conjoint analysis and multidimensional scaling: A complementary approach," *Journal of Advertising Research*, 27, 21-27.

Green, P. E., Krieger, A. M., and Schaffer, C. M. (1985), "Quick and simple benefit segmentation," *Journal of Advertising Research*, 25, 9-17.

Green, P. E., and Maheshwari, A. (1969), "Common stock perception and preference: An application of multidimensional scaling," *Journal of Business*, 42, 439-457.

Green, P. E., and Maheshwari, A. (1970), "A note on the multidimensional scaling of conditional proximity data," *Journal of Marketing Research*, 7, 106-110.

Green, P. E., Maheshwari, A., and Rao, V. R. (1969), "Self concept and brand preference: An empirical application of multidimensional scaling," *Journal of the Market Research Society*, 11, 343-360.

Green, P. E., and Rao, V. R. (1969a), "A note on proximity measures and cluster analysis," *Journal of Marketing Research*, 6, 359-364.

Green, P. E., and Rao, V. R. (1969b), "Configuration in variance in nonmetric scaling: An empirical study," *Proceedings of the Cincinnati Educators Meeting of the American Marketing Association*, Chicago: American Marketing Association.

Green, P. E., and Rao, V. R. (1971), "Multidimensional scaling and individual differences," *Journal of Marketing Research*, 8, 71-77.

Green, P. E., and Rao, V. R. (1972a), *Applied Multidimensional Scaling: A Comparison of Approaches and Algorithms*. New York: Holt, Rinehart, and Winston.

Green, P. E., and Rao, V. R. (1972b), "Configural synthesis in multidimensional scaling," *Journal of Marketing Research*, 9, 65-68.

Green, P. E., and Rao, V. R. (1977), "Nonmetric approaches to multivariate analysis in marketing," in J. N. Sheth (ed.), *Research for Marketing,* Chicago: American Marketing Association, pp. 237-254.

Green, P. E., and Robinson, P. J. (1971), "Nonmetric methods in the analysis of multivariate data," in G. Fisk (ed.), *New Essays in Marketing Theory*, Newton, MA: Allyn and Bacon, pp. 73-102.

Green, P. E., and Schaffer, C. M. (1999), "Cluster-based market segmentation: Some further comparisons of alternative approaches," *Journal of Marketing Research Society*, 40, 155-163.

Green, P. E., Schaffer, C. M., and Patterson, K. M. (1988), "A reduced-space approach to the clustering of categorical data in market segmentation," *Journal of the Market Research Society*, 30, 267-288.

Green, P. E., and Wind, Y. (1973), *Multiattribute Decisions in Marketing*, Hinsdale, IL: Dryden.

Grover, R., and Srinivasan, V. (1989), "An approach for tracking within-segment shifts in market shares," *Journal of Marketing Research*, 26, 230-236.

Harshman, R. A., and Lundy, M. E. (1984), "The PARAFAC model for three-way factor analysis and multidimensional scaling," in H. G. Law, C. W. Snyder, J. A. Hattie, and R. P. McDonald (eds.), *Research Methods for Multimode Data Analysis*, New York: Praeger, pp. 372-402.

Heiser, W. J. (1981), *Unfolding Analysis of Proximity Data*, unpublished doctoral dissertation, University of Leiden.

Heiser, W. J., and de Leeuw, J. (1979), "How to Use SMACOF-III," Research Report, Leiden: Department of Data Theory.

Helsen, K., and Green, P. E. (1991), "A computational study of replicated clustering with an application to market segmentation," *Decision Sciences,* 22, 1124-1141.

Hinkle, C., Robinson, P. J., and Green, P. E. (1969), "Cluster analysis in industrial marketing," *Journal of Purchasing*, 5, 49-58.

Holman, E. W. (1978), "Completely nonmetric multidimensional scaling," *Journal of Mathematical Psychology*, 18, 39-51.

Hubert, L., and Arabie, P. (1985), "Comparing partitions," *Journal of Classification*, 2, 193-218.

Hubert, L., and Arabie, P. (1994), "The analysis of proximity matrices through sums of matrices having (anti-)Robinson forms," *British Journal of Mathematical and Statistical Psychology*, 47, 1-40.

Hubert, L., and Arabie, P. (1995a), "The approximation of two-mode proximity matrices by sums of order-constrained matrices," *Psychometrika*, 50, 573-605.

Hubert, L., and Arabie, P. (1995b), "Iterative projection strategies for the least-squares filling of tree structures to proximity data," *British Journal of Mathematical and Statistical Psychology*, 48, 281-317.

Hubert, L. J., Arabie, P., and Meulman, J. (1997), "Linear and circular unidimensional scaling for symmetric proximity matrices," *British Journal of Mathematical and Statistical Psychology*, 50, 253-284.

Hubert, L. J., Arabie, P., and Meulman, J. (1998), "Graph-theoretic representations for proximity matrices through strongly-anti-Robinson or circular strongly-anti-Robinson matrices. *Psychometrika*, 63, 341-458.

Hubert, L. J., Arabie, P., and Meulman, J. (2001), "Modeling dissimilarity: Generalizing ultrametric and additive tree representations," *British Journal of Mathematical and Statistical Psychology*, 64, 103-123.

Iacobucci, D., Arabie, P., and Bodapati, A. (2000), "Recommendation agents on the Internet," *Journal of Interactive Marketing*, 14 (3), 2-11.

Jardine, C. J., Jardine, N., and Sibson, R. (1967), "The structure and construction of taxonomic hierarchies," *Mathematical Biosciences*, 1, 173-179.

Johnson, S. C. (1967), "Hierarchical clustering schemes," *Psychometrika*, 32, 241-254

Kim, Y., Chatterjee, R., and DeSarbo, W. S. (1999), "Incorporating context effects in the multidimensional scaling of choice data," *International Journal of Research in Marketing*, 16, 35-56.

Kim, C., Rangaswamy, A., and DeSarbo, W. S. (2000), "A fixed point non-metric unfolding procedure," *Multivariate Behavioral Research*, 34, 143-180.

Krieger, A. M., and Green, P. E. (1999), "A generalized Rand-Index method for consensus clustering of separate partitions of the same data base," *Journal of Classification*, 16, 63-89.

Kruskal, J. B. (1964a), "Multidimensional scaling by optimizing goodness of fit to a nonmetric hypothesis," *Psychometrika*, 29, 1-27.

Kruskal, J. B. (1964b), "Nonmetric multidimensional scaling: A numerical method," *Psychometrika*, 29, 115-129.

Kruskal, J. B. (1965), "Analysis of factorial experiments by estimating monotone transformations of the data," *Journal of the Royal Statistical Society, Series B*, 27, 251-263.

Kruskal, J. B. (1977), "The relationship between multidimensional scaling and clustering," in J. Van Ryzin (ed.), *Classification and Clustering*, New York: Academic Press, pp. 17-44.

Kruskal, J. B., and Carmone, F. J., Jr. (1969), "MONANOVA: A FORTRAN IV program for monotone analysis of variance (non-metric analysis of factorial experiments)," *Behavioral Science*, 14, 165-166.

Kruskal, J. B., and Carroll, J. D. (1969), "Geometrical models and badness-of-fit functions," in P. R. Krishnaiah (ed.), *Multivariate Analysis II*, New York: Academic Press, pp. 639-671.

Kruskal, J. B., and Wish, M. (1978), *Multidimensional Scaling*, Newbury Park, CA: Sage.

Lance, G. N., and Williams, W. T. (1967), "A general theory of classificatory sorting strategies, I. Hierarchical systems," *Computer Journal*, 9, 373-380.

Leclerc, B. (1998), "Consensus of classifications: The case of trees," in A. Rizzi, M. Vichi, and H.-H. Bock (eds.), *Advances in Data Science and Classification*, Heidelberg: Springer-Verlag, pp. 81-90.

Luce, R. D., and Tukey, J. W. (1964), "Simultaneous conjoint measurement: A new type of fundamental measurement," *Journal of Mathematical Psychology*, 1, 1-27.

MacCallum, R. C. (1977), "Effects of conditionality on INDSCAL and ALSCAL weights," *Psychometrika*, 42, 297-305.

MacQueen, J. (1967), "Some methods for classification and analysis of multivariate observations," in L. M. Le Cam and J. Neyman (eds.), *Proceedings of the Fifth Berkeley Symposium on Mathematical Statistics and Probability*, Vol. 1, Berkeley: University of California Press, pp. 281-297.

Mahajan, V., and Jain, A. K. (1978), "An approach to normative segmentation," *Journal of Marketing Research*, 15, 338-345.

McLachlan, G. J., and Basford, K. E. (1988), *Mixture Models: Inference and Applications to Clustering*, New York: Marcel Dekker.

Meulman, J. J., Heiser, W. J., and SPSS, Inc. (1999), *CATEGORIES*, Evanston, IL: SPSS, Inc.

Milligan, G. W. (1989), "A validation study of a variable weighting algorithm for cluster analysis, *Journal of Classification*, 6, 53-71.

Milligan, G. W. (1996), "Clustering validation: Results and implications for applied analyses," in P. Arabie, L. J. Hubert, and G. De Soete (eds.), *Clustering and Classification*, River Edge, NJ: World Scientific, pp. 341-375.

Milligan, G. W., and Cooper, M. C. (1986), "A study of the comparability of external criteria for hierarchical cluster analysis," *Multivariate Behavioral Research*, 21, 441-458.

Ogawa, K. (1987), "An approach to simultaneous estimation and segmentation in conjoint analysis," *Marketing Science*, 6, 56-81.

Pruzansky, S. (1975), *How to Use SINDSCAL: A Computer Program for Individual Differences in Multidimensional Scaling*, Murray Hill, NJ: AT&T Bell Laboratories.

Punj, G., and Stewart, D. W. (1983), "Cluster analysis in marketing research: Review and suggestions for application," *Journal of Marketing Research*, 20, 134-148.

Ramsay, J. O. (1977), "Maximum likelihood estimation in multidimensional scaling," *Psychometrika*, 42, 241-266.

Ramsay, J. O. (1980), "The joint analysis of direct ratings, pairwise preferences, and dissimilarities," *Psychometrika*, 45, 149-165.

Ramsay, J. O. (1983), "MULTISCALE: A multidimensional scaling program," *American Statistician,* 34 326-327.

Richardson, M. (1938), "Multidimensional psychophysics," *Psychological Bulletin*, 35, 659-660. (Abstract).

Schaffer, C. M., and Green, P. E. (1998), "Cluster-based market segmentation: Some further comparisons of alternative approaches," *Journal of the Market Research Society*, 40, 155-163.

Schaffer, C. M., Green, P. E., and Carmone, F. J., Jr. (2000), "An investigation of the efficacy of univariate screening measures in defining market structure," *Journal of Segmentation in Marketing*, 4, 107-125.

Shepard, R. N. (1962a), "The analysis of proximities: Multidimensional scaling with an unknown distance function. I," *Psychometrika*, 27, 125-140.

Shepard, R. N. (1962b), "The analysis of proximities: Multidimensional scaling with an unknown distance function. II," *Psychometrika*, 27, 219-246.

Shepard, R. N., and Arabie, P. (1979), "Additive clustering: Representation of similarities as combinations of discrete overlapping properties," *Psychological Review*, 86, 87-123.

Shepard, R. N., and Carroll, J. D. (1966), "Parametric representation of nonlinear data structures," in P. R. Krishnaiah (ed.,) *Multivariate Analysis*, New York: Academic Press, pp. 561-592.

Sinha, I., and DeSarbo W. S. (1998), "An integrated approach toward the spatial modeling of perceived customer value," *Journal of Marketing Research*, 35, 236-249.

SYSTAT, Version 10 (2002), Richmond, CA: SYSTAT Software Inc.

Takane, Y., Young, F. W., and de Leeuw, J. (1977), "Nonmetric individual differences multidimensional scaling: An alternating least squares method with optimal scaling features," *Psychometrika*, 42, 7-67.

Torgerson, W. S. (1952), "Multidimensional scaling: I. Theory and method," *Psychometrika*, 17, 401-419.

Torgerson, W. S. (1958), *Theory and Methods of Scaling*, New York: Wiley.

Wedel, M., and DeSarbo, W. S. (1993), "A latent class binomial logit methodology for the external analysis of paired comparison choice data: An application of reinvesting the determinants of perceived risk," *Decision Sciences*, 24, 1157-1170.

Wedel, M., and DeSarbo, W. S. (1994), "A review of recent developments in latent structure regression models," in R. P. Bagozzi (ed.), *Advanced Methods in Marketing Research*, Oxford: Blackwell, pp. 352-388.

Wedel, M., and DeSarbo, W. S. (1995), "A mixture likelihood approach to generalized linear models," *Journal of Classification*, 12, 21-55.

Wedel, M., and DeSarbo, W. S. (1996), "An exponential-family multidimensional scaling mixture methodology," *Journal of Business and Economic Statistics*, 14, 447-459.

Wedel, M., and Kamakura, W. A. (2000), *Market Segmentation: Conceptual and Methodological Foundations* (2nd ed.), Norwell, MA: Kluwer Academic.

Wedel, M., Kamakura, W., and DeSarbo, W. S. (1995), "Implications for asymmetry, nonproportionality, and heterogeneity in brand switching from piece-wise exponential mixture hazards," *Journal of Marketing Research*, 32, 457-463.

Weinberg, S. L., and Menil, V. C. (1993), "The recovery of structure in linear and ordinal data: INDSCAL versus ALSCAL," *Multivariate Behavioral Research*, 28, 215-233.

Wind, Y. (1978a), "Introduction to special section on market segmentation research," *Journal of Marketing Research*, 15, 315-316.

Wind, Y. (1978b), "Issues and advances in segmentation research," *Journal of Marketing Research*, 15, 317-337.

Wind, J., Green, P. E., Shifflet, D., and Scarbrough, M. (1989), "Courtyard by Marriott: Designing a hotel facility with consumer-based marketing models," *Interfaces*, 19 (January-February), 25-47.

Young, G., and Householder, A. (1938), "Discussion of a set of points in terms of their mutual distances," *Psychometrika*, 3, 19-22.

Zenor, M. J., and Srivastava, R. K. (1993), "Inferring market structure with aggregate data: A latent-segment approach," *Journal of Marketing Research*, 30, 369-379.

PART FOUR: ENABLING TECHNOLOGIES

The rise of the World Wide Web has dramatically increased the data available for marketing research. The Web offers opportunities to design and implement broad studies quickly and flexibly. Online clickstreams also provide an efficient way of collecting running documentation of the entire purchase process, from search and information gathering to narrowing of choice sets to purchase transactions to after-sale satisfaction. This is customer data that researchers once could only infer or gain through painstaking study. In Chapter 4, Wolfgang Gaul considers some of the implications of Web usage data for the study of marketing and the practice of marketing research.

Chapter 4

Market Research and the Rise of the Web: The Challenge

Wolfgang Gaul
Institut für Entscheidungstheorie und Unternehmensforschung,
Universität Karlsruhe

Today's possibilities to communicate with each other or with devices designed to provide desired services, e.g., via the Internet or by mobile phone, have influenced our private life and have had continuing effects on such scientific disciplines as market research and marketing.

Labels such as e-intelligence, e-marketing, and m-commerce indicate that the growth of media-assisted business activities has attracted people who have investigated different ways of interaction.

These developments have been accompanied by a tremendous growth of corresponding data (by which I do not mean data needed for the operation of communication systems, but those that have been called content data and usage data). Given the irresistible power of attraction that interesting sources of information exert on data analysts (and the data sources created by the development just mentioned are considered to belong to the fastest growing ones in the world), it could be of interest to say a few words about the following hypothetical situation: What would have happened if all this had taken place earlier? How would Paul Green have reacted? – I think he would have tackled this challenge.

The worst that could have happened (in the case that he had started to be more and more engaged in findings for the underlying situation) is that some of the well-known papers that Paul Green and coworkers from his different research groups have published would not have appeared. That would have been a great pity. On the other hand, we would have nice results (additional to those that we already know) within research directions of instantaneously growing importance.

WEB USAGE DATA AS STARTING POINT

For the following discussion a restriction is made to situations in which mainly Web usage data are considered, because a treatment of the overall problem (for all kinds of data that make up the media challenge mentioned before) is too ambitious for a short contribution.

For a given Web site, one could begin by asking how efforts to attract Internet users to visit the underlying site can be optimized (or the percentage of potential contacts for which these efforts failed to establish a visitor relationship can be minimized), and continue by considering how site visitors can be influenced to return to and/or buy from the site, as well as how buyers can be convinced to become repeat buyers and so forth.

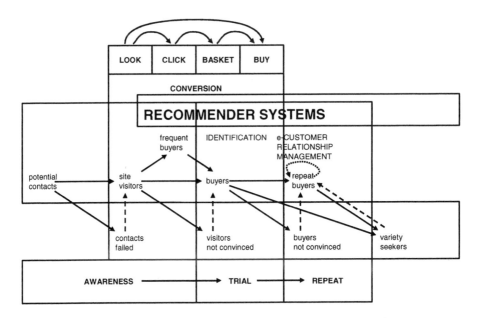

Figure 4-1. Possibility of Web Usage Data Analysis

Figure 4-1 illustrates the possibilities for using Web data. While the problems as such are not new for marketing and could be discussed within the well-known awareness-trial-repeat approach, the determination of new so-called *e-metrics* (NetGenesis 2000) and *conversion rates* (Future Now 2001) derivable from the Web usage behavior of site visitors allows refined measures on which improved marketing activities can be based. As an example, the obvious possibility to compute micro-conversion rates from Web usage data is mentioned where the labels "look," "click," "basket," and "buy" are nearly self-explaining ("look" stands for the phase in which a site visitor takes in first impressions about what is offered; "click" covers the situation in which the site visitor decides on the hyperlink to click; "basket" denotes the action of putting a chosen product into the electronic market basket; and "buy" concludes the buying contract). The "basket-to-buy" rate, for example, describes the percentage of products contained in the e-basket that were finally bought.

At the latest, before completion of the purchase a Web user has to provide identification, although registration procedures at earlier time points try to transform unknown browsing individuals into site visitors with known navigational behavior with respect to fields of interest and buying habits. To registered visitors, e-customer relationship management strategies can be applied, and well-designed recommender systems are useful tools to operate sites and to tighten ties to visitors and customers.

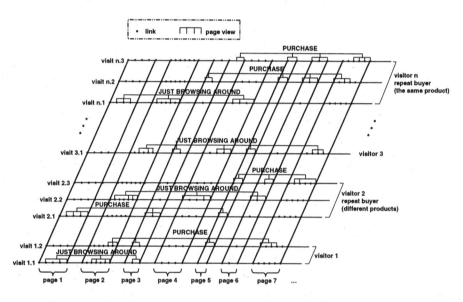

Figure 4-2. Web User Behavior and Site Structure Described via "Links, Page Views, Visits"

Figure 4-2 depicts how connections between Web user behavior and site structure can be described in terms of "links," "page views," and "visits." This Web usage data can be used to determine the attraction level, or "e-attractivity," of (parts of) single pages, counts of (parts of) pages visited together, visit times, and other information for the characterization of visitors and their visits as well as for site design measures. A discussion of some obvious problems, e.g., how usage data of human beings can be distinguished from those of Web robots or how single Web server logfile entries can be correctly assigned to the "right" user, has to be omitted because of length restrictions for this contribution. For more on this topic, see Gaul and Schmidt-Thieme (2000, 2002) and Schmidt-Thieme and Gaul (2002).

RECOMMENDER SYSTEMS

A recommender system is software that collects and aggregates information about site visitors (e.g., buying histories, products of interest, hints concerning desirable search dimensions, or other FAQ) and their actual navigational and buying behavior, and returns recommendations (e.g., based on customer demographics, past behavior of the actual visitor, and/or user patterns of top sellers with fields of interest similar to those of the actual contact). These recommendations have to be created in such a way that they are valuable for transitory browsers as well as frequent visitors and loyal repeat buyers on the one side and site owners on the other side. Currently, recommender systems are installed in more and more commercial sites not only to assist consumers in better/faster accessing useful information, but also to assist site owners in converting browsers to buyers, in stimulating cross- and up-sales, and in establishing customer loyalty as part of the activities to improve electronic customer care. See Gaul, Geyer-Schulz, Hahsler, and Schmidt-Thieme (2002) and Schafer, Konstan, and Riedl (2000) for descriptions of recommender systems in terms of input/output features and lists of examples from the application side.

"Recommender systems" could be the label for an area in which computer science is combined with market research and marketing to give answers to the just mentioned challenge. In the following, to be more specific, a recommender system approach based on the navigational behavior of Internet users is formulated in mathematical terms.

For such a description, the succession of visited resources of the underlying site (which is information that was not depicted in Figure 4-2) is now needed.

Let R be an arbitrary set (the set of resources of a Website). The set $R^* := \bigcup_{n \in N} R^n$ of all tuples of R is called the set of sequences of R and serves as basis to model user navigation paths or "clickstreams."

A sequence $p = (p_1, ..., p_{|p|}) \in R$ describes a path as sequence of resources of R, its length is denoted as $|p|$. Sometimes, the tuple-notation is replaced by just putting the corresponding resources one after the other, i.e., $p_1, p_2, ..., p_{|p|}$. A substructure space of R^* is defined as pair $(A, \leq)$ of a set A and a relation $\leq$ on $A \times R^*$ where $a \in A$ is called substructure of $p \in R^*$ if

$a \leq p$. Examples of substructures for navigation paths $p \in R^*$ are (where $P(R)$ denotes the powerset of R):

1. *Sets* $(P(R), \subseteq)$: Here, a set of resources $a \in P(R)$ is defined to be a substructure of a path p if all resources $x \in a$ occur in path p.

2. *Sequences* $(R^*, \leq_{ct})$: Here, a sequence $a \in R*$ is defined to be a substructure of a path p if it is a contiguous subsequence, i.e., it exists $i_0 \in \{0, ..., |p| - |a|\}$ with $a_i = p_{i_0+i}$ for all $i = 1, ..., |a|$.

3. *Generalized sequences* $((R \cup \{*\})^*, \leq_{gen})$: Here, sequences consist of elements of R and an additional symbol $*$ used as wildcard, where a generalized sequence $a \in (R \cup \{*\})^*$ is defined to be a substructure of a path p if it is a generalization of a (contiguous) subsequence of p and *generalization* means that arbitrary parts of the sequence may be replaced by wildcards (see Gaul and Schmidt-Thieme (2000) for an exact definition).

4. *Simple generalized sequences* $(R^*, \leq_{nct})$: Here, a (simple generalized) sequence $a \in R^*$ is defined to be a substructure of a path p if it is a non-contiguous subsequence with the following meaning: It exists $j: \{1, ..., |a|\} \rightarrow \{1, ..., |p|\}$ strictly increasing with $a_i = p_{j(i)}$ for all $i = 1, ..., |a|$, i.e., in the context of generalized sequences, if $a_1 * a_2 * ... * a_{|a|} \leq_{gen} p$.

The space of simple generalized sequences can be viewed as a subspace of the space of generalized sequences where a wildcard is interspersed between each two resources. Notice that, in practical applications, only generalized sequences without a wildcard at the first and/or last position (i.e., $a \in (R \cup \{*\})^*$ with $a_1, a_{|a|} \in R$) are of interest. These sequences are called *path fragments*.

For any substructure space the symbol $\varnothing$ describes the empty substructure (i.e., the empty set or the empty sequence, respectively) and $|a|$ the substructure complexity of $a \in A$ defined as cardinality (for sets) or length (for sequences).

Now, we can define a path feature to be a pair (Φ, φ) where Φ is an arbitrary set called *feature space* and $\varphi: R^* \rightarrow \Phi$ the *feature map* mapping paths to features. For a path $p \in R^*$ we call $\varphi(p)$ the feature of p.

Trivial examples for path features are its length (φ: $R^* \to N$, $p \to |p|$) and its entry point (φ: $R^* \to R$, $p \to p_1$). More interesting features are obtainable via substructures.

Feature spaces based on substructures turn out to have the disadvantage of high dimensionality because they contain – for every path p – a binary vector indicating whether an element $a \in A$ is a substructure of p or not, e.g., the feature space build from subsets has dimension $2^{|R|}$, the one build from finite sequences (if subsequences are restricted to length n) has dimension $\sum_{i=0}^{n} |R|^i$. Therefore – given an underlying (multi)set of navigation paths S that has to be analyzed (where *(multi)set* denotes a set with eventually multiple membership of elements) – one is looking for interesting subsets of substructures that result in a smaller number of dimensions but that still carry as much information as possible for a description of the objects of (multi)set S *(feature selection)*. We call a dimension sparse with respect to S if the corresponding entry in the binary vector is zero for almost all paths of (multi)set S: In applications, one often can drop a vast number of sparse dimensions and restrict to those dimensions for which the percentage of non-zero entries in the binary vector exceeds a lower bound.

Dependent on this bound, called "minsup," frequent substructures of the paths of S can be determined beforehand. For a substructure $a \in A$ one defines its relative frequency

$$\frac{\sup(a)}{S} := \frac{|\{p \in S \mid a \le p\}|}{|S|}$$

as support of a in S: The task to compute all frequent substructures, i.e., the set $\Phi_{(S, \text{minsup})} := \{a \in A \mid \sup_S(a) \ge \min \sup\}$ of all substructures with at least a given minimum support minsup $\in R_o^+$, is well known and accomplished by the à priori algorithm for sets (Agrawal and Srikant 1994), sequences (Agrawal and Srikant 1995), and generalized sequences (Gaul and Schmidt-Thieme 2000), respectively. Building the feature space from the frequent substructures $\Phi_{(S, \text{minsup})}$ only, instead of using all substructures of A, can reduce the dimensionality dramatically (depending on the minimum support and the structure of S, of course).

Given all the mathematical notations just explained, a recommender system based on navigation paths is a map:

$$r: R^* \to P(R)$$

and the set *r(p)* is called *recommendation set* for $p \in R^*$.

Starting point for an evaluation of such recommender systems is the (multi)set *S* of paths or "clickstreams." Each path $p \in S$ can be split at position $i \in \{1, ..., |p| - 1\}$ in a history $h_i(p) : = (p_1, ..., p_i)$ and future $f_i(p) : = (p_{i+1}, ..., p_{|p|})$. p_i is called *recommendation point*.

Figure 4-3 explains this situation, reminds us of the fact that parts of the historical navigation behavior (that may be not important or unknown) can be replaced by wildcards, and helps us to understand how the quality of recommendations can be considered in the underlying case.

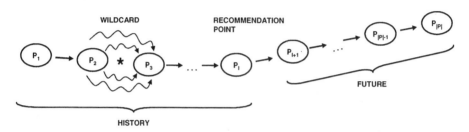

Figure 4-3. "Clickstream" Depiction

Here, a general definition for a *recommendation quality measure* can be given by

$$q : R_1 \times R_2 \times R_3 \quad \rightarrow \quad R_o^+$$
$$(h, f, r) \quad \rightarrow \quad q(h, f, r)$$

where R_1 describes the history space, R_2 the future space, and R_3 the space of (sets of) recommendations $r(h)$ derived from $h \in R_1$. Various choices of R_1, R_2, and R_3 are possible. $q(h,f,r)$ measures the quality of recommendations (e.g., by choosing $h = h_{i(p)}$ and comparing $r = r(h_{i(p)})$ with $f = f_{i(p)}$ for a path p).

For the crucial point on how "best" recommender systems based on clickstreams can be designed, the reader has to be referred to Gaul and Schmidt-Thieme (2002) and Schmidt-Thieme and Gaul (2001). Figure 4-4 does show that, given the recommendation point $h_{|h|}$ of a clickstream history *h*, different designs of recommender subsystems can be combined for the construction of an optimal system (where "optimal" must be related to additional restrictions that have to be fulfilled).

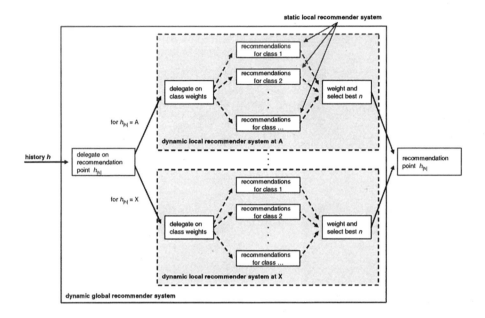

Figure 4-4. **Possible Architecture of a Recommender System Based on Clickstream Histories**

THE CHALLENGE REVISITED

In the beginning of this contribution I postulated that Paul Green would have tackled the challenge. Now, after my attempt to outline the contours of this challenge, I hope that my original guess is still valid. Of course, the determination of straightforward e-business measures would not be a challenge to Green from an intellectual point of view, although such measures are to some extent indispensable for the construction of more sophisticated "marketing-modeling-oriented" and "market-research-techniques-based" recommender systems.

If, on the right hand side of Figure 4-1, we have (repeat) buyers or, at least, frequent site visitors whom we can "persuade" to participate in data-collecting activities needed for the application of some of the well-known approaches that Paul Green, his coworkers, and other researchers with similar interests have developed, then we are back to the "good old models" discussion. I think of *conjoint analysis* (e.g., Green and Wind 1975; Green and Srinivasan 1978, 1990; Baier and Gaul 2001), *correspondence analysis* (e.g., Carroll, Green, and Schaffer 1986, 1987; Nishisato and Gaul 1988, 1990), multidimensional scaling variants via *stochastic ideal points* (e.g., De Soete, Carroll, and DeSarbo 1986; Böckenholt and Gaul 1986; Baier and Gaul

1999), or *preference vectors* (e.g., De Soete and Carroll 1983; Baier and Gaul 2001), generalizations of cluster analysis as *overlapping clustering* (e.g., Arabie, Carroll, DeSarbo, and Wind 1981; Gaul and Schader 1994; Baier, Gaul, and Schader 1997), *multimode clustering* (e.g., Arabie, Carroll, and DeSarbo 1987), and *product line optimization* (e.g., Green and Krieger 1985, 1987a, 1987b; Gaul, Aust, and Baier 1995), to mention just a few examples in which I have tried to mix results by Paul Green and scholars with my own contributions, mainly for the purpose of showing how much I have benefited from these research groups.

One area for further work would be to investigate to what extent such known methodologies could be combined with the efforts to build recommender systems for the various tasks and for the different target groups that one has in mind. Another would be to consider what one can do if the data collected are not yet in a condition that would allow the application of known approaches.

Above all, the incorporation of Web usage data and/or the combination of such data with other information obtained or obtainable in connection with efforts to support site owners and/or site visitors opens a wide field for future research for which, as one example, the analysis of clickstreams or navigation path data by recommender systems has been sketched in the previous section. Here, national law may require that one has to apply for permission from Web users if the intention is to evaluate such data on an individual level. This could be the starting point for another discussion on "personalization" issues, one that has to be postponed to a later occasion.

REFERENCES

Agrawal, R., and Srikant, R. (1994), "Fast algorithms for mining association rules," in J. B. Bocca, M. Jarke, and C. Zaniolo (eds.), *Proceedings of the 20th International Conference on Very Large Data Bases* (VLDB'94), pp. 487-499.

Agrawal, R., and Srikant, R. (1995), "Mining sequential patterns," in P. S. Yu and A. L. P. Chen (eds.), *Proceedings of the Eleventh International Conference on Data Engineering*, IEEE Computer Society, pp. 3-14.

Arabie, P., Carroll, J. D., and DeSarbo, W. S. (1987), *Three-Way Scaling and Clustering*, Sage, Newbury Park.

Arabie, P., Carroll, J. D., DeSarbo, W. S., and Wind, J. (1981), "Overlapping clustering: A new method for product positioning," *Journal of Marketing Research*, 18, 310-317.

Baier, D., and Gaul, W. (1999), "Optimal product positioning based on paired comparison data," *Journal of Econometrics*, 89, 365-392.

Baier, D., and Gaul, W. (2001), "Market simulation using a probabilistic ideal vector model for conjoint data," in A. Gustafsson and A. Herrmann (eds.), *Conjoint Measurement, Methods and Applications* (2nd ed.), Springer, pp. 97-120.

Baier, D., Gaul, W., and Schader, M. (1997), "Two-mode overlapping clustering with applications to simultaneous benefit segmentation and marketing structuring," in R. Klar and O. Opitz (eds.), *Classification and Knowledge Organization, Studies in Classification, Data Analysis, and Knowledge Organization*, pp. 557-566.

Böckenholt, I., and Gaul, W. (1986), "Analysis of choice behavior via probabilistic ideal point and vector models," *Applied Stochastic Models and Data Analysis*, 2, 209-226.

Carroll, J. D., Green, P. E., and Schaffer, C. M (1986), "Interpoint distance comparison in correspondence analysis," *Journal of Marketing Research*, 23, 271-280.

Carroll, J. D., Green, P. E., and Schaffer, C. M. (1987), "Comparing interpoint distances in correspondence analysis: A clarification," *Journal of Marketing Research*, 24, 445-450.

De Soete, G., and Carroll, J. D. (1983), "A maximum likelihood method for fitting the wandering vector model," *Psychometrika*, 48, 553-566.

De Soete, G., Carroll, J. D., and DeSarbo, W. S. (1986), "The wandering ideal point model: A probabilistic multidimensional unfolding model for paired comparisons data," *Journal of Mathematical Psychology*, 30, 28-41.

Future Now (2001), *Increasing Conversion Rates: One Step at a Time*, Future Now, Inc.

Gaul, W. (1998), "Data mining: A new label for an old problem?" in *Proceedings of Workshop on Data Mining and Knowledge Discovery in Business Applications*, Osaka, Japan, pp. 1-11.

Gaul, W., Aust, E., and Baier, D. (1995), "Gewinnorientierte Produktliniengestaltung unter Berücksichtigung des Kundennutzens," *Zeitschrift für Betriebswirtschaftslehre*, 65, 835-854.

Gaul, W., Geyer-Schulz, A., Hahsler, M., and Schmidt-Thieme, L. (2002), "eMarketing mittels Recommendersystemen," *Marketing ZFP,* 24 (47), 47-56.

Gaul, W., and Schader, M. (1994), "Pyramidal classification based on incomplete dissimilarity data," *Journal of Classification*, 11, 171-193.

Gaul, W., and Schader, M. (1996), "A new algorithm for two-mode clustering," in H.-H. Bock and W. Polasek (eds.), *Data Analysis and Knowledge Organization: Studies in Classification, Data Analysis, and Knowledge Organization*, Springer, pp. 15-23.

Gaul, W., and Schmidt-Thieme, L. (2000), "Frequent generalized subsequences – a problem from web mining," in W. Gaul, O. Opitz, and M. Schader (eds.), *Data Analysis – Scientific Modeling and Practical Application*: *Studies in Classification, Data Analysis, and Knowledge Organization*, Springer, pp. 429-445.

Gaul, W., and Schmidt-Thieme, L. (2002), "Recommender systems based on user navigational behavior in the internet," *Behaviormetrika*, 29 (1), 1-22.

Green, P. E., and Krieger, A. M. (1985), "Models and heuristics for product line selection, *Marketing Science*, 4 (1), 1-19.

Green, P. E., and Krieger, A. M. (1987a), "A simple heuristic for selecting 'good' products in conjoint analysis," *Applications of Management Science*, 5, 131-153.

Green, P. E., and Krieger, A. M. (1987b), "A consumer-based approach to designing product line extensions," *Journal of Product Innovation Management*, 4, 21-32.

Green, P. E., and Srinivasan, V. (1978), "Conjoint analysis in consumer research: issues and outlook," *Journal of Consumer Research*, 5, 103-123.

Green, P. E., and Srinivasan, V. (1990), "Conjoint analysis in marketing: new developments with implications for research and practice," *Journal of Marketing*, 54, 3-19.

Green, P. E., and Wind, Y. (1975), "New ways to measure consumers' judgments," *Harvard Business Review*, 53, 107-117.

Net Genesis (2000), *E-Metrics: Business Metrics for the New Economy*, NetGenesis Corp.

Nishisato, S., and Gaul, W. (1988), "Marketing data analysis by dual scaling," *International Journal of Research in Marketing*, 5, 151-170.

Nishisato, S., and Gaul, W. (1990), "An approach to marketing data analysis: the forced classification procedure of dual scaling," *Journal of Marketing Research*, 27, 354-360.

Schafer, J. B., Konstan, J. A., and Riedl, J. (2000), "Electronic commerce recommender applications," *Journal of Data Mining and Knowledge Discovery*, 5 (1/2), 115-152.

Schmidt-Thieme, L., and Gaul, W. (2001), "Frequent patterns in structured data – a general framework with applications to web usage mining," Working Paper of the Institut für Entscheidungstheorie und Unternehmensforschung, Universität Karlsruhe.

Schmidt-Thieme, L., and Gaul, W. (2002), "Aufzeichung des Nutzungsverhaltens – Erhebungstechniken und Datenformate," in H. Hippner, M. Merzenich, K.D. Wilde (Hrsg.), Handbuch *Web Mining im Marketing*, Vieweg, pp. 35-52.

PART FIVE: CONJOINT ANALYSIS

Conjoint analysis arose from a recognition of the limits of other earlier approaches to modeling consumer preferences, particularly for new products. Applying approaches from psychometrics, it offers an elegant way to identify the specific features and benefits that shape judgments. The judgments are decomposed into partworths. Since conjoint was introduced to marketing by Green and Rao, both the practice of conjoint and the development of choice models have developed considerably. In Chapter 5, Paul Green, Abba Krieger, and Jerry Wind offer an overview of the development of conjoint methodologies from their distinctive vantage point as central contributors to its development. In Chapter 6, John Hauser and Vithala Rao offer more detail on the development of conjoint analysis. In Chapter 7, Green, Krieger, and Wind provide insights on the application of buyer choice simulators, optimizers, and dynamic models to these data. Finally, in Chapter 8, Jordan Louviere, Deborah Street, and Leonie Burgess offer an overview of two decades of research in choice experiments.

Chapter 5

Thirty Years of Conjoint Analysis: Reflections and Prospects[1]

Paul E. Green
Abba M. Krieger
Yoram (Jerry) Wind
The Wharton School, University of Pennsylvania

Conjoint analysis is marketers' favorite methodology for finding out how buyers make tradeoffs among competing products and suppliers. Conjoint analysts develop and present descriptions of alternative products or services that are prepared from fractional factorial, experimental designs. They use various models to infer buyers' partworths for attribute levels, and enter the partworths into buyer choice simulators to predict how buyers will choose among products and services. Easy-to-use software has been important for applying these models. Thousands of applications of conjoint analysis have been carried out over the past three decades.

Readers of *Interfaces* are no strangers to multiattribute utility models (Keeney and Raiffa 1976; Starr and Zeleny 1977; Bell, Raiffa, and Tversky 1988). Thomas Saaty (1980) introduced a different approach to multiattribute utility measurement: the analytic hierarchy process (AHP). Both approaches emphasized small numbers of decision makers facing high-level decisions. Operations researchers and management scientists have applied both methods extensively to important problems in management and government decision making.

OR/MS researchers may be less familiar with another method – conjoint analysis – that has been applied for over 30 years, primarily by researchers in marketing and business. Conjoint analysis evolved from the seminal research of Luce and Tukey (1964). Their theoretical contributions were put to use by a number of psychometricians, including Carroll (1969), Kruskal (1965), and Young (1969). These researchers developed a variety of nonmetric models for

117

computing partworths (attribute-level values) from respondents' preference orderings across multiattributed stimuli, such as descriptions of products or services.

Conjoint analysis is, by far, the most used marketing research method for analyzing consumer tradeoffs. Surveys conducted by Wittink and Cattin (1989) and Wittink, Vriens, and Burhenne (1994) attest to its worldwide popularity.

It is not difficult to see why researchers developed and applied conjoint analysis so rapidly. Conjoint analysis deals with a central management question: Why consumers choose one brand or one supplier over another? Also, marketing research practitioners want to be part of something new, and computer software for implementing the methodology became readily available.

THE BASIC IDEAS OF CONJOINT ANALYSIS

Conjoint analysis is one of many techniques for handling situations in which a decision maker has to deal with options that simultaneously vary across two or more attributes. The problem the decision maker faces is how to trade off the possibility that option X is better than option Y on attribute A while Y is better than X on attribute B, and various extensions of these conflicts.

Conjoint analysis concerns the day-to-day decisions of consumers – what brand of toothpaste, automobile, or photocopying machine to buy (or lease)? Marketing researchers may collect tradeoff information for hundreds or even thousands of respondents. Data collection and processing techniques must be fairly simple and routinized to handle problems of this scope.

Conjoint analysis is a technique for measuring tradeoffs for analyzing survey responses concerning preferences and intentions to buy, and it is a method for simulating how consumers might react to changes in current products or to new products introduced into an existing competitive array. Researchers have used conjoint analysis for consumer and industrial products and services and for not-for-profit offerings.

To understand the basic concepts of conjoint analysis, assume that a marketer of credit cards wishes to examine the possibility of modifying its current line of services. One of the first steps in designing a conjoint study is to develop a set of attributes and corresponding attribute levels to characterize the competitive domain. Focus. groups, in-depth consumer interviews, and internal corporate expertise are some of the sources researchers use to structure the sets of attributes and levels that guide the rest of the study.

Table 5-1. These attributes (and levels within attributes) describe the set of potential services that would be offered to credit card subscribers.

Annual price ($)

    0   10   20   50   80   100

Cash rebate (end-of-year, on total purchases)

    None   ½%   1%

800 number for message forwarding

    None   9-5 weekdays   24 hours per day

Retail purchase insurance

    None   90 days' coverage

Common carrier insurance (death, injury)

    None $50,000 $200,000

Rental car insurance (fire, theft, collision, vandalism)

    None $30,000

Baggage insurance

    None $2,500 depreciated cost $2,500 replacement cost

Airport club admission (based on small entrance fee)

    No admission $5 per visit $2 per visit

Card acceptance

    Air, hotel, rental cars (AHC)

    AHC and most restaurants (AHCR)

    AHCR and most general retailers (AHCRG)

    AHCR and department stores only (AHCRD)

24-hour medical/legal referral network

    No   Yes

Airport limousine to city destination

    Not offered   Available at 20% discount

800 number for emergency car service

    Not offered   Available at 20% discount

In an actual study of credit-card suppliers, researchers used a set of 12 attributes with two to six levels, for a total of 35 levels (Table 5-1). However, the total number of possible combinations of levels is 186,624. Conjoint analysts make extensive use of orthogonal arrays (Addelman 1962) and other types of fractional factorial designs to reduce the number of stimulus descriptions that a respondent sees to a small fraction of the total number of combinations. In this problem, an array of 64 profiles (less than 0.04 percent of the total) is sufficient to estimate all attribute-level main effects on an uncorrelated basis. Since the study designers used a hybrid conjoint design (Green and Krieger 1996), each respondent was asked to consider only eight (balanced) profile descriptions drawn from the 64 profiles.

For such studies, researchers may prepare prop cards (Figure 5-1). After the respondent sorts the prop cards in terms of preference, each card is rated on a 0 to 100 likelihood-of-acquisition scale. In small conjoint studies (for example, six or seven attributes, each at two or three levels), respondents are given all of the full profiles – 16 to 32 prop cards. In these cases, respondents typically sort the prop cards into four to eight ordered categories before they give likelihood-of-purchase ratings for each separate profile within each category.

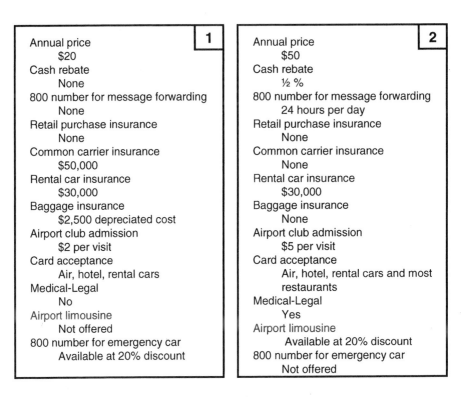

Annual price **1**	Annual price **2**

Annual price · $20 — Cash rebate · None — 800 number for message forwarding · None — Retail purchase insurance · None — Common carrier insurance · $50,000 — Rental car insurance · $30,000 — Baggage insurance · $2,500 depreciated cost — Airport club admission · $2 per visit — Card acceptance · Air, hotel, rental cars — Medical-Legal · No — Airport limousine · Not offered — 800 number for emergency car · Available at 20% discount

Annual price · $50 — Cash rebate · ½ % — 800 number for message forwarding · 24 hours per day — Retail purchase insurance · None — Common carrier insurance · None — Rental car insurance · $30,000 — Baggage insurance · None — Airport club admission · $5 per visit — Card acceptance · Air, hotel, rental cars and most restaurants — Medical-Legal · Yes — Airport limousine · Available at 20% discount — 800 number for emergency car · Not offered

Figure 5-1. **These prop cards illustrate specific services that a credit card could offer. For each card the respondent indicates how likely she would be to subscribe to the credit card on a 0-100 point scale.**

Types of Conjoint Data Collection

Four major types of data collection procedures are currently used for conjoint analysis:

(1) In *full-profile techniques,* each respondent sees a complete set of the full-profile prop cards. After sorting the cards into ordered categories, the respondent rates each card on a 0 to 100 likelihood-of-purchase scale.

(2) In *compositional techniques,* such as the CASEMAP procedure (Srinivasan 1988), each respondent rates the desirability of each set of attribute levels on a 0 to 100 scale and then rates the attributes on an importance scale. (This approach is typically called self-explicated preference-data collection.)

(3) In *hybrid techniques,* each respondent performs a self-explicated evaluation task and evaluates a subset of the full-profile cards (Green, Goldberg, and Montemayor 1981). The resulting utility function is a composite of data obtained from both tasks.

(4) In *adaptive conjoint analysis,* a hybrid technique developed by Sawtooth Software (Johnson 1987), each respondent first performs a self-explication task and then evaluates a set of partial-profile descriptions, two at a time. Partial profiles usually consist of two or three attributes per stimulus card. Researchers vary the partial profile descriptions depending upon responses to earlier paired comparisons. The respondent evaluates each pair of partial profiles on a graded, paired comparisons scale. Both tasks are administered by computer (Johnson 1987).

Conjoint Models

Most conjoint analysts fit what is known as the *partworth model* to respondents' evaluative judgments, whether they obtain these judgments using full-profile, self-explicated, or hybrid approaches. However, they occasionally use vector and ideal point models. We assume that there are P attributes and J stimuli used in the study design. For a given respondent, we let y_{jp} denote the desirability of the pth attribute for the jth stimulus; we first assume that y_{jp} is inherently continuous. The *vector* model assumes that the respondent's preference s_j for the jth stimulus is given by

$$s_j = \sum_{p=1}^{P} w_p y_{jp}$$

where w_p denotes the respondent's importance weight for each of the P attributes (Figure 5-2).

Preference

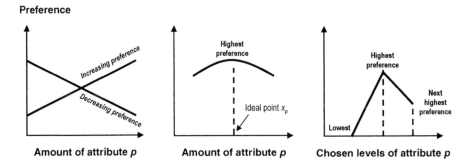

Figure 5-2. **These diagrams illustrate what is meant by linear preferences, ideal point preferences, and discrete (partworth) preferences. The third graph shows three partworths.** *(From Green, P.E., and Srinivasan, V. (1978),* Journal of Consumer Research, 5, *103-123.)*

In the *ideal-point model,* the analyst posits that preference s_j is inversely related to the weighted squared distance d_j^2 of the location y_{jp} of the jth stimulus from the individual's ideal point x_p, where d_j^2 is defined as

$$d_j^2 = \sum_{p=1}^{P} w_p \left(y_{jp} - x_p \right)^2.$$

In the *partworth model,* the analyst assumes that

$$s_j = \sum_{p=1}^{P} f_p \left(y_{jp} \right)$$

where y_{jp} is the category level and f_p is a function denoting the partworth corresponding to level y_{jp}. In practice, the analyst estimates $f_p(y_{jp})$ for a selected set of discrete levels of y_{jp}.

In Figure 5-3, we show illustrative (averaged) partworths for the attribute levels described in Table 5-1. Partworths are often scaled so that the lowest partworth is zero, within each attribute. Strictly speaking, analysts evaluate partworth functions at discrete levels for each attribute. However, in many applications, analysts interpolate between levels of continuous attributes, such as price, when they enter the partworths in buyer-choice simulators. The scaling (vertical axis) is common across all attributes; this allows the analyst to add up partworths across each attribute level to obtain the overall (product or service) utility of any profile composable from the basic attribute levels.

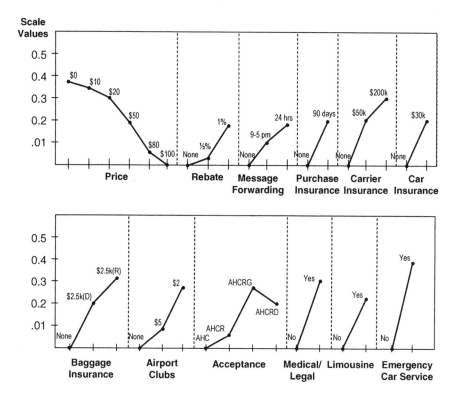

Figure 5-3. This chart illustrates how partworth scale values depend on price, message forwarding, ... emergency car service. For example, the most preferred price is $0 and the least preferred price is $100.

Stimulus Presentation

In collecting conjoint data, analysts currently emphasize the full-profile and hybrid procedures, including Sawtooth's adaptive conjoint analysis. While they still employ paragraph descriptions of attribute levels in some industry studies, they usually use profile cards with terse attribute-level descriptions (Figure 5-1). Analysts increasingly use pictorial material; these kinds of props make the respondent's task more interesting and convey information easily with little ambiguity. Moreover, conjoint methods are increasingly being applied to the design of *physical* products (for example, foods and beverages, fragrances, and personal-care products). In these cases, researchers use actual, experimentally designed prototypes.

PRECURSORS TO CONJOINT ANALYSIS

How did conjoint analysis come about? For marketing researchers working in data analysis and modeling, the 1970s provided a rich bounty of tools and techniques. Unlike the 1960s (a decade of borrowing tools from operations researchers), the late '60s and early '70s saw the strong influence of developments in the behavioral sciences (primarily psychometrics and mathematical psychology) on marketing research methods. In particular, three techniques – cluster analysis, multidimensional scaling (MDS), often called perceptual and preference mapping, and conjoint analysis – were introduced to marketing at that time.

Cluster analytic methods almost immediately found application in market segmentation (Green, Frank, and Robinson 1967). Unlike a priori market segmentation, where researchers assume they know segment identifiers at the outset, cluster analysis provided researchers and practitioners with tools for implementing post hoc, or cluster-based segmentation. Researchers could then base segmentation on the needs or benefits sought, brand preferences, problem-solving alternatives, psychographics, and a host of other variables. The idea of cluster-based segmentation was to let the data speak for themselves in terms of finding groups of consumers who share similar needs, attitudes, tradeoffs, or benefits.

Multidimensional scaling methods also received considerable attention in the 1970s. Marketing researchers learned the value of constructing attractive "maps" for pictorially representing large two-way (or multi-way) numerical tables as point or point and vector geometric representations in two (or possibly three) dimensions. They could also profitably combine MDS with hierarchical clustering methods to augment two-dimensional configurations with cluster-based representations based on solutions in higher dimensionalities. Carroll and Green (1997) summarize the history of the MDS field.

As early appliers of MDS found (often to their dismay), the brand-positioning maps generated using MDS techniques appeared to be largely of *diagnostic* rather than predictive value. Researchers who wanted to use MDS to develop new or restaged products faced a two-part problem: translating brand scores on perceived dimensions to manipulable dimensions, and relating manipulable attribute levels to their counterparts in perceptual or preference space.

These problems illustrate the general problem of *reverse engineering*, in which back-translation from perceived attributes to physical and chemical product characteristics is typically not one-to-one (Kaul and Rao 1994). It is little wonder that conjoint analysis, with its emphasis on *researcher-specified* attribute levels, provided a basis for relating preference or choice responses to *explicit* arguments, including physical attributes as well as verbal descriptions of product and service attribute levels.

THE ERA OF CONJOINT ANALYSIS

Conjoint analysis has been blessed with several sets of parents. The seminal precursory paper to conjoint analysis, Luce and Tukey's paper on conjoint measurement, appeared in the *Journal of Mathematical Psychology* in 1964. The authors focused on axiomatic approaches to fundamental measurement. The idea was to obtain ordered metric scale data from rank-order response data and a set of factorially designed stimuli. Not surprisingly, the initial conjoint algorithm, called MONANOVA, designed by Kruskal (1965) and programmed by Kruskal and Carmone, used ranked response data.

In the late 1960s, Green and his colleagues (Vithala Rao, Frank Carmone, and Arun Jain) started running numerous experiments with the MONANOVA program. A working paper by Green and Rao appeared in 1969, followed by the first marketing journal article on conjoint analysis (Green and Rao 1971). Following this, Johnson (1974) and Westwood, Lunn, and Beazley (1974) published articles on Johnson's two-attributes-at-a-time tradeoff model.

Users of Kruskal's MONANOVA and Shocker and Srinivasan's (1977) LINMAP programs (both nonmetric models) soon learned, however, that ratings-based dependent variables analyzed with dummy-variable regression techniques provided a robust alternative to ordinally based data procedures (Cattin and Wittink 1976; Carmone, Green, and Jain 1978). Orthogonal main-effects plans, based on Addelman's (1962) fractional factorial designs, significantly reduced respondents' cognitive burdens in responding to full-profile descriptions.

Hence, in the mid-1970s conditions were ripe for the quick diffusion of metric methods of conjoint analysis, using dummy-variable regression. In the mid-1980s, Johnson (1987) introduced his adaptive conjoint analysis program that used graded paired comparisons as one set of inputs to the model. About the same time, Herman (1988) introduced a PC-based package that used full profile stimuli based on orthogonal designs. Both packages contained conjoint simulators. Both software packages were also easy to use and moderately priced for commercial research firms. The advent of PC-based conjoint packages opened a large and eager market for applying the methodology.

By the late 1970s, conjoint analysis had truly come of age. Wittink and his co-authors (Wittink and Cattin 1989; Wittink, Vriens, and Burhenne

1994), provided extensive surveys attesting to the rapidity with which conjoint analysis was being adopted by researchers. Myers, Massy, and Greyser (1980) used conjoint analysis as a canonical case of how new ideas diffuse throughout the research community. Green and Srinivasan (1978) published a review of conjoint's progress, which they followed with a further review 12 years later (Green and Srinivasan 1990). The impetus behind conjoint's diffusion reflected the joint influence of academic and practitioners' contributions to the methodology, the availability of easy-to-use software, and the early credibility of results from business applications.

Conjoint analysis, unlike MDS and clustering, dealt with central problems – measuring buyer tradeoffs for developing new or reformulated products and estimating price-demand functions. In contrast, cluster analysis and MDS tools are often used as ancillary techniques for data analysis and presentation. Both, however, have been gainfully employed in conjoint studies involving buyer segmentation (Green and Krieger 1991) and in presenting perceptual maps of conjoint results (Green, Krieger, and Carroll 1987).

Distant relatives to conjoint analysis include the decompositional approaches of Hoffman, Slovic, and Rorer (1968) and the functional measurement approach of Anderson (1970). However, the seminal paper by Luce and Tukey (1964) and the experimental-design papers by Addelman (1962) and Plackett and Burman (1946), among others, provided key theoretical underpinnings and motivation for developing conjoint analysis. In particular, orthogonal main-effects designs and their more sophisticated extensions still constitute a major activity in the continuing development of efficient experimental designs. Considerable new research (Anderson and Wiley 1992; Kuhfeld, Tobias, and Garratt 1994; Lazari and Anderson 1994; Huber and Zwerina 1996) on this topic occurred during the 1990s.

The most publicized early paper on conjoint analysis appeared in *Harvard Business Review* (Green and Wind 1975). Ironically, Green and Wind (1973) had earlier published a research monograph on conjoint analysis and multiattribute decision making that met with much less reader interest.

Conjoint Development in the 1980s

Technical developments in conjoint analysis have proceeded swiftly over the past two decades, accompanied by thousands of methodological contributions (Table 5-2). During the 1980s, two developments stand out with regard to model development and application:

- Choice-based conjoint models, and
- Hybrid conjoint models, including Johnson's adaptive conjoint analysis model.

Table 5-2. **A Partial List of Contributions to Conjoint Analysis 1974-2000**

Choice-based conjoint (McFadden 1974; Gensch and Recker 1979; Batsell and Lodish 1981; Mahajan, Green, and Goldberg 1982; Louviere and Woodworth 1983)

Three-way multivariate conjoint analysis (DeSarbo, Carroll, Lehmann, O'Shaughnessy 1982)

Number of attribute levels effects on derived conjoint importance (Wittink, Krishnamurthi, and Nutter 1982)

Constrained parameter estimation in conjoint analysis (Srinivasan, Jain, and Malhotra 1983)

Hybrid models for conjoint analysis (Green, Goldberg , and Montemayor 1981; Green 1984)

Introduction in 1985 of Bretton-Clark's full profile conjoint techniques (Herman 1988)

Introduction in 1985 of Sawtooth Software's *Adaptive Conjoint Analysis* (Johnson 1987)

Factor analytic approaches to individualized conjoint analysis (Hagerty 1985)

Conjoint analysis and MDS in tandem (Green, Krieger, and Carroll 1987)

Reliability and validity testing (Bateson, Reibstein, and Boulding 1987)

Simultaneous conjoint parameter estimation and segmentation (Kamakura 1988)

Bretton-Clark's second generation, full-profile suite of programs (Herman 1988)

Conjunctive-compensatory self-explicated models (Srinivasan 1988)

Componential segmentation with optimization features (Green, Krieger, and Zelnio 1989)

Compensatory model problems in negatively correlated environments (Johnson, Meyer, and Ghose 1989)

New experimental designs for conjoint (Steckel, DeSarbo, and Mahajan 1991)

A reservation price model for optimal pricing (Kohli and Mahajan 1991)

A review of experimental choice analysis (Batsell and Louviere 1991)

Latent class conjoint analysis (DeSarbo, Wedel, Vriens, and Ramaswamy 1992)

Constrained partworth estimation (van der Lans and Heiser 1992)

Modeling hierarchical conjoint processes (Oppewal, Louviere, and Timmermans 1994)

Concomitant variable latent class modeling (Kamakura, Wedel, and Agrawal 1994)

Hierarchical Bayes (HB) models for conjoint analysis (Allenby, Arora, and Ginter 1995; Allenby and Ginter 1995; Lenk, DeSarbo, Green, and Young 1996)

A comparison of metric conjoint models (Vriens, Wedel, and Wilms 1996)

Utility balanced experimental designs (Huber and Zwerina 1996)

Competitive interaction simulators (Choi, DeSarbo, and Harker 1990; Green and Krieger 1997)

Mixture models for segmentation (Wedel and Kamakura 1998)

Commercial windows-based, choice-based conjoint (Sawtooth Software 1999)

Krieger and Green's hybrid choice-based conjoint model (Vavra, Green, and Krieger 1999)

Latent class conjoint analysis (Ramaswamy and Cohen 2000)

HB applied to Internet recommendation systems (Ansari, Essegaier and Kohli 2000)

Response latencies and conjoint analysis (Haaijer, Kamakura, and Wedel 2000)

In traditional conjoint analysis, respondents typically rate various product or supplier profiles, presented one at a time, on a likelihood-of-purchase scale. In choice-based conjoint analysis, respondents typically see profile descriptions of two or more explicit competitors, which vary on one or more attributes. In this case, the task is either to pick one's most preferred profile from the set or alternatively to allocate 100 points across the set of profiles, reflecting one's relative strength of preferences.

In choice-based conjoint analysis, analysts typically employ multinomial logit models, although occasionally they use probit-based models. They usually employ traditional conjoint analysis when a new product is entering a new or stable market in which competitors are either nonexistent or treated as "passive" in terms of responding competitively to the new entry. In choice-based conjoint analysis, however, the analyst assumes active competitors who can modify their profiles (including price and nonprice attributes) as well. Sawtooth Software's Adaptive Conjoint Analysis is a traditional (hybrid) conjoint model. Its choice-based conjoint model deals with the case of explicit, active competitors. In choice-based conjoint analysis, analysts originally estimated parameters at the total sample level. Newer methods (hierarchical Bayes) now permit measurement of individual differences as well.

The seminal precursory paper to choice-based conjoint (using the multinomial logit model) was written by an econometrician (McFadden 1974). McFadden's work was soon recognized and adopted by a number of marketing researchers, including Punj and Staelin (1978). Gensch and Recker (1979) also used this model in developing an alternative to regression for analyzing cross-sectional choice data. Batsell and Lodish (1981) illustrated the multinomial logit's use in modeling individual choices over replicated choice sets. Their model yields a share-of-choice prediction for alternatives in competitive choice sets. They indicate that the model can be profitably applied to market segments, as well. Mahajan, Green, and Goldberg (1982) applied Theil's logit model to a choice-based conjoint problem.

Louviere and Woodworth (1983) extended the preceding research. They discuss experimental designs that lend themselves to choice-based conjoint problems. They also provide an extensive and rich set of empirical examples based on various sets of fractional factorial designs. They focus on aggregate (pooled-over individuals) consumer choice studies. This paper spawned subsequent research for dealing with the more complex experimental designs needed for choice-based conjoint analysis.

Choice-based conjoint studies can be a mixed blessing. The respondent's tasks are extensive, since respondents may have to evaluate 10 (or more) scenarios. Each scenario could contain eight or more brands, each with several attributes and with several levels within attributes. Nonetheless, choice-based conjoint analysis has markedly increased in popularity because it can deal with the complexity of choosing among two or more competitive profiles, each of which can vary idiosyncratically across attributes and levels

In the early 1980s, hybrid models (Green, Goldberg, and Montemayor 1981; Green 1984) appeared in direct response to the increasing popularity of conjoint analysis. Along with conjoint's increased application came the desire to expand the number of attributes and the levels that could be accommodated. Hybrid models employ self-explicated data collected on both the desirability and the importance of attributes and levels. Respondents then consider small subsets of the full profiles to evaluate.

The early hybrid models initially used stagewise regression to fit simplified compositional models to the self-explicated data, later augmented by decompositional models (fitted at the segment level). The value of these models lies in the greater accuracy they achieve, compared to non-hybrid models, in within-attribute estimation. The full-profile responses mainly serve to refine self-explicated attribute importances.

More recently, Green and Krieger (1996) extended hybrid models to allow parameter estimation at the individual level. They describe four separate models of increasing generality. Again, the objective is to use the self-explicated data primarily for within-attribute partworth estimation while using the full-profile analysis to produce improved estimates of attribute importances.

The most used commercial conjoint model is Johnson's Adaptive-Conjoint-Analysis (ACA) program. ACA is a hybrid model that incorporates self-explicated desirabilities and importances, followed by the presentation of pairs of partial profiles (typically consisting of levels on two or perhaps three attributes) drawn from the full set of attributes. A respondent is asked to choose between the members of each pair and to include his or her preference intensity as well via graded paired comparison; ACA developers (Sawtooth Software 1999) have continued to introduce useful refinements to the original version (Johnson 1987).

Conjoint Developments in the 1990s

Probably the most far-reaching developments in the 1990s use hierarchical Bayesian modeling of individual differences in choice-based models. Before this, choice-based models were either estimated from data pooled across all individuals or by latent class methods (partial dissaggregation) as applied by DeSarbo, Wedel, Vriens, and Ramaswamy (1992) and Ramaswamy and Cohen (2000).

The work of Allenby, Arora, and Ginter (1995), Allenby and Ginter (1995), and Lenk, DeSarbo, Green, and Young (1996) has enabled choice-based conjoint users to obtain individual-level, partworth estimates based on hierarchical Bayesian methods. (Sawtooth Software has recently added this type of module to its choice-based conjoint software.) To the extent that an individual's parameters are both self-consistent and different from the aggre-

Table 5-3. **Illustrative Applications of Conjoint Analysis**

Antidumping litigation – AT&T vs. Pacific-rim manufacturers legal dispute regarding small business telephone equipment; case adjudicated in AT&T's favor

AT&T's first cellular telephone – Chicago-based study of 1,000 drivers' reactions to cell phone features of the new "honey-comb" relay system

Continental vs. American Airlines litigation – study of travel agents' tradeoffs among airline flight selections

Courtyard by Marriott – used to design new hotel chain catering to business travelers (largest known conjoint project in terms of attributes and levels)

E-Z Pass – used to design new electronic toll collection service in northeast U.S.

FedEx new services study – tradeoff study of customer reactions to new methods for tracking delayed and lost letters and packages

Ford Fairlane – used in redesign of Ford to reflect automotive downsizing objectives

Health maintenance plans – study conducted by the American Association of Retired Persons; results submitted to Congress

IBM RISC 6000 workstation – measured potential buyer reactions to variations in performance and reliability features of a new workstation

Intermittent windshield wipers litigation – study to determine consumer evaluations of the derived "willingness to pay" for the intermittent wiper feature

Japanese cable TV – survey of Japanese consumers' tradeoffs among services and prices of satellite TV

Marriott time-share units – development of optimal interior and exterior decors, services, and price

MasterCard and Diner's Club – new travel and entertainment features evaluated

Monsanto's herbicide packaging study – consumer reactions to advanced packaging devices for liquids, solids, and aerosols

Polaroid's instant camera design – study of consumer reactions to new features and camera design aesthetics

Squibb's captopril antihypertensive – six-country study of physicians' evaluations of Capoten's efficacy and safety features

Tagamet (SKF) and Zantac (Glaxo) ulcer drugs – competitive pricing and analysis of demand elasticities

TrafficPulse – a study of consumer reactions to a new system for providing updates on traffic conditions

Ritz Carlton – used to develop hotel decor and services

UPS services study – examined customers' evaluations of four major suppliers of overnight letter and package delivery

US Navy reenlistment benefit packages – used to develop menu of plans based on individual differences in types of duties, health needs, sign-over bonuses

---

aggregated data, the individual's data will receive more weight in the estimation of his or her partworths. Individuals whose partworths are estimated poorly (that is, with large error in his or her own data) will receive more weight from the aggregate data.

Recently, Vavra, Green, and Krieger (1999) proposed another approach to the choice-based conjoint problem. They developed a hybrid choice-based model and simulator that combines self-explicated data with full-profile responses. This model requires no weighted averaging of an individual's data with that from the entire group. On the downside, however, it requires self-explicated (in addition to full-profile) data.

Illustrative Applications

Of the extensive list (Table 5-3) of conjoint applications, three are of particular interest: the customer-driven design of Marriott's Courtyard Hotels (Wind, Green, Shifflet, and Scarbrough 1989), the design and evaluation of the New Jersey and New York E-Z Pass electronic toll collection system (Vavra, Green, and Krieger 1999), and the TrafficPulse system for receiving updates on traffic conditions (Krieger, Green, Lodish, D'Arcangelo, Rothey and Thirty 2002).

Courtyard by Marriott

To the best of our knowledge, *Courtyard by Marriott* is the largest project in terms of attributes and levels ever undertaken using conjoint analysis. In the early 1980s, Marriott management wished to design an "optimal" hotel chain catering primarily to business travelers who had no need for many of the features provided by up-scale hotels, such as Marriott and Hyatt.

In addition to price, the study design included seven hotel facets: external decor, room decor, food service, lounge facilities, general services, leisure activities (for example, a fitness club), and security features. Analysts developed some 50 attributes with a total of 160 attribute levels. The models included hybrid conjoint and an early type of choice-based conjoint. The analysts also used computer simulators. The study made extensive use of visual props (pictures and three-dimensional models) as well as experimental rooms in which the furnishings and decor were systematically varied according to experimental designs.

By all counts, the Courtyard study was a success. Marriott implemented almost all of the design recommendations, and later extended the approach to other new products (for example, Marriott Suites) and used the findings in the design of Courtyard advertisements and brochures. By 1990, Marriott had over 300 Courtyards, employing more than 15,000 people. Today, there are 450 Courtyards worldwide, with annual sales in the billions of dollars.

Marriott has since used conjoint analysis in such related endeavors as designing time-share vacation units and in-room and amenities pricing.

E-Z Pass

In the E-Z Pass toll collection project, New Jersey and New York developed a genuinely new product aimed at speeding up and simplifying vehicle passage on their toll highways, bridges, and tunnels. Commuters use an electronic tag (transponder) attached to the vehicle's inside windshield. As the vehicle approaches a toll lane, an antenna in the lane reads the customer's vehicle and account information embedded in the tag. The information is electronically forwarded to an in-line computer. The computer, in turn, deducts the toll from the customer's account.

The project began in 1992. There were two main questions:

- How should E-Z Pass be configured?
- What level of resources should be allocated to its implementation?

The two states conducted a large conjoint study (over 3,000 respondents) by a telephone-mail-telephone procedure in which qualified respondents received a packet of questionnaire materials and a video cassette. The video contained an 11-minute infomercial that described the problems associated with the current toll road system and the benefits provided by E-Z Pass.

Analysts used seven conjoint attributes dealing with such issues as number of lanes available, tag acquisition, cost, toll prices, invoicing, and other uses of the tag. The study designers analyzed the individual respondents' data at both the overall sample level and by region and facility. The overall (at equilibrium) forecast made in 1992 of "take rate" was 49 percent usage. The actual take rate (seven years later) was 44 percent; future usage is expected to be higher than 49 percent. (Even David Letterman liked the system!)

The TrafficPulse System

The study of TrafficPulse also addressed the challenge of assessing reactions to a "really new" product, a new service that enables subscribers to obtain continuous 24/7 updates on traffic conditions, travel times, and alternate routes, should congestion occur. In the process, the researchers embellished traditional conjoint analysis to educate the prospective consumer and then obtain relevant information about consumer evaluations of the service prior to their actual introduction and use.

The study, with responses from 401 prospective consumers in the Pittsburgh market, helped the sponsoring company (Mobility Technologies, Inc.) to assess the attributes that would have the most value for different segments and the optimal bundle pricing strategies for different combinations of delivery mode add-ons, cost per call, and payment mode.

The project provided concrete feedback to Mobility Technologies and also advanced research and practice by developing strategies for handling restrictions on which attribute levels can appear together across which attributes, for paying more attention to the "no interest case" and emphasizing the use of market "norms" in converting respondents' buying intention scores into purchase likelihoods.

These projects illustrate the ability of conjoint analysis to lead to actionable findings that provide customer-driven design features and consumer usage or sales forecasts.

Future Prospects

After 30 years of development and application, conjoint analysis seems to have survived the test of time. While new breakthroughs may well be less frequent, the method continues to grow in depth and breadth of usage. We expect to see the following further developments:

- New simulator-optimizers that can maximize either financial return or market share (Vavra, Green, and Krieger 1999);

- New classes of problems, including menu selection and bundling models for telecommunications and banking services (Ben-Akiva and Gershenfeld 1998);

- More realistic imagery for describing attribute levels, for example, using virtual reality displays;

- Continued extensions of conjoint applications to such fields as tourism, entertainment, health maintenance, gambling, and legal disputes;

- New application venues, such as conjoint's recent implementation on the Internet, including such sites as activebuyersguide.com, personalogic.com, and conjointonline.com, that typically use hybrid conjoint models to elicit buyer preferences for Web-based merchandise (Ansari, Essegaier, and Kohli 2000);

- Additional studies of conjoint reliability and validity (Vriens, Wedel, and Wilms 1996; Haaijer, Kamakura, and Wedel 2000);

- Extension of consumer-based applications to other stakeholder groups, such as employees, suppliers, stockholders, and municipalities;

- New "dynamic" conjoint simulators that consider competitive action-reaction sequences (Choi, DeSarbo, and Harker 1990; Green and Krieger 1997); and

- Prototype simulators (for example, test cars) that permit analysts to measure respondents' preferences for type of ride, acceleration, cornering, and so forth, in realistic surroundings.

In short, despite its maturity, conjoint analysis is still far from stagnant. Because the methods deal with the pervasive problem of buyer preferences and choices, conjoint's future promises continued development and application.

THE ROLE OF SOFTWARE DEVELOPMENT IN THE DIFFUSION OF CONJOINT ANALYSIS

Throughout the development of conjoint analysis and the precursory techniques of cluster analysis and MDS, the availability of inexpensive and easy-to-use software has been crucial to their dissemination. Early on, Bell Laboratories and the Marketing Science Institute played important roles in making mainframe software available to both academic and industry users. With the growth of the personal computer, Johnson's Sawtooth Software and Herman's Bretton-Clark companies provided affordable PC software to business users and academic versions for teaching purposes. Sawtooth Software has maintained contact with business and academia through its newsletters, annual meetings, and continued development of software (Sawtooth 1999) to implement new research ideas, such as choice-based models. The American Marketing Association's annual Advanced Research Techniques Forum provides a meeting place for the fruitful exchange of ideas between academics and practitioners.

A SCIENCE VS. ENGINEERING POSTSCRIPT

From its inception, conjoint analysis has drawn on ideas from mathematical psychologists, psychometricians, statisticians, econometricians, and operations researchers. These ideas concern experimental design, parameter estimation, descriptive model building, normative model building, and the comparative evaluation of various models' reliability and validity. The method's practical consequences attest to its value and staying power (Gustaffsson, Hermann, and Huber 2000).

Through the interplay of theoretical contributions and practical applications, conjoint methodology continues to grow, as academics and practitioners learn useful things from each other.

NOTES

[1] Adapted from *Interfaces*, 31 (3), Part 2 of 2, May/June 2001, S56-S73.

ACKNOWLEDGMENTS

We thank Eric Bradlow and Wes Hutchinson of the Wharton School, an anonymous reviewer, and the editors for helpful comments on the paper's initial draft.

REFERENCES

Addelman, S. (1962), "Orthogonal main-effect plans for asymmetrical factorial experiments," *Technometrics*, 4 (1), 21-46.

Allenby, G. M., Arora, N., and Ginter, J. L. (1995), "Incorporating prior knowledge into the analysis of conjoint studies," *Journal of Marketing Research*, 32 (May), 152-162.

Allenby, G. M., and Ginter, J. L. (1995), "Using extremes to design products and segment markets," *Journal of Marketing Research*, 32 (May), 152-162.

Anderson, D. A., and Wiley, J. B. (1992), "Efficient choice set designs for estimating cross-effects models," *Marketing Letters*, 3 (October), 357-70.

Anderson, N. H. (1970), "Functional measurement and psychophysical judgment," *Psychological Review*, 77 (3) 153-70.

Ansari, A., Essegaier, S., and Kohli, R. (2000), "Internet recommendation systems," *Journal of Marketing Research*, 37 (August), 363-375.

Bateson, J. E. G., Reibstein, D. J., and Boulding, W. (1987), "Conjoint analysis reliability and validity: A framework for future research," in M. J. Houston (ed.), *Review of Marketing*, Chicago, IL: American Marketing Association, pp. 451-481.

Batsell, R. R., and Lodish, L. M. (1981), "A model and measurement methodology for predicting individual consumer choice," *Journal of Marketing Research*, 18 (February), 1-12.

Batsell, R. R., and Louviere, J. J. (1991), "Experimental analysis of choice," *Marketing Letters*, 2 (August), 199-214.

Bell, D. F., Raiffa, H., and Tversky, A. (eds.) (1988), *Decision Making: Descriptive, Normative, and Prescriptive Interactions*, New York, NY: Cambridge University Press.

Ben-Akiva, M., and Gershenfeld, S. (1998), "Multi-featured products and services: Analyzing pricing and bundling strategies," *Journal of Forecasting*, 17, 175-196.

Carmone, F. J., Green, P. E., and Jain, A. K. (1978), "The robustness of conjoint analysis: Some Monte Carlo results," *Journal of Marketing Research*, 15, 300-303.

Carroll, J. D. (1969), "Categorical conjoint measurement," Meeting of Mathematical Psychology, Ann Arbor, MI.

Carroll, J. D., and Green, P. E. (1997), "Psychometric methods in marketing research: Part II, multidimensional scaling," *Journal of Marketing Research*, 34 (May), 193-204.

Cattin, P., and Wittink, D. R. (1976), "A Monte Carlo study of metric and nonmetric estimation techniques," Paper 341, Graduate School of Business, Stanford University.

Choi, S. C., DeSarbo, W. S., and Harker, P. T. (1990), "Product positioning under price competition," *Management Science*, 30, 175-199.

DeSarbo, W. S., Carroll, J. D., Lehmann, D. R., and O'Shaugnhessy, J. (1982). "Three-way multivariate conjoint analysis," *Marketing Science*, 1 (Fall), 323-350.

DeSarbo, W. S., Wedel, M., Vriens, M., and Ramaswamy, V. (1992), "Latent class metric conjoint analysis," *Marketing Letters*, 3 (July), 273-288.

Gensch, D. H., and Recker, W. W. (1979), "The multinominal multiattribute logit choice model," *Journal of Marketing Research*, 16 (February), 124-132.

Green, P. E. (1984), "Hybrid models for conjoint analysis: An expository review," *Journal of Marketing Research*, 21 (May), 155-159.

Green, P. E., Frank, R. E., and Robinson, P. J. (1967), "Cluster analysis in test market selection," *Management Science*, 13, B387-400.

Green, P. E., Goldberg, S. M., and Montemayor, M. (1981), "A hybrid utility estimation model for conjoint analysis," *Journal of Marketing*, 45 (Winter), 33-41.

Green, P. E., and Krieger, A. M. (1991), "Segmenting markets with conjoint analysis," *Journal of Marketing*, 55 (October), 20-31.

Green, P. E., and Krieger, A. M. (1996), "Individualized hybrid models for conjoint analysis," *Management Science*, 42 (June), 850-867.

Green, P. E., and Krieger, A. M. (1997), "Using conjoint analysis to view competitive interaction through the customer's eyes," in G. S. Day and D. J. Reibstein (eds.), *Wharton on Dynamic Competitive Strategy*, New York, NY: John Wiley & Sons, pp. 343-367.

Green, P. E., Krieger, A. M., and Carroll, J. D. (1987), "Conjoint analysis and multidimensional scaling: A complementary approach," *Journal of Advertising Research*, 27 (October/November), 21-27.

Green, P. E., Krieger, A. M., and Zelnio, R. N. (1989), "A componential segmentation model with optimal design features," *Decision Sciences*, 20 (Spring), 221-238.

Green, P. E., and Rao, V. R. (1971), "Conjoint measurement for quantifying judgmental data," *Journal of Marketing Research*, 8 (August), 355-363.

Green, P. E., and Srinivasan, V. (1978), "Conjoint analysis in consumer research: Issues and outlook," *Journal of Consumer Research*, 5 (September), 103-123.

Green, P. E., and Srinivasan, V. (1990), "Conjoint analysis in marketing: New developments with implications for research and practice," *Journal of Marketing*, 54 (October), 3-19.

Green, P. E., and Wind, Y. (1973), *Multiattribute Decisions in Marketing: A Measurement Approach*, Hinsdale, IL: The Dryden Press..

Green, P. E., and Wind, Y. (1975), "New way to measure consumers' judgments," *Harvard Business Review*, 53 (July-August), 107-117.

Gustaffsson, A., Hermann, A., and Huber, F. (eds.) (2000), *Conjoint Measurement: Methods and Applications*, Berlin, Germany: Springer-Verlag.

Haaijer, R., Kamakura, W., and Wedel, M. (2000), "Response latencies in the analysis of conjoint choice experiments," *Journal of Marketing Research*, 37 (August), 376-382.

Hagerty, M. R. (1985), "Improving the predictive power of conjoint analysis: The use of factor analysis and cluster analysis," *Journal of Marketing Research*, 22 (May), 168-184.

Herman, S. (1988), "Software for full-profile conjoint analysis," in M. Metegrano (ed.), *Proceedings of the Sawtooth Conference on Perceptual Mapping, Conjoint Analysis, and Computer Interviewing*, Ketchum, ID: Sawtooth Software, pp. 117-130.

Hoffman, P. J., Slovic, P., and Rorer, L. G. (1968), "An analysis of variance model for the assessment of configural cue utilization in clinical judgment," *Psychological Bulletin*, 69, 338-349.

Huber, J., and Zwerina, K. (1996), "The importance of utility balance in efficient choice designs," *Journal of Marketing Research*, 33 (August), 307-317.

Johnson, E., Meyer, R. J., and Ghose, S. (1989), "When choice models fail: Compensatory models in negatively correlated environments," *Journal of Marketing Research*, 26 (August), 255-270.

Johnson, R. M. (1974), "Trade-off analysis of consumer values," *Journal of Marketing Research*, 11 (May), 121-127.

Johnson, R. M. (1987), "Adaptive conjoint analysis," in *Sawtooth Software Conference on Perceptual Mapping, Conjoint Analysis, and Computer Interviewing*, Ketchum, ID: Sawtooth Software, pp. 253-265.

Kamakura, W. (1988), "A least squares procedure for benefit segmentation with conjoint experiments," *Journal of Marketing Research*, 25 (May), 157-167.

Kamakura, W., Wedel, M., and Agrawal, J. (1994), "Concomitant variable latent class models for conjoint analysis," *International Journal of Research in Marketing*, 11, 451-464.

Kaul, A., and Rao, V. R. (1994), "Research for product position and design decisions: An integrative review," *International Journal of Research on Marketing*, 12, 293-320.

Keeney, R. L., and Raiffa, H. (1976), *Decisions with Multiple Objectives: Preferences and Value Trade-offs*, New York, NY: Wiley.

Kohli, R., and Mahajan, V. (1991), "A reservation price model for optimal pricing of multiattribute products in conjoint analysis," *Journal of Marketing Research*, 28 (August), 347-354.

Krieger, A., Green, P., Lodish, L., D'Arcangelo, J., Rothey, C., Thirty, P. (2002), Consumer Evaluations of "Really New" Services: The TRAFFICPULSE System," Working Paper, The Wharton School Marketing Department.

Kruskal, J. B. (1965), "Analysis of factorial experiments by estimating monotone transformations of the data," *Journal of the Royal Statistical Society*, Series B, 27, 251-263.

Kuhfeld, W. F., Tobias, R. D., and Garratt, M. (1994), "Efficient experimental designs with marketing research applications," *Journal of Marketing Research*, 31 (November), 545-557.

Lazari, A. G., and Anderson, D. A. (1994), "Designs of discrete choice set experiments for estimating both attribute and availability cross effects," *Journal of Marketing Research*, 31 (August), 375-383.

Lenk, P. J., DeSarbo, W. S., Green, P. E., and Young, M. R. (1996), "Hierarchical Bayes conjoint analysis: Recovery of partworth heterogeneity from reduced experimental designs," *Marketing Science*, 15, No. 2, 173-191.

Louviere, J., and Woodworth, G. (1983), "Design and analysis of simulated consumer choice or allocation experiments, *Journal of Marketing Research*, 20 (November), 350-367.

Luce, R. D., and Tukey, J. W. (1964), "Simultaneous conjoint measurement: A new type of fundamental measurement," *Journal of Mathematical Psychology*, 1, 1-27.

Mahajan, V., Green, P. E., and Goldberg, S. M. (1982), "A conjoint model for measuring self- and cross-price demand relationships," *Journal of Marketing Research*, 19 (August), 334-342.

McFadden, D. (1974), "Conditional logit analysis of qualitative choice behavior," in P. Zarembka (ed.), *Frontiers on Econometrics,* New York, NY: Academic Press, pp. 105-421.

Myers, J. G., Massy, W. F., and Greyser, S. A. (1980), *Marketing Research and Knowledge Development,* Englewood Cliffs, NJ: Prentice-Hall..

Oppewal, H., Louviere, J., and Timmermans, H. (1994), "Modeling hierarchical conjoint processes with integrated choice experiments," *Journal of Marketing Research*, 31 (February), 92-105.

Plackett, R. L., and Burman, J. P. (1946), "The design of optimum multifactorial experiments," *Biometrika*, 33, 305-325.

Punj, G. N., and Staelin, R. (1978), "The choice process for graduate business schools," *Journal of Marketing Research,* 15 (November), 588-598.

Ramaswamy, V., and Cohen, S. H. (2000), "Latent class models for conjoint analysis," in A. Gustafsson, A. Hermann, and F. Huber (eds.), *Conjoint Measurement: Methods and Applications*, Berlin, Germany: Springer-Verlag.

Saaty, T. L. (1980), *The Analytical Hierarchy Process*, New York, NY: McGraw-Hill.

Sawtooth Software (1999), *CBC for Windows*, Sequim, WA.

Shocker, A. D., and Srinivasan, V. (1977), "LINMAP (Version II): A FORTRAN IV computer program for analyzing ordinal preference (dominance) judgments via linear programming techniques and for conjoint measurement," *Journal of Marketing Research*, 14, 101-103.

Srinivasan, V. (1988), "A conjunctive-compensatory approach to the self-explication of multiattributed preferences," *Decision Sciences*, 19 (Spring), 295-305.

Srinivasan, V., Jain, A. K., and Malhotra, N. K. (1983), "Improving the predictive power of conjoint analysis by constrained parameter estimation," *Journal of Marketing Research*, 20 (November), 433-438.

Starr, M. K., and Zeleny, M. (1977), *Multiple Criteria Decisions Making*, Amsterdam, Holland: North-Holland.

Steckel, J. H., DeSarbo, W. S., and Mahajan, V. (1991), "On the creation of feasible conjoint analysis experimental designs," *Decision Sciences*, 22, 435-442.

van der Lans, I. A., and Heiser, W. H. (1992), "Constrained partworth estimation in conjoint analysis using the self-explicated utility model," *International Journal of Research in Marketing*, 9, 325-344.

Vavra, T. G., Green, P. E., and Krieger, A. M. (1999), "Evaluating E-Z Pass," *Marketing Research*, 11 (Summer), 5-16.

Vriens, M., Wedel, M., and Wilms, T. (1996), "Metric conjoint segmentation methods: A Monte Carlo comparison," *Journal of Marketing Research*, 33 (February), 73-85.

Wedel, M., and Kamakura, W. A. (1998), *Market Segmentation: Conceptual and Methodological Foundations*, Boston, MA: Kluwer..

Westwood, D., Lunn, T., and Beazley, D. (1974), "The trade-off model and its extensions," *Journal of the Market Research Society*, 16, 227-241.

Wind, J., Green, P. E., Shifflet, D., and Scarbrough, M. (1989), "*Courtyard by Marriott*: Designing a hotel facility with consumer-based marketing models," *Interfaces* 19 (January-February), 25-47.

Wittink, D., and Cattin, P. (1989), "Commercial use of conjoint analysis: An update," *Journal of Marketing*, 53 (July), 91-96.

Wittink, D. R., Krishnamurthi, L., and Nutter, J. B. (1982), "Comparing derived importance weights across attributes," *Journal of Consumer Research*, 8 (March), 471-474.

Wittink, D., Vriens, M., and Burhenne, W. (1994), "Commercial use of conjoint in Europe: Results and critical reflections," *International Journal of Research in Marketing*, 11, 41-52.

Young, F. W. (1969), "Polynomial conjoint analysis of similarities: Definitions for a special algorithm," Research paper No. 76, Psychometric Laboratory, University of North Carolina.

Chapter 6

Conjoint Analysis, Related Modeling, and Applications

John R. Hauser, *Massachusetts Institute of Technology*
Vithala R. Rao, *Cornell University*

Conjoint analysis has as its roots the need to solve important academic and industry problems. Paul Green's work on conjoint analysis grew out of his contributions to the theory and practice of multidimensional scaling (MDS) to address marketing problems, as discussed in Chapter 3. MDS offered the ability to represent consumer multidimensional perceptions and consumer preferences relative to an existing set of products.

THE DEVELOPMENT OF CONJOINT ANALYSIS

Recognizing the strengths and weaknesses of MDS, Green sought ways to augment its power. Drawing upon his extensive experience in product development from his days at DuPont, Green sought a means to decompose consumer preferences into the partial contribution (partworth) of product features. In this manner, researchers could not only explain the preferences of existing products, but could simulate preferences for *entirely new products* that were defined by feature combinations. Such a method could also be used to decompose perceptions if a perceptual variable – say "ease of use" – was used as the dependent measure rather than "preference." This would solve the problem of reverse mapping in MDS – the challenge of translating a point from perceptual space into a corresponding point (or set of points) in product-feature space.

This mapping challenge was related to axiomatic work in psychometrics. Authors such as Luce and Tukey (1964) and Krantz, Luce, Suppes, and Tversky (1971) were exploring the behavioral axioms that would enable a decomposition of an overall judgment into its parts. In a seminal paper (Green and Rao 1971), Green drew upon this conjoint measurement theory, adapted it to the solution of marketing and product-development problems, considered carefully the practical measurement issues, and opened a floodgate of research opportunities and applications. (As an indication of the pathbreaking nature of this work, the reviewers of the article by Green and Rao were quite apprehensive of the value of this approach. But, the editor at the time, Professor Ralph Day, had the vision to see the enormous potential for this research stream.)

Conjoint Measurement or Conjoint Analysis

Conjoint measurement offered a theory to decompose an ordinal scale of holistic judgment into interval scales for each component attribute. The theory details how the transformation depends on the satisfaction of various axioms such as additivity and independence. However, in real problems we expect that such axioms are approximate at best. The real genius is making appropriate tradeoffs so that real consumers in real market research settings are answering questions from which useful information can be inferred.

In the thirty years since the original conjoint analysis article, researchers in marketing and other disciplines, led by the insight and creativity of Paul Green, have explored these tradeoffs. While valid and interesting intellectual debates remain today and while the field continues to advance with new insights, theory, and methodology, we are left with the legacy of an elegant theory transformed into an evolving research stream of great practical import. Whereas the earlier, axiomatic work is often called conjoint *measurement,* we choose to call the expanded focus conjoint *analysis.*

Paul Green's Contributions

Paul Green himself has contributed almost 100 articles and books on conjoint analysis. He was there in the beginning and he is there now. He has embraced (or led) new developments including the move to metric measures (Carmone, Green, and Jain 1978), evaluations of non-additivity (Green and Devita 1975), hybrid methods to combine data sources and reduce respondent burden (Green 1984), and new estimation methods such as hierarchical Bayes methods (Lenk et al. 1996). He has further led the way with seminal applications such as the application of conjoint analysis to really new products such as Marriott's Courtyard (Wind et al. 1989) and the E-Z Pass system (Green, Krieger, and Vavra 1999). It is safe to say that conjoint analysis would not be where it is today without Green's leadership.

In this paper we pay homage to Green by reviewing some of the enormous breadth of research in conjoint analysis. We highlight some of the major theoretical and practical issues and we illustrate many of the contributions of the past thirty years.

CONJOINT ANALYSIS IS A JOURNEY NOT A DESTINATION

The essence of conjoint analysis is to identify and measure a mapping from more detailed descriptors of a product or service onto an overall measure of the customer's evaluation of that product. We begin with an example from Green's classic paper (with Jerry Wind) that was published in the *Harvard Business Review* (1975). Green and Wind were designing a carpet cleaner and chose to describe the carpet cleaners by five features:

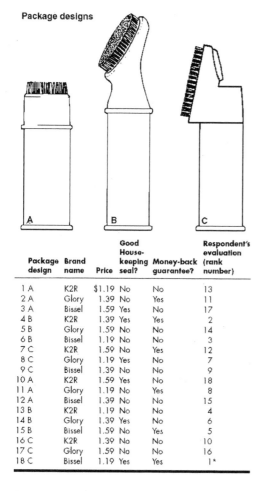

Package design	Brand name	Price	Good Housekeeping seal?	Money-back guarantee?	Respondent's evaluation (rank number)
1 A	K2R	$1.19	No	No	13
2 A	Glory	1.39	No	Yes	11
3 A	Bissel	1.59	Yes	No	17
4 B	K2R	1.39	Yes	Yes	2
5 B	Glory	1.59	No	No	14
6 B	Bissel	1.19	No	No	3
7 C	K2R	1.59	No	Yes	12
8 C	Glory	1.19	Yes	No	7
9 C	Bissel	1.39	No	No	9
10 A	K2R	1.59	Yes	No	18
11 A	Glory	1.19	No	Yes	8
12 A	Bissel	1.39	No	No	15
13 B	K2R	1.19	No	No	4
14 B	Glory	1.39	Yes	No	6
15 B	Bissel	1.59	No	Yes	5
16 C	K2R	1.39	No	No	10
17 C	Glory	1.59	No	No	16
18 C	Bissel	1.19	Yes	Yes	1*

Figure 6-1. **Experimental Design for Carpet Cleaner**
From Green and Wind (1975)

- package design – one of three levels illustrated in Figure 6-1
- brand name – one of three brand names – K2R, Glory, and Bissell
- seal – either the carpet cleaner had a Good Housekeeping seal of approval or it did not
- guarantee – either the carpet cleaner had a money-back guarantee or it did not
- price – specified at the three discrete levels of $1.19, $1.39, and $1.59

Respondents were given a fractional factorial design of profiles, each of which was described by the levels of the features it contained, and were asked to rank order cards representing the profiles in order to indicate their preferences for the profiles. Because a full 3x3x2x2x3 design would have yielded 108 profiles, they chose a balanced orthogonal design that kept the respondent's task within reason – each respondent had to rank but 18 profiles.

When the data collection was complete, Green and Wind assumed that the overall preference was an additive sum of the "partworths" of the features, represented each feature by a series of dummy variables, and used monotonic regression to estimate the contribution of each feature to overall preference. In this manner, partworths were obtained for each respondent, enabling the researchers flexibility to (1) cluster the partworths to identify segments and (2) simulate preferences for new products by adding those products to the respondents' choice sets and re-computing the implied preferences. (Here they assumed that each respondent would purchase their most preferred product.)

In the twenty-seven years since this article was published (thirty-one years since the pioneering Green and Rao 1971 article), much has changed, but the basic structure of the conjoint challenge remains. We organize this short review around the elements pioneered by Green and provide examples of how each element has evolved. Because of the sheer breadth of today's applications, we have space but to highlight the most common examples. The basic elements of our review are:

- how a product or service is decomposed (additive function of five features in 1975)
- stimuli representation (cards in 1975)
- methods to reduce respondent burden (orthogonal factorial design in 1975)
- data collection format (rank order of cards in 1975)
- estimation (monotonic regression in 1975)

In a field so vast, we can provide but an overview. Our focus is on the measurement and representation of consumer preferences. In the next chapter, Green, Krieger, and Wind address how conjoint estimates are used in models to segment the market, identify high-potential product designs, plan product lines, and forecast purchase potential. We encourage readers to explore this field further.

Decomposing the Product or Service

There are at least two considerations in decomposing the product or the service: (1) the elements into which the product is decomposed and (2) the function by which the elemental decomposition is mapped onto overall preference.

In the carpet-cleaner example, the elemental decomposition was into physical features. This has been the most common application of conjoint analysis in the last thirty years and is the most relevant if the product-development team is facing the decision about which features to include in a product design. However, conjoint analysis has also been used with more qualitative features such as "personalness," "convenience," and "quality" of health care, (e.g., Hauser and Urban 1977). Such applications occur early in the product-development process when the team is trying to understand the basic perceptual positioning of the product or service.

The key consideration in the decomposition is that the elements be as complete as feasible, understandable to the respondents, useful to the product-development team, and as separable as feasible. Researchers have used detailed qualitative interviews, focus groups, contextual engineering, and lead-user analyses to identify the appropriate elements. In some cases, more elaborate methods are used in which detailed phrases (obtained from customer interviews) are clustered based on similarity or factor-analyzed based on evaluations to identify groups of phrases which are then represented by a summary feature (e.g., Green, Carmone, and Fox 1969; Green and McMennamin 1973; Griffin and Hauser 1993; Hauser and Koppelman 1979; Rao and Katz 1971).

If the features are chosen carefully, then they will satisfy a property known as "preferential independence." Basically, two features, f_1 and f_2, are preferentially independent of the remaining features if tradeoffs among f_1 and f_2 do not depend upon the remaining features. Preferential independence is extremely important to the researcher because if each set of features is preferentially independent of its complement set, then the (riskless) conjoint function can be represented by an additive (or multiplicative) decomposition (Keeney and Raiffa 1976, Theorem 3.6). Whenever preferential independence is not satisfied, the conjoint function is more difficult to estimate and interactions among features are necessary, as illustrated for food menus by Green and Devita (1975) and Carmone and Green (1981). There are many decompositional forms and related independence conditions.

In some cases, the preference is defined over risky features – that is, the features are described by a probability density function rather than simply as known features. In this case, some researchers have represented the features as lotteries and have applied von Neumann-Morgenstern utility measurement (Eliashberg 1980; Eliashberg and Hauser 1985; Hauser and Urban 1979). See Farquhar (1977) for a review of related independence conditions and functional forms.

Representation of Stimuli

In the carpet-cleaner example, Green and Wind represented the product profiles by verbal and pictorial descriptions on cards that were then sorted by respondents. In the past thirty years, stimuli representations have been limited only the by imagination of the researchers. For example, in the design of the E-Z Pass system, Vavra, Green, and Krieger (1999) sent videotapes and other descriptive materials to respondents so that they fully understood the innovation and its features. Wind et al. (1989) used combinations of physical models, photographs, and verbal descriptions. Recently, with the development of the Internet, researchers have begun to exploit the rich multi-media capabilities of the Web to provide virtual prototypes to Web-based respondents (Dahan and Srinivasan 2000). Indeed, this area of conjoint analysis is growing rapidly, with many firms providing panels of literally millions of respondents who can respond within days (Buckmann 2000; Dahan and Hauser 2002; Gonier 1999; Nadilo 1999).

Have Mercy on the Respondents

From the beginning, researchers have recognized that conjoint-analysis estimates are only as good as the data from which they are obtained. In the carpet-cleaner example, Green and Wind were concerned with respondent wear-out if respondents were asked to rank 108 product profiles. To avoid such wear-out, they chose an orthogonal design to reduce the number of profiles (to 18) that any respondent would see. Of course, this design was not without tradeoffs – an orthogonal design implicitly assumes preferential independence and does not allow any interactions to be estimated. Researchers have developed many methods to reduce respondent burden, tailored to the information required for the managerial application, the feature structure, and respondent task.

We review briefly a few of the methods that have been proposed. As early as 1978, Carmone, Green, and Jain (p. 300) found that most applications demanded a dozen or more features, but that it was difficult for customers to rank more than a dozen profiles. Many researchers have documented that the respondents' task can be burdensome and have suggested that accuracy degrades as the number of questions increases (Bateson, Reibstein, and Boulding 1987; Green, Carroll, and Goldberg 1981, p. 34; Green, Goldberg, and Montemayor 1981, p. 337; Huber et al. 1993; Lenk et al. 1996, p. 183;

Malhotra 1982, 1986, p. 33; Moore and Semenik 1988; Srinivasan and Park 1997, p. 286). When appropriate, efficient experimental designs are used so that the respondent need consider only a small fraction of all possible product profiles (Addelman 1962; Kuhfeld, Tobias, and Garratt 1994). Tradeoff analysis presents respondents with two attributes at a time and has them evaluate the reduced sets (Jain et al. 1979; Johnson 1974; Segal 1982). Two stages can be introduced in which respondents eliminate unacceptable products, unacceptable attributes, or use prior sorting tasks to simplify the evaluation task (Acito and Jain 1980; Green, Krieger, and Bansal 1988; Klein 1988; Malhotra 1986; Srinivasan 1988). Hierarchical integration provides a means to measure preferences among higher-level benefits and then again for features that drive those benefits (Oppewal, Louviere, and Timmermans 1994; Wind et al. 1989; Srinivasan and Park 1997).

Many researchers combine these methods with intensity questions (interval and ratio scales) or with self-explicated tasks (Griffin and Hauser 1993; Hauser and Shugan 1980; Neslin 1981; Srinivasan and Wyner 1988; Wilkie and Pessemier 1973). Other researchers have simplified the task. In choice-based conjoint analysis (CBC) respondents simply choose one profile each from many sets of profiles (Carroll and Green 1995; Elrod, Louviere, and Davy 1992; Haaijer, Kamakura, and Wedel 2000; Haaijer et al. 1998; Oppewal, Louviere, and Timmermans 1994; Orme 1999). Hybrid conjoint analysis combines self-explicated tasks for each respondent with a master design across respondents of profile-based questions (Akaah and Korgaonkar 1983; Green 1984; Green, Goldberg, and Montemayor 1981). Finally, Hierarchical Bayes (HB) methods improve the predictability of the partworths that have been collected by other means (Lenk et al. 1996; Johnson 1999; Sawtooth 1999) and thus, in theory, enable the researcher to obtain estimates with fewer questions.

Each of these methods, when used carefully and responsibly, reduces the respondents' burden and is feasible in large commercial applications. As this remains an area of active research, we expect further developments and, specifically, we expect researchers to experiment with many hybrid combinations of these methods.

Formats of Data Collection

Conjoint analysis was born in the belief that the data collection method should ask as little of the respondents as feasible and infer the rest. Like most early researchers, Green and Wind asked their respondents to rank order the profiles of carpet cleaners. Even the linear-programming methods transformed overall rank orders into rank orders among pairs (Srinivasan and Shocker 1973a, 1973b). However, toward the end of the 1970s, both academic and industrial researchers began to notice that respondents could, indeed, provide interval, or even ratio, data on preferences among product or service profiles.

For example, Carmone, Green, and Jain (1978) state: "(in industrial applications) rating scales ... have substituted for strict ranking procedures. ... metric analysis ... is very robust." In parallel, in their well-known Assessor model, Silk and Urban (1978) and Urban and Katz (1983) were using constant-sum-paired-comparison preference measurements for extremely accurate forecasts for new products. During this period, researchers experimented with many different formats for collecting data on preferences.

Research into question formats continues today with new forms, such as configurators, being used with success. However, this area remains one of strongly-held beliefs and debates. For example, in their defense of the choice-based (CBC) format, Louviere, Hensher, and Swait (2000) state: "We suggest that researchers consider transforming ratings data in this way rather than blindly assuming that ratings produced by human subjects satisfy demanding measurement properties." Green, Krieger, and Wind (2001) take a more two-sided view and, while acknowledging the potential benefits of the format, suggest that "choice-based conjoint studies can be a mixed blessing. The respondent's tasks are extensive." Finally, Orme (1999) suggests that "(CBC) often press the limits of how much information can be successfully evaluated before respondents either quit, glaze over, or start to employ sub-optimal shortcut methods for making choices."

We do not take a stand on which format is best, primarily because each format has its strengths and weaknesses and because the researcher should choose the format carefully as appropriate to the managerial problem and the stimuli being presented. We instead review five major formats: full-profile, partial-profile, stated preferences (CBC), self-explicated preferences, and configurators.

Full-Profile Evaluations

Full-profile stimuli are similar to those in Figure 6-1. Each product is described by the levels of the features that it contains. The respondent can be asked to rank order all stimuli or to provide a metric rating of each stimulus. In some hybrid methods, the experimental designs are blocked across respondents. Full-profile analysis remains the most common form of conjoint analysis and has the advantage that the respondent evaluates each profile holistically and in the context of all other stimuli. Its weakness is that the respondent's burden grows dramatically with the number of profiles that must be ranked or rated.

Partial-Profile Evaluations

Whenever preferential independence is satisfied, perhaps approximately, tradeoffs among a reduced set of features do not depend upon the levels of the other features. In this case, respondents can evaluate partial profiles in which some of the features are explicit and the other features are assumed constant. While the number of stimuli can vary from two to many, two stimuli are most common. Although the respondent can be asked only to choose among the partial profiles, it is common to obtain an interval evaluation of the profiles. Figure 6-2a illustrates a pairwise partial-profile evaluation in which the respondent is asked to provide a metric rating to indicate his or her strength of preference. In fixed designs, the partial stimuli are chosen from a partial design. Recently, there has been significant research on the most efficient manner in which to choose the partial profiles (e.g., Kuhfeld, Tobias, and Garratt 1994).

Because partial profiles are well suited to presentation on computer monitors, researchers have developed adaptive methods in which the nth set of partial profiles presented to respondents is based on the answers to the preceding $n-1$ sets of partial profiles. The best-known example of such adaptive selection of partial profiles is Johnson's (1987) adaptive conjoint analysis (ACA). In ACA, respondents are first asked a set of self-explicated questions (see below) to establish initial estimates of importances. Then, ordinary-least-squares (OLS) regression, based on the initial importances and the preceding $n-1$ metric paired-comparison questions, provides intermediate estimates of the partworths of each feature and level. The nth pair of profiles are chosen so that they are as equal as feasible in terms of estimated preference – a procedure known as utility balance. ACA has proved robust in practice and is, perhaps, the second most common form of conjoint analysis. Recently, researchers have re-estimated the partworths obtained from ACA with Hierarchical Bayes (HB) methods. (That is, OLS estimates the intermediate partworths that are used to select questions, but, once the data collection is complete, the partworths are re-estimated with HB.) HB appears to be quite effective when fewer questions are asked of each respondent than are typical in the standard ACA interview.

The advantage of ACA is that the questions are chosen for high information content. However, because it is OLS-based, ACA has the potential for endogeneity bias, that is, the nth question, and hence the nth set of independent variables, depend upon the answers, and hence the errors, in the first $n-1$ questions. Furthermore, the utility-balance criterion suggests that this bias is always upward and is greater for features that have higher (true) partworths (Hauser, Simester, and Toubia 2002). However, to date, there has been no research to establish whether or not this theoretical bias is managerially relevant.

Recently, new methods for adaptive question selection have been proposed that are not OLS based and, instead, choose questions to minimize the uncertainty in parameter estimation. In these "polyhedral" methods, each question constrains the feasible set of partworths. Multiple constraints imply that the set of partworths is a multi-dimensional polyhedron in partworth-space. The polyhedron is approximated with an ellipsoid and the longest axis of the ellipsoid provides the means to select the next question. Specifically, if the question vector is selected parallel to the longest axis, then the constraints imposed by the next answer are perpendicular to that axis and are most likely to result in the smallest new polyhedron. In addition, this question vector is most likely to lead to constraints that intersect the feasible polyhedron. In this manner, the questions reduce the set of feasible partworths as rapidly as

(a) Partial Profile (Metric Pairs)

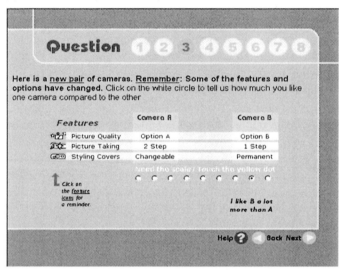

(b) Stated Preference (CBC)

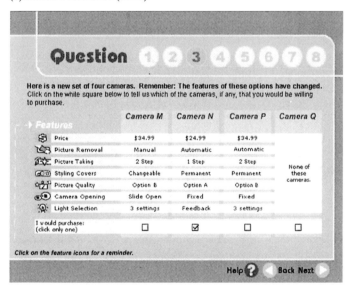

Figure 6-2a and b. Examples of Data-Collection Formats
From Toubia, Simester, Hauser, and Dahan 2003; Toubia, Hauser, and Simester (2003)

possible. In initial applications and simulations, these question-select methods appear superior to OLS-based utility-balance estimates (Toubia, Simester, Hauser, and Dahan 2003). These methods are available as stand-alone options (e.g., FastPace) and are now offered as an option within ACA. In addition, other major suppliers are developing polyhedral-based methods.

(c) Self-explicated Questions

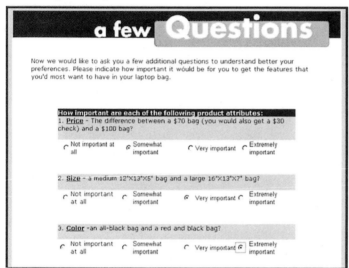

(d) Configurators

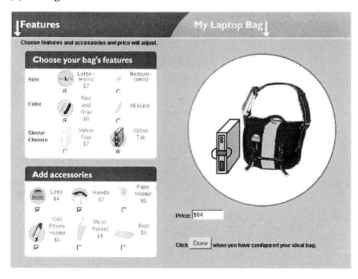

Figure 6-2c and d. **Examples of Data-Collection Formats**
From Toubia, Simester, Hauser, and Dahan (2003); Toubia, Hauser, and Simester (2003)

Stated Preferences

In 1974 McFadden provided a random utility interpretation of the logit model, renewing interest in disaggregate choice models in transportation demand analysis and in econometrics. In random utility models (RUM), the respondent's utility is represented as a (usually linear-in-the-parameters) combination of product or service features, plus an error term. Then, based on the distributional assumptions that are made about the error term, a researcher can calculate the probability that a product, defined by its features, is purchased. For example, if the error terms are independent Gumbel extreme value random variables, then we obtain the logit model. If the error terms are multivariate normal, we obtain the probit model. Initially, such RUM were estimated based on observing (1) the product features of existing products and (2) the choices made by individual consumers. Because such partworths are "revealed" by the marketplace such models became known as "revealed preference models."

While RUM models have many advantages, they suffer from sample selection bias when the set of existing products represents an efficient frontier of the product space. Very often, the data upon which RUM are based is highly collinear. If a new product "stretches" a feature not currently in the data, predictions are difficult. Thus, RUM models have been extended to stated preferences in which the researcher creates product profiles to span the set of feature combinations. The respondent's task is redefined as a choice among product profiles (cf. Louviere, Hensher, and Swait 2000). In this form, RUM models have all the characteristics of conjoint analysis, except that the data collection format is varied. (See Figure 6-2b.) Specifically, rather than ranking or rating the full product profiles, respondents are asked to choose one profile from each choice set. Each respondent sees multiple choice sets and, usually, the experimental design is completed across many respondents. A null product is often included in the choice sets so that forecasts can be calibrated. The partworths are estimated either with standard RUM analysis (logit or probit) or, increasingly, with Hierarchical Bayes estimation.

Unlike OLS estimation, the experimental design that maximizes efficiency depends upon the parameters of the model, e.g., the partworths. Thus, recent papers have explored "aggregate customization" in which data are collected with an initial experimental design, parameters are estimated, and the experimental design is re-optimized. See, for example, Huber and Zwerina (1996), Arora and Huber (2001), and Sandor and Wedel (2001).

More recently, polyhedral methods have been extended to the choice-based format and provide a means to customize experimental designs within respondents. Early research suggests that, for some levels of heterogeneity and for some levels of uncertainty the polyhedral methods produce experimental designs that lead to better estimates than those obtained by aggregate customization (Toubia, Simester, and Hauser 2003).

Self-explicated Methods

In the carpet-cleaner example, Green and Wind <u>decomposed</u> each respondent's preferences into partworths which represented the values of the various levels of the carpet-cleaner features. However, it is possible to *compose* preferences by asking respondents questions about the features themselves. Such compositional methods require two types of questions. First, the respondent must provide the relative value of each level within a feature and, second, provide the relative value of the features. Figure 6-2c provides examples of the latter.

In theory, it should be difficult for respondents to provide such judgments, but empirical experience suggests that they are quite accurate. For example, one conjoint method, Casemap, relies entirely on self-explicated judgments and has proven to predict well (Bucklin and Srinivasan 1991; Srinivasan 1988; Srinivasan and Wyner 1988). For an interesting review of self-explicated models, see Wilkie and Pessemier (1973) and for a comparison of alternative formats, see Griffin and Hauser (1993).

Self-explicated methods have also proven powerful when used in conjunction with decompositional methods. For example, Green has used self-explicated methods effectively in hybrid conjoint analysis – a method in which each respondent's self-explicated partworths modify overall partworths that are estimated with an experimental design that is blocked across respondents. ACA, reviewed earlier, is another hybrid in which self-explicated and metric partial profile data are combined effectively to enhance accuracy.

Configurators

Configurators represent a relatively recent form of conjoint-analysis data. With configurators, the respondent is given the choice of all levels of all features and uses a Web interface to select his or her preferred set of features. For example, at Dell.com potential computer purchasers "configure" their machine by choosing memory, processor speed, peripherals, and other features. Figure 6-2d is an example of a configurator for laptop computer bags. The form of data collection is relatively new. Applications include Franke and von Hippel (2002), Liechty, Ramaswamy, and Cohen (2001), Urban and Hauser (2002) and von Hippel (2001).

Estimation Methods

Because Green and Wind asked their respondents to rank order the eighteen carpet-cleaner profiles, the natural choice for estimation was monotonic regression. Since 1975, researchers have expanded greatly the repertoire of estimation tools. We review here five classes of estimation methods.

Regression-Based Methods

The basic conjoint problem is to estimate the partworths that best explain the overall preference judgments made by respondents. If the preference judgment is an approximately interval scale, then the partworths can be represented by dummy variables and ordinary least-squares (OLS) regression is a natural and relatively straightforward means with which to estimate the partworths.[1] If the data are only monotonic, then the least-squares criterion is replaced with a "stress" criterion. Further, if there are known constraints, such as the constraint that a lower price is preferred to a higher price, then such constraints can be added to either the metric or monotonic regressions. One particularly interesting form of regression is the Linmap algorithm (Srinivasan and Shocker 1973a, 1973b). In Linmap, the profile ranks are converted to pairwise ranks and the resulting inequality constraints are noted. A linear loss function is defined such that any violations of the constraints are weighted by the magnitude of the violation and a linear program is used to minimize the sum of these violations. Not only has Linmap proven accurate in a number of applications, but it provides a natural structure to handle constraints.

The advantages of the regression-based methods are their simplicity and the wide availability of software with which to perform estimations. If all the appropriate normality assumptions are satisfied, then regression may be the most efficient. However, regression requires at least as many observations as parameters. This presents a real challenge with large conjoint designs (many features and levels). In some cases respondent fatigue suggests much smaller designs. Even when the number of observations exceeds the number of parameters, the number of degrees of freedom may not be sufficient for good estimation. Fortunately, researchers have mitigated this problem by combining data from self-explicated preferences with data from either full- or partial-profile methods (Green 1984; Johnson 1987). Such hybrid methods have been used very successfully in large conjoint applications (e.g., Wind et al. 1989).

Random-Utility Models

When the data are choice-based (CBC), researchers have turned to random-utility models (RUM). The basic idea is that the assumption of utility maximization combined with distributional assumptions on the unobserved errors implies a known function that maps the partworth levels onto the probabilities that each profile is chosen from a given choice set. Many specifications of RUM lend themselves nicely to maximum-likelihood estimation (MLE). The most common models are the logit model (Gumbel errors), the probit model (multivariate normal errors), and the nested-logit model (generalized extreme value errors). See Ben-Akiva and Lerman (1985), Louviere, Hensher, and Swait (2000), or McFadden (2000).

The advantages of RUM models are that they are derived from transparent assumptions about utility maximization, that they lend themselves naturally to efficient MLE estimation, that estimation software is widely available, and that they are a natural means to estimate partworths from choice-based data. Not only have they proven accurate, but Louviere, Hensher and Swait (2000) review sixteen empirical studies in marketing, transportation, and environmental valuation in which stated-choice models (CBC) provide estimates similar to those obtained by revealed preference choice models.[2] The disadvantage of the RUM models is that, prior to HB estimation, the number of choice observations required for partworth estimation was too large to obtain practical estimates for each respondent. Most experimental designs are blocked across respondents. However, like regression-based hybrids, this, too, can be mitigated with the judicious use of self-explicated importances (Ter Hofstede, Kim, and Wedel 2002).

Hierarchical Bayes Estimation

One of the greatest practical challenges in conjoint analysis is to get sufficient data for partworth estimates with relatively few questions. This leads to tension in the experimental design. The researcher would like partworth estimates for each respondent so that (1) he or she could capture the heterogeneity of preferences, (2) design a product line, and (3) segment the market if necessary. On the other hand, if the respondent is asked too many questions, the respondent might become fatigued and either quit the interview, especially in Web-based formats, or provide data that are extremely noisy.

Hierarchical Bayes (HB) estimation addresses this tension in at least three ways. First, HB recognizes that the researcher's goals can be achieved if he or she knows the distribution of partworths. Second, while consumers are heterogeneous, there is information in the population distribution that can be used to constrain the estimates of the partworths for each respondent. And, third, prior information and beliefs can be used effectively. In addition, the philosophy is changed slightly. The researcher does not attempt to estimate point-values of the partworths, but endeavors to fully characterize the uncertainty about those estimates (mean and posterior distribution).

The basic idea behind HB is quite simple. For each respondent, the uncertainty about that respondent's partworths is characterized by a known distribution. However, the parameters of that distribution are themselves distributed across the population (hence the hierarchy). We then establish prior beliefs and update those beliefs based on the data and Bayes theorem. The challenge is that the equations do not lend themselves to simple analytical solutions. Fortunately, with the aid of Gibbs sampling and the Metropolis Hastings Algorithm, it is feasible to obtain updates for the specified parameters (Allenby and Rossi 1999; Arora, Allenby, and Ginter 1998; Johnson 1999; Lenk et al. 1996; Liechty, Ramaswamy, and Cohen 2001; Sawtooth Software 1999). HB estimates have proven quite accurate in simulation and in empirical applications (Andrews, Ansari, and Currim 2002; Lenk et al. 1996, Toubia et al. 2003). Hierarchical Bayes estimates appear particularly useful for situations in which the partworths are relatively homogeneous and/or there is significant response errors (Toubia, Simester, Hauser, and Dahan 2003; Toubia, Hauser, and Simester 2003).

The details of HB estimation are beyond the scope of this paper. However, we note that HB estimation has been applied to all forms of conjoint analysis data collection. For example, although ACA uses a form of OLS for intermediate estimates and FastPace uses analytic-center methods for intermediate estimates, both have used HB successfully to re-estimate partworths after all data have been collected.

Direct Computation Based on Self-Explicated Importances

In methods such as Casemap, the partworths are computed directly. In addition, as discussed above, such direct computations can be combined with other forms of estimation.

Estimation Based on New Optimization Methods

In the last few years, researchers have recognized the power of new optimization methods. These optimization methods run extremely fast on today's computers and provide the means to do extensive computations between questions (for intermediate estimates) or after all the data are collected (for revised estimates). There are many such approaches. We review three.

Analytic-center estimation. When there are fewer questions than there are partworths to be estimated, the questions can be viewed as constraints on the parameter space. The resulting feasible region is a multidimensional polyhedron. One estimate is the center of the polyhedron. Such estimates are justified based on either uniform priors or the proven (local) robustness of equally-weighted models (Dawes and Corrigan 1974; Einhorn 1971; Huber 1975; Moore and Semenik 1988; Srinivasan and Park 1997). Although computing the true center of a polyhedron is computationally intractable, the analytic center provides an extremely close approximation and can be computed rapidly (Freund 1993; Nesterov and Nemirovskii 1994; Sonnevend 1985a, 1985b; and Vaidja 1989).[3] Furthermore, for state-preference data, the analytic-center is analogous to a maximum-likelihood criterion. For the specific algorithm, and methods to handle response errors for metric-pairs data, see Toubia, Simester, Hauser, and Dahan (2003). For methods based on stated-preference data, see Toubia, Hauser, and Simester (2003). Simulations suggest that AC estimation is quite accurate and provides relative advantages when the partworths are heterogeneous and/or response errors are not too large. It is particularly useful for estimates when there are fewer questions than there are parameters.

Support-vector machines. One challenge in conjoint has been the specification of the preference function. If each pair of features is not preferentially independent of its complement set, then the preference function is not separable. However, estimating all interactions often requires more data than are feasible to collect. Evgeniou, Boussios, and Zacharia (2002) propose a solution using support-vector machines (SVM). SVMs are common in machine learning and artificial intelligence. The basic idea is to create new variables to represent both interactions and non-linearities, but to write the function as linear in its parameters. This leads to a large number of parameters to be estimated. However, SVM machines control for this complexity either by imposing a constraint on the sum of squares of the linear parameters or using this sum of squares in the objective function. A quadratic program then identifies the key parameters. Early applications suggest strong promise for the method.

Genetic algorithms. Conjoint analysis identifies high-potential product concepts by first estimating the partworths of the features of those products. Recently, researchers have experimented with genetic algorithms to identify those product concepts directly (Affinnova.com). As in conjoint analysis, each product is represented by its features and these features are reinterpreted as "genes." A respondent is shown a representative set of concepts, each of which is a set of genes. The respondent rates the product on a three-point scale (green, yellow, red). This rating determines the likelihood that the product concept will "reproduce" into the next generation. Then, following a genetic algorithm, new progeny concepts are generated based on the genes of their parents. These progeny concepts are shown to further respondents and the process continues until the population stabilizes on a small set of product concepts.

CONJOINT ANALYSIS IS ALIVE, WELL, AND GROWING

Little could anyone have known, when Green pioneered conjoint analysis, that the field would grow to be what it is today. Theory and practice have exploded to address a myriad of issues. But the journey is not over; indeed it has just begun. We are confident that the field will continue to be as vibrant for many years to come. With this vibrancy come challenges. We review a few of those challenges here, arranged by pragmatic issues, conceptual issues, and methodological issues.

Pragmatic Issues

Conjoint analysis has solved many managerial problems and will continue to do so. Such applications encourage a focus on both expanding the frontier of capabilities and on tradeoffs along that frontier. Some of these pragmatic issues include the following:

1. Analysis of tradeoffs between complexity of analysis, cost and difficulty of data collection, and managerial application. Currently, no method dominates in all situations with each method providing both strengths and weaknesses. To date there is no comprehensive theory to guide decisions among methods.

2. Matching analysis methods to new forms of data collection, including Web-based methods, rich multimedia representations, configurators (e.g., Dell.com) and computational applets that run during data collection. With more computing power available during data collection, new heuristics, new methods, and new representations are now feasible.

3. Meta-analyses of the varied applications under a variety of managerial problems, e.g., tourism, entertainment, health maintenance, gambling, development of complex products and systems, legal disputes, and corporate acquisitions. There are literally hundreds, perhaps thousands, of applications completed each year. Meta-analyses of these applications could raise interesting research hypotheses.

4. Comparative empirical studies of the reliability and validity including internal validity, convergent validity, and external validity. It is common to test internal validity (e.g., holdout profiles), but much less common to test external validity. More importantly, there is ample opportunity to test the *comparative* strengths of the various methods.

5. Methods to handle larger numbers of features, especially, for use in the new product development processes. Complex products such as automobiles and office equipment (e.g., copiers) often require consumer information on hundreds of features. More importantly, the fuzzy front end of product development is focused on screening large numbers of potential features to identify opportunities. New methods such as HB, polyhedral methods, and hybrid methods have greatly expanded the data collection capabilities of conjoint analysis. But industry demands continue for even larger numbers of features and levels.

Conceptual Issues

It is common in any scientific field that new applications and new challenges spawn new theory. This is certainly true in the field of conjoint analysis. We cite here but a few of the conceptual issues.

1. One of the most hotly debated issues in the field is the relative merits of the various data-collection methods. We see substantial opportunities for an underlying theory coupled with empirical tests to explore which situations favor one or more of the various forms of data collection including full-profile ratings, (metric) paired comparison data, self-explicated data, and (quantal) stated preference.

2. Price plays a special role in consumer preferences. It is not a feature of a product *per se*, but rather that which the consumer pays in return for features. It can be a signal, interact with the prices of other products, and be a strategic weapon. See, for example, Rao and Sattler (2000) and Foutz, Rao, and Yang (2002). Among the many price-related issues are:
    a. Effects of reference points on partworth measurement and evaluation
    b. Relative accuracy of price partworths (across methods and data collection) and their relationship to pricing decisions

3. Conjoint analysis provides an exacting measurement of consumer preferences, but to design a product or set marketing variables a firm must often do so in light of the actions and potential actions of its competitors. We are now beginning to see equilibrium (or non-equilibrium) models, which include the reactions of firms, competitors, and customers, coupled to conjoint analyses. One example is Kadiyali, Sudhir, and Rao (2001).

4. Conjoint analysis is based on measurements that inform respondents about product features. However, in real markets such information diffuses and does not happen instantaneously. Thus, we expect further development of methods that combine the diffusion of information among customers with models of how customers will choose based on that information and with models of how markets will evolve.

5. Conjoint analysis is based on consumer measurement. But consumer measurement means real consumers answering questions about potential behavior in situations that may differ from the situation of the measurement. This opens opportunities for research on learning, wear-out, self-perception biases, and other phenomena such as task presentation and task order.

Methodological Issues

As application and theory advance, so will methodology. Today we can handle larger designs, with more complex tasks, and more relevant stimuli. These advancements will continue. Among the methodological issues are:

1. With the advent of Web-based interviewing, each consumer can be asked multiple types of questions. We can also imagine studies in which the type of question is varied across respondents. Hybrid methods such as Green's Hybrid Conjoint Analysis and Johnson's Adaptive Conjoint Analysis have been successful. We anticipate further exploration of hybrid methods that combine data from multiple data sources.

2. A related issue is the use of information from other respondents to inform each respondent's partworth estimates. This includes methods such as:
   a. Hybrid Conjoint approaches
   b. Hierarchical Bayes methods
   c. Classical Bayes methods to combine population data with individual respondent estimation.
   d. Use aggregate market shares and product archeology(e.g., see the models proposed by Berry, Levinsohn, and Pakes 1995, 1998).

3. Improved methods for adaptive data collection based on data from either prior respondents (aggregate customization), prior questions, or both.

4. Many new methods have been proposed in the last few years. There are ample research opportunities to evaluate these many methods including:
   a. Support-vector machines for higher-level interactions
   b. Genetic algorithms for question design
   c. Data tries for adaptive full profile tasks
   d. Polyhedral question design for CBC and for metric paired comparisons
   e. Analytic center estimation
   f. Neural networks for improved estimation
   g. Genetic programming methods for analysis (Koza 1992)
   h. Bayesian methods to "listen in" on trusted Internet agents.

5. And, finally, managers are always seeking insight with which to make cost vs. benefit tradeoffs. This includes the analysis of the value of sample information to effect tradeoffs between the cost of a study and the value of the study. This is particularly relevant in the early stages of product development.

CONCLUDING THOUGHTS

Thirty years ago, in the time before time, or at least before the PC, he took pen in hand and scribbled a few equations. Conjoint analysis was born. Looking back, we can simply say that we've come a long way, but that the journey continues. And Paul Green will continue to lead the way.

NOTES

[1] Naturally, there is dependence among the dummy variables for a feature. One value can be set arbitrarily.

[2] By similar, we mean similar *relative* values of the partworths. Stated-preference partworths may need to be rescaled for choice predictions if they are to provide the same predictions as revealed-preference models (Louviere, Hensher, and Swait 2000). It depends on the application.

[3] The analytic center is the point that minimizes the geometric mean of the distances to the faces of the polyhedron.

REFERENCES

Acito, F., and Jain, A. K. (1980), "Evaluation of conjoint analysis results: A comparison of methods," *Journal of Marketing Research*, 17 (February), 106-112.

Addelman, S. (1962), "Orthogonal main-effect plans for asymmetrical factorial experiments," *Technometrics*, 4, 1 (February), 21-46.

Addelman, S. (1962), "Symmetrical and asymmetrical fractional factorial plans," *Technometrics*, 4, 1 (February), 47-58.

Akaah, I. P., and Korgaonkar, P. K. (1983), "An empirical comparison of the predictive validity of self-explicated, Huber-hybrid, traditional conjoint, and hybrid conjoint models," *Journal of Marketing Research*, 20 (May), 187-197.

Allenby, G. M., and Rossi, P. E. (1999), "Marketing models of consumer heterogeneity," *Journal of Econometrics*, 89 (March/April), 57-78.

Andrews, R. L., Ansari, A., and Currim, I. S. (2002), "Hierarchical Bayes versus finite mixture conjoint analysis models: A comparison of fit, prediction, and partworth recovery," *Journal of Marketing Research*, 39 (February), 87-98.

Arora, N., Allenby, G. M., and Ginter, J. L. (1998), "A hierarchical Bayes model of primary and secondary demand," *Marketing Science*, 17, 1, 29-44.

Arora, N., and Huber, J. (2001), "Improving parameter estimates and model prediction by aggregate customization in choice experiments," *Journal of Consumer Research*, 28 (September), 273-283.

Bateson, J. E. G., Reibstein, D., and Boulding, W. (1987), "Conjoint analysis reliability and validity: A framework for future research," in M. Houston (ed.), *Review of Marketing*, 451-481.

Ben-Akiva, M., and Lerman, S. R. (1985), *Discrete Choice Analysis*, Cambridge, MA: MIT Press.

Berry, S., Levinsohn J., and Pakes, A. (1995), "Automobile prices in market equilibrium," *Econometrica,* 63 (4), 841-890.

Berry, S., Levinsohn, J., and Pakes, A. (1998), "Differentiated products demand systems from a combination of micro and macro data: The new car market," Working Paper, New Haven, CT: Yale University.

Bucklin, R. E., and Srinivasan, V. (1991), "Determining interbrand substitutability through survey measurement of consumer preference structures," *Journal of Marketing Research*, 28 (February), 58-71.

Buckman, R. (2000), "Knowledge Networks' Internet polls will expand to track Web surfers," *Wall Street Journal*, (September 7).

Carmone, F. J., and Green, P. E. (1981), "Model misspecification in multiattribute parameter estimation," *Journal of Marketing Research*, 18 (February), 87-93.

Carmone, F. J., Green, P. E., and Jain, A. K. (1978), "Robustness of conjoint analysis: Some Monte Carlo results," *Journal of Marketing Research*, 15 (May), 300-303.

Carroll, J. D., and Green, P. E. (1995), "Psychometric methods in marketing research: Part I, conjoint analysis," *Journal of Marketing Research*, 32 (November), 385-391.

Cattin, P., and Punj, G. (1984), "Factors influencing the selection of preference model form for continuous utility functions in conjoint analysis," *Marketing Science*, 3, 1 (Winter), 73-82.

Cattin, P., and Wittink, D. R. (1982), "Commercial use of conjoint analysis: A survey," *Journal of Marketing*, 46 (Summer), 44-53.

Corstjens, M. L., and Gautschi, D. A. (1987), "Formal choice models in marketing," *Marketing Science,* 2 (Winter), 19-56.

Dahan, E., and Hauser, J. R. (2002), "The Virtual Customer," forthcoming, *Journal of Product Innovation Management*, 19, 5 (September), 332-354.

Dahan, E., and Srinivasan, V. (2000), "The predictive power of Internet-based product concept testing using visual depiction and animation," *Journal of Product Innovation Management*, 17, 99-109.

Dawes, R. M., and Corrigan, B. (1974), "Linear models in decision making," *Psychological Bulletin*, 81 (March), 95-106.

Einhorn, H. J. (1971), "Use of nonlinear, noncompensatory, models as a function of task and amount of information," *Organizational Behavior and Human Performance*, 6, 1-27.

Eliashberg, J. (1980), "Consumer preference judgments: An exposition with empirical applications," *Management Science*, 26, 1 (January), 60-77.

Eliashberg, J., and Hauser, J. R. (1985), "A measurement error approach for modeling consumer risk preference," *Management Science*, 31, 1 (January), 1-25.

Elrod, T., Louviere, J., and Davey, K. S. (1992), "An empirical comparison of ratings-based and choice-based conjoint models," *Journal of Marketing Research* 29, 3 (August), 368-377.

Evgenoiu, T., Boussios, C., and Zacharia, G. (2002), "Generalized robust conjoint estimation," Working Paper, Fontainebleau, France: INSEAD.

Farquhar, P. H. (1977), "A survey of multiattribute utility theory and applications," *Studies in Management Sciences,* 59-89.

Foutz, Y., Zhang N., Rao V. R., and Yang, S. (2002), "Incorporating consumer reference effects into choice-based conjoint analysis: An application to online and offline channel choices" Working paper, Ithaca, NY: Johnson Graduate School of management, Cornell University.

Franke, N., and von Hippel, E. (2002), "Satisfying heterogeneous user needs via innovation toolkits: The case of Apache security software," Working Paper #4341-02, Cambridge, MA: MIT Sloan School of Management.

Freund, R. (1993), "Projective transformations for interior-point algorithms, and a superlinearly convergent algorithm for the w-center problem," *Mathematical Programming*, 58, 385-414.

Gonier, D. E. (1999), "The emperor gets new clothes," Paper presented at the Advertising Research Foundation's On-line Research Day and available at www.dmsdallas.com. (January).

Green, P. E. (1974), "On the design of choice experiments involving multifactor alternatives," *Journal of Consumer Research*, 1 (September).

Green, P. E. (1984), "Hybrid models for conjoint analysis: An expository review," *Journal of Marketing Research*, 21 (May), 155-169.

Green, P. E., Carmone, F. J., and Fox, L. B. (1969), "Television programme similarities: An application of subjective clustering," *Journal of the Market Research Society*, 11, 1, 70-90.

Green, P. E., Carroll, J. D., and Carmone, F. J. (1977-78), "Superordinate factorial designs in the analysis of consumer judgments," *Journal of Economics and Business*, 30, 1977-78.

Green P. E., Carroll, J. D., and Goldberg, S. M. (1981), "A general approach to product design optimization via conjoint analysis," *Journal of Marketing*, 45 (Summer), 17-37.

Green, P. E., DeSarbo, W. S, and Kedia, P. K. (1980), "On the insensitivity of brand choice simulations to attribute importance weights," *Decision Sciences*, (July), 11, 439-450.

Green P. E., and Devita, M. (1974), "A complementary model of consumer utility for item collections," *Journal of Consumer Research,* 1 (December), 56-67.

Green, P. E., and Devita, M. T. (1975), "An interaction model of consumer utility," *Journal of Consumer Research*, 2 (September), 146-153.

Green, P. E., Goldberg, S. M., and Montemayor, M. (1981), "A hybrid utility estimation model for conjoint analysis," *Journal of Marketing*, 45, 1 (Winter), 33-41.

Green, P. E., Goldberg, S. M., and Wiley, J. B. (1982), "A cross validation test of hybrid conjoint models," in *Advances in Consumer Research*, 10, R. P. Bagozzi and A. M. Tybout (eds.), Ann Arbor, MI: Association for Consumer Research, pp. 147-150.

Green, P. E., and Helsen, K. (1989), "Cross-validation assessment of alternatives to individual-level conjoint analysis: A case study," *Journal of Marketing Research*, 24, 3 (August), 346-350.

Green, P. E., Helsen, K., and Shandler, B. (1988), "Conjoint internal validity under alternative profile presentations," *Journal of Consumer Research*, 15 (December), 392-397.

Green P. E., and Krieger, A. M. (1991), "Product design strategies for target-market positioning," *Journal of Product Innovation Management*, 8 (Fall), 189-202.

Green P. E., and Krieger, A. M. (1992), "An application of a product positioning model to pharmaceutical products," *Marketing Science*, 11, 2 (Spring), 117-132.

Green, P. E., and Krieger, A. (1996), "Individual hybrid models for conjoint analysis," *Management Science,* 42, 6 (June), 850-867.

Green, P. E., and Krieger, A. (1985), "Choice rules and sensitivity analysis in conjoint simulations," *Journal of the Academy of Marketing Science,* (Spring) 1988.

Green, P. E., and Krieger, A. (1985), "Models and heuristics for product line selection," *Marketing Science*, 4, 1 (Winter), 1-19.

Green, P. E., and Krieger, A. (1989), "Recent contributions to optimal product positioning and buyer segmentation," *European Journal of Operational Research*, 41, 2, 127-141.

Green, P. E., Krieger, A., and Agarwal, M. K. (1991), "Adaptive conjoint analysis: Some caveats and suggestions," *Journal of Marketing Research*, 23, 2 (May), 215-222.

Green, P. E., Krieger, A., and Bansal, P. (1988), "Completely unacceptable levels in conjoint analysis: A cautionary note," *Journal of Marketing Research*, 25, 3 (August), 293-300.

Green P. E., Krieger, A. M., and Vavra, T. (1999), "Evaluating E-Z Pass: Using conjoint analysis to assess consumer response to a new tollway technology," *Marketing Research* 11 (Summer),, 5-16.

Green, P. E., Krieger, A. M., and Wind, Y. (2001), "Thirty Years of Conjoint Analysis: Reflections and Prospects," *Interfaces,* 31, 3, Part 2 (May-June), S56-S73.

Green, P. E., and McMennamin, J. L. (1973), "Market position analysis," in S. H. Britt and N. F. Guess (eds.), *Marketing Manager's Handbook*, Chicago IL: Dartnell Press), pp. 543-554.

Green, P. E., and Rao, V. R. (1971), "Conjoint measurement for quantifying judgmental data," *Journal of Marketing Research*, 8 (August), 355-363.

Green, P.E., and Rao, V. R. (1972), *Applied Multidimensional Scaling,* Dryden Press.

Green, P. E., Rao, V. R., and DeSarbo, W. (1978), "A procedure for incorporating group-level similarity judgments in conjoint analysis," *Journal of Consumer Research,* 5 (December), 187-193.

Green, P. E., and Srinivasan, V. (1990), "Conjoint analysis in marketing: New developments with implications for research and practice," *Journal of Marketing*, 54, 4 (October), 3-19.

Green, P. E., and Srinivasan, V. (1978), "Conjoint analysis in consumer research: Issues and outlook," *Journal of Consumer Research*, 5, 2 (September), 103-123.

Green, P. E., and Wind, J. (1975), "New way to measure consumers' judgments," *Harvard Business Review*, (July-August),107-117.

Green, P. E., Wind, Y., and Jain, A. K. (1972), "Preference measurement of item collections," *Journal of Marketing Research*, 9 (November), 371-377.

Green, P. E., and Wind, J. (1973), *Multiattribute Decisions in Marketing,* Dryden Press.

Griffin, A. J., and Hauser, J. R. (1993), "The voice of the customer," *Marketing Science*, 12 (Winter), 1-27.

Haaijer, R., Wedel, M., Vriens, M., and Wansbeek, T. (1998), "Utility covariances and context effects in conjoint MNP models," *Marketing Science*, 17, 3, 236-252.

Haaijer, R., Kamakura, W., and Wedel, M. (2000), "Response latencies in the analysis of conjoint choice experiments," *Journal of Marketing Research* 37 (August), 376-382.

Hauser, J. R., and Koppelman, F. S. (1979), "Alternative perceptual mapping techniques: Relative accuracy and usefulness," *Journal of Marketing Research*, 16, 4 (November), 495-506.

Hauser, J. R., and Shugan, S. M. (1980), "Intensity measures of consumer preference," *Operation Research*, 28, 2 (March-April), 278-320.

Hauser, J. R., Simester, D. I., and Toubia, O. (2002), "Configurators, utility balance, and managerial use," working paper, Cambridge, MA: Center for Innovation in Product Development, MIT, (June).

Hauser, J. R., and Urban, G. L. (1977), "A normative methodology for modeling consumer response to innovation," *Operations Research,* 25, 5 (July-August), 579-619.

Hauser, J. R., and Urban, G. L. (1979), "Assessment of attribute importances and consumer utility functions: von Neumann-Morgenstern theory applied to consumer behavior," *Journal of Consumer Research*, 5 (March), 251-262.

Huber, J. (1975), "Predicting preferences on experimental bundles of attributes: A comparison of models," *Journal of Marketing Research*, 12 (August), 290-297.

Huber, J. (1987), "Conjoint analysis: How we got here and where we are," *Proceedings of the Sawtooth Software Conference on Perceptual Mapping, Conjoint Analysis, and Computer Interviewing*, pp. 237-252.

Huber, J., Wittink, D. R., Fiedler, J. A., and Miller, R. (1993), "The effectiveness of alternative preference elicitation procedures in predicting choice," *Journal of Marketing Research*, 105-114.

Huber, J., and Zwerina, K. (1996), "The importance of utility balance in efficient choice designs," *Journal of Marketing Research*, 33 (August), 307-317.

Jain, A. K., Acito, F., Malhotra, N. K., and Mahajan, V. (1979), "A comparison of the internal validity of alternative parameter estimation methods in decompositional multiattribute preference models," *Journal of Marketing Research*, 16 (August), 313-322.

Johnson, R. (1974), "Tradeoff analysis of consumer values," *Journal of Marketing Research*, (May), 121-127.

Johnson, R. (1987), "Accuracy of utility estimation in ACA," Working Paper, Sequim, WA: Sawtooth Software, (April).

Johnson, R. (1991), "Comment on adaptive conjoint analysis: Some caveats and suggestions," *Journal of Marketing Research*, 28 (May), 223-225.

Johnson, R. (1999), "The joys and sorrows of implementing HB methods for conjoint analysis," Working Paper, Sequim, WA: Sawtooth Software, (November).

Kadiyali, V., Sudhir, K., and Rao, V. R. (2000), "Structural analysis of competitive behavior," *International Journal of Research in Marketing*, 18, 161-185.

Keeney, R., and Raiffa, H. (1976), *Decisions with Multiple Consequences: Preferences and Value Tradeoffs*, New York, NY: John Wiley & Sons.

Klein, N. M. (1988), "Assessing unacceptable attribute levels in conjoint analysis," *Advances in Consumer Research,* 14, 154-158.?

Koza, J. R. (1992), *Genetic Programming,* Cambridge, MA: The MIT Press.

Krantz, D. H., Luce, R. D., Suppes, P., and Tversky, A. (1971), *Foundations of Measurement*, New York, NY: Academic Press.

Kuhfeld, W. E., Tobias, R. D., and Garratt, M. (1994), "Efficient experimental design with marketing research applications," *Journal of Marketing Research*, 31, 4 (November), 545-557.

Lenk, P. J., DeSarbo, W. S., Green, P. E., and Young, M. R. (1996), "Hierarchical Bayes conjoint analysis: Recovery of partworth heterogeneity from reduced experimental designs," *Marketing Science*, 15, 2, 173-191.

Liechty, J., Ramaswamy, V., and Cohen, S. (2001), "Choice-menus for mass customization: An experimental approach for analyzing customer demand with an application to a web-based information service," *Journal of Marketing Research*, 38, 2 (May).

Louviere, J. J., Hensher, D. A., and Swait, J. D. (2000), *Stated Choice Methods: Analysis and Application*, New York, NY: Cambridge University Press.

Luce, R. D., and Tukey, J. W. (1964), "Simultaneous conjoint measurement: A new type of fundamental measurement," *Journal of Mathematical Psychology*, 1, 1-27.

Malhotra, N. (1982), "Structural reliability and stability of nonmetric conjoint analysis," *Journal of Marketing Research*, 19 (May), 1999-207.

Malhotra, N. (1986), "An approach to the measurement of consumer preferences using limited information," *Journal of Marketing Research*, 23 (February), 33-40.

McFadden, D. (1974), "Conditional logit analysis of qualitative choice behavior," in P. Zarembka (ed.), *Frontiers in Econometrics*, New York: Academic Press, pp. 105-142.

McFadden, D. (2000), "Disaggregate behavioral travel demand's RUM side: A thirty-year retrospective," Working Paper, University of California, Berkeley, (July).

Montgomery, D. B., and Wittink, D. R. (1980), "The predictive validity of conjoint analysis for alternative aggregation schemes," in D. B. Montgomery and D. R. Wittink (eds.), *Market Measurement and Analysis: Proceedings of the 1979 ORSA/TIMS Conference on Marketing*, Cambridge, MA: Marketing Science Institute, pp. 298-309.

Moore, W. L. (1980), "Levels of aggregation in conjoint analysis: An empirical comparison," *Journal of Marketing Research*, 17, 4 (November), 516-523.

Moore, W.L., and Semenik, R. J. (1988), "Measuring preferences with hybrid conjoint analysis: The impact of a different number of attributes in the master design," *Journal of Business Research,* 261-274.

Nadilo, R. (1999), "On-line research: The methodology for the next millennium," *Advertising Research Foundation Journal*, (Spring). Available at www.greenfield.com.

Neslin, S. A. (1981), "Linking product features to perceptions: Self-stated versus statistically revealed importance weights," *Journal of Marketing Research*, 18 (February), 80-86.

Nesterov, Y., and Nemirovskii, A. (1994), "Interior-point polynomial algorithms in convex programming," SIAM, Philadelphia.

Oppewal, H., Louviere, J. J., and Timmermans, H. J. P. (1994), "Modeling hierarchical conjoint processes with integrated choice experiments," *Journal of Marketing Research*, 31 (February), 92-105.

Orme, B. (1999), "ACA, CBC, or both?: Effective strategies for conjoint research," Working Paper, Sequim, WA: Sawtooth Software..

Rao, V. R. (1977) " Conjoint measurement in marketing analysis," in J. Sheth (ed.), *Multivariate Methods for Market and Survey Research*, Chicago: American Marketing Association, pp. 257-286.

Rao, V. R., and Katz, R. (1971), "Alternative multidimensional scaling methods for large stimulus sets," *Journal of Marketing Research*, 8 (November), 488-494.

Rao, V. R., and Sattler, H. (2000), "Measurement of informational and allocative effects of price," in A. Gustafsson, A. Herrmann, and F. Huber (eds.), *Conjoint Measurement: Methods and Applications*, Berlin: Springer-Verlag, pp.47-66.

Reibstein, D., Bateson, J. E. G., and Boulding, W. (1988), "Conjoint analysis reliability: Empirical findings," *Marketing Science*, 7, 3 (Summer), 271-286.

Sandor, Z., and Wedel, M. (2001), "Designing conjoint choice experiments using managers' prior beliefs," *Journal of Marketing Research*, 38, 4 (November), 430-444.

Sawtooth Software, Inc. (1996), "ACA system: Adaptive conjoint analysis," *ACA Manual*, Sequim, WA: Sawtooth Software, Inc.

Sawtooth Software, Inc. (1999), "The ACA/HB module for Hierarchical Bayes estimation," *ACA/HB Manual*, Sequim, WA: Sawtooth Software, Inc.

Segal, M. N. (1982), "Reliability of conjoint analysis: Contrasting data collection procedures," *Journal of Marketing Research*, 19, 139-143.

Silk, Al. J., and Urban, G. L. (1978), "Pre-test-market evaluation of new packaged goods: A model and measurement methodology," *Journal of Marketing Research*, 15 (May), 171-191.

Sonnevend, G. (1985a), "An 'analytic' center for polyhedrons and new classes of global algorithms for linear (smooth, convex) programming," *Proceedings of the 12th IFIP Conference on System Modeling and Optimization*, Budapest.

Sonnevend, G. (1985b), "A new method for solving a set of linear (convex) inequalities and its applications for identification and optimization," Preprint, Department of Numerical Analysis, Institute of Mathematics, Eötvős University, Budapest, 1985.

Srinivasan, V. (1988), "A conjunctive-compensatory approach to the self-explication of multiattributed preferences," *Decision Sciences*, 19 (Spring), 295-305.

Srinivasan, V., and Park, C. S. (1997), "Surprising robustness of the self-explicated approach to customer preference structure measurement," *Journal of Marketing Research*, 34 (May), 286-291.

Srinivasan, V., and Shocker, A. D. (1973a), "Estimating the weights for multiple attributes in a composite criterion using pairwise judgments," *Psychometrika*, 38, 4 (December), 473-493.

Srinivasan, V., and Shocker, A. D. (1973b), "Linear programming techniques for multidimensional analysis of preferences," *Psychometrika*, 38, 3 (September), 337-369.

Srinivasan, V., and Wyner, G. A. (1988), "Casemap: Computer-assisted self-explication of multiattributed preferences," in W. Henry, M. Menasco, and K. Takada (eds.), *Handbook on New Product Development and Testing*, Lexington, MA: D. C. Heath, pp. 91-112.

Ter Hofstede, F., Kim, Y., and Wedel, M. (2002), "Bayesian prediction in hybrid conjoint analysis," *Journal of Marketing Research*, 36 (May), 253-261.

Toubia, O., Simester, D., Hauser, J. R, and Dahan, E. (2003), "Fast polyhedral adaptive conjoint estimation," forthcoming *Marketing Science*, 22.

Toubia, O., Simester, D., and Hauser, J. R. (2003), "Adaptive choice-based conjoint analysis with polyhedral methods," Working Paper, Cambridge, MA: Center for Innovation in Product Development, MIT, (February).

Urban, G. L., and Hauser, J. R. (2002), "'Listening in' to find consumer needs and solutions," Working Paper, Cambridge, MA: Center for Innovation in Product Development, MIT, (January).

Urban, G. L., and Katz, G. M. (1983), "Pre-test market models: Validation and managerial implications," *Journal of Marketing Research*, 20 (August), 221-34.

Vaidja, P. (1989), "A locally well-behaved potential function and a simple Newton-type method for finding the center of a polytope," in N. Megiddo (ed.), *Progress in Mathematical Programming: Interior Points and Related Methods*, New York: Springer, pp. 79-90.

Vavra, T. G., Green, P. E., and Krieger, A. (1999), "Evaluating E-Z Pass," *Marketing Research*, 11, 3 (Summer), 5-16.

von Hippel, E. (2001), "Perspective: User toolkits for innovation," *Journal of Product Innovation Management*, 18, 247-257.

Wilkie, W. L., and Pessemier, E. A. (1973), "Issues in marketing's use of multi-attribute attitude models," *Journal of Marketing Research*, 10 (November), 428-441.

Wind, J., Green, P. E., Shifflet, D., and Scarbrough, M. (1989), "Courtyard by Marriott: Designing a hotel facility with consumer-based marketing models," *Interfaces*, 19, 25-47.

Wittink, D. R., and Cattin, P. (1981), "Alternative estimation methods for conjoint analysis: A Monte Carlo study," *Journal of Marketing Research*, 18 (February), 101-106.

Wittink, D. R., and Cattin, P. (1989), "Commercial use of conjoint analysis: An update," *Journal of Marketing*, 53, 3 (July), 91-96.

Wittink, D. R., and Montgomery, D. B. (1979), "Predictive validity of tradeoff analysis for alternative segmentation schemes," in N. Beckwith (ed.), *1979 AMA Educators' Conference Proceedings,* Chicago, IL: American Marketing Association.

Wright, P., and Kriewall, M. A. (1980), "State-of-mind effects on accuracy with which utility functions predict marketplace utility," *Journal of Marketing Research*, 17 (August), 277-293.

Chapter 7

Buyer Choice Simulators, Optimizers, and Dynamic Models

Paul E. Green
Abba M. Krieger
Yoram (Jerry) Wind
The Wharton School, University of Pennsylvania

Collecting and analyzing respondents' conjoint data is an essential part of the analytical process. As noted by John Hauser and Vithala Rao in their excellent discussion of conjoint analysis over the past 30 years (see Chapter 6), marketing researchers have expended intense efforts on data collection and partworth estimation. Partworths have been estimated by full profile, Adaptive Conjoint Analysis, hybrid conjoint, and categorical conjoint, with or without empirical or hierarchical Bayes enhancement. Partworth measurement and estimation processes are central to the accuracy and usefulness of all conjoint studies. Accordingly, much has been written about the pros and cons of various conjoint data collection and parameter estimation methods.

At the end of the day, however, it is *what is done with the partworths* that interests marketing managers. Hence, an important part of the applications process involves the design and use of "if–then" models: simulators and optimizers that provide bottom-line forecasts and comparisons of alternative strategic options.

Ironically, descriptions of simulators/optimizers have received much less attention in the literature than they deserve. This chapter attempts to redress this imbalance. Our main objective is to describe a variety of descriptive and prescriptive models whose goal is to forecast (or optimize) the sponsor firm's share or financial return position, given a set of actions that are played out in the simulator/optimizer modules. We try to show that such descriptive (or prescriptive) models are essential to both the tactical and strategic roles that conjoint models play in finding good (or even optimal) courses of action. The chapter also includes a real world application of conjoint modeling, as used in the design of the Northeast U.S.A.'s E-Z Pass travel system.

Most conjoint software distributors (e.g., Sawtooth Software and SPSS CATEGORIES) provide a market simulator in the software packages. These simulators, while highly useful, are not meant to fully cover the various features that a simulator/optimizer could have. Hence, we describe more elaborate simulation modules that consulting firms (in particular) have developed to extend the range of commercial conjoint applications.

We start from a set of basic operations and progress to more elaborate models that are typically proprietary to a specific consulting firm. We describe three classes of models:

- *Simulators,* designed to implement if–then tactics on the part of a single supplier (with competitors)
- *Optimizers,* that solve for the highest market share or return product configuration, conditioned on known (or assumed) competitors' strategies, and
- *Dynamic optimizers*, that examine longer-term returns that reflect several "rounds" of competitive interplay (and the associated concept of Nash equilibrium).

COMMERCIAL CONJOINT SIMULATORS

Both Sawtooth Software and SPSS conjoint procedures have serviceable and easy-to-use simulators. Sawtooth's simulator is considerably more elaborate than that of SPSS and has the virtue of being appropriate for each of its three tradeoff models – Adaptive Conjoint Analysis (ACA), Conjoint Value Analysis (CVA), and Choice-Based Conjoint (CBC) – as well as its ancillary software, such as hierarchical Bayes, Latent Class, and ICE. The SPSS simulator is a basic choice simulator that is modeled after Bretton-Clark's package (which is no longer being promoted). The SPSS simulator utilizes holdout profiles (for reliability and validity checks) and computes a preference score for each respondent. It offers three choice rules: max utility, the Bradley-Terry-Luce probability of choice model, and logit, which uses the natural log of the utilities before normalizing market shares. The SPSS simulator also computes attribute importances from the partworths. In addition, Pearson's R and Kendall's tau are computed as summary measures of goodness-of-fit. Both Sawtooth and SPSS produce basic simulator outputs. However, Sawtooth's simulator is considerably more flexible in its ability to handle simulations for all of its conjoint models (ACA, CVA, and CBC) on a standardized basis.

Table 7-1. **Typical Characteristics of Buyer Choice Simulators**

- Product simulation flexibility
  - o Single product (vs. status quo)
- Likelihood-of-purchase (averaged response)
- Proportion of respondents whose predicted likelihood of purchase exceeds a user-supplied criterion level
  - o Multiple products (sponsors and competitors): share received by each
  - o Sponsor's product bundle (vs. competitors' products): share received by bundle and its separate components
- Choice rules for the multiple-product and bundle cases
  - o Max-utility rule
  - o Share of utility (STL) rule
  - o Logit rule
- Other substantive features of choice simulators
  - o Interpolation of partworths
  - o Base-case entry with adjusted current-product comparisons
- Parametric confidence intervals around output measures
- Nonparametric (bootstrapped) intervals
  - o Frequency tabulations and histograms of responses
  - o Replicated cases in a single run
  - o Inclusion of price and cost parameters
  - o Brand-switching matrices
  - o Derived attribute-level importances (based on choice data)
- Consumer characteristics
  - o Respondent background data for market-segment summaries
  - o Respondent importance weights
  - o Respondent perceptual distributions of brand attributes
  - o Individual/respondent output file (for additional analyses)
- Sensitivity features
  - o Runs through all levels of a single attribute
  - o Flexibility for fixing attribute levels at user-present values (in all runs)
- Cosmetic features
  - o Menu-driven
  - o Graphics output
- Pie charts and histograms of market share; partworth graphs
- Average partworths for total sample and segments

Some consulting firms have developed their own simulator, which accompanies each of their completed conjoint studies. While detailed information on these tailor-made simulators is difficult to obtain, Table 7-1 contains a reasonable set of features that a commercial conjoint simulator could (or should) have. Some consulting firms also offer a sensitivity simulator, in addition to their primary simulator. Table 7-2 shows the typical characteristics of a sensitivity analysis simulator.

Table 7-2. **Illustrative Outputs of Sensitivity Analysis Simulator**

- Preliminary detail-proportion of sample selecting each attribute level as displaying the highest partworths, by attribute

- Sensitivity analyses (assuming a bundle of two or more new products) to compute bundle share (and individual item-shares), given:

  o   Deletion of each item in bundle, in turn

  o   Change levels of each attribute of each product, holding all others at initial levels

  o   Fixing or lowering all status quo utilities by a fixed (user-supplied) percentage

  o   Selection of a specified segment (based on background-variable categories or cluster-based segments)

  o   Random selection of K bundles (up to 1,000) where random bundles can be constrained to include user-specified profiles and/or restricted attribute-level variation

- Additions to basic sensitivity analyses

  o   Inclusion of attribute-level returns to the user's product line

  o   Inclusion of price vs. utility relationship for adjusting respondent utilities to price increases/decreases

  o   Inclusion of effect on firm's existing products (cannibalization) due to new product(s) introduction

---

In sum, most of the early conjoint simulators, commercial or consultant-based, have similar choice rule capabilities and some have sensitivity analysis features as well. Until recently, this was pretty much the state of practice.

CONJOINT OPTIMIZERS

More recently, there has been a trend toward increasing the sophistication of simulators to handle attribute-level costs, thus leading to the potential development of conjoint optimizers. To the best of our knowledge, consultants' optimizers, at least tentatively, are proprietary models, rather than being offered for outright sale (although Sawtooth Software will soon be marketing a conjoint optimizer). Optimizers require the firm's management to be able to estimate variable costs at the product attribute level. Moreover, the researcher may also want to add associated price increments to the enhancement levels of a basic attribute offering. For example, hotel rooms may carry different prices according to room size and the extent of the room's amenities. These components naturally complicate the model and make additional demands on already difficult-to-estimate parameters.

We begin by describing three simulation/optimization models: CONJOINT DISPLAY, SIMOPT, and SIMACT. The first, CONJOINT DISPLAY, is a simulator that utilizes partworths typically estimated from ratings data, as obtained from Sawtooth's ADAPTIVE CONJOINT ANALYSIS (ACA) procedure. SIMOPT and SIMACT are typically (but not necessarily) used for choice-based conjoint data. CONJOINT DISPLAY, SIMOPT, and SIMACT are all proprietary (i.e., not-for-sale) software. We then describe SIMDYN (SIMulation via DYNamic modeling), which extends the capabilities of conjoint optimizing models to consider dynamic competitive moves.

CONJOINT DISPLAY

CONJOINT DISPLAY is a versatile simulator that typically utilizes partworths obtained from conjoint ratings data, e.g., Sawtooth's ACA data collection procedure. The input to CONJOINT DISPLAY consists of each individual's:

- Set of partworths (including intercept term)
- Set of desired attribute importances
- Most preferred level within each attribute
- Set of background-variable category assignments
- Respondent weights (optional)

These inputs can, incidentally, be obtained from almost any conjoint data collection procedure, including Sawtooth software or SPSS's CATEGORIES software.

CONJOINT DISPLAY then produces the following results:

- Displays (with pie charts) the market shares and most preferred levels within each attribute across respondents.
- Displays each attribute's partworths in terms of a dollar metric, where each enhanced attribute level is expressed in dollar terms, relative to the price attribute's base (or least-preferred) level.
- Displays derived attribute importances, at either the total-sample level or by any user-selected background (e.g., demographic) attribute. In addition, the user can compose a selected segment

and find the associated attribute importances for only members of this composed segment.

- Composes one or more product profiles and finds the share of choices received by each profile, either for the total sample or for a segment composed by the user.
- Includes two kinds of simulations. In the single product case, the user selects one product profile (from those composed) and finds the group-average probability that it will be chosen. One can also find the number of consumers whose probability of selecting the profile exceeds a user-specified cutoff (say, 80%) value.
- In the multiple product case, the simulator can compose two or more profiles and obtain estimated market shares of each. CONJOINT DISPLAY's choice rule employs a flexible model that can emulate share of utility, max utility (winner takes all), or gradations in between.
- Employs a bootstrapping (resampling) procedure to show the degree of possible variation around the expected market shares of each profile.
- With the compose-a-segment module, CONJOINT DISPLAY prepares an a priori segment description and shows how it behaves throughout various descriptive and analytical operations in the software package.
- With the perceptual mapping module, CONJOINT DISPLAY selects any background attribute (e.g., age) and obtains a similarities map that relates attribute importance to the various age categories. Alternatively, one can also show attribute importances and demographics in terms of a hierarchical tree (based on two up to six dimensions in the multidimensional space obtained from the mapping).
- In sum, CONJOINT DISPLAY has been designed to incorporate descriptive summaries, choice simulations, and perceptual mapping/clustering in a coherent package that combines user flexibility with attractive graphics.

The SIMOPT Model

SIMOPT (SIMulation and OPTimization) is an optimal product-positioning model that can be used for either the single-product or the product-line case. Its principal inputs are a matrix of K buyers' partworths and a set of competitive product profiles. As in CONJOINT DISPLAY, the partworths may come from any conjoint procedure, including the programs of

Sawtooth and SPSS. In particular, partworths obtained from hybrid conjoint models are appropriate.

In addition to input matrices of buyer partworths and competitive-supplier profiles, the model has options for including:

- Buyer importance weights (reflecting buyers' frequency and/or amount of purchase)
- Demographic or other background attributes
- Demographic weights for use in market-segment selection and market-share forecasting
- Current market-share estimates of all supplier (brand) profiles under consideration (used in model calibration), and
- Costs/returns data, measured at the individual-attribute level.

SIMOPT uses a general choice rule, based on share of utility. This rule is called the alpha rule, and is capable of mimicking the more traditional Bradley-Terry-Luce (BTL), logit, or max-utility choice rules. The alpha rule assumes that the probability, π_{ks}, of buyer k selecting brand s is given by:

$$\pi_{ks} = \frac{U_{ks}^{\alpha}}{\sum\limits_{s=1}^{S} U_{ks}^{\alpha}}$$

where U_{ks} is the utility of buyer k for brand s; α (which is typically set to at least 1.0) is chosen by the user; and S is the number of suppliers. If $\alpha = 1$, the model mimics the BTL share-of-utility rule; as α approaches infinity the model mimics the max-utility rule.

The primary data input to the SIMOPT model consists of a matrix of K individuals' partworths. In the simple case where no interaction effects are included, the general entry is

$p_{i,j}^{(k)}$ = partworth for level i of attribute j for individual k; $i = 1, \ldots L_j$; $j = 1, \ldots, M$;

$a^{(k)}$ = intercept term for individual k,

where L_j denotes the number of levels for attribute j, and M is the number of attributes. Each vector of partworths enables the user to compute a utility for any product/supplier profile for any individual k. A profile is defined by its levels $(i_1, \ldots i_M)$. The utility of this profile to individual k is given by

$$U_k(i_1,...,i_M) = \sum_{j=1}^{M} p_{i_j,j}^{(k)} + a^{(k)}.$$

We assume that in any given run of SIMOPT, each supplier is represented by a profile vector i_s; s = 1, 2, ..., S. Hence, we can compute

$$U_{k,s} = U_k(i_s)$$

as the utility of individual k for supplier s. The "market share" of individual k for supplier s is

$$\pi_{k,s} = \frac{U_k^\alpha(i_s)}{\sum_{s=1}^{S} U_k^\alpha(i_s)}$$

for a specified value of α.

Once we have computed the $\pi_{k,s}$, we can combine them into a total market share by using $\sum_{k=1}^{K} W^{(k)} \pi_{k,s}$ where $W^{(k)}$, the weight for individual k, is non-negative with $\sum_{k=1}^{K} W^{(k)} = 1$. The individual weights can be further modified by considering various market segments. We generally assume that an input matrix of demographic (or general background) classification variables is available. We let

> $D_n^{(k)}$ = the demographic category of individual k for variable n; n = 1, 2, ..., N, where N denotes the total number of demographic variables.

We also have weights E_n, one weight for each of the N demographics: $E_n > 0$; $\sum_{n=1}^{N} E_n = 1$.

In SIMOPT we can specify the number of demographics H we want to use, which demographics, $t_1, t_2, ..., t_H$, and the level for each demographic, l_h. More than one level within demographic can be included (but for expository purposes only one level for each demographic is shown here). We then have

$$V^{(k)} = W^{(k)} \sum_{h=1}^{H} I_h^{(k)} E_{t_h}$$

where

$$I_h^{(k)} = \begin{cases} 1 & \text{if } D_{t_h}^{(k)} = I_h, \\ 0 & \text{otherwise.} \end{cases}$$

and

$$V^{(k)} = \frac{V^{(k)}}{\sum\limits_{k=1}^{K} V^{(k)}}.$$

The overall market share for supplier product s is given by

$$M_s^* = \sum_{k=1}^{K} V^{(k)} \pi_{k,s}.$$

(Note that M_s^* implicitly depends on the profiles of each of the S suppliers.)

Starting conditions for applying the model entail a set of initial supplier profiles and initial market shares, I_s. These initial supplier profiles are associated with market shares M_s^* and, hence, multipliers given by $f_s \equiv I_s/M_s^*$.

The adjusted market shares are the given by:

$$\hat{M}_s = \frac{f_s M_s^*}{\sum\limits_{s=1}^{S} f_s M_s^*}.$$

Costs/Returns

Finally, the model can incorporate costs and returns and can optimize over this measure (as well as over market share). First, we let $R_{i,j}$ = return for level

i of attribute j. (Note: the default value is $R_{i,j} = 1/M$ for all j and i.) We can then compute total return as:

$$T(i_1, i_2, ..., i_M) = \sum_{j=1}^{M} R_{i_j, j}.$$

Hence, for each supplier we have a total return: $T_s = T(i_s)$. This gives us, respectively, an adjusted and an unadjusted return for each supplier of:

$$O_s^* = M_s^* T_s, \quad \hat{O}_s = \hat{M}_s T_s.$$

SIMOPT's Features

The SIMOPT model's outputs consist of market shares or dollar contributions to overhead and profits for each supplier. In the latter case, direct (or variable) costs/returns have to be estimated at the individual-attribute level for each supplier – a daunting task in most real-world settings. In any given run of the model, the user obtains market share (return) for each supplier on both an unadjusted and adjusted (for initial share) basis. Outputs can be obtained for both the total market and for any segment defined by the user from the available demographic variables.

The user is then able to perform four types of analysis:

1. A sensitivity analysis. This shows how shares (returns) change for all suppliers as one varies the levels within each attribute, in turn.

2. An optimal attribute-level analysis. If this option is chosen, the model computes the best attribute profile for a given supplier, conditioned on specified attribute levels for all competing suppliers.

3. A cannibalization analysis. The user can also specify one or more ancillary products. If so, the model finds the optimal profile that maximizes share (return) for the set of chosen products (that can include the firm's existing products). This profile can be compared to the best product for a given supplier that does not take into account interactions with the firm's existing products.

4. A Pareto frontier analysis. In most real-world problems the marketing strategist is not only interested in finding the "best" product in terms of (say) return, but also wishes to get some feel

for the tradeoff between return and market share. SIMOPT provides a capability to trace out the (Pareto) frontier of all profiles that are undominated with respect to return and share. The user can then find out what the potential value may be in giving up some amount of return for an increase in market share.

Practical Implications

As we have tried to show, SIMOPT has been designed as a practical model that can be operationalized by market-based, conjoint data. We believe its value lies in its versatility for considering:

- market share and/or profit-return optimization;
- total market and/or individual-segment forecasts;
- sensitivity analysis as well as optimal profile seeking;
- cannibalization issues related to product complementarities and line-extension strategies;
- calibration of results to existing market conditions;
- constrained optimization, through fixing selected attribute levels for any or all suppliers;
- a decision parameter (alpha) that can be used to mimic any of the principal conjoint choice rules (max utility, logit, BTL);
- sequential competitive moves, such as line extensions or competitor actions/reactions; and
- detailed information on who chooses which product under any specified set of conditions.

Like any model, SIMOPT no doubt will be modified and extended as further information about its performance and user reception is obtained. Perhaps its most significant contribution lies in illustrating how current conjoint-based simulators can be extended beyond their traditional application to estimating market shares for a few user-selected profiles.

Additional Features of SIMOPT

There are two additional aspects of the SIMOPT model that are of interest:

1. ALPH, the model used to find the *optimal* value of alpha, and
2. The divide-and-conquer heuristic, used to find optimal products and product lines in SIMOPT.

The ALPH Model

For any value of α, we obtain a set of predicted market shares, $\hat{\Pi}_1(\alpha), ..., \hat{\Pi}_S(\alpha)$. We also assume that we have *external* market shares Π_1, ..., Π_S. The problem is to find α such that the vector $\hat{\Pi} = \hat{\Pi}_1(\alpha), ..., \hat{\Pi}_S(\alpha)$ is as close as possible to $\Pi = (\Pi_1, ..., \Pi_S)$.

There are many possible distance metrics between the probability measures that can be considered. The ones most commonly employed are:

1. chi-squared:

$$d_c(\hat{\Pi},\Pi) = \sum_{s=1}^{S}(\hat{\Pi}_s - \Pi_s)^2 / \Pi_s$$

2. entropy:

$$d_E(\hat{\Pi},\Pi) = \sum_{s=1}^{S}\Pi_s \ln\Pi_s / \hat{\Pi}_s$$

3. Kolmogorov-Smirnov:

$$d_K(\hat{\Pi},\Pi) = \underset{s}{\max}\ |\Pi_s - \hat{\Pi}_s|$$

4. absolute:

$$d_A(\hat{\Pi},\Pi) = \sum_{s=1}^{S}|\Pi_s - \hat{\Pi}_s|$$

The problem is to find the α that minimizes the distance function.

Clearly, if there is an α such that $\hat{\Pi}(\alpha) = \Pi$, then all four distance measures would lead to the same α, since all distances are non-negative and equal to zero when $\Pi = \hat{\Pi}$. When no such α exists, then the choice of an α that minimizes distance depends on the metric that is used. In practice, α does not vary widely across d_c, d_E, d_K and d_A. The differences arise because in comparing α₁ to α₂, $\hat{\Pi}_1(\alpha_1)$ could be closer to Π_1 than $\hat{\Pi}_1(\alpha_2)$, but $\hat{\Pi}_2(\alpha_1)$ could be farther from Π_2 than $\hat{\Pi}_2(\alpha_2)$. Which is viewed as superior would then depend on the metric.

Since there is no strong theoretical basis for choosing among d_C, d_E, d_K and d_A, on practical grounds we choose the distance metric that has useful mathematical properties. It can be shown that d_C, d_K and d_A are *not* unimodal in α. Although the value of α that minimizes each of the three distance metrics can be found by a numerical search procedure, this is time-consuming and not very elegant. In contrast, it can be shown that d_E is convex in α so there is only *one* optimum.

The Divide-and-Conquer Heuristic

To find the best product profile, conditional or specified competitive product configurations, SIMOPT employs a divide-and-conquer heuristic. We now discuss the nature of this heuristic.

In implementing the heuristic, we want to find the levels $(i_1^*,...,i_M^*)$ that maximize share or return for the supplier of interest, possibly in an environment in which the supplier has more than one product in the product class. The objective we want to maximize can be written in the form $\Phi(i_1, ..., i_M)$, where i_m denotes the attribute level for attribute m; $m = 1, ..., M$.

The levels $(i_1^*,...,i_M^*)$ that maximize Φ can be found by complete enumeration. The number of possible solutions is $B = \prod_{m=1}^{M} L_m$. In practice, B could be large, although with high-speed computing if $b \leq 1,000,000$, this is certainly a viable approach. Alternatively, we can divide the attributes into subsets. To see how this approach works, assume that we divide the M attributes into two subsets, so that attributes 1 to M_1 define subset 1 and attributes $(M_1 + 1)$ to M define subset 2.

We begin the process by finding levels $(i_1, ..., i_M)$ that are reasonable first approximations to $(i_1^*,...,i_M^*)$. One approach is to average the partworths within each level of each attribute and choose the level, within attribute, that has the highest average. Label these levels as $[i_1^{(0)},...,i_M^{(0)}]$. We find $[i_1^{(p)},...,i_M^{(p)}]$ from $[i_1^{(p-1)},...,i_M^{(p-1)}]$ in two steps:

1. Find $[i_1^{(p)},...,i_M^{(p)}]$ by choosing the levels for attributes 1, ..., M_1 that maximize $\Phi[i_1,...,i_{M1},i_{M_1+1}^{(p-1)},...,i_M^{(p-1)}]$.

2. Find $[i_1^{(p)},...,i_M^{(p)}]$ by choosing the levels for attributes $M_1 + 1$, ..., M_1 that maximize $\Phi[i_1^{(p)},...,i_{M_1}^{(p)},i_{M_1+1},...,i_M]$.

If $\Phi(i^{(p)}) = \Phi(i^{(p-1)})$, then stop. Since Φ cannot decrease at each iteration, this approach leads to a local optimum.

Of course, the procedure can be extended to an arbitrary number of subsets. It should be pointed out that the effect of increasing the number of subsets is to reduce the amount of computation at the risk of not finding the global optimum.

There is no foolproof way of knowing whether this "divide-and-conquer" approach has produced the global optimum except by checking it with complete enumeration. In applications where we have applied this technique, the optimum *was* found. If we were to simulate data that are independently and identically distributed, then, intuitively, divide-and-conquer would work very well. Environments in which there are many interactions among attributes are ones in which the divide-and-conquer heuristic could potentially lead to a suboptimal solution.

SIMOPT is designed so that the user can specify the subset compositions. In general, subsets should be formed so as to minimize the correlation of partworths *across* subsets of attributes. Intuitively, attributes that are more closely related to each other should be assigned to the same subset and attributes that are more nearly independent should be assigned to different subsets. This suggests that we might like to cluster attributes based on distances between attributes.

We need a distance measure between attributes that reflects the extent to which individual's partworths for levels of one attribute are related to the partworths for levels of the other attribute. We propose two reasonable, albeit ad hoc, measures. Consider two attributes with I and J levels, respectively. We can create an $I \times J$ contingency table with entry n_{ij} indicating the number of individuals whose preferred levels are i for the first attribute and j for the second attribute. The distance between the two attributes can be defined as a $(1 - \text{p-value})$ of the chi-squared test; we use P-values for calibration when the number of levels differ across attributes and a $(1 - \text{p-value})$ so that similar attributes have small distances.

Another possibility is to create an $I \times J$ matrix where the (i, j) entry is the squared correlation between the partworths of level i of the first attribute and level j of the second attribute. Then, $1 - \overline{R}^2$ defines another measure where $\overline{R}^2$ is the average of the IJ entries in this matrix. (In either case the SIMOPT model contains an option where the user can choose the make-up of the subsets in the divide-and-conquer heuristic; as noted above, the subsets can be designed in several different ways.)

The SIMACT Model

The SIMACT model represents an extension of SIMOPT that has the following features:

- The researcher can estimate (via hierarchical Bayes) two-way interactions for the non-price attributes.
- The user can also factorially generate various sets of scenario descriptions, against which one can compute optimal returns for any selected scenario.
- SIMACT includes confidence levels around selected output measures (e.g., market shares, returns) of interest.

In so doing, SIMACT also maintains all of the features found in SIMOPT.

The SIMDYN Model

As described above, the SIMOPT and SIMACT models are basically static optimizing models where competitor's product profiles and consumers' tastes (i.e., partworths) are assumed to remain fixed over the firm's planning horizon. SIMDYN (SIMulation via DYNamic modeling) extends the SIMOPT model to explicitly consider a sequence of competitive moves and countermoves. (See Choi, DeSarbo, and Harker 1990; Hauser and Simmie 1988; and Hauser and Shugan 1983.)

In addition, SIMDYN allows the user to input differential attribute-level costs, by competitor, and to fix certain attribute levels (e.g., brand name). SIMDYN maintains a running record of each competitor's optimal profile (when it makes a move) and associated market shares and returns (i.e., contributions to overhead and profits) for all competitors at any stage in the sequence.

Thus, SIMDYN is concerned with game theoretic modeling in which a group of competitors are allowed to sequentially choose product/price formulations, based on strategies adopted by earlier competitive moves. The main practical use of SIMDYN so far has been in the examination of those attributes and levels, for a given competitor (i.e., "your" supplier), that are reasonably robust to rational competitive retaliations.

How can conjoint analysis of two or more competitors be brought together into a model of competitive interactions? The key idea is the concept of Nash equilibrium. To understand Nash equilibrium, imagine two or more competing suppliers, each independently trying to formulate its competitive strategy to maximize its own profits, given a specific set of competitive products, market strategies, and consumers' preferences. Since the market shares of competing products would usually be affected by a given firm's strategy, we would expect their attribute levels to change in response to the initiating firm's actions. The Nash equilibrium represents a market situation (perhaps unattainable) where no individual firm can make further gains for itself by *unilaterally* departing from the Nash equilibrium.

There are two iterative problems available for finding a Nash equilibrium: simultaneous and sequential. In the latter case, players (competitors) select strategies, in turn, in a predetermined order. We believe that the sequential approach is a more realistic portrayal of real action/reaction sequences; this is the approach considered here.

To answer these questions we construct a small, fictitious example involved three competing firms: Alpha, Beta, and Gamma. However, our account is based on real conjoint data obtained from an actual study of cellular phone buyers. For illustrative purposes, we assume the role of Alpha's management.

Table 7-3. **List of Attributes and Levels in Cellular Phone Application**

Attribute	Level	Features (Absent = 1 or Present = 2)
Initial Price		High-strength battery (15 hours)
$125	1	9-number speed dialing
$175	2	Programmable for two different
$250	3	numbers
		Cigarette lighter battery charger
		Large-size (100 numbers) memory
		Portable car-roof antenna
		Low-battery warning beep
		Electronic lock
		Missed-call counter
		Mute function (for privacy)
		Extra (rechargeable) battery included
Brand		
Alpha	1	
Beta	2	
Gamma	3	
Warranty		
3 years	1	
1 year	2	
Weight		
7.5 ounces	1	
8.5 ounces	2	
9.5 ounces	3	

A Study Using the SIMDYN Model

Alpha's management commissioned a hybrid conjoint study among potential cellular phone buyers in the southwestern United States. Prospective buyers were defined as those who expressed interest in purchasing (primarily for personal use) a cellular phone during the next six months. Interviewing was conducted via a telephone-mail-telephone procedure. Initial screening of qualified respondents was done by telephone and followed by a mailing of questionnaires and conjoint materials. This, in turn, was followed by the main telephone call in which the conjoint exercise was conducted and responses were recorded. A total of 600 questionnaires were completed.

Color photographs and detailed descriptions of each telephone feature were included with the questionnaire booklet. The list of 15 attributes and their levels is shown in Table 7-3. Respondents' self-explicated desirability ratings on each attribute's level were obtained, along with a constant-sum importance point assignment across the 15 attributes.

Following the self-explicated tasks, each respondent received eight profile cards drawn from a master orthogonal design of 32; each set of eight cards represented a balanced block from the set of 32. After examining all eight cards, the respondent sorted them into three graded piles: least desirable, neutral, most desirable. Profiles were then ranked within subgroup. Starting from the top-ranked profile, the respondent rated each of the ranked profiles on a 0-100 likelihood-of-purchase scale. The respondents then answered some demographic questions. Conjoint (averaged) partworths are shown in Figure 7-1.

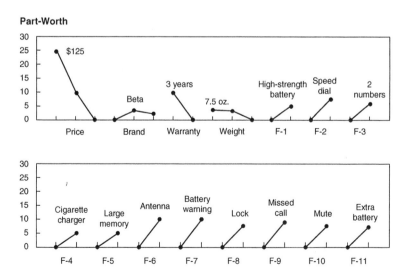

Figure 7-1. **Partworths for Convex Combination Model**

Experimental Assumptions

There are many factors that could influence competitive responses. In this experiment, we focused on two key variables: the cost structure of competitors and their participation in the market. For each of these variables, we examine two different assumptions:

1. Cost structure
   a. All competitors are assumed to have the *same* variable costs (viz., those costs associated with Alpha).
   b. Competitors are allowed to have different variable costs; see Table 7-4.
2. Active vs. passive participation
   a. All competitors are assumed to be active, that is, participate in the action/reaction sequence.
   b. One (out of three) competitors is assumed to be passive and does *not* change its product-price profile in response to others' moves.

Attribute-level variable costs were estimated (crudely) by the sponsoring firm. Net prices per unit are shown first, followed by variable costs per unit for each attribute level. Under the initially-assumed *equal* cost condition, Alpha's cost data apply to all three competitors. Table 7-4 shows the cost structures.

Table 7-4. Estimated Attribute-Level Cost Structures

Attribute	Levels		
	Alpha	Beta	Gamma
Net price	75; 105; 150	75; 105; 150	65; 95; 140
Brand	0; 0; 0	0; 0; 0	0; 0; 0
Warranty	-10; 0	-15; 0	-5; 0
Weight	-20; -10; 0	-30; -15; 0	-15; -5; 0
Battery	0; -2	0; -2	0; -2
Speed dialing	0; -2	0; -2	0; -2
Program numbers	0; -4	0; -2	0; -2
Battery charger	0; -5	0; -2	0; -4
Larger memory	0; -5	0; -5	0; -5
Antenna	0; -8	0; -7	0; -5
Low-battery beep	0; -5	0; -7	0; -5
Lock	0; -5	0; -7	0; -10
Missed call	0; -9	0; -8	0; -10
Mute function	0; -5	0; -2	0; -10
Extra battery	0; -10	0; -5	0; -15

The SIMDYN model was first applied to the equal costs and active participation case. There are six different sequences by which competitive moves can be initiated and reacted to, that is, six permutations. We started with the sequence: Alpha, Beta, Gamma, and continued through the five remaining sequences. A Nash equilibrium was achieved when three moves in a row resulted in the same shares and returns.

A Nash equilibrium was found in all six sequences, although the number of moves required to reach equilibrium varied from as few as 6 to as many as 11. By sequence, the number of moves required for equilibrium were:

Sequence	Number of Moves
Alpha, Beta, Gamma	7
Alpha, Gamma, Beta	6
Beta, Gamma, Alpha	6
Beta, Alpha, Gamma	8
Gamma, Alpha, Beta	11
Gamma, Beta, Alpha	9

As noted, when Alpha initiates the sequence, equilibrium occurs with as few as six moves. When Gamma initiates the sequence, as many as 11 moves are needed before equilibrium is reached.

Table 7-5 shows the history of the equilibrium process for one sequence: Alpha, Beta, Gamma. (In all cases, we permit all attributes to vary, except brand name.) We first examine the initial conditions and note that shares for Alpha, Beta, and Gamma are, respectively, 20.4%, 33.7%, and 45.9%, with associated unit returns of $6.73, $17.53, and $13.31. These results correspond to the initial profile conditions of:

Alpha	11231
Beta	22112
Gamma	13231

where 11231 denotes $125, Alpha, one-year warranty, 9.5 oz., and no high-strength battery, as shown in Table 7-5.

We next optimize Alpha's profile, conditioned on fixed profiles for Beta and Gamma. As Table 7-5 shows, the best levels for Alpha for the first five attributes are 31132, which, respectively, are $150, Alpha, three-year warranty, 9.5 oz., and high-strength battery. As it turns out, in all cases, the optimal levels for the ten 2-state attributes, 6 through 15, are the *presence* of the feature (coded 2). We also note that when the Alpha profile is optimized, the share for Alpha increases to 61.1%, with an associated return of $48.90.

We next shift from Alpha's perspective to Beta's. Given Alpha's newly optimized product, how should Beta optimize its own product? The process is updated as the sequence continues. Finally, we note that at move 5, the Nash

Table 7-5. **Equilibrium History Based on the Alpha, Beta, Gamma Sequence (Equal Costs)**

Move Initiator	Brand	Profile: First Five Attributes	Market Shares	Returns	Sum
Initial	Alpha	11231	20.4%	$	
Conditions	Beta	22112	33.7	6.73	
	Gamma	13231	45.9	17.53	37.56
				13.31	
Alpha	Alpha	31132	61.1	48.90	
	Beta	(best)	15.1	7.84	
	Gamma		23.8	6.90	63.64
Beta	Alpha		34.2	27.39	
	Beta	32132	44.1	35.30	
	Gamma		21.6	6.27	68.69
Gamma	Alpha		26.2	20.95	
	Beta		29.5	23.63	
	Gamma	33122	44.3	31.01	75.59
Alpha	Alpha	31112	38.6	23.13	
	Beta		25.0	19.99	
	Gamma		36.3	25.52	58.64
Beta	Alpha		33.0	19.81	
	Beta	32112	37.8	22.67	Equilibrium
	Gamma		29.2	23.35	
Gamma	Alpha		33.0	19.81	
	Beta		37.8	22.67	Equilibrium
	Gamma	33132	29.2	23.35	
Alpha	Alpha	31112	33.0	19.81	
	Beta		37.8	22.67	Equilibrium
	Gamma		29.2	23.35	

Note: The *initial* (starting) conditions include battery strength as the fifth attribute (which is a 2-level feature). As the analysis turned out, for each of the eleven 2-level features, level 2 of each feature was *always* preferred to level 1; that is, having the feature was always preferred to not having it.

equilibrium is initiated; and at moves 6 and 7, the solution has stabilized with returns of $19.81, $22.67, and $23.35, respectively, for Alpha, Beta, and Gamma.

It is worth noting that at equilibrium, all three brands are charging the highest price ($150). All three brands also offer a three-year warranty, but Alpha's and Beta's weight is 7.5 oz. while Gamma's optimal weight is 9.5 oz.

Note that the optimal profile after competitive interactions are considered is different from the initial optimal profile. As shown in Table 7-5, Alpha's short-term optimal profile (31132) changes to 31112 at equilibrium, where the weight changes from 9.5 oz. to 7.5 oz. We also note that Beta's initially optimized profile (32132) moves to 32112 at equilibrium, and Gamma's initially optimized profile (33122) moves to 33132 at equilibrium. Hence, optimal weight appears to be sensitive to the sequence of moves.

We conclude that for these conditions each competitor should offer all 11 features, a three-year warranty, and a $150 price. However, optimal phone weight still varies by brand. It is worth noting that at initial conditions, the returns vary relatively widely, with a low of $6.73 (Alpha) to a high of $17.53 (Beta). However, at equilibrium, the returns are much less varied; Gamma is now highest at $23.35.

The Unequal Costs Case

A similar analysis was conducted for the unequal costs case (Table 7-6). Starting conditions were the same as before; the only characteristic that

Table 7-6. Equilibrium History Based on the Alpha, Beta, Gamma Sequence (Unequal Costs)

Move Initiator	Brand	Profile: First Five Attributes	Market Shares	Returns	Sum
Initial	Alpha	11231	20.4%	$ 6.73	
Conditions	Beta	22112	33.7	15.17	
	Gamma	13231	45.9	8.26	30.16
Alpha	Alpha	31132	61.1	48.90	
	Beta	(best)	15.1	6.78	
	Gamma		23.8	4.28	59.96
Beta	Alpha		34.7	27.39	
	Beta	32122	44.1	35.95	
	Gamma		21.6	3.89	67.13
Gamma	Alpha		26.2	20.95	
	Beta		29.5	25.39	
	Gamma	33122	44.3	26.13	72.47
Alpha	Alpha	31112	38.6	23.13	
	Beta		25.0	21.49	
	Gamma		36.5	21.52	Equilibrium
Beta	Alpha		38.6	23.13	
	Beta	32132	25.0	21.49	Equilibrium
	Gamma		36.5	21.52	
Gamma	Alpha		38.6	23.13	
	Beta		25.0	21.49	Equilibrium
	Gamma	33122	31.5	21.52	

varied was the assumption of different attribute-level costs across brands. Again, a Nash equilibrium was reached over all six sequences of moves. Table 7-6 shows the results from the sequence Alpha, Beta, Gamma.

As noted in Table 7-6, equilibrium was reached after six moves. In comparing Table 7-6 to Table 7-5, we note that under initial conditions, the returns for Beta and Gamma differ from the equal costs case because of the different cost structure assumptions. Although not shown in the table, we found, as before, that it was optimal to have all 10 features. The equilibrium profile for Alpha (31112) is the same as it was in the equal costs case of Table 7-5. The equilibrium profile for Beta (32132) differs, however; the optimal weight is now 9.5 oz. (rather than 7.5 oz.). The equilibrium profile for Gamma (33122) also differs in that the optimal weight is now 8.5 oz. (rather than 9.5 oz.). We also note that the initially optimum profile for Alpha changes from a weight of 9.5 oz. to a weight of 7.5 oz. at equilibrium.

Finally, we again see less disparity in returns across the three brands when the Nash equilibrium returns are compared to those associated with the initial conditions. It is also interesting to note that at equilibrium, Alpha's return is the highest of the three, even though it was lowest at the initial conditions stage.

The Passive Products Case

Suppose one competitor does not actively respond to the moves of its rivals? Companies sometimes choose to ignore moves of competitors or, if recognized, fail to respond to them. The analysis was repeated with the assumption that two companies were active and one was passive. Illustratively, we look at only the unequal cost condition. Again, Nash equilibria were obtained.

Table 7-7 shows the results for active products Alpha and Beta, and passive product, Gamma, under the unequal cost condition. An equilibrium is reached after only four moves. In this case, the players converge to an equilibrium more quickly if one player is passive. The profile of products may also differ. We use the same starting conditions as those shown in Table 7-6. At equilibrium, Alpha's profile (first five attributes) is the same as that shown in Table 7-6. Such is not the case for Beta. In Table 7-7, Beta's optimal weight is 8.5 oz. while in Table 7-6 its optimal weight is 9.5 oz. Apparently, the passivity of Gamma has an effect on the optimal profile for Beta (but not on Alpha).

Table 7-7. Equilibrium History Based on the Alpha, Beta Sequence
(Gamma Passive, Unequal Costs)

Move Initiator	Brand	Profile: First Five Attributes	Market Shares	Returns	Sum
Initial	Alpha	11231	20.4%	$ 6.73	
Conditions	Beta	22112	33.7	15.17	
	Gamma	13231	45.9	8.26	30.16
Alpha	Alpha	31132	61.1	48.90	
	Beta	(best)	15.1	6.78	
	Gamma		23.8	4.28	59.96
Beta	Alpha		34.2	27.39	
	Beta	32132	44.1	37.95	
	Gamma		21.6	3.89	69.23
Alpha	Alpha	31112	41.5	29.04	
	Beta		38.2	32.84	
	Gamma		20.3	3.66	Equilibrium
Beta	Alpha		41.5	29.04	
	Beta	32122	38.2	32.84	Equilibrium
	Gamma		20.3	3.66	

Conclusions

As illustrated by the case just discussed, recognizing the potential moves of competitors can have an impact on optimal product design. In the cellular telephone case, when competitor moves are considered, the optimal products are often different from those in the initial optimization. In addition, the SIMDYN model permits managers to optimize their product under a variety of assumptions, allowing them to anticipate a variety of competitive situations (such as different cost structures) or competitive moves (such as a passive competitor). For this case, interactions among competitors did, in fact, converge to Nash equilibria. The speed of convergence, however, depended on the order in which companies made their moves.

In the complex and dynamic world where consumer preferences do change, where individual competitors may not try to optimize their strategies, and where new firms can enter and old firms can exit, it should be realized that the Nash equilibrium is essentially a theoretical concept, not a practical reality. Still, as many theoretical concepts have demonstrated, the Nash equilibrium concept can provide a useful way to study real competitive behavior by providing a rational norm and framework for examining a firm's strengths and weaknesses, under the concept's assumptions. (Indeed, the laws of physics are idealizations as well; their predictions of empirical phenomena are always subject to statistical fluctuations.)

In addition, the cost of making attribute-level changes, internal constraints on which attribute levels can be changed, and the difficulty of accurately measuring attribute-level variable costs present serious research challenges. Also, more study is needed of the so-called first-move advantage and the possible muted effect of "me-too" followers that try to emulate innovative product designs.

Even with these limitations (many of which apply to any model), this dynamic approach to conjoint analysis can offer a powerful tool for developing strategy. At the minimum, it can point out those components of one's current brand profile that are most resistant to competitors' retaliations. Just as earlier work in conjoint analysis has proved very valuable to marketers, this extended model offers an important tool for the study of competitive interplay.

PRODUCT BUNDLING: A NEW AREA FOR APPLYING CONJOINT ANALYSIS

An additional new area in which a conjoint-like approach can be used is *bundling*. Specifically, in addition to the main attributes that form the product, one adds features that can be present or absent. For example, in long-distance calling plans, besides the main contract, there are added features such as call-waiting, unlimited minutes in a certain geographical area, calling-friend plants, etc. Besides being able to purchase individual features at a specified price, a customer is often given the option of purchasing a subset of features at a price that is lower than the aggregate costs of each of the separate features.

There are three phases for determining optimal bundles and their associated costs. The first phase is the questionnaire instrument. In this phase, an individual's "willingness to pay" for each feature needs to be elicited. One approach is to simply ask the respondent directly, "How much extra would you pay for feature x?" There are two problems with this approach. First, there is a tendency for individuals to understate the amount they are willing to pay. Second, if an individual has a budget constraint, then this will not be captured by direct questioning of the amount each individual is willing to pay for each feature separately.

An alternative approach is to present bundles of features in a conjoint framework. Each of the features is viewed as an attribute with two levels: present or absent. Hence, a profile that specifies the levels for each feature is equivalently representing a bundle of these features consisting of those features that are present. Prices can also be embedded, thereby determining, through an appropriate estimation method, an individual's willingness to pay.

The second phase of the analysis is to estimate the parameters. One parametric form assumes that one's willingness to pay for the features can be characterized by a multivariate normal distribution with some unknown covariance matrix. A budget constraint can then be included as an additional parameter, based on a censoring model. Since it would be difficult to estimate the parameters separately at the individual level, a hierarchical Bayes approach can be employed.

Finally, in the third stage, the optimal bundles and associated prices can be determined from the underlying multivariate normal behavior for willingness-to-pay variables. In a seminal paper, Schmalensee (1984) considered the case of two features. An area for further research is to extend the problem to more than two features in the pure bundling and mixed bundling (features can also be purchased separately in addition to in bundles) cases.

NEW OPPORTUNITIES FOR THE
APPLICATION OF CONJOINT ANALYSIS

Conjoint analysis is far from becoming moribund. As shown in Chapter 5 (Table 5-3, p. 130), high-profile applications of conjoint have included both consumer and industrial goods and a host of services: credit cards, cellular phones, employee benefit packages, time share units, and overnight letter/package delivery, to name a few.

To illustrate the nature of conjoint applications, we discuss one study in more detail: The E-Z Pass Electronic Toll Collection System, originally developed for New York and New Jersey and later extended to Delaware, Maryland, Pennsylvania, and Massachusetts.

The E-Z PASS Electronic Toll System

The E-Z Pass case is noteworthy in that it involved high technology applied to a common and pervasive problem: traffic congestion. The project also had a fair amount of drama – the study team's overseeing committee did not always see eye-to-eye with one another or, for that matter, with the study team, as well.

The Product

The E-Z Pass electronic toll collection (ETC) works like this: Commuters use an electronic "tag"' (transponder) about the size of an audio tape cassette which is attached to a vehicle's inside windshield. As an equipped vehicle approaches a toll lane, an antenna alongside the lane reads the customer's vehicle and account information embedded in the tag. Using high frequency radio waves, the technology sends the information to an in-lane computer that checks the driver's data against a database of valid tags and active accounts, deducts the appropriate toll from the customer's account, and approves passage or raises a tollgate to allow the vehicle to pass through the toll plaza.

Each commuter's tag emits a signal assigned specifically to him or her. This enables the commuter's use of all ETC-equipped facilities to be tracked and logged. ETC users set up a prepaid account, which is debited for each use of an ETC-equipped roadway, bridge, or tunnel. (The tags are particularly advantageous to fleet operators who otherwise would have to advance cash to drivers for tolls or engage in time-consuming cash reimbursement.) Each tag contains an identification number, data identifying the issuing agency, tag type, a description of the vehicle, and other agency-specific data. The tag ID, agency ID, and tag type are encoded by the vendor and cannot be altered, The tag is based on read-write technology capable of storing highway entry and exit points for toll calculations in closed systems (i.e., where the toll is based on distance traveled). Vehicle gross weight (for toll calculations based on weight, or for checking on maximum highway weight) also can be obtained.

Issues to be Investigated

Ultimately, seven major design attributes, with varying numbers of levels, were selected as most likely to benefit from the research with potential users. They were:

1. How many facilities would the user need to open an E-Z Pass account and, therefore, how many periodic invoices would the user receive (two levels)?
2. How and where would a user apply and pay for a new E-Z Pass account (six levels)?
3. How many lanes would be available for E-Z Pass at a typical toll plaza and how would they be controlled (five levels)?
4. Would the E-Z Pass tag be transferable to different vehicles (two levels)?

5. What would be the acquisition cost (if any) for E-Z Pass and would there be a periodic service charge (four levels)?
6. What would the toll price be with E-Z Pass (four levels)?
7. What other uses, if any, such as parking at local airports or purchasing gasoline, would commuters find valuable for using E-Z Pass (three levels)?

Given the complexity of the design, a hybrid conjoint analysis model was chosen that incorporated a fractional factorial design. (A full factorial would have resulted in 5,760 possible combinations of products $[2 \times 6 \times 5 \times 2 \times 4 \times 4 \times 3]$ – obviously an impractical number on which to gather preferences.) With this design, only 49 product descriptions were required.

Commuter Recruitment and Questionnaire Administration

Commuters (contacted through RDD telephone interviews) were informed of the survey and asked if they would participate. While a modest gratuity was offered (the opportunity to win one of 10 U.S. Savings Bonds each valued at $100), the main inducement was providing them with an opportunity to voice their preferences for improvements in the area's automobile commuting situation. More than 6,500 potential participants were recruited within a three-week period.

The centerpiece of the survey was a videotape demonstration, accompanied by a set of survey materials to be examined and thoughtfully responded to. Instead of simply placing the materials in an envelope, the research team decided to "dimensionalize" the kit. A self-mailing box was designed with customized graphics and the E-Z Pass logo. The special illustration and the box helped ensure that the material would be examined and the survey completed. Kits were mailed to all 6,500 commuters recruited for the survey.

In addition to the videotape, the kit contained a glossary of terms (to serve as a reference for participants as they answered the questions), a questionnaire measuring self-explicated importance weights for the major options, and an envelope containing the eight scenario cards, where one card was a common reference card, appearing in each profile set. The sequence of the self-administered interview was clearly indicated in three steps on the inside flap of the box. Participants were asked to complete the importance rating questions first, then proceed to rate each of the eight scenario cards in terms of their likelihood of using the service.

To ensure that data were collected from a maximum number of participants, responses were collected by telephone, rather than relying on a mail return. Participants were given the choice of either waiting to be contacted by a telephone interviewer, or calling a toll-free number at a convenient time for them to complete the interview. Of the 6,500 commuters recruited, 3,369 respondents successfully completed interviews within three weeks. The 52% response rate was considered quite satisfactory, given the complexity of the survey.

Conjoint Results

Results were analyzed at three levels: the total sample level (a view of the New York-New Jersey commuter), the agency level (an agency's typical commuter), and the facility level (the user of a bridge or tunnel). Some differences emerged at the facility level (probably as a result of commuters' adaptation to the different operational and pricing practices instituted over the years at particular facilities). At the agency level, however, only a few significant differences emerged. This finding allowed the committee to endorse an area-wide configuration as long as it was practical.

Among the seven design options, the option: "How many lanes would be available and how would they be controlled?" was judged by commuters as the most important. (See Table 7-8). This result was not anticipated by the committee members for the Interagency Group (IAG); the committee had thought that commuters would be more concerned with the "acquisition costs for the tag" option. The emergence of the "available lanes" option was interesting for another strategic reason: Some of the implementation levels of this option would have negated many of the promised advantages of E-Z Pass, had the system been implemented in these ways. Clearly, the high priority that commuters assigned to this attribute showed they understood the full benefits of the new system and did not want them compromised. The committee responded by placing a high priority on the implementation levels that were most desired. Table 7-8 shows the derived relative importance of each of the seven attributes. Price did enter as a concern, but in a more practical sense. The price of the toll with E-Z Pass was the second most important attribute. But acquisition cost for E-Z Pass and a periodic service charge were relegated to the middle of the priority listing. This ordering clearly showed commuters' willingness to undertake reasonable costs to enjoy the potential benefits of the E-Z Pass system.

Table 7-8. **Judged Importance of E-Z Pass Design Attributes**

Attribute (Feature)	Importance Rating
How many lanes would be available and how would they be controlled?	21%
Price of the toll with E-Z Pass	18%
How and where a user would apply and pay for a new E-Z Pass account	17%
The acquisition cost for E-Z Pass and any periodic service charges	15%
Number of E-Z Pass accounts necessary/number of periodic invoices received	13%
Would the E-Z Pass tag be transferable to different vehicles	12%
Other potential uses for the E-Z Pass tag	4%
	100%

The Forecast

As the process of working with the conjoint design placed committee members in a more "customer-centered" perspective, they began to speculate about the preferences that consumers might have for the levels within attributes. They also became more aware of the need to estimate the demand for the E-Z Pass system. Substantial capital investments needed to be made, not only for the purchase of electronic tags for distribution to users, but also for equipping toll gates for the hundreds of toll plazas operated by these agencies.

As results were presented and discussed, the most pressing issue for committee members was, "How many commuters will adopt E-Z Pass within the first year?" The research team had planned on answering this question in two ways: through use of a simulation model, and from answers to verbal purchase questions asked of each survey participant. The SIMPRO simulation model, developed by Green and Krieger, was first employed to produce overall service adoption estimates. SIMPRO requires the researcher to specify a configuration for the product tested. With this configuration, the model then predicts an adoption rate, using a function of the sum of each respondent's partworths for the attributes.

When the SIMPRO model was employed in the E-Z Pass project, very attractive adoption rates, on the order of a 45% penetration, were predicted. The committee was hesitant to trust these high rates, which essentially indicated that one out of every two area commuters would apply for an E-Z

Pass account. Still, the research team had confidence in the model. Fortunately, verbal purchase data were also available, so the research team turned to this source for corroboration.

Two versions of the verbal purchase data were used: the top two boxes (ratings of 10 or 9 on the "definitely would subscribe" scale) and top box only. While the verbal purchase rates were somewhat lower, either version still seemed too high to the committee. The high acceptance scores were heartening, but both the committee and the research team wanted to be certain they were valid and not the result of "demand bias" (the willingness of respondents to comply with their perceptions of a test's intention or an experimenter's hoped-for outcome). Ultimately the scores were factored down, using close to a "worst-case scenario" which was fed into the simulator as an indication of the lowest likely level of interest.

What's the E-Z Pass Penetration in 2002?

In 1999, the penetration rate of E-Z Pass approached 45 percent. In 2002, at the time of this writing, penetration rates have either been sustained or somewhat increased. Interestingly, this penetration rate was achieved with few expenditures on either advertising or promotion.

Some Unintended Consequences

Although the technological aspects of E-Z Pass continue to be lauded by most commuters, New Jersey's former governor Whitman has recently been excoriated by the state's Democrats, regarding her handling of the *financial* aspects of E-Z Pass.

In 2002, the new (Democratic) governor, James McGreevy, announced that E-Z Pass now faces a huge deficit. Unlike the governor of Massachusetts, former governor Whitman did not want the state to pay its share. She depended on the $25 fines of toll cheats to finance much of the system.

In 2001, the plan called for $101.8 million in fines; only $10.3 million was actually collected. With one million users – 15 percent more than expected – customer service costs also soared. The result: New Jersey E-Z Pass now loses money on each new user. Hence, E-Z Pass has turned out to be a technical success but a financial embarrassment.

An additional prediction: E-Z Pass discounts will soon disappear. To add to McGreevy's troubles, in the future, $50 million will be needed to replace the system's battery depletions in 2004. Such are the vagaries of modeling large-scale governmental developments.

REFERENCES

Choi, S. C., DeSarbo, W., and Harker, P. T. (1990), "Product positioning under price competition," *Management Science*, 35 (February), 175-199.

Hauser, J. R., and Simmie, P. (1988), "Profit maximizing perceptual positions: An integrated theory for the selection of product features and price," *Management Science*, 27 (1), 33-56.

Hauser, J. R., and Shugan, S. M. (1983), "Defensive marketing strategies," *Marketing Science*, 2, 319-360.

Schmalensee, R. (1984), "Gaussian demand and commodity bundling", *Journal of Business*, 57 (1), S 211-S 230.

Chapter 8

A 20+ Years' Retrospective on Choice Experiments

Jordan Louviere, *School of Marketing*
Deborah J. Street, *Department of Mathematical Sciences*
Leonie Burgess, *Department of Mathematical Sciences*
University of Technology, Sydney, Australia

Paul Green inspired many of us who work in conjoint analysis and related areas, such as stated preference discrete choice experiments, and all of us who undertake research in understanding and modeling preferences have benefited from his work. Knowing Paul Green, his impact and contributions will continue during his "retirement." Our thanks to him for so many of the advances that we now often take for granted, but without which we would not be where we are today.

In tribute to Paul Green, this paper provides a brief history of choice experiments, how the results of choice experiments relate to real market behavior, and progress that has been made in the design of choice experiments. We conclude by discussing several aspects of choice experiments, such as the interactions of subjects with experiments, model complexity and the scientific understanding of choice behavior compared with mere predictions of choices.

A BRIEF HISTORY OF CHOICE EXPERIMENTS

Choice experiments have a long and distinguished history, beginning with Thurstone's (1927) seminal contributions to random utility theory (RUT) and the method of paired comparisons. Luce's (1959) book on multiple choices not only promoted the scientific study of multiple choices, but also underscored the limitations of paired comparisons, providing a new and compelling reason to study and understand choices among multiple options.

Looking back on the early years, it is somewhat surprising that so many empirical choice studies were designed in an ad hoc manner for so many years, often by using ad hoc combinations of pairs and triples or triples and quadruples. That is, there was little recognition that choice experiments could be designed like other statistical experiments, which would allow researchers to conduct appropriate hypothesis tests as well as provide more efficient estimates of the parameters of the models of interest.

Indeed, by the early 1980s Randy Batsell and his collaborators (Batsell and Lodish 1981; Batsell and Polking 1985) had recognized that if there were M total choice objects/options, there were exactly 2^m possible sets of choice sets, including the null set. However, surprisingly, there seemed to be little recognition that this was a combinatorial problem that could be mapped into well-known experimental design solutions. Louviere appears to be the first to have recognized this link between the design of choice sets and experimental design(s), which led to the Louviere and Woodworth (1983) paper on the design and analysis choice experiments.

In particular, Louviere and Woodworth noted that choice experiments that were characterized by first designing m objects/options and then using some design strategy to put the objects into sets, could be treated as a problem of selecting a suitable fractional factorial design from the general class of 2^m factorial designs. Unfortunately, they also showed that this design strategy generally leads to experiments in which numbers and compositions of choice options vary from set to set, which has the limitation that as the number of options, m, increases, the average set size (or number of options per set) increases. The latter can lead to large, practically unmanageable set sizes.

To deal with this limitation, Louviere and Woodworth proposed what they called "fixed choice set" designs that could be created by random assignment of designed attribute profiles (treatments) to a fixed number of overarching (labeled) choice options or by treating all attributes of all choice options as a collective factorial and selecting suitable fractions from that collective factorial (called an L^{mk} design approach – e.g., see Louviere, Hensher, and Swait 2000). Of course, fixed choice set designs also can be made from balanced or partially balanced incomplete block designs, solving the problem of set sizes increasing with m, as discussed by Bunch, Louviere, and Anderson (1996).

Early Applications of "Fixed Choice Set"

Concomitant with the development of designed choice experiments by Louviere and associates in the late 1970s and early 1980s was their application to obtain data to estimate choice models and forecast market behavior. The first applications of this approach were in Australia in 1978-

1980, followed shortly thereafter by applications at the University of Iowa in 1980-1981. The advances in understanding and design in Australia were due to the visionary financial support of Dr. Terry Cutler, then VP for Strategy of Telecom Australia (now Telstra) in 1981-1983, and now a member of the Board of CSIRO. Cutler's support led to several high-profile forecasting projects, such as consumer choices of itemized long distance bills at various costs, consumer choices between air travel and various possible configurations and prices of a new ocean-going ferry between mainland Australia and Tasmania, and worker choices among possible residential options for a new diamond mine in Western Australia. These projects yielded accurate forecasts of actual choices, which led to considerable interest in the new design and associated modeling and forecasting technology.

Rapid scientific developments in choice modeling occurred from 1983 to 1990, but there was little additional progress in choice experiments. After 1990 papers began to appear that attempted to deal with the many unresolved problems in the original Louviere and Woodworth (1983) approach. For example, Don Anderson and colleagues pioneered designs for the most general choice models in the Generalized Extreme Value family, known as "mother logit" models (Anderson and Wiley 1992; Lazari and Anderson 1994), which are called "availability" or "cross-effects" designs. These designs allow one to estimate the model proposed by McFadden, Tye, and Train (1978), which is a random utility version of the fixed utility model of Batsell and Polking (1985). Several scholars published papers in this genre, including Kuhfeld, Tobias, and Garratt (1994) and Huber and Zwerina (1996).

Minimal vs. Large-Scale Design Strategies: The Search for Statistical Efficiency

Since 1983, many researchers interested in the design of choice experiments have focused on minimal design strategies for model estimation and/or ways to improve the statistical efficiency of estimated models. Looking at this body of work, including the early work of Louviere and Woodworth (1983), it is unclear why researchers focused on design minima, but it may be that many researchers interested in choice experiments also were familiar with or trained in conjoint analysis methods that typically relied on design minima for individual-level model estimation. Of course, it is now obvious that in many, if not most cases, design minima are inappropriate for choice experiments; instead one should try to use the largest design possible for the resources one has available (e.g., Louviere, Hensher, and Swait 2000). One possible exception to the foregoing is the use of minimal designs as a way to study and capture preference heterogeneity, which generally is not necessary, but might make sense in some applications.

More recently, several papers have appeared that propose various ways to design choice experiments to optimize the statistical efficiency of the parameters of assumed models of choice processes, such as Grasshoff, Grossmann, Holling, and Schwabe (2002); Grossmann, Grasshoff, Holling, and Schwabe (2001); Grossmann, Holling, and Schwabe (2002); Grossmann, Holling, Grasshoff, and Schwabe (2002); and Kanninen (2002). Additionally, Street and her colleagues recently derived formal proofs for the efficiency properties of choice experiments that now permit the statistical efficiency of any designs in the general logistic regression family to be compared. Specific examples are discussed in Street, Bunch, and Moore (2001); Street and Burgess (2003); and Burgess and Street (2002). Thus, progress has been and probably will continue to be rapid as interest in this area continues.

RELATING THE RESULTS OF CHOICE EXPERIMENTS TO REAL MARKET BEHAVIOR

Morikawa (1989) revolutionized the way that many researchers in the choice experiment paradigm view their research and the way(s) in which they conduct basic and applied research (see also Ben-Akiva and Morikawa 1990a, 1990b). That is, Morikawa deduced that RUT predicted a link between preferences stated in surveys and experiments and actual market choices and/or behavior. Specifically, if stated and revealed market preferences are the same, the systematic utility component parameters estimated from both sources of preference data should be proportional, and the constant(s) of proportionality should be equal to the ratio(s) of the variance(s) of the respective random utility components. Swait and Louviere (1993) extended this notion to all sources of preference data consistent with RUT (see also Louviere, Hensher, and Swait 1999, 2000; Hensher, Louviere, and Swait 1999). Numerous academic papers since 1991 have tested his deduction in marketing, transport, tourism/leisure, and applied areas of economics; and it is notable that there have been few serious rejections (e.g., see Louviere 2001; Louviere, Meyer, et al. 1999; Louviere, Hensher, and Swait 2000; Louviere, Street, et al. 2002; McFadden 2001).

Despite the considerable empirical evidence suggesting that stated preference methods yield the same estimates of preferences that one obtains from well-conditioned and well-behaved revealed preference data, there is a notable absence of empirical tests of non-choice experiment conjoint methods, and academic marketing researchers in particular seem to have paid little attention to these advances. Thus, there is an urgent need to show that preferences estimated by various preference elicitation methods used in academic marketing research and by marketing research practitioners are consistent with the preferences and behavior of consumers in real markets. For example, Louviere, Fox, and Moore (1993) show that not all elicitation methods provide consistent results, a result also reported recently by Cameron, Poe, Etheir, and Schulze (2002). Interest in stated preference elicitation methods is growing rapidly in many fields; hence, it is important for marketing and other fields to begin to understand which methods are consistent with RUT and by implication, real market behavior, and which are not. Indeed, as of this writing, academic marketing seems to be in danger of surrendering leadership in preference elicitation methods, as it lags behind other fields in testing the external validity of preference elicitation methods in real markets.

In a related vein, it is worth noting that most conjoint and related methods that claim to be able to elicit preferences can be transformed to be consistent with random utility theory (see, e.g., Louviere, Fox, and Moore 1993; Hensher, Louviere, and Swait 1999; Louviere, Hensher, and Swait 1999, 2000). Thus, these preference elicitation methods can be tested against one another on the level playing field created by random utility theory, and more importantly, they can be tested against the real behavior of real consumers in real markets. Hopefully, such tests now will become common, if not required, in the marketing literature, particularly in so far as the theory to undertake them has been available for more than a decade, and the literature associated with the theory and empirical tests of the theory on real market behavior is large and growing.

PROGRESS IN UNDERSTANDING THE STATISTICAL PROPERTIES OF CHOICE EXPERIMENTS

There has been considerable recent progress in understanding the statistical efficiency of choice experiments, and designing optimally efficient choice experiments. For example, in the case of the multinomial logit (MNL) model, D-optimality often has been used as a basis for design comparisons, although other criteria like orthogonality, item balance, level balance, minimal overlap, and utility balance have been used to compare designs.

Orthogonality often is termed "proportional frequency" in mathematics and statistics. Let $N_i [x]$ be the number of times that level x of attribute I appears in the design and let $N_j [y]$ be the number of times that level y of attribute J appears in the design. Let $N_{ij} [x,y]$ be the number of times that levels x and y of attributes I and J appear in a design in the same profile. Attributes I and J are said to be *orthogonal* if $N_{ij} [x,y] = n_i [x] n_j [y] / n$, where there are n profiles in a design, and extensive discussion of arrays of this type can be found in Dey (1985).

Apparently due to Green (1974), *item balance* means that each item appears in a choice set with every other item equally often; Green used this notion to construct choice sets of size 2 based on the blocks of a partially balanced incomplete block design. *Level balance* means that the levels of each attribute occur with equal frequency (so applies only to discrete attributes), an idea commonly used in linear models. *Minimal overlap* is used to indicate that there are as few overlaps of levels as possible for each attribute in each choice set. Thus, if choice sets are of size m and all attributes have $> m$ levels, no level of any attribute is repeated in any choice set. The latter idea apparently is due to Bunch, Louviere, and Anderson (1996), and was subsequently used by Huber and Zwerina (1996). *Utility balance* seeks to improve the information matrix associated with a particular design by designing options in choice sets so that they are as close to one another in attractiveness as possible (e.g., Huber and Zwerina 1996).

Most results for design optimality assume that all attributes have levels chosen from discrete sets of possible levels and focus on D-optimality because it is widely used as a general design optimality criterion. That is, if C is the information matrix of the p parameters that we want to estimate, the *D-efficiency* of any design is given by $[\det(C) \, / \, \det(C)_{\text{optimal}}]^{1/p}$. For choice experiment designs that estimate main effects, $p = k$; for designs that estimate both main effects and two factor interactions, $p = (k+k(k-1)/2)$. The latter assumes knowledge of the optimal design, but one can compare the *D*-efficiency of any two designs with the same formula. Typically, two information matrices have been discussed in the literature: one assumes that all items are equally likely to be chosen, and the second uses estimates of the β_i to estimate the probability that any item in any choice set is chosen. We will denote these matrices by C_0 and C_p, respectively.

Developments in Choice Experiments with Two-Level Attributes

Quenouille and John (1971) provided an early example of the use of design theory to construct choice experiments. They discuss the case of k attributes, each with two levels, and compare the performance of various subsets of a complete round-robin paired comparison design to a complete round-robin design for estimation of main effects and interactions of all orders.

Green (1974) discussed how to use symmetric and asymmetric orthogonal arrays to chose subsets of treatments (profiles) from a complete set of profiles. A complete set of profiles is defined by a full factorial, which may/may not be asymmetric. Only profiles in a subset of profiles are used to construct a choice experiment, and Green suggested using blocks from a partially balanced incomplete block design to define the choice sets. Green (1974) also discussed the case in which only a subset of attributes is allowed to appear within each choice set, which may reduce task complexity (if one believes this is necessary). Green suggested using blocks from balanced incomplete block designs (BIBDs) to determine which attributes would differ in each choice set. That is, each block of a BIBD is treated as a "design condition," and a separate design is constructed for each design condition using only the attributes in that block. Subjects evaluate only the design in one of the blocks.

A number of results for optimal paired comparison designs are due to El-Helbawy and various collaborators. For example, El-Helbawy and Bradley (1978) derived optimal 2^3 paired comparison designs to test if one two-factor interaction equals 0, and/or whether all interactions involving one factor equal 0. Elaborations of these ideas are due to El-Helbawy and Ahmed (1984), and El-Helbawy, Ahmed, and Alharbey (1994) extended these ideas to the case of asymmetrical factorial paired comparison experiments. Berkum (1987a) constructed D-optimal paired comparison designs to estimate main effects and two-factor interactions for two-level attributes.

Street, Bunch, and Moore (2001) extended results for optimal paired comparison designs for two-level attributes to the class of competing designs in which all pairs with i attributes at different levels appear equally often. They used this framework to derive optimal sets of pairs to estimate main effects, main effects + two-attribute interactions and main effects + two- and three-attribute interactions. The resulting designs are very large because they are based on complete factorials. Smaller optimal and near-optimal sets of pairs for two-level attributes were derived by Street and Burgess (2003) using fractional factorial designs. Results in Street, Bunch, and Moore (2001) also can be used to calculate the best possible information matrix for any number of attributes; hence the efficiency of any proposed design can be calculated relative to the most efficient design for a particular problem.

Burgess and Street (2002) derived optimal choice experiment designs for two-level attributes for any choice set size, and now are extending these results to apply to attributes with any number of levels and for symmetric or asymmetric designs. Designs developed in this way have the advantage of being defined by main effects plans and a number of generators, making design construction straightforward. A working paper that discusses how to construct optimal choice sets of any size to estimate the main effects of two-level attributes is available from these authors.

Sandor and Wedel (2001) proposed using prior information about likely model parameter values to make designs with improved information matrices. They compared the algorithm that they derived for this case and the designs that it generates with designs for the same number of attributes with the same number of levels provided by Huber and Zwerina (1996). They showed that the Bayesian designs produced with their approach are more efficient for the situations that they considered.

Grasshoff et al. (2002) constructed optimal pairs to estimate two-attribute interactions when *s* of the attributes may vary. Grossmann, Holling, and Schwabe (2002) compare their design for the case described in Green (1974) and show that the relative efficiency of these two designs is 42%. Grossmann, Holling, Grasshoff, and Schwabe (2002) also provide an example of empirical benefits gained from using optimal designs to measure preferences.

Paired Choice Experiments with Continuous Attributes

Results for paired choice experiments in which attributes are continuous were derived by Berkum (1987a, 1987b, 1989), including a general method for constructing such designs (Section 4, 1987a). However, for any particular problem the desired designs must be obtained iteratively (illustrated in Section 5, 1987a). He also discusses how to construct designs with fewer pairs (Berkum 1989); although the designs that result may not be optimal, their optimality properties should be reasonably good.

Offen and Littell (1987) derived optimal paired comparison designs for treatments with one quantitative attribute. If the degree of curvature in the model specification is unknown a priori, tradeoffs may be necessary, such as deciding to allow for a cubic specification, but finding that the specification in fact is quadratic after the fact. Offen and Littell (1987) discuss the relative performance of seven designs for this case.

Grossmann, Grasshoff, Holling, and Schwabe (2001) derived efficient designs for one continuous attribute for polynomial representations of degree 1, 2 and 3 (i.e., linear, quadratic, and cubic). They also considered a two-attribute additive model and showed that a cross-product design of the two marginal models is optimal. They compared their designs to the quadratic designs of Berkum (1987a) that allow for cross-product terms.

Kanninen (2002) discussed how to construct D-optimal designs for multinomial choice experiments for cases in which all attributes are continuous using a two-stage process. Her analysis shows that it is best to convert continuous attributes to two-level attributes and use the levels of one of these attributes to manipulate the probabilities that different options will be chosen. Her results give no insights into designing experiments if there might be interaction effects, which she acknowledges in her concluding remarks.

OTHER ISSUES ASSOCIATED WITH CHOICE EXPERIMENTS

The behavior of human subjects in choice experiments is impacted by types of choice tasks and their underlying designs, such that some layouts and designs lead to more difficult tasks. Because task difficulty can increase with increasing numbers of attributes, numbers of choice options, and/or difficulties in choosing between options due to the use of utility balance or similar methods, the variability in subjects' responses also can increase with these factors (e.g., see Louviere 2001; Louviere et al. 2002). This variability manifests itself in the variance of the random utility component; hence it can decrease statistical efficiency. We now know that this occurs and can be demonstrated empirically, but we do not yet fully understand the mechanism(s) by which it occurs, which would provide guidance for those who design and implement choice experiments. However, we are optimistic that this will be resolved in the near future because progress is being made in conceptual understanding and empirical results (e.g., see Severin, 2000; Louviere 2001; Louviere et al. 2002).

There has been great progress in the development of more general and hence more complex choice model specifications (Ben-Akiva et al. 2002; Louviere et al. 2002), as well as rapid progress in methods for estimating such models, including forms of simulation estimation and Bayesian estimation (Revelt and Train 1998; McFadden and Train 2000). Increased complexity, however, comes at the expense of a number of assumptions that may be hard to verify or test, such as joint multivariate normality of utility parameter distributions. Moreover, choice experiment data frequently are characterized by significant proportions of subjects who either never choose an option, or always choose an option. For example, as we write this paper an experiment involving possible new transport infrastructure options exhibits about 35% of subjects who never chose any options other than what they used last, and about 17% choose a new option in every choice set. Carson and Jeon (2002) shows that parameter estimates for such cases are indeterminate, and that at best the distribution of willingness-to-pay only can be bounded. Related cases are discussed by Louviere et al. (2002), who review growing evidence that at least some behavioral assumptions underlying such models may need rethinking.

Unresolved Issues and Areas for Further Study

Other issues associated with some complex model forms remain unresolved, such as potential confounds in models that estimate parameter distributions across individuals who not only may have different systematic utility functions, but who also may have different random components. In the latter case, differences in random component variances may lead to distributions of scale parameters that are confounded with utility parameter distributions. Another issue concerns failures to take into account choice patterns that result from individuals with different scale origins and attribute utility scale units and/or different underlying choice process models and/or utility functions. Light could be shed on the foregoing issues by developing ways to model single individuals and/or to develop statistically optimal designs for choice experiments that permit tests for differences and/or allow one to gain insights into underlying differences.

Finally, it is worth noting that confusion remains in various literatures about the "validity" of models that fit and predict well in empirical applications. That is, recent advances in the ability to formulate and test complex models seem to have overshadowed the scientific quest for understanding choice and decision processes as opposed to evaluating models purely on fit and/or predictive ability. Many complex (and simple!) models fit and predict well to the data from which they are estimated, and also perform well in cross-validations on holdout choice sets or "out of sample" predictions. Good fits and cross-sample validations can have little to do with the scientific validity of models, although they do provide information about predictive validity. There needs to be more recognition that imposing particular forms of choice process models, estimating the parameters of the associated utility function(s) and/or utility parameter distributions, and demonstrating relatively high levels of fit, is not the same as showing that models are accurate reflections of unknown underlying data-generation processes.

To wit, many published papers impose complex models of choice processes with relatively simplistic strictly additive or similar utility forms. Reviewers and authors often seem to argue about the superiority of particular forms and associated computational methods. However, such discussions miss the fundamental issue that little is actually known about what individuals actually do and/or the choice processes that they use. Imposing models and estimating them is not the same as designing experiments and data collection methods to shed more light on process instead of focusing only on prediction. Literature in several fields contains cases in which violations of distributional assumptions manifest themselves as "invalid" results like positive price estimates. Yet when such results arise, researchers, reviewers, and editors do not seem to ask if the methods themselves are flawed because the maintained assumptions imposed on the modeling process may mask various possible behavioral processes at individual or small group levels. Instead, questions are asked about whether continuous or discrete distributions are more appropriate and/or whether ·normal or other distributions are "better" able to capture violations. In such instances, science is likely to be better served by questioning methods that fail to shed light on underlying processes than by trying to "fix" paradigms by varying the maintained assumptions.

REFERENCES

Anderson, D. A., and Wiley, J. B. (1992), "Efficient choice set designs for estimating availability cross-effects models," *Marketing Letters*, 3, 4, 357-370.

Batsell, R. R., and Lodish, L. M. (1981), "A model and measurement methodology for predicting individual consumer choice," *Journal of Marketing Research*, 18, 1-12.

Batsell, R. R., and Polking, J. C. (1985), "A generalized model of market share," *Marketing Science*, 4, 177-198.

Ben-Akiva, M., and Morikawa, T. (1990a), "Estimation of travel demand models from multiple data sources," in M. Koshi (ed.), *Transportation and Traffic Theory*, North Holland: Elsevier, 461-476.

Ben-Akiva, M., and Morikawa, T. (1990b), "Estimation of switching models from revealed preferences and stated intentions," *Transportation Research A*, 24A, 6, 485-495.

Ben-Akiva, M., McFadden, D., Train, K., Walker, J., Bhat, C., Bierlaire, M., Bolduc, D., Boersch-Supan, A., Brownstone, D., Bunch, D. S., Daly, A., de Valme, A., Gopinath, D., Karlstrom, A., and M. A. Munizaga (2002) "Hybrid choice models: Progress and challenges," *Marketing Letters*, 13, 3, 163-176.

Berkum, E. E. M. van (1987a), "Optimal paired comparison designs for factorial and quadratic models," *Journal of Statistical Planning and Inference*, 15, 265-278.

Berkum, E. E. M. van (1987b), "Optimal paired comparison designs for factorial experiments," *CWI Tract*, 31, Amsterdam.

Berkum, E. E. M. van (1989), "Reduction of the number of pairs in paired comparison designs and exact designs for quadratic models," *Computational Statistics and Data Analysis*, 8, 93-107.

Bunch., D. S., Louviere, J. J., and Anderson, D. A. (1996), "A comparison of experimental design strategies for choice-based conjoint analysis with generic-attribute multinomial logit models," Working Paper, Graduate School of Management, University of California, Davis, (May).

Burgess, L., and Street, D. J. (2002), "Optimal designs for 2^k choice experiments," Research Report, Department of Mathematical Sciences, University of Technology, Sydney.

Cameron, T. A., Poe, G. L., Etheir, R. G., and Schulze, W. D. (2002), "Alternative nonmarket value-elicitation methods: Are the underlying preferences the same?" *Journal of Environmental Economics and Management*, 44, 391-425.

Carson, R. T., and Jeon, Y. (2002), "On overcoming informational deficiencies in estimating willingness to pay distributions," Working Paper, Department of Economics, University of California, San Diego, (September).

Dey, A. (1985), *Orthogonal Fractional Factorial Designs*, New York: John Wiley & Sons, Inc.

El-Helbawy, A. T., and Ahmed, E. A. (1984), "Optimal design results for 2^n factorial paired comparison experiments," *Communications in Statistics – Theory and Methods*, 13, 2827-2845.

El-Helbawy, A. T., Ahmed, E. A., and Alharbey, A.H. (1994), "Optimal designs for asymmetrical factorial paired comparison experiments," *Communications in Statistics – Simulation*, 23, 663-681.

El Helbawy, A. T., and Bradley, R. A. (1978), "Treatment contrasts in paired comparisons: large-sample results, applications and some optimal designs," *Journal of the American Statistical Association*, 73, 831-839.

Grasshoff, U., Grossmann, H., Holling, H., and Schwabe, R. (2002), "Optimal comparison designs for first order interactions," available at http://www.math.uni-magdeburg.de/~schwabe/Preprints/2002.

Green, P. E. (1974), "On the design of choice experiments involving multifactor alternatives," *Journal of Consumer Research*, 1, 61-68.

Grossmann, H., Grasshoff, U., Holling, H., and Schwabe, R. (2001), "Efficient designs for paired comparisons with a polynomial factor," in A. C. Atkinson, B. Bogacka, and A. Zhigljavsky (eds.), *Optimum Design 2000*, Dordrecht: Kluwer, 45-56.

Grossmann, H., Holling, H., Grasshoff, U., and Schwabe, R. (2002), "On the empirical relevance of optimal designs for the measurement of preferences," available at http://www.math.uni-magdeburg.de/~schwabe/Preprints/2002.

Grossmann, H., Holling, H., and Schwabe, R. (2002), "Advances in optimum experimental design for conjoint analysis and discrete choice models," *Econometric Models in Marketing*, 16, 91-115.

Hensher, D., and Bradley, M. (1993), "Using stated response choice data to enrich revealed preference discrete choice models," *Marketing Letters*, 4, 2, 139-151.

Hensher, D.A., Louviere, J. J., and Swait, J. (1999), "Combining sources of preference data," *Journal of Econometrics*, 89, 197-221.

Huber, J., and Zwerina, K. (1996), "The importance of utility balance in efficient choice designs," *Journal of Marketing Research*, 33, 307-317.

Kanninen, B. J. (2002), "Optimal design for multinomial choice experiments," *Journal of Marketing Research*, 39, 214-227.

Kuhfeld, W. F., Tobias, R. D., and Garratt, M. (1994), "Efficient experimental design with marketing research applications," *Journal of Marketing Research*, 545-557.

Lazari, A. G., and Anderson, D. A. (1994), "Design of discrete choice set experiments for estimating both attribute and availability cross effects," *Journal of Marketing Research*, 31, 375-383.

Louviere, J. J. (2001), "Response variability as a behavioral phenomenon," *Journal of Consumer Research*, 28, 506-511.

Louviere, J. J., and Woodworth, G. (1983), "Design and analysis of simulated consumer choice or allocation experiments: An approach based on aggregated data," *Journal of Marketing Research*, 20, 350-367.

Louviere, J. J., Fox, M., and Moore, W. (1993), "Cross-task validity comparisons of stated preference models," *Marketing Letters*, 4, 205-213.

Louviere, J. J., Hensher, D. A., and Swait, J. (1999), "Conjoint analysis methods in the broader context of preference elicitation methods," in A. Gustafson, A. Hermann, and F. Huber (eds.), *Conjoint Measurement: Methods and Applications*, Berlin: Springer-Verlag, 279-318.

Louviere, J. J., Hensher, D. A., and Swait, J. D. (2000), *Stated Choice Methods: Analysis and Application*, Cambridge, U.K.: Cambridge University Press.

Louviere, J. J., Meyer, R. J., Bunch, D. S., Carson, R. T., et al. (1999), "Combining sources of preference data for modeling complex decision processes," *Marketing Letters*, 10, 3, 187-204.

Louviere, J. J., Street, D., Carson, R., Ainslie, A., et al. (2002), "Dissecting the random component of utility," *Marketing Letters*, 13, 3, 177-193.

Luce, R. D. (1959), *Individual Choice Behavior: A Theoretical Analysis*, New York: John Wiley & Sons, Inc.

McFadden, D. (2001), "Disaggregate behavioral travel demand's RUM side: A 30-year retrospective," in D. A. Hensher (ed.), *Travel Behavioral Research: The Leading Edge*, Amsterdam: Pergamon, 17-64.

McFadden, D., and Train, K. (2000), "Mixed MNL models for discrete response," *Journal of Applied Econometrics*, 15, 447-470.

McFadden, D., Tye, W., and Train, K. (1978), "An application of diagnostic tests for the independence from irrelevant alternatives property of the multinomial logit model," *Transportation Research Record*, 637, 39-46.

Morikawa, T. (1989), *Incorporating Stated Preference Data in Travel Demand Analysis*, Unpublished PhD Dissertation, Department of Civil Engineering, M.I.T.

Offen, W. W., and Littell, R. C. (1987), "Design of paired comparison experiments when treatments are levels of a single quantitative variable," *Journal of Statistical Planning and Inference*, 15, 331-346.

Quenouille, M. H., and John, J. A. (1971), "Paired comparison design for the 2^n-factorials," *Applied Statistics*, 20, 16-24.

Revelt, D., and Train, K. (1998), "Mixed logit with repeated choices: Households' choices of appliance efficiency level," *Review of Economics and Statistics*, 80, 1-11.

Sandor, Z., and Wedel, M. (2001), "Designing conjoint choice experiments using managers' prior beliefs," *Journal of Marketing Research*, 38, 430-444.

Severin, V. C. (2000), *Comparing Statistical Efficiency and Respondent Efficiency in Choice Experiments*, Unpublished PE Thesis, Faculty of Economics and Business, University of Sydney, Australia.

Street, D. J., Bunch, D. S., and Moore, B. (2001), "Optimal designs for 2^k paired comparison experiments," *Communications in Statistics – Theory and Methods*, 30, 2149-2171.

Street, D. J., and Burgess, L. (2003), "Optimal and near-optimal pairs for the estimation of effects in 2-level choice experiments," *Journal of Statistical Planning and Inference*, forthcoming.

Swait, J., and Louviere, J. J. (1993), "The role of the scale parameter in the estimation and use of generalized extreme utility models," *Journal of Marketing Research*, 30, 305-314.

Thurstone, L. L. (1927) "A law of comparative judgment," *Psychological Review*, 34, 273-286

Chapter 9

Evolving Conjoint Analysis: From Rational Features/Benefits to an Off-the-Shelf Marketing Database

Howard R. Moskowitz
Moskowitz Jacobs, Inc.

This chapter presents the author's experiences in the business applications of conjoint analysis, combining technical developments and business applications spanning a three-decade range. The points of view are those of the author, who has attempted to intertwine research methodology with business applications.

BUSINESS ISSUE LEADS TO A NEW APPROACH TO CONJOINT

In 1979-1980 the author was involved in a marketing research venture, Developmetrics Inc., a division of a marketing services company, Weston Group Inc. The focus of this venture was on the rapid, accelerated development of products and concepts. One of the key aspects was that Weston Group did not deal with the research community as a research company, but rather dealt with marketers. This change in client would thus introduce the author to a different realm of individuals in business, with different types of problems, and without the necessary background to talk in "research-speak." The author's clients were not research cognoscenti. This would make all the difference.

At a meeting in Toronto, Canada, then-general manager of Colgate Canada, the late Mr. Court Shepard, asked the author and a colleague whether it would be possible to estimate the impact or utility of different messages (promises, benefits, emotions) for toothpaste. The three ingoing assumptions for this problem were the following:

1. *Complexity*: Marketers had to deal with complexity and multiplicity of stimuli, not simple stimuli to which researchers had grown accustomed. There might be as many as 90+ elements (far greater than the conventional conjoint at the time).
2. *Reality*: The promises, benefits, and emotions needed to be combined into reasonable offers to a consumer rather than evaluated singly (so-called "benefit testing," then popular). The results had to be useful for copy development.
3. *Evolution & Optimization*: The results had to allow for the recombination of these elements into new and more powerful combinations.

Although the problem posed by Shepard sounded vaguely like it could be handled by the conventional conjoint approaches, the reality of the matter was that the number of elements was far too large. The 90 might well grow to 100 or more if new elements could be found. Conventional tradeoff methods would simply not work to answer the question.

It was at that time the author had begun experiments with dummy variable regression analysis, using the personal computer available then (Apple II Plus), with rudimentary software. With 90 elements, with concepts that comprise 3-5 elements, and with the need to have many more cases than elements, it soon became apparent that the problem of creating an experimental design was quite different from that in conventional conjoint analysis. To make a long story short, the author succeeded in developing a manual approach, using VisiCalc and a rotation strategy. The spreadsheet, run on an Apple II Plus, enabled the creation of a large number of concepts (e.g., 2X, where X is the number of concept elements). Analysis of the design by simple statistical programs run on the Apple II Plus showed whether or not the elements were statistically independent of each other.

The output of the foregoing procedure generated 180 concepts, or two concepts for each element in the conjoint analysis. This strategy ensured a sufficient value for the degrees of freedom. The test concepts were scanned by the researcher and the client, printed out from the word processing program, arranged in booklets, in a rotated order, and tested among consumers. The rather rudimentary approach worked very well. Although it could not be said to match the conventional conjoint approach, the method led to dummy variable modeling between the presence/absence of the 90 concept elements and the percent of interested respondents. Interest was defined by the conventional market research way: those who said that they would probably or definitely buy the toothpaste based upon what they read.

The same algorithmic approach was done through the entire 1980s, beginning with the 90 elements, but typically reaching 200-300 elements in any study. Clients such as Playtex found the procedure to work for a variety of issues. The most remarkable aspects of the approach were:

1. *Reliability*: The method worked consistently.
2. *Statistical validity & robustness*: The use of regression up front to test the viability of the design ensured that the approach would work each time.
3. *Changes were easy to make*: Clients could read the hundreds of concepts before the study and point out inconsistencies, and the changes in elements could be made easily and the statistical up-front work redone to ensure that the regression model would run.
4. *Clarity*: The data were interpretable, and made a great deal of sense.
5. *Positive, encouraging feedback*: Clients in marketing became extremely comfortable with the approach and results. Many marketing researchers began to accept it as well, or at least went along with the marketers.
6. *Multi-media possibilities*: Pictures were introduced as part of the approach early in the game.
7. *Emotional elements crept into the study and stayed in*: Some researchers had averred that the conjoint methods should not mix together emotional and rational statements, heritages and benefits, pictures and description in this systematic fashion. In contrast, for the most part marketers were all in favor of pushing the system to the limits and incorporating as many different elements as possible. The author followed the marketers, both because he believed their point of view (always a plus in research), and because they paid the bills and thus "called the shots."
8. *The limiting factors were recognized early in the game, and dealt with*: The limiting factors were:
   a. the number of concepts to be created (typically 2x the number of elements, which could reach 350 elements or 700 concepts),
   b. the need to ensure that illogical combinations were eliminated, and
   c. the need to fund large-scale studies. With many combinations the client needed to run a study with many more respondents, in order to develop a reasonable base of respondents behind each concept.

9. *Actual adoption was fairly easy, and the number grew from year to year*: Ultimately, this decomposition approach to conjoint proved eminently feasible, was used in hundreds of commercial projects, and was eventually implemented in various countries around the world. The toll of the approach was on the development of the concept elements. Many evenings were spent creating the concepts, pasting in the pictures where appropriate, checking that the concept booklets were properly created, that a sufficient number were prepared for any market, and that every market received the proper number of such booklets in advance of the session.

10. *Execution was straightforward, although the sessions were long*: The sessions ran smoothly, with respondents participating for 2-3 hours. During the session respondents read the concepts, and rated each on a variety of attributes, ranging from purchase intent to ratings of communication of specific and general benefits (e.g., uniqueness, communication of masculine/feminine, and the like).

DEVELOPING INDIVIDUAL-LEVEL MODELING

One of the key aspects of marketing is the use of the data to predict choice behavior. Such predictions rely upon measuring behavior at the individual aggregate level. Although many marketers and marketing researchers are content to measure responses at the group level, deeper understanding of consumers can come about far more rapidly with more fine-grained, albeit disciplined, analysis at the micro-level.

Individual-level modeling with conjoint models or dummy variable additive (decomposition) models is reasonably straightforward with a short list of concept elements. Each respondent need only see a limited number of concept elements (e.g., 20-30). The creation of an experimental design wherein the elements are reasonably balanced is feasible; and in some cases the solution has already been found and is available in a textbook or other collection of experimental designs. The problem with individual modeling becomes much more severe and eventually intractable when the situation calls for hundreds, if not many dozens of elements, when the elements must obey pairwise restrictions, and when new elements can be inserted into the element mix at any time, and at any place. The requirement that the categories (or attributes, in common conjoint parlance) be balanced so as to contain equal numbers of elements, is also not necessary. To anyone ever involved in practical research, last-minute changes in the number of test stimuli and a total disregard of formal statistical considerations not only occurs, but appears to be the general rule. Porting conjoint analysis to this type of world – to be used by marketers, advertising agencies, as well as product development researchers – requires re-thinking the entire design and analysis process.

RETHINKING CONJOINT DESIGNS TO ACCOMMODATE MANY ELEMENTS AND INDIVIDUAL MODELS

The traditional conjoint design can be reengineered by considering the following six aspects. These have been incorporated as key features in a computer system known as IdeaMap® (Moskowitz and Martin 1993):

1. *Basic Design Structure*: There should be one fundamental design (called the basic design structure). This basic structure should comprise an extremely powerful fractional factorial design, fairly but not completely saturated.

2. *Pairwise Restrictions*: It should be possible to create a file listing those pairs of concept elements that can never appear with each other. With 10-15 concept elements, there may be a dozen or more pairwise restrictions. With 200+ elements there may be upwards of 500 pairs of concept elements that cannot appear with each other.

3. *Scalability:* The design structure should be set up so that it can select concept elements from the full set of elements. It should not matter how many elements are used in the study, as long as the basic design structure is "whole," in and of itself, and can be analyzed by dummy variable regression analysis.

4. *Data Imputation*: With conventional research methods, and with consumers, it is impossible to have studies that last a very long time, wherein the respondent evaluates hundreds of combinations. With today's time-pressured consumers and professionals, one is lucky to have a respondent for a half-hour on the Internet, and about 1-2 hours in a well-remunerated central location study. Data imputation is a method that allows the research to work within the constraints of a short study, obtain data from part of the stimulus set and estimate the likely response to elements that were not directly tested. Moskowitz and Martin (1993) presented an approach for data imputation based upon the profiling of concept elements by semantic scaling, and the subsequent estimation of missing data through the location of the concepts in the semantic space.

5. *Simple Modeling*: One of the key issues in the practical application of conjoint measurement is the type of modeling.

Most applied researchers are not familiar with regression models, much less with logit models. Applied researchers do understand regression when explained to them, and can grasp ordinary least squares. Although technically not as good as logit, ordinary least squares applied to data provides the type of answer that a client needs – viz., the utility values of the particular elements. Thus, for the sake of computational efficiency and client comprehension, ordinary least squares estimations were adopted. The independent variables were the presence/absence of elements, coded as 0 (to denote absence from the concept) or coded as 1 (to denote presence), respectively. The dependent variable, at the individual level, was either the rating of interest (typically on a 9-point scale), or a binary value (0 if the concept were rated 1-6, to denote low interest; or 100 if the concept were rated 7-9 to denote high interest).

6. *Acquisition of Rating Scales, Latency of Response, and Immediate Data Processing*: In applied consumer work, rapid data acquisition and processing in an almost turnkey fashion is desirable. By making the system fairly automatic, and by incorporating latency as an additional dependent variable, it became possible to expand the business applications of conjoint, both in capacity and in types of analyses.

By implementing the foregoing, it soon became possible to run rather large studies effortlessly. Table 9-1 shows the set up for a typical IdeaMap study for credit cards (Moskowitz, Cohen, Krieger, and Rabino 2001).

Table 9-1. Number of concept elements for the credit card study, by category

Category	Elements
Visuals (card types)	9
Application incentives	26
Approval benefits	26
Ongoing benefits	36
Heritage/image	21
Convenience	46
Service	26
Renewal benefits	22
Competitive claims	12
User and usage emotional statements	27
Pricing	17
Total categories	9
Total number of elements	238

A sense of the type of data that emerge from this appears in Table 9-2. Through the technology one can see the degree to which different concept elements drive consumer interest. The numbers in the body of the table are utilities, which are defined as the conditional probability that a concept will go from not interesting (rating of 1-6) to interesting (7-9) if the element is introduced into the concept.

THE DRIVE TO SELF-AUTHORING SYSTEMS

In the late 1990s, the drive to create do-it-yourself research and analysis packages began to pick up steam. A chance meeting with Chris Robinson and John Abraham, two licensees of IdeaMap®, at the 1996 ESOMAR Congress in Istanbul surfaced the goal of these licensees to have a small version of conjoint measurement that they could run themselves. As part of the drive to create a self-authoring system, the author and several colleagues at Moskowitz Jacobs Inc. asked a number of clients to provide ideas. The basic ideas kept coming down to rapid, inexpensive, and error-proof. Using these general guides, a task force of programmers and brand managers began the job of convening the innards of IdeaMap to a self-authored system that the researcher could run automatically and efficiently. Control of the conjoint process would be handed over to individuals who were not necessarily experts in the field, but who demanded lower prices, faster turnaround, and oversight of the process. Or so they said.

Although the promise at that time of self-authoring was that it would soon popularize conjoint, we were somewhat over-optimistic. Our biggest problem was something we couldn't foresee – problems with data processing involving the manual task of compacting the files. The success rate was high overall, but everyone made mistakes in the sequence of operations. These operations in the manual analysis of the data eventually limited the success of the PC-based self-authoring system.

Internet Based Self-Authoring

The popularity of the Web opened up a vast new opportunity for conjoint analysis without the problems encountered with PC-based self-authoring systems. First, the Internet was intrinsically interesting in the early years, and there were many respondents ready to participate in all sorts of surveys. During the late 1990s and early 2000, so much interest was focused on the Web that it seemed a natural course of events to create a self-authoring system. The goal was to make the system robust. The lessons learned with the creation of the PC-based systems came down to making the manipulation of

Table 9-2. Winning elements for each of the two key concept response segments emerging from the credit card data.

	Total	Seg 1	Seg 2
Base Size	167	58	67
Additive Constant	40	44	45
Winners – Segment #1 ("Stuff")			
As a card holder you get 1 AIRMILE for every £15 spent	4	7	4
Interest-free repayment period of up to 56 days	5	7	3
With your application you get an offer for cheap BA flights	4	6	4
Follow your dreams	4	6	3
As a card holder you will get a chance to win 1 of 5 all-expenses-paid trips for two to an European Grand Prix	6	6	9
Transfer a balance of £500 for 6 months or more and get 500 free AIRMILES	3	6	3
Premium insurance benefits, including car rental and travel accident insurance	3	6	1
Winners – Segment #2 ("Life Style Experience")			
With your application you get an opportunity to win a day at the Formula One test tracks	6	4	10
On acceptance of your application you will be entered into a draw for tickets to the Monaco Grand Prix	6	5	10
For every month you use your card 10 times or more (as long as the total spent is £500 or more), you will get a chance of a lifetime to drive the Jordan race car at Silverstone	5	3	10
On acceptance of your application, you get an opportunity to win a helicopter ride and tickets to the Monte Carlo Grand Prix	6	3	9
For every time you spend £500 or more on your card, you will get a chance of a lifetime to drive the Jordan race car at Silverstone	5	3	9
As a card holder you will get a chance to win 1 of 5 all-expenses-paid trips for two to any European Grand Prix	6	6	9
On acceptance of your application, participate in a competition – 25 winners get an all-expenses-paid trip for two to a Formula One Grand Prix event in Japan	6	4	8
For every time you spend £500 or more on your card, you will get a chance to win one of ten pairs of tickets to tour the Jordan factory in the United Kingdom, watch the Jordan test day at Silverstone and meet Damon Hill	4	3	8
As a card holder, get additional AIRMILES to Japan, to see the last Grand Prix of the year	5	3	8

files error free. To the extent that this cumbersome operation could be removed, a stumbling block to acceptance would be eliminated.

The eventual Web-based conjoint system was launched in March 2001, and was an immediate success. Almost no one had any problems logging on and completing the interview. The automatic file handling, the creation of the necessary files, and even the analysis of the data into subgroups on an automatic basis effectively overcame the procedural problems that had caused such havoc with the PC version. The results from Internet-based research showed good agreement with studies run on the PC even down to the subgroup level, as shown in Figure 9-1. The study dealt with a conjoint analysis of political statements about candidate Al Gore. Each of the 24 points is a concept element. The agreement is high for total panel, and for subgroups (results from Moskowitz et al., 2000).

The use of conjoint spread rather quickly. A variety of users on the Web tried it, validated against other methods, and began to use it regularly. Over the years since it was introduced, we learned about small glitches, such as capacity on the server, sending out invitations, and the like. The biggest problems appeared to be analysis of the data (how to do cross-tabulations), higher-level analysis (i.e., segmentation), and the ever-present issues of test execution. The executional problems no longer had to do with the sequence of activities, but rather the sequencing of respondents. All in all, however, the self-authoring system proved to be successful, easy to do, and accepted by clients.

CREATING A MARKETING DATABASE

The last part of the story (as of 2002) concerns the creation of a marketing and R&D database. During the 2001 Food Update Conference, held yearly in April and involving executives in the food industry, the question was posed as to whether there were any data that could help marketers and product developers understand the concept of "craveability." This rather innocent hall conversation with two professionals from a well known QSR company in California prompted the author to consider how conjoint analysis method might deal with the emotion-laden attribute craveability. The answer was relatively simple, at least superficially. One could present the respondents with different phrases about a food, conjoined into a test concept, and obtain the rating of craveability. Craveability, just like purchase interest, was a cognitively driven dependent variable. The partworth utilities would show quite clearly which particular elements in the concept were driving this rating of craveability.

The author and a colleague, Jacqueline Beckley of the Insight & Understanding Group, used a two-phase research strategy to answer the question, little realizing where the research would take them in the next year.

We established a two-phase structure – a pilot and then a broader study sponsored by McCormick & Company. We identified 20 foods (later

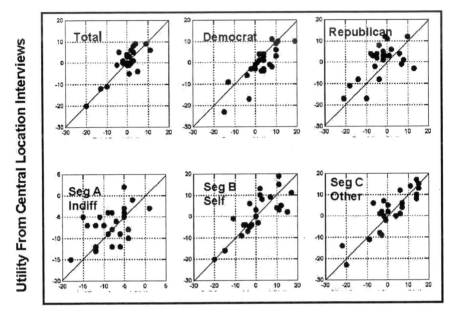

Utilities - From Internet Interviews

Figure 9-1. **Agreement between central location and Internet utilities.**

increased to 30), and developed a procedure whereby the study would comprise two linked parts. The first part comprised 36 concept elements. Each concept element had a raison d'être. For example, the first nine concept elements dealt with the description of the food, the second set dealt with the emotions, etc. In this way the structure for the study was basically laid out. It was left as a task for the actual researches to fill in the blanks. The second part of the interview comprised an extensive classification questionnaire. This classification questionnaire was essentially the same across all of the foods, with the specific questions particularized only slightly. The classification questions dealt with a variety of factors, such as:

1. the conventional geo-demographics (age, income, gender, market),
2. a checklist of factors relevant to the product (e.g., when do they crave the food; where do they crave the food),
3. what sensory and marketing features lead to craving, and
4. a checklist about their physiological state (hunger, state of the mouth).

The vision of Crave It! was a database showing, cross-sectionally, the algebra of the customers as revealed by conjoint analysis. The following paragraph, from an abstract for the ESOMAR congress in Barcelona in 2002, summarizes The Crave It! study, and the subsequent studies and databases dealing with topics such as health foods (Healthy You!), insurance (Protect It!), and the buying experience (Buy It!).

> We have developed a new set of 'mega' databases, using conjoint analysis to understand the customer mind and to provide practical guidance for marketers, product developers, and advertising agencies. Each database comprises approximately 30 related conjoint studies in a general area (e.g., buying situations, insurance, beverages, good-for-you foods, craved foods, the driving experience, the workspace environment, etc.). The World of It! provides a cross-sectional and tracking system to show what specifics drive customer interest. We reveal new segments, who they are, how to talk to them, what to say, what to avoid. Meta-analyses within a database of related studies reveal newly emerging trends, and areas of opportunity, for companies entering the category and for companies seeking unique opportunities in a crowded environment (Moskowitz & Beckley 2002).

Specifics of the Database

The devil is in the details. So it is for any research project. It is worth spending the final sections of this paper on some of the key aspects of the "It!" databases, and how they have expanded the scope of conjoint measurement. These studies provide the foundation for conjoint measurement as a tracking device, and thus enhancing its ultimate business value.

1. *Getting Respondents.* In any research study one of the biggest headaches is the recruitment of panelists. Fortunately, panelist recruitment is quite affordable in the Internet world. There are opt-in services that provide e-mails inviting respondents to participate and thus become eligible for a drawing prize. Through the use of such sweepstakes, and through a dynamic system that allowed respondents to choose any study, it became possible to recruit respondents in a cost-effective way for the 30 studies. Figure 9-2 shows an example for the Buy It! study. We created similar walls for Crave It!, Healthy You!, Protect It!, and the like. The rationale was that respondents could be directed towards a

wall, and could choose the study or studies that interested them. Furthermore, we directed respondents to participate in different studies as they wished, in order to increase the chances of winning the sweepstakes. At the same time, we inserted a cookie into the respondent's Internet browser in order to prevent participation in the same study more than once.

2. *Motivating Respondents.* Another way to motivate respondents besides sweepstakes is to provide them with immediate feedback about their responses. People like to know how they score. The Internet provides a wonderful opportunity to share information with respondents about how they perform versus how others who participate perform. By computing the results immediately we created an optimum concept for the respondent, and compared that optimum with the concept that would be best, on the average, for everyone who participated previously. This approach proved very popular. The respondent was presented with these two concepts at the end of the session, virtually immediately upon the completion of the classification questionnaire.

3. *Providing Immediate Feedback to the Researcher.* There is a breed of researchers who exhibit an increasing loss of patience when they have to wait for data. We discovered that a key aspect of a successful program was to provide the team with instant gratification. This gratification took the form of the ability to look at the results for the total panel as the ratings came in. That is, the system was programmed to compute the additive model for each respondent, locate that respondent in the database, and then compute the average utility value for each concept elements across all completed interviews. This feature proved important from a motivation point of view, because it satisfied the researcher's curiosity and reduced any researcher anxiety about the progress of the study. Of course, the feedback did not affect the study, but the fact that the information was available was sufficient for the researcher.

4. *Creating Results Tables Automatically and Relatively Rapidly at the End of the Fieldwork.* A key feature of today's marketplace is the need for immediate information. Whether information is actually needed as quickly as is demanded remains a moot point. What is becoming obvious, however, is the tightening of deadlines. Researchers servicing corporations no longer have the luxury of thinking about the results in a relaxed fashion. Rather, they are requested again and again to deliver the results in a

"timely" and generally accelerated manner. Fortunately, conjoint results are easy to understand, and do not need to be pored over for a picture to emerge. The issue with conjoint results is to provide them rapidly, almost automatically. The interpretation of the conjoint utilities is easy because it consists of scanning a page of easy-to-read numbers, in order to find a common thread. All the hard intellectual work is done up-front, in the design phase, which may well take weeks or months as each of the participants in the research project gets a chance to think about the elements, modify them, and make new suggestions.

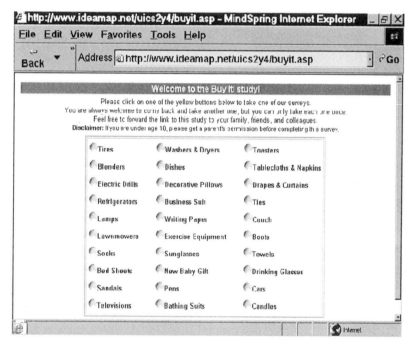

Figure 9-2. Screen shot of the Buy It!® 'wall,' which allowed the respondent to select the study or studies in which to participate.

An Example of the Results from the "Buy It!" Study

A good way to understand the results of the study is by looking at a single large-scale study – the "Buy It!" Foundation study. The full set of 30 shopping studies categories appears in Table 9-3. It is worth remarking that a Foundation study requires the exploration of product and service categories that are usually not explored by conjoint analysis, because they are out of the mainstream, or have no budget to warrant large-scale research, or are simply not particularly interesting in and of themselves, respectively. The Foundation study, locating them in the context of similar topics, makes these less-explored topics far more interesting.

Table 9-3. The 30 topics for the "Buy It!" Foundation study

Household Items	Personal Items	Big Ticket Items
Toaster	Bathing suit	Car
Blender	Sandals	Television
Dishes	Boots	Refrigerator
Towels	Business suit	Couch
Bed sheets	Ties	Lawnmower
Tablecloths and napkins	Socks	Tires
Candles	Sunglasses	Washer and dryer
Electric drill	Pens	
Decorative pillows	Exercise equipment	
Drapes and curtains	Writing paper	
Lamps	New baby gift	

Looking Across Shopping Situations with a Foundational Database

In addition to examining a specific category such as business suits, the database also allows researchers to explore the data across other shopping situations (e.g., versus boots, dishes, and refrigerators, just to name three others). Since the structure is the same; the researcher or marketer can explore the values of the brand names in different shopping situations, the value of emotional benefits, of large selections, etc. These are questions that have been traditionally difficult to answer, but with a database, answering the question becomes quite simply a matter of a table-sort or two. Two of the elements in the Buy It! study dealt with self service ("Self service ... no one to get in your way or slow you down") and price ("Offering a GREAT DEAL on the suggested retail price").

As shown in Table 9-4, these elements perform rather differently across the 30 shopping situations, as evaluated by males and females. What holds for a business suit may not hold for a candle, a decorative pillow or a car. Only through experimentation, and preferably through a powerful decomposition tool such as conjoint analysis, can one begin to see how the same feature operates in different situations.

Table 9-4. How two concept elements perform in the Foundational database, for 30 different shopping situations, among total panel, males and females, respectively. The numbers in the body of the table are the utilities of the elements.

Element: Self service ... no one to get in your way or slow you down	Total	Male	Fem	Element: Offering a GREAT DEAL on a suggested retail price	Total	Male	Fem
Socks	9	7	10	Sunglasses	11	7	12
Pens	9	11	9	Bathing suit	11	3	11
Sunglasses	9	6	11	Dishes	10	-2	11
Candles	9	10	9	Refrigerator	10	12	10
Towels	9	4	9	Television	9	7	11
Writing paper	9	12	8	Blender	9	0	11
Dishes	8	11	8	New baby gift	9	-4	9
Drinking glasses	8	7	8	Towel	8	-2	9
New baby gift	7	6	7	Washer and dryer	8	18	7
Ties	6	5	8	Socks	8	2	10
Decorative pillow	6	5	6	Exercise	8	5	9
Sandals	6	-5	7	Writing paper	8	4	8
Toaster	6	3	7	Drinking glasses	7	8	7
Tablecloth	6	11	5	Toaster	7	-7	10
Exercise	5	5	5	**Business suit**	**7**	**4**	**9**
Boots	5	7	5	Lamps	7	1	8
Couch	5	19	4	Couch	6	3	7
Refrigerator	5	9	4	Tablecloth	6	2	6
Bathing suit	5	9	4	Car	6	4	7
Blender	5	-3	7	Decorative pillow	5	-4	6
Drapes	4	0	5	Ties	5	4	6
Bed sheets	4	-2	5	Bed sheets	5	8	5
Car	4	7	1	Lawnmower	5	4	6
Television	4	6	3	Boots	5	4	5
Electric drill	4	3	5	Drapes	5	14	4
Lamps	3	-6	4	Pens	5	5	5
Washer and dryer	1	1	1	Tires	4	1	9
Business suit	**0**	**1**	**-1**	Electric drill	4	4	4
Lawnmower	-1	2	-3	Candles	4	-8	4
Tires	-3	0	-8	Sandals	3	2	3

EVOLVING CONJOINT TO A BUSINESS

When conjoint analysis was first introduced to the academic community no one openly discussed its potential. The evolution from theory to academic investigation to business process was, in fact, fairly smooth. As conjoint evolved into a business tool it did not lose its luster among academicians.

Far less established, but of potential equal magnitude, is the evolution of conjoint from a method used in high-level research. In the research community, databases abound. Most databases deal with observations of behavior, such as store audits. Other databases deal with attitude. Virtually no databases deal with the algebra of the customer's mind in the way that the Crave It! and Buy It! databases do. It will be interesting to chart the evolution of this conjoint-based business, to see where it gains acceptance and where it meets with rejection. The jury is still out on the ultimate outcome. What is known, however, is that databasing an area using 30 different conjoint studies certainly forces the researcher to explore many topics not usually explored at all by research. Thus, if nothing else, the database idea will create a matrix of knowledge for aspects of consumer life that are less explored today. Indeed, the results for the Buy It! database reveal that winning ideas in one area of shopping may or may not work for other areas, and that winning ideas for males may not do particularly well among females, and vice versa. Such insights, important in business, may yet prove to be foundational in the study of the deeper aspects of the consumer mind.

ACKNOWLEDGEMENTS

For their key work in the Buy It! database, the author would like to acknowledge Jacqueline Beckley, Hollis Ashman, and Melanie Cushman from the Understanding and Insight Group, and Rachel Katz and Barbara Itty of Moskowitz Jacobs. The Crave It! database was sponsored by and continues to be supported by McCormick & Company. The Buy It! database was sponsored by the Kelly School of Business, Department of Marketing, Indiana University. The author would like to acknowledge the ongoing help of Frank Acito, Chair of the Department, and Gil Frisbie, Clinical Professor.

REFERENCES

Moskowitz, H. R. (1996), "Segmenting consumers world-wide: An application of multiple media conjoint methods," *Proceedings of the 49th ESOMAR Congress*, Istanbul, 535-552.

Moskowitz, H. R. and Beckley, J. (2002), Presentation at the 55th ESOMAR Congress, Barcelona.

Moskowitz, H. R., Cohen, D., Krieger, B., and Rabino, S. (2001), "Interest and reaction time analysis of credit card offers – managerial implications of high level research procedures," *Journal of Financial Services Marketing*, 6, 172-189.

Moskowitz, H. R., Gofman, A., Tungaturthy, P., Manchaiah, M., and Cohen, D. (2000), "Research, politics and the web can mix: Considerations, experiences, trials, tribulations in adapting conjoint measurement to optimizing a political platform as if it were a consumer product," *Proceedings of the ESOMAR World Wide Internet Conference and Exhibition,* Dublin, 109-130.

Moskowitz, H. R., and Martin, D. G. (1993), "How computer-aided design and presentation of concepts speeds up the product development process," *Proceedings of the 46th ESOMAR Conference*, Copenhagen, Denmark, 405-419.

PART SIX: REFLECTIONS

A mix of personal and professional recollections begins, in Chapter 10, with comments by Paul Green on his own development as a marketing scholar and on the evolution of marketing research methodology and collaboration. In Chapter 11, Green and colleagues Richard Johnson and William Neal review the evolution of the field of marketing research and four decades of growth of one of its central publications, the Journal of Marketing Research. *We then turn in Chapter 12 to the more personal reflections of colleagues and students of Paul Green on his contributions and career – from anecdotes to poems and songs. And concluding this section, in Chapter 13, Jerry Wind and Paul Green describe the continuing legacy of Wroe Alderson.*

Chapter 10

The Vagaries of Becoming (and Remaining) a Marketing Research Methodologist[1]

Paul E. Green
The Wharton School, University of Pennsylvania

Recently, I received an e-mail from Terry Clark, editor of the *Journal of Marketing*'s Book Review section, asking me to:

> ... talk about your development over the years as a marketing scholar. Why did Paul Green get into marketing? Who/what influenced him? What twists and turns has his career taken? How does he go about doing research? How does he pick his topics? What are his idiosyncrasies?

This essay represents an attempt to respond to Terry's questions and, in the process, comment on some recent trends in research. (However, I'll go easy on the idiosyncrasies.)

The Early Years

> *Random walk:* the path taken by a point or quantity that moves by steps, where the direction of each step is determined randomly.

In the fall of 1946, armed with a university scholarship and the GI Bill, I began my freshman year at the University of Pennsylvania's College of Arts and Sciences. Starting in the fifth grade, I had maintained an almost single-minded interest in chemistry. Most of my spending money went for home laboratory equipment. Fortunately, I managed to avoid blowing up the lab (with me in it), though I had a few close calls along the way. Once, while running some experiments with a Tesla high voltage coil, I accidentally brushed against a standing water pipe in our attic; the results were not pretty.

When I entered Penn, I fully intended to major in chemistry and eventually become a research chemist. To my dismay, all the chemistry courses I wanted to take were being reserved for GIs who were majoring in pre-med, so I decided to major in mathematics and – being ever mindful of eventually needing a job – in economics as well. I put my background and interest in music to good use by performing a few nights a week with some other part-time musicians. We worked in a variety of local bars and bistros, all of dubious reputation.

After the first year of college, I found that I quite liked my dual economics/mathematics major and decided to stick with it. Meanwhile, the music gigs provided ample income for a full-time student. I resisted an offer to go on the road with a traveling combo; summer jobs at the New Jersey shore provided sufficient fun and thrills.

Graduating from Penn in January 1950, I landed a job at the Sun Oil Company's home office in Philadelphia. After a one-month mandatory stint in the mail room, I was given my first real job as a statistical research analyst. Because Penn offered graduate courses in statistics, I decided to enroll part-time in the university's master's degree program and earn an A.M. degree. I was extremely lucky to have Simon Kuznets (later a Nobel Prize winner in economics) as my master's thesis advisor.

Three years later (armed with the master's degree), I was approached by the Lukens Steel Company in Coatesville, Pennsylvania, to work in its marketing research department. This relatively new department was engaged in carrying out business-to-business market studies for its major steel plate and weldments customers. While at Lukens, I became engrossed in the then-fledgling field of operations research (OR). The company sent me to several OR short courses taught by West Churchman and Russ Ackoff at the Case Institute of Technology. My manager asked me to start a small OR group at Lukens, and I jumped at the chance. Our three-person group quickly got involved in work scheduling, inventory control, and simulation problems. The work was sufficiently interesting to management for it to give me the opportunity to enroll (part-time) in Penn's doctoral program in statistics. In 1958, while still at Lukens, I was approached by a recruiting firm to explore a job opening in market planning at DuPont's Wilmington headquarters. I took this job and, with my new manager's approval, continued (part-time) the doctoral program in statistics at Penn.

In 1961, eight years after receiving the A.M. degree, I received a Ph.D. in statistics. My dissertation was in the then-arcane fields of Bayesian statistics and Von Neumann-Morgenstern utility theory. I was able to use these new concepts in some real-world research at DuPont. My doctoral dissertation advisor and longtime friend, Morris Hamburg, introduced me to Bayesian inference and expected utility concepts, I became an ardent proponent of these ideas, particularly as they related to the modeling of the cost versus value of marketing research information (Green 1963).

Wroe Alderson and My Beginning Years as an Academic

During my last couple of years in Penn's doctoral program, I had the pleasure of sitting in on some of Wroe Alderson's lectures in the marketing department. Wroe was a major figure in the world of marketing research. Earlier, he had headed his own research firm, Alderson and Sessions. After selling his interest in the firm, he focused his considerable energies on teaching and academic research.

Wroe's first book, *Marketing Behavior and Executive Action* (Alderson 1957), was a landmark publication; many of its concepts are as fresh today as when they first appeared. During the last two years of my doctoral studies, I had the opportunity to spend a lot of time with Wroe. When he asked me if I would be interested in an academic appointment, I was overjoyed.

In the summer of 1962 I left DuPont and started, full-time, in Wharton's Marketing Department. I also joined Wroe as a consultant in his new research firm, Behavior Systems. I was pleasantly surprised to learn that DuPont was interested in my consulting services. I spent a year and a half in this capacity while still teaching at Wharton.

During this same time, Wroe and I completed a book together, called *Planning and Problem Solving in Marketing* (Alderson and Green 1964). Here, I had the opportunity to show how some relatively new tools, including Bayesian analysis, could be used to address marketing problems. A couple of years later Don Tull and I published the text *Research for Marketing Decisions* (Green and Tull 1966). This book was completed through the mails, because Don was then at California State University, Fullerton. (The book was published and on the market before we had the opportunity to meet in person.)

Wroe's influence on marketing science was broad and deep. In the mid-1950s, he initiated the marketing theory seminars (held in alternate years at the University of Vermont and the University of Colorado). We Young Turks were treated to the experiences and wisdom of the early marketing scholars, including Leo Aspinwall, Lyndon Brown, Richard Clewett, Paul Converse, Ewald Grether, Edmund MeGarry, and Hugh Wales, to name a few. The seminars continued until Wroe's death in 1965 at the age of 68.

The Marketing Science Institute

In the early 1960s, Wroe was also instrumental in persuading Thomas McCabe, president of Scott Paper Company, to found the Marketing Science Institute (MSI). Wendell Smith was selected as its first director and Patrick Robinson and Michael Halbert were hired as principal investigators. The institute's quarters were only a stone's throw from Wharton.

Meanwhile, Wharton's Marketing Department was acquiring an impressive portfolio of new talent – Ron Frank, Jerry Wind, Len Lodish, Scott Armstrong, Peter FitzRoy, and Irv Gross all arrived in the mid-to-late 1960s. Several of us were asked to consult on MSI's research projects.

During one such project, involving experimental gaming on how managers process and act on "noisy" information, Peter FitzRoy and I became interested in psychometric techniques as related to correlates of risk aversion (Green, FitzRoy, and Robinson 1967). One thing led to another, and before I knew it, I was deeply involved in multidimensional scaling (MDS) and clustering methods; this epiphany occurred in the mid-1960s. I have been interested in these areas ever since. After the experimental gaming project was completed, Frank Carmone (then at MSI) and I were able to meet and work with some of the major psychometricians of the 1960s, including Clyde Coombs, Warren Torgerson, Roger Shepard, Joe Kruskal, and Doug Carroll. Doug, in particular, became my MDS mentor and has continued to keep me up to date ever since. Out of that beginning came the Workshop on Multidimensional Scaling, sponsored by Bell Labs and the University of Pennsylvania, held at Penn in June 1972. Scholars came from around the world to present papers.

Between 1968 and 1972, I was involved in producing three monographs – two on MDS (Green and Carmone 1970; Green and Rao 1972) and one on conjoint analysis (Green and Wind 1973). Research in MDS clustering, conjoint analysis, discrete choice, latent class analysis, and general multivariate data analysis still proceeds apace. Major contributors to this area include Wayne DeSarbo, Michel Wedel, Wagner Kamakura, Jordan Louviere, Moshe Ben Aikiva, Greg Allenby, Eric Bradlow, and Roland Rust, to name just a few.

Starting in the late 1960s (and continuing to the present day), I learned much about scaling techniques from Doug Carroll, my friend and collaborator for many years, and currently the Board of Governors Professor of Management and Psychology at Rutgers University. He and I wrote two hooks together (Green and Carroll 1976, 1978) and have another on the way (coauthored with Jim Lattin). Other researchers who have influenced my thinking include Jerry Wind, with whom I have worked the longest – since 1966 when he joined Wharton – Frank Carmone at Wayne State University,

Vithala Rao at Cornell, and Wayne DeSarbo at Pennsylvania State University have all collaborated with me on various articles over the years. (I have, indeed, been fortunate in the company I have kept.)

The Past 20 Years or So

My interest in marketing research methodology started in the 1960s and continues to this day. My principal collaborator during the last two decades has been Abba Krieger, the Robert Steinberg Professor of Statistics at Wharton. Abba's technical background in theoretical mathematics, OR, and statistics (with degrees from the Massachusetts Institute of Technology and Harvard) is outstanding. Helped by Abba's creativity and diverse skills, my interest in data analysis and descriptive modeling has taken a turn toward optimization modeling. The research that Abba and I have done over the past two decades reflects an emphasis on normative modeling, such as conjoint simulators and optimizers, competitive pricing models, customer satisfaction optimization, optimal reach analysis, and a variety of other efforts that have led to decision support models.

Meanwhile, we continue to work on clustering methods, conjoint modeling, market segmentation, and various kinds of hybrid models for preference analysis. In summary, my old areas of research have not disappeared – they have been revisited and extended. More important, I am still interested in models and techniques that have (actual or potential) relevance for managerial decision making.

One of the fringe benefits of working with cluster analysis, MDS, conjoint analysis, and other multivariate techniques is that their application often leads to practical (and sometimes high-profile) results:

- Cluster analysis has been used in IBM's change from an industry-based to a needs-based segmentation strategy (entailing personal computers). Other examples of clustering include the development of AT&T's "Reach out and touch someone" advertising campaign and a psychographic-based cluster analysis for General Motors' Chevrolet division.
- A variety of problems have been tackled by the use of MDS methods, including tracing the results of Life cereal's advertising campaign (involving moving earlier perceptions of the cereal as a strictly nutritional product to one that also appeals to children). Also, MDS was used in developing Coca-Cola's slogan, "It's the real thing!"
- Conjoint analysis has been applied to a host of applications, including hotel design (Matriott's Courtyard and Ritz Carlton's

offering of deluxe services), AT&T's first cellular telephone, the E-Z Pass toll collection system (now used in New York, New Jersey, and parts of Pennsylvania), and IBM's RISC 6000 and AS-4OO computer designs and pricing.

- Thousands of conjoint studies have been carried out over the past 30 years. Commercial software is readily available for most of these techniques, and all the larger marketing firms provide consulting help on their application.

Now that I have discussed my own research and the sizable impact of my colleagues on that research, a few more general comments on research practice may be of interest.

THE SOCIOLOGY OF RESEARCH

Over the past 40 years it seems to me that research in marketing has moved rapidly away from the single-author articles and more toward collaboration among scholars. This is also true in marketing research methodology. The inducements are many – friendships, complementary and compatible skills, similarity of interests, and ticking tenure clocks are just a few reasons.

On examining my curriculum vitae recently, I noted that over the past 40 years, I have collaborated with 55 different coauthors, 23 of whom were academics, 10 are former doctoral students of mine, and 22 are research practitioners. I have thoroughly enjoyed working with every one or them. Rare is the case that I have not learned something from collaborations with my colleagues, whether they were peers, students, or practitioners.

For the fun of it, I took my top seven collaborators (using a cutoff of at least 12 joint publications with me). Their rank order in terms of number of coauthored publications is as follows: Krieger, Carroll, Carmone, Wind, Rao, Schaffer, and DeSarbo. These scholars, representing 13% of my coauthors, accounted for more than half of my joint publications. Although I have not attempted to replicate the venerable "20/80 rule," my publication history seems to reflect the tendency (at least in my case) to stay with scholars with whom common interests and respect remain over extended periods of time.

Big ideas in market research methodology are rare, and any researcher is fortunate to be associated with one, let alone several, over the course of a career. I have tried to develop the methodological skills needed to tackle various substantive problems, be they research questions on segmentation, pricing, competition, product positioning, or whatever. (This is not the same as learning a technique and going around solely looking for cases in which it can be applied.)

For me, the research process generally starts with a problem. Then I draw on the set of skills and models that offer promise for useful solutions. Other researchable problems stem from critiquing others' research, accepting consulting assignments, trying to answer students' or colleagues' questions, and even self-critiquing my own prior research.

As I see it, there are two kinds of researchers in marketing research methodology. The first has a broad range of interests and becomes attracted to interesting and often off-beat problems that appear to be amenable to solutions. Typically, the solutions are interesting and creative but often lack transfer value to other classes of problems. The second type of researcher starts out with a related set of topics (e.g., interest in clustering methods) and spends time researching the literature, looking for unsolved aspects of the methodology, and tackling one or more of these unsolved problems. The second approach has the added value of leading to cumulative research contributions that relate to a specific domain, such as conjoint analysis or hierarchical clustering. Although the second approach tends to be more time consuming, it also prompts the researcher to look for incompletely solved subproblems or new problems that arise with new findings. Over time, this type of researcher usually has the better chance of making more interconnected contributions to the field.

With few exceptions, my research has focused on methodologies that promise to help practitioners cope with certain classes of problems, such as market segmentation, product positioning, price/demand relationships, distribution, product design, customer satisfaction, and so on. Researchers who take this path do so on the expectation that the client/decision maker will make better decisions if these tools and techniques are correctly used.

Of course, this is not the only type of research strategy that methodologists need follow. Quite the contrary: Several new research niches have emerged in recent years. Examples include causal modeling and covariance structure analysis, economic modeling of marketing phenomena, and game theory. Because each has attained a critical mass of researchers whose work now appears in top marketing journals, I say a few words about each.

Causal Modeling

With the introduction of sophisticated statistical techniques (Bentler 1985; Jöreskog and Sörbom 1978; Wold 1985), causal models began appearing in marketing (Bagozzi 1980) during the late 1980s, and their growth accelerated during the 1990s. Although causal modeling is not without its critics (e.g., Cliff 1983; Freedman 1987), it has attracted considerable attention, particularly among consumer behavior researchers. Causal modeling is currently concerned more with the descriptive aspects of behavior and ways to test theories of how buyers (and managers) make decisions than with normative prescription. The presence of such studies in the journals and research textbooks is a testimony to their growing importance. An area of emerging applicability for causal modeling seems to be customer satisfaction, in which industry practitioners are beginning to investigate the potential value of covariance structure analysis and partial least squares models in tracking and analyzing customer satisfaction problems.

Economic Modeling

Another area of intense research activity is economic modeling. Moorthy (1993) provides a clear and non-technical description of this research stream. He views economic modeling as consisting of the following components:

1. The researcher observes a phenomenon.
2. The researcher constructs an economic model to explain the phenomenon.
3. The researcher develops a set of assumptions to help define the model.
4. The researcher explores the logical consequences of the model: (a) the consequences should be at least consistent with the observed phenomenon; (b) some of these consequences should be empirically testable; and (c) other consequences might describe the phenomenon if the model were perturbed, that is, if the decision maker's environment were different.

These guidelines do not rule out other (possibly better) models. Note also that the approach is basically descriptive. The theoretical model builder does not have to make normative recommendations or tell the business person how to make better decisions. This is in contrast with decision support models that are designed to provide a mathematical description of a managerial problem with the intent of finding an improved (possibly optimal) solution to some aspect of current business practice. Economic modeling has become a fast-growing enterprise. Applications of the approach routinely appear in *Marketing Science*, and articles are also starting to appear in *Journal of Marketing Research* (Hauser and Wernerfelt 1989; Lal 1990) and *Marketing Letters* (Ingene and Parry 1998).

Game Theory

Although game theory also relies heavily on economic modeling, its principal feature entails two or more players whose fates are intertwined in various ways. Examples include Moorthy's (1984) work on buyer self-selection. Green and Krieger (1997) describe the application of Nash equilibrium in the context of new product design, in which researchers' interest is in long-term return optimization, given the responses of rational opponents. Choi and DeSarbo (1993) and Choi, DeSarbo, and Harker (1990) also discuss related competitive issues in the context of choice modeling.

My limited experience with game theory leads me to believe that game-theoretic notions – even under highly simplifying assumptions – can still offer useful insights into product design decisions, such as identifying product attribute levels that are reasonably resistant to rational competitive retaliation. Although game-theoretic model formulations employ highly simplifying assumptions, they can provide help in tracing out the possible consequences of short-term actions on long-term payoffs. Although marketing researchers' acceptance of causal modeling approaches has been more or less universal, I believe that all three research niches – causal modeling, economic modeling, and game theory – will continue to attract young scholars with theoretical interests and methodological training. The main problem seems to be in constructing interesting marketing theories in which the methodology can be fruitfully used.

A SUMMING UP

As I look back over my research career of over 40 years (my first publication was in 1957 when I was at the Lukens Steel Company), I like to think that my many collaborators and I have made some useful contributions to marketing research methodology. In turn, I have had the pleasure and honor of working with extremely talented colleagues, ranging from those in the early years (Jerry Wind, Ron Frank, Frank Carmone, Doug Carroll, Arun Jain, Vithala Rao, and Wayne DeSarbo) to those later on (including Cathy Schaffer and particularly, Abba Krieger, my latest coauthor). Abba and I have coauthored 45 articles in the approximately two decades that we have worked together.

If my thoughts are at least close to the mark, researchers in marketing are entering the age of research "pluralism" in which methodologists, economic modelers, and consumer behaviorists will live side by side and learn from one another. They will need at least four skill sets: teaching basic material (possibly remote from their own specialty), tolerating others' specialties, being mindful of the needs of business practitioners, and engaging in self-criticism of their research. Hopefully, the expected fragmentation will nonetheless continue to produce useful scholarly output, at least in the long run. Because marketing academics work for business schools, it would be a decided plus if the output were eventually important to somebody, say, the business practitioner or the MBA student.

As for future scholarly research, I still see a need for prescriptive research methodology that can help managers make more informed decisions. I also find it useful and refreshing to open the door to researchers who are less interested in prescriptive modeling than in understanding how the marketing world works, be it first-mover advantage, competitive duopoly, vertical structure analysis, or what have you. Prescriptive and descriptive researchers can easily live side by side. Often, both talents exist in the same researcher.

As for me, it is comforting to know that everything is not brand new. As I write this essay, I note that empirical and hierarchical Bayesian techniques are now quite the rage in choice modeling and related areas. They are more sophisticated than the Bayesian concepts I learned in the early 1960s; still, it is nice to know that "new wine in old bottles" is something more than a catchphrase.

As far as the vagaries of remaining a marketing research methodologist are concerned, it now seems inevitable that I have stayed a marketing researcher. With no talent for, or interest in, administration, I successfully avoided making the mistake of believing I had either.

NOTES

[1] Reprinted from *Journal of Marketing*, 64 (July 2001), 104-108.

REFERENCES

Alderson, W. (1957), *Marketing Behavior and Executive Action,* Homewood. IL: Richard D. Irwin.

Alderson, W., and Green, P.E. (1964), *Planning and Problem Solving in Marketing,* Homewood, IL: Richard D. Irwin.

Bagozzi, R. P. (1980), *Causal Models in Marketing,* New York: John Wiley & Sons.

Bentler, P. M. (1985), *Theory and Implementation of EQS: A Structural Equations Program,* Los Angeles: BMDP Statistical Software.

Choi, S. C., and DeSarbo, W. S. (1993), "Game theoretic derivations of competitive strategies in conjoint analysis," *Marketing Letters*, 4 (4), 337-348.

Choi, S. C., and Harker, P. T. (1990), "Product positioning under price competition," *Management Science*, 36 (2), 175-199.

Cliff, N. (1983), "Some cautions concerning the application of causal modeling methods," *Multivariate Behavioral Research*, 18 (1), 115-126.

Freedman, D. A. (1987), "As others see us: A case study in path analysis," *Journal of Educational Statistics*, 12 (Summer), 101-128.

Green, P. E. (1963), "Bayesian decision theory in pricing strategy," *Journal of Marketing*, 27 (January), 5-14.

Green, P. E., and Carmone, F., Jr. (1970), *Multidimensional Scaling and Related Techniques in Marketing Analysis*, Boston: Allyn and Bacon.

Green, P. E., and Carroll, J. D. (1976), *Mathematical Tools for Applied Multivariate Analyses*, New York: Academic Press.

Green, P. E., and Carroll, J. D. (1978), *Analyzing Multivariate Data*, Hinsdale, IL: The Dryden Press.

Green, P. E., FitzRoy, P. T., and Robinson, P. J. (1967), *Experiments on the Value of Information in Simulated Marketing Experiments*, Boston: Allyn & Bacon.

Green, P. E., and Krieger, A. M. (1997), "Using conjoint analysis to view competitive interaction through the consumer's eyes," in G. Day and D. Reibstein (eds.), *Wharton on Dynamic Competitive Strategy*, New York: John Wiley & Sons, pp. 343-67.

Green, P. E., and Rao V. R. (1972), *Applied Multidimensional Scaling*, Hinsdale, IL: Holt, Rinehart & Winston.

Green, P. E., and Tull D. S. (1966), *Research for Marketing Decision*, Englewood Cliffs, NJ: Prentice Hall.

Green, P. E., and Wind Y. (1973), *Multiattribute Decisions in Marketing*, Hinsdale, IL: Holt, Rinehart & Winston.

Hauser, J., and Wernerfelt, B. (1989), "The competitive implications of relevant set/response analysis," *Journal of Marketing Research*, 26 (November), 391-405.

Ingene, C. A., and Parry, M. E. (1998), "Manufacturer-optimal wholesale pricing when retailers compete," *Marketing Letters*, 9 (February), 65-78.

Jöreskog, C., and Sörborn, D. (1978), *LISREL - Analysis of Linear Structural Relationships by the Method of Maximum Likelihood*, Chicago: International Educational Services.

Lal, R. (1990), "Manufacturer trade deals and retail price promotions," *Journal of Marketing Research*, 2 (November), 428-444.

Lattin. J., Carroll, J. D., and Green, P. E. (2002), *Analyzing Multivariate Data*, Belmont, CA: Duxbury Press.

Moorthy, K. S. (1984), "Market segmentation, self-selection, and product line design," *Marketing Science*, 3 (Fall), 288-305.

Moorthy, K. S. (1993), "Theoretic modeling in marketing," *Journal of Marketing*, 57 (April), 92-106.

Wold, H. (1985), "Partial least squares," in S. Katz and N. L. Johnson (eds.), *Encyclopedia of Statistical Sciences*, Vol. 6, New York: John Wiley & Sons, pp. 581-591.

Chapter 11

The *Journal of Marketing Research*: Its Initiation, Growth, and Knowledge Dissemination[1]

Paul E. Green, *The Wharton School, University of Pennsylvania*
Richard M. Johnson, *Sawtooth Software*
William D. Neal, *SDR Consulting*

It seems hard to believe that the *Journal of Marketing Research* (*JMR*) has been around for almost 40 years. Since its inception in 1964, hundreds of articles have appeared. Much of what we now know of marketing research methodology first showed up in the pages of *JMR*. How did this all come about? And where does the journal appear to be headed in the future?

We first describe the history of *JMR* and illustrate how its content has changed as new technical developments have come to the fore. Because those technical developments have been facilitated by a dramatic increase in computer resources, we also provide a brief history of the computer's role in the development of marketing research methodology. We then discuss the important role of *JMR* and its sponsoring organization, the American Marketing Association, in knowledge dissemination and real-world application of research techniques.

JMR: FOUR DECADES OF GROWTH AND CHANGE

Encapsulating the broad sweep of marketing research methodology over the last 40 years is a daunting task for mere mortals. So many new developments have emerged from marketing researchers' efforts that the mind falters in searching for a single, dominant theme (or even a small number of themes) to cover its progress.

Perhaps a good place to start is to turn to Bob Ferber (*JMR*'s first editor) and his words of wisdom, as excerpted from Myers, Massy, and Greyser's book, *Marketing Research and Knowledge Development* (1980), pp. 8-9:

> Market behavior is a multivariate, multidisciplinary problem. ... this is not to deny statistical laws of aggregate market behavior, such as the negative binomial for consumer purchases. These regularities can be useful for certain marketing problems, but they can't provide an explanation of the factors underlying market behavior.... Largely spurious is the long-standing distinction, or controversy, between the quantitative and qualitative approaches to marketing research.... One may specialize in either approach, but to be most effective one must be able to use each method as the situation demands.... Marketing researchers are becoming aware that they face the same problems that econometricians did about twenty years go ... the systems analyst appears to be to the 1960s what the motivation researcher was to the 1940s (and let's hope that he comes to a more glorious end).... Paradoxically, marketing research is becoming more intricate and specialized at the same time that awareness for a simple comprehension of marketing problems is increasing.

One natural and straightforward approach is historical: to describe who did what, when, how, and why, and what were the consequences. While this theme is not particularly off-beat or insightful, it does keep us on track. This approach also serves as a springboard for discussing more recent trends in research and their implications for academics and practitioners. In particular, we later describe some of the newer developments of latent class, hierarchical Bayes, and the growing role of the computer in marketing research.

Researchers or practitioners, we are all interested in learning about newer methods and when and when not to use them. In short, most of us are interested in knowledge development and transfer and the replications of these developments for management practice.

Developments Preceding the Introduction of *JMR*

As has been amply documented by many authors, research in marketing had been going on long before the appearance of *JMR*. As far back as 1911, Charles Coolidge Parlin, the acknowledged founder of marketing research, had been plying his trade under the auspices of the Curtis Publishing Company. Other pre-1964 luminaries included Wroe Alderson, George Katona, Paul Lazersfeld, and Malcolm McNair.

Table 11-1 shows a list of modeling/methodology books that appeared either before, or shortly after, *JMR*'s appearance. Their contents cover a variety of areas: mathematical models, statistical techniques, marketing and the computer, and statistical decision theory, to name a few. These books all reflect, to some extent, the relatively new role of statistics, operations research, and the computer in marketing research.

Table 11-1. **1960s (or Earlier) Book Contributions to Modeling/Methodology in Marketing**

Ferber, Robert A. (1949), *Statistical Techniques in Marketing Research,* McGraw-Hill.

Alderson, Wroe (1957), *Marketing Behavior and Executive Action,* Irwin.

Bass, Frank M. et al. (1961), *Mathematical Models and Methods in Marketing,* Irwin.

Frank, Ronald E., Alfred A. Kuehn, and William F. Massy (1962), *Quantitative Techniques in Marketing Analysis,* Irwin.

Alderson, Wroe and Stanley J. Shapiro, eds. (1963), *Marketing and the Computer,* Prentice Hall.

Alderson, Wroe and Paul E. Green (1964), *Planning and Problem Solving in Marketing,* Irwin.

Langhoff, Peter, ed. (1965), *Models, Measurement, and Marketing,* Prentice Hall.

The Decade of the Sixties

The decade of the sixties reflected not only the appearance of new disciplines, such as operations research and management science. To a large extent, this decade also ushered in a new brand of marketing instructor. The Ford and Carnegie Foundations played a seminal role in the development of teaching programs featuring many of the OR/MS tools. Several marketing instructors took advantage of these programs by expanding and sharpening their quantitative skills. *JMR* became one of the beneficiaries of this retooling.

Not surprisingly, misguided attempts to apply OR/MS methodology, *without* modification, led to some early failures in such marketing areas as advertising allocation, media scheduling, and brand switching models. Problems typically centered around the paucity of customer response data.

Still, the 1960s ushered in a variety of new techniques, several of which were borrowed from multivariate statistics, OR/MS, and microeconomics.

Table 11-2 shows a partial list of the many techniques that marketers borrowed from the quantitative sciences of the 1960s and earlier.

Table 11-2. **Decade of the Sixties**

Models and Methods

- Bayesian decision theory
- Canonical analysis, discriminant analysis, factor analysis, and cluster analysis
- Dynamic programming
- Experimentation and the analysis of variance and covariance
- Heuristic programming
- Linear programming in media selection
- Markov brand switching and learning models in consumer behavior
- Probability models for brand loyalty
- Queuing models for customer service planning
- Simulation of marketing processes
- Simultaneous-equation regression
- Warehouse and other spatial location models

The Decade of the Seventies

The decade of the 1970s was marked by a swing from OR/MS toward the psychometricians, i.e., the descriptive model builders. Since the mid-sixties, developments in cluster analysis and multidimensional scaling were proceeding at a rapid rate. Bell Laboratories was a hotbed of activity, involving several outstanding psychometricians and statisticians, including Roger Shepard, Joe Kruskal, and Doug Carroll. In addition, other scholars from other locations (e.g., Norm Cliff and Jan de Leeuw) were also major contributors to the MDS and clustering literature.

Marketing researchers' use of cluster analysis and MDS owes much to the techniques of these early developers. Bell Laboratories was gracious enough to distribute its extensive suite of mainframe computer programs, including the FORTRAN source code, free of charge to interested takers. Many of the Bell Labs' early algorithms wound up in the assorted software packages of marketing research organizations. The Bell Labs' programs were eagerly applied by marketing research firms and contributed markedly to the strides made in analyzing consumers' perceptions, preferences, attitudes, and choices.

The 1970s also ushered in the development and application of conjoint analysis and computer simulations using respondents' partworths data. Marketing researchers' problems with interpreting high-dimensional perceptual/preference maps led to the idea of composing factorially-designed stimuli at the outset. In this way, one could obtain respondents' implicit attribute-level values from their reactions to complete product or service profiles – what has come to be known as full-profile conjoint analysis. In addition, each individual's partworths could be entered into a choice simulator and various "if - then" scenarios could be played out as managers varied the attribute levels of the various competitive products.

Choice simulations could, in turn, be used to estimate market shares for each competitive product/service and predictions of new market shares as various product features were changed. Such early simulators have been extensively modified to encompass optimization modules (including mass customization products), dynamic modules that reflect action/reaction sequences in the marketplace, and potential equilibrium solutions. Table 11-3 illustrates some of the many marketing research developments of the seventies.

Table 11-3. **Decade of the Seventies**

Measurement and Scaling

- Carroll's PREFMAP 2
- Conjoint analysis of consumer tradeoffs and computer choice simulation
- Hierarchical and partitional cluster analysis of judgments data and market segmentation
- Individual differences modeling via the INDSCAL perceptual mapping technique
- Perceptual mapping of consumers' similarity judgments, preferences, or product ratings
- Preference mapping of consumers' rank order preference judgments
- Two-way correspondence and multiple correspondence analysis

---

Myers, Massy, and Greyser (1980) describe the diffusion-of-information process, using the introduction of conjoint analysis as an example. They refer to the seminal research of Luce, Tukey, Thurstone, and others and illustrate how Green and Rao utilized this information to develop what they called conjoint analysis.

Interestingly enough, Richard Johnson, then at Market Facts, independently proposed a two-factor-at-a-time tradeoff approach. Both Green and Rao and Johnson published articles on their methodology. Myers, Massy, and Greyser cite this case as an example of how research ideas can permeate the marketplace, either through publications and/or successful applications. Figure 11-1 (taken from Myers, Massy, and Greyser) illustrates the process.

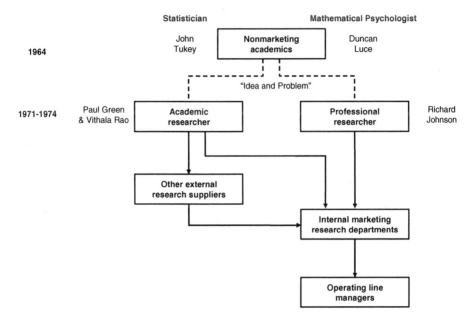

Figure 11-1. **Persons and Institutions Involved in the Creation and Diffusion of Conjoint Analysis** (Reproduced with permission from Myers, Massy, and Greyser, 1980)

The Decades of the Eighties and Nineties

Many research events occurred during the 1980s and 1990s. A major development has been the emergence of decision support models, as pioneered by John Little and his colleagues at MIT. Little, Glen Urban, John Hauser, and colleagues have been prime movers in the development of decision support models and Little's idea of the "decision calculus."

One of the novelties of this approach is the model builder's use of subjective estimates provided by expert decision makers, given the absence of hard data. User-supplied estimates can be useful pieces of information in cases where reliable data are either non-existent or fraught with error.

Decision support systems combine some of the well-known tools of OR/MS (e.g., sensitivity analysis) with both hard and soft data, as the need dictates. While Little and colleagues continue to lead this area, Table 11-4 shows that, over the past 20 years, researchers have embraced a variety of decision support models, as well as created a variety of research niches.

Table 11-4. **Decades of the Eighties and Nineties**

Decision Support Models
• Blend of descriptive and prescriptive model building
• Detailed behavioral measurement coupled with more flexible "optimization" procedures, including heuristics

Characteristics of Decision Support Models
- Recurring, high-stake decisions
- Reasonably well-structured problems, e.g., media selection, sales force allocation, test market evaluation
- Common structure across many types of businesses
- Amenable to specialized software development

Internally-based Decision Support Models

- Examples
  - BRANDAID
  - CALLPLAN
  - EXPRESS
- Characteristics
  - Data may be generated internally
  - Explicit inclusion of judgments

- Philosophy
  - John Little's Decision Calculus
    Make models increasingly comprehensive as data quality and quantity increase

Illustrative Decision Support Models

- ASSESSOR (Silk & Urban)
- BASES (Lin)
- BEHAVIORSCAN (Information Resources Inc.)
- BRANDAID (Little)
- BUNDOPT (Green & Krieger)
- CALLPLAN (Lodish)
- CLUSEQ (Green & Krieger)
- CONJOINT DISPLAY (Green & Krieger)

- DEFENDER (Hauser & Shugan)
- PENETRATOR (Parker)
- PERCEPTOR (Urban)
- PRODEGY (Urban, Johnson, Hauser)
- PROMOTER (Abraham and Lodish)
- PROMOTIONSCAN (Abraham & Lodish)
- SCAN-PRO (Nielsen)
- SIMOPT/SIMDYN (Green & Krieger)
- VOICE (Green & Krieger)

Expansion of Old and Rise of New Research Niches
- Brand equity analysis
- Causal modeling and covariance structure analysis
- Clustering techniques for mixtures of quantitative and qualitative variables
- Customer acquisition and retention
- Customer life-time value measurement
- Customer satisfaction modeling
- Data base management and data mining
- Empirical and hierarchical Bayesian analysis
- Expert systems and hybrid models of man and computer
- Game theory
- Generalized additive regression models; genetic and simulated annealing algorithms
- MARS-type regression modeling
- Mixture model fitting, including latent class and clusterwise regression
- Neural networks – unsupervised learning algorithms for cluster analysis
- "No-fat" economic (or theoretical) modeling
- Relationship marketing
- Tree classification techniques: CHAID, CART, ANSWER TREE

The Decade Ahead

We are now in the early years of the first decade of the new millennium. What can be said about 21st century marketing research? New models and techniques continue to appear. In addition, new research niches entailing economic modeling and game theory are being explored, particularly by some of the younger members of our profession. Table 11-5 shows a variety of recent measurement and modeling ideas, adding to the richness of marketing research methodology.

Table 11-5. **Into the New Century**

Research Supplier-directed Modeling and Methodology

- Conjoint analysis, discrete choice modeling, and buyer behavior simulation/ optimization
- Cluster and latent class analysis
- Hierarchical and empirical Bayes
- Multidimensional scaling, correspondence analysis, and classification and regression trees
- Multivariate methods for prediction, discrimination, and data summarization
- Prescriptive models for marketing mix allocation, sales force and territory planning, product and product line design, price/demand analysis, media management, and customer switching behavior

Specialized Research Methodologies and Models

- Behavioral decision theory
- Experimental economics
- Game theoretic and competitive models
- LISREL, partial least squares, and other approaches to covariance structure analysis
- "No-fat" economic modeling

Algorithms

- Fitting by splines
- Greedy and divide-and-conquer heuristics
- Lagrangian relaxation methods for constrained optimization
- Probit and "mother" logit models
- Tabu search; genetic algorithms; simulated annealing

Clearly, the field of research methodology shows no signs of drying up. In particular, we have all noted the advances made in discrete choice modeling by a host of young and talented scholars. Drawing on the pioneering work of Daniel McFadden (recent Nobel Prize winner), Jordan Louviere and his colleagues introduced discrete choice models to the existing array of conjoint modeling methods in marketing research. In particular, he and his colleagues have developed experimental designs tailored to the special characteristics of discrete choice modeling.

Discrete choice modeling has extended the breadth and value of conjoint analysis well beyond its initial roots. Now, with the advent of hierarchical Bayesian methods, analysts can estimate partworths at the individual level from aggregated individuals' data. This major event (and other technical developments, including mixture models and latent class modeling) has extended the marketing researcher's domain to include increasingly powerful statistical methods.

Many highly trained researchers, including (alphabetically) Greg Allenby, Eric Bradlow, Wayne DeSarbo, Wagner Kamakura, Abba Krieger, Peter Lenk, Jordan Louviere, Peter Rossi, and Michel Wedel have contributed to the major innovation that hierarchical Bayes and related techniques have brought to the analyst's table. These developments are excellent examples of how statisticians and marketing researchers, working together, can develop useful and important techniques for choice modeling, multiple regression, and other multivariate tools of interest to marketers.

In sum, the foregoing (and brief) overview of technical developments hardly does justice to the strides made in marketing research methodology over the past four decades. What we have seen, however, is a dramatic and sustained reaching out to other disciplines (e.g., microeconomics, OR/MS, statistics, psychometrics, etc.) for new tools and techniques that can be adapted to marketing problems. Conversely, marketing practitioners have provided feedback to the technique developers on how the initial methods could (or should) be modified to provide even more useful tools for applications-oriented researchers.

In concert with all of these new methods, there has been a dramatic increase in the use of computers and algorithms that often entail hundreds of thousands of iterations. Hierarchical Bayes is a prime example of the vital role that computers are beginning to play in implementing much of the newer choice-based methodology. We now turn to a discussion of the rapid rise of computers in marketing research and practice.

THE IMPACT OF EXPANDING COMPUTATIONAL RESOURCES

A reader of the first issue of *JMR* would have been stunned if he or she had encountered an issue from the year 2003. The marketing research field has experienced radical growth in the number and variety of methodologies now in common use. Most of these are computer-intensive, and in the early

1960s they were either not yet invented or not feasible due to lack of computational facilities.

In the current age of easy computer accessibility, it is sometimes hard to remember how different life was 40 years ago. There were no small computers. Large computers became available on university campuses but, within industry, their use was often limited to accounting, and they were rarely available for marketing research applications. Software for marketing research was mostly limited to tabulating. Techniques such as regression analysis and factor analysis had existed for many years, but had not been computationally feasible except for very small data sets.

The increasing availability of computers had a dramatic effect on marketing research, but developments in programming languages were equally important. In the early '60s higher-level programming languages were being developed, and FORTRAN compilers were becoming available at many computer centers. This led to an explosion of methodological developments. Many individuals began writing their own software to do statistical analyses.

The expanding availability of computational resources led to new types of methodological research at many academic institutions and at a few outstanding commercial ones, such as Bell Labs. This resulted in wholly new methods for performing analyses that were becoming available for marketing research practitioners, such as multidimensional scaling, which helped managers visualize market structures, and cluster analysis for dividing potential buyers into relatively homogeneous market segments. In 1970 the AMA sponsored a workshop on Multivariate Methods at the University of Chicago. Those papers eventually appeared in a volume edited by Jagdish Sheth (1977). (The table of contents of that volume provides an excellent overview of the state of the art at the beginning of the '70s.)

However, as dramatic as the changes of the '60s had been, there was much more to come. With the 1970s came two major developments: time sharing and minicomputers. Previously, when working with "mainframe" computers, computational jobs were submitted by physically delivering a deck of punched cards to a computer center; there was often a delay of hours or sometimes even days before results were available.

Time-sharing provided a way for a researcher to submit computational jobs remotely, without having to be present at a computer center. The user had the illusion of having the computer to oneself and results were available quickly. This made software development much easier, and also prompted more marketing researchers to interact directly with computers, rather than depending on data processing departments to do their work for them.

"Minicomputers" provided another step in the direction of enabling more people to work directly with computers. The term did not refer to what we think of today as a small computer, but rather to a computer that filled a small room rather than a large one. By the early '70s it was possible to buy a minicomputer for less than $100,000 that had more memory and speed than had been available a decade earlier in much larger machines costing millions of dollars.

Minicomputers offering time sharing provided the first sufficiently cost-effective capability for computers to be used for interviewing survey respondents. In the late '70s, Market Facts, Inc. undertook a conjoint analysis study of recruiting incentives for the U.S. Army in which hundreds of teenage males in many locations throughout the country were interviewed simultaneously by a computer in Chicago. The cost of the study was far less than it would have been without using the computer as an interviewer; also, the results were available much more quickly, and respondents enjoyed the experience.

The appearance of microcomputers in the late '70s triggered a further surge of increased computer availability for marketing researchers. The first commercially successful microcomputer was the Apple II, which provided much of the capability of the preceding generation's minicomputers in a package that weighed about 30 pounds and cost approximately $2,000. In the early 1980s IBM introduced the PC, a machine of similar size and capability but with higher reliability and a dramatically improved video display.

The '80s and '90s could reasonably be called the decades of the personal computer. During that period PCs increased in speed and memory size by factors of several hundred. By the year 2000, PCs were in nearly every office and about 60% of the homes in the U.S. By the mid-1990s the Internet had developed so far that e-mail had become one of the most frequently used means of communication among marketing researchers. Web-administered surveys had become one of the most widely used ways to interview respondents, and electronic transmission of documents had become a common way of distributing manuscripts.

This dramatic increase in computer resources over the past 40 years has had great impact on the practice of marketing research. Its effect, while still increasing, has been so vast that we are probably not aware of all its facets. However, several of the more noteworthy aspects are as follows:

- *A large proportion of the population in developed nations has access to computers.* Since so many potential survey respondents have computer access and familiarity, a large and growing proportion of marketing research data collection is now done using interviews administered by computer. Indeed, a whole new industry has sprung up to provide software for computer-based interviewing, which has resulted in lower costs, faster results, and higher-quality data.

- *Most marketing researchers have become computer users themselves.* We now type our own e-mail messages and compose our written text using computers; and many use computers for data analyses. This has been facilitated by the availability of user-friendly PC-based software for commonly used techniques such as regression, perceptual mapping, cluster analysis, and conjoint analysis.
- *Methodology that was once restricted to "experts" is available to all.* Just as one can drive a car skillfully without knowledge of electronics or thermodynamics, one can now use software for many sophisticated methodologies without complete knowledge of the underlying mathematical or statistical principles. The availability of user-friendly software for conjoint analysis, for example, has contributed to its widespread adoption by marketing researchers.
- *Researchers now think in multivariate rather than univariate terms.* In the '60s it was common for surveys to ask about perceptions of products on many attributes. But practitioners seldom attempted to study relationships among attributes. If products were rated on, say, 30 characteristics, the results were usually treated as if the characteristics were independent of one another. By contrast, today researchers often consider multidimensional market structures, and multiattribute preference models are common.
- *The unit of analysis has moved from the population to the individual.* We are now much better able to recognize heterogeneity in preference. In the '60s we lacked techniques to deal with heterogeneity, and aggregate-level analyses were the rule. Analysis methods for market segmentation became available in the '70s, as did conjoint analysis, which permitted analysis of values at the individual level. Most recently, hierarchical Bayes methods have provided a way to obtain yet more precise estimates of individual's values by (perhaps ironically) considering information from other individuals.

In sum, the vital role of computers (and their current ubiquity) has dramatically changed the kinds of things that can now be done in marketing research and practice. Fast, inexpensive computation has put a new face on analyses that were once considered formidable, if implementable at all.

However, major developments in methodology and computation would be interesting curiosities were it not for the critical role that industry *application* plays in furthering (and expanding) the boundaries of marketing research.

Fortunately, *JMR* and the American Marketing Association's "outreach" programs have played essential roles in furthering the *practice* of marketing research.

GETTING THE WORD OUT: *JMR* RESEARCH, MSI, THE AMA, AND THEIR IMPACT ON MARKETING PRACTICE

New marketing research ideas without application and feedback are, at best, tentative and incomplete. Industry practitioners play a vital role in testing the practicality and usefulness of new models and techniques. Through practitioner feedback, technique developers can learn valuable information about how the new ideas can be improved upon in terms of reliability, validity, and impact.

Ideas that work well with docile and cooperative business students may not suit the respondent population at large. In short, real-world practitioner feedback is critical to the research process. Fortunately, marketing researchers can look to three key sources – the Marketing Science Institute, the American Marketing Association, and commercial research firms (including software firms such as SPSS and SAS) – to provide knowledge transfer and field testing of ideas that may very well have been generated by *JMR* authors. We first describe the early days of the Marketing Science Institute and show how this institution has contributed significantly to the generation and dissemination of research methods.

The Marketing Science Institute

The Marketing Science Institute owes much to the foresight and doggedness of two men: Thomas McCabe, then president of Scott Paper Company, and Wroe Alderson, then faculty member at Wharton. Prior to the beginning of the Institute, starting in the mid-fifties, Wroe initiated the Marketing Theory Seminar (held in alternate years at the University of Vermont and the University of Colorado).

It was in these bucolic surroundings that young marketing instructors were treated to the musings and pronouncements of the "grand old men," Leo Aspinwall, Lyndon Brown, Richard Clewett, Paul Converse, Ed Grether, Ed McGarry, and Hugh Wales, among others. (The seminars continued until Wroe's death in 1965.)

In the early 1960s Thomas McCabe coaxed many top executives to contribute funds to the founding of MSI in 1961. Is initial location was in Philadelphia. Wendell Smith was selected as its first president; Patrick Robinson and Michael Halbert came on board as principal investigators. The

Institute's first location was hardly patrician; it was nestled on Walnut Street between a bowling alley and a pizza parlor! (Subsequently, it was moved to a somewhat more prestigious address on Market Street.)

A large number of academic "young turks" came to MSI to work on projects. These included Bill Massy, Ron Frank, Jerry Wind, Peter Fitz Roy, Irwin Gross, David Luck, and Paul Green.

In the latter part of the 1960s, MSI moved to Cambridge, Massachusetts, where it has remained. MSI maintains regular contact with the business world and one of its primary objectives is to design conferences where both research practitioners and academics can get together and discuss research progress and priorities. MSI also maintains an active library of research papers, proceedings, and assorted reviews of new research findings.

Table 11-6 lists the current and past presidents and executive directors of the Marketing Science Institute. And what a distinguished list it has turned out to be. Clearly, MSI has been an important source of practitioner feedback.

Table 11-6. **Presidents and Directors of the Marketing Science Institute**

Presidents (1961-2002)	**Executive Directors** (1968-2002)
Wendell R. Smith	Robert D. Buzzell, Georgetown University
Edwin L. Morris	Stephen A. Greyser, Harvard University
Thomas B. McCabe, Jr.	E. Raymond Corey, Harvard University
Alden G. Clayton	Louis W. Stern, Northwestern University
F. Kent Mitchel	John U. Farley, Dartmouth College
H. Paul Root	Frederick E. Webster, Jr., Dartmouth College
William A. Ghormley	George S. Day, University of Pennsylvania
William H. Moult	Richard Staelin, Duke University
	Donald R. Lehmann, Columbia University
	David B. Montgomery, Stanford University
	Rohit Deshpandè, Harvard University
	David J. Reibstein, University of Pennsylvania
	Donald R. Lehmann, Columbia University (current)

The American Marketing Association

In 1937, the National Association of Teachers in Marketing and the American Marketing Society decided to merge and create the American Marketing Association (AMA). Since this beginning, the AMA has become a leader in the generation and dissemination of marketing research information. The AMA's mission statement pretty much sums up its role: "to empower marketers, through the supply of information, education, and resources that will enrich their professional development and careers, and to advance the thought, application, and ethical practice of marketing."

However, by the middle of the 1950s, marketing research was evolving into its own separate field of specialization within the marketing community and the AMA. In 1958, the AMA formed the Marketing Research Division with a separate management group and advisory council. One of the early results of this trend was the launch of AMA's Attitude Research Conference. The Division's first conference exclusively for marketing researchers was held on a cruise ship bound for Bermuda; many of marketing's top academics and practitioners addressed issues and solutions related to attitude measurement and analysis (including multivariate methods). For over two decades thereafter, the AMA's annual Attitude Research Conference continued as a primary event for disseminating applied marketing research methods and techniques to both educators and practitioners.

In 1980, the AMA launched its First Annual Marketing Research Conference. Now in its 23rd year, this conference is still designed to keep the research community abreast of "best practices" by featuring applied research results at the business unit level. The conference also provides a forum for the annual Charles Coolidge Parlin Award – the oldest and most prestigious award in the field of marketing research.

One rather quiet event, that apparently has not been previously documented, occurred in early 1987. The Marketing Research Division Council of the AMA developed a strategic plan (its first) that called for renewed efforts to improve marketing research training and knowledge dissemination. This plan guided the activities of the Marketing Research Division over ten years. Four initiatives from the plan were to have considerable impact on the diffusion of marketing research knowledge.

The first initiative called for the delivery of targeted training in marketing research. Each of the AMA's conferences was to be expanded to include tutorials before and after the main conference proceedings. The tutorials were initially planned as four-hour programs, designed to provide in-depth treatment of best practices, ranging from an introduction to conjoint analysis to cluster analysis. Well-respected practitioners and academics were recruited to teach these programs. The first tutorials were presented at the Attitude Research Conference in 1987. The programs were very well received and continue today as a key feature of every AMA research conference.

From these tutorial programs there evolved another conference format, named the Applied Research Methods Conference. The AMA Research Division now offers this program twice each year. Primarily, it is a conference of tutorials only. Attendees may pick from a wide variety of two-hour and four-hour sessions ranging from questionnaire design to advanced topics in market segmentation. It is estimated that over 4,000 marketing researchers have attended at least one of these tutorials since their inception.

The second initiative of the 1987 Marketing Research Division Council called for the development of a *basic* training program in marketing research principles that could be delivered, on-site, to anyone wishing to learn marketing fundamentals. This initiative was presented to, and endorsed by, the Research Industry Leadership Forum in 1988. Malcolm McNiven, then head of the Masters degree in Marketing Research program at the University of Georgia, and William Neal designed and developed the initial program.

The Principles of Marketing Research Program is currently available worldwide, both online and offline. The program has ten modules that provide training in all of the fundamentals of marketing research. The program has been endorsed by leading marketing research organizations worldwide and has been adopted by many large firms as a basic training requirement for their marketing research staffs.

The AMA's third strategic initiative entailed an expansion of its professional development conferences. In the 1980s, the field of marketing research was itself beginning to specialize along both functional lines (e.g., data analysis, sampling, media research, field management, account management) and by industry specialty (e.g., pharmaceuticals, energy, chemicals, travel, and tourism). The strategic plan called for developing smaller format, targeted conferences that would address specific functional and specialty areas of marketing research practice.

By the mid 1980s, Sawtooth Software had developed PC-based software for computer interviewing, perceptual mapping, and conjoint analysis, and wished to broaden the awareness of its capabilities among marketing researchers. In 1987 the first of a series of annual Sawtooth Software conferences was held on the use of computers in marketing research. The first conference drew 250 participants, mostly practitioners from data collection services, full-service marketing research, and end-user organizations. Attendees were excited about the potential increases in marketing research capabilities related to these new PC developments; this excitement, in turn, led to a high degree of openness and congeniality among the conference participants.

Representatives of the AMA Marketing Research Council who attended the Sawtooth conferences saw them as useful and enlightening. In 1991, with Sawtooth Software's blessing, the AMA initiated its first annual Advanced Research Techniques (A/R/T Forum) conference. It was patterned after the Sawtooth conferences.

The A/R/T Forum

The A/R/T Forum is now in its thirteenth year. Mindful of the need to provide a healthy climate and scenic beauty, the A/R/T Forum designers have chosen lovely sites along the way, including Amelia Island, Keystone, Vail, Monterey, and Santa Fe. The most recent meeting was held in Vail (fortunately, prior to the forest fires). The conference was chaired by Peter Fader and, by any measure, was an outstanding success.

In addition to plenary presentations, the Forum's designers include seminars on a variety of topics entailing new models and techniques. The presenters are tops in their respective specialty areas. Plenty of time is provided for audience questions and feedback. In addition, informal discussion groups are routinely set up for speaker and audience participation.

Poster sessions are also designed by presenters who choose this avenue to discuss their work. Discussions are lively and informative. Speaking for ourselves, we find the A/R/T Forum to be an exceptionally well-run conference. For marketing researchers interested in the latest tools and applications, this is clearly the conference to attend. Its format and content are fully in sync with *JMR* and its objectives.

Other AMA Researcher/Practitioner Events

AMA's service to practitioners extends to other areas as well. Its fourth initiative resulted in the birth of a new journal. *Marketing Research*, an AMA magazine for management and marketing research practitioners, has begun its fourteenth volume, under the current stewardship of Chuck Chakrapani. *Marketing Research* has a lively (and sometimes irreverent) group of authors who often hold strong opinions about what kinds of industry research should be done and how one should go about doing it.

Marketing Research features two regular columns: one by Gordon Wyner on research methods and one by Donna Gillin on legislative and regulatory issues. One of its principal sections is "Back Talk," a free-for-all section where various researchers can challenge, bicker, and otherwise excoriate fellow researchers in spirited debate. *Marketing Research* is a mixture of developments in methodology and the reactions and experiences of practitioners who have tried these techniques, many initially published in *JMR*. Such feedback is useful for researchers and practitioners alike.

Marketing Research provides an excellent companion to *JMR* by providing "voice of the customer" feedback, namely practitioner-consultants or intra-firm marketing research personnel who have a major stake in the thoughtful application of new research techniques and the refurbishing of older research methods. AMA and the Marketing Science Institute provide important dissemination and feedback roles in furthering technical developments, often spearheaded by *JMR* authors. Nor do these activities exhaust AMA's role in technique diffusion. A variety of conferences on special topics for different interest groups (and associated publications) are also part of AMA's many activities for broadening the base of marketing practice and research.

In sum, the four strategic initiatives developed by the Marketing Research Division to improve marketing research training and enhance the dissemination of marketing research knowledge continue today. The AMA Marketing Research Division also continues to experiment with new conference topics, new formats, and new technologies. We are all most appreciative of the time and creative efforts of those volunteers who have served on the Council over its extensive lifetime.

POINT US TO TOMORROW

Our attempt to cover, in one article, 40 years of progress in marketing research methodology is presumptuous, at best. We have shown our biases in favor of techniques that have led to extensive, real-world application (or potential application). These include:

- Cluster analysis: partitional and hierarchical
- MDS and correspondence analysis
- Conjoint analysis and discrete choice modeling
- Computer choice simulation
- Decision-support modeling (including simulated test marketing)
- Price/demand marketing
- Economic modeling and game theory
- Covariance structure modeling and hypothesis testing

Decision areas that have benefited from these models include:

- Market segmentation
- Market experimentation
- Attitude measurement
- Voice of the customer modeling
- New product/service development
- Analysis of competitive behavior
- Advertising measurement, sales force deployment, and technical service evaluation.

Additional areas of research should be noted. These include the pioneering work of Frank Bass and Vijay Mahajan on product diffusion modeling, the economic modeling of Sridhar Moorthy, Pradeep Chintagunta, Rajeev Lal, and Jagmohan Raju (to name a few of the top scholars in this area), and the important work of Jerry Wind and his collaborators on market segmentation and industrial buying behavior. The list of possible application areas in marketing seems to go on and on.

Wagner Kamakura, in his inaugural note to the *JMR* readership (2001), succinctly listed three basic conceptual and methodological perspectives for *JMR* direction and content:

- Quantitative (e.g., statistics, econometrics)
- Behavioral (e.g., psychology, sociology)
- Managerial (e.g., strategy, organizational behavior).

Independently, the current authors have historically examined what has transpired over the first 40 years of *JMR* methodology and noted virtually the same themes:

- Quantitative methods including OR/MS, econometrics, and statistics
- Psychometrics and measurement
- Managerial, in the context of decision support models.

Wagner further describes the *JMR* audience as made up of both educators and practitioners, the latter representing almost 60% of *JMR* subscribers. Our review supports the importance of this segment, and reinforces the need for pushing the technical envelope while keeping in mind the pragmatic issues of implementation, information transfer, and practitioner feedback. We believe that the combined efforts of the American Marketing Association and the Marketing Science Institute have implemented these missions with talent, foresight, and energy.

Table 11-7. **Journal of Marketing Research Editors: 1964-2003**

Robert Ferber	1964-1968
Ralph L. Day	1969-1971
Frank M. Bass	1972-1974
Harper W. Boyd	1975-1977
Gilbert A. Churchill, Jr.	1978-1982
William D. Perreault, Jr.	1983-1985
Robert A. Peterson	1986-1988
Michael J. Houston	1989-1991
Barton A. Weitz	1992-1994
Vijay Mahajan	1995-1997
Russell S. Winer	1998-2000
Wagner A. Kamakura	2001-2003

The remarks made here are both fleeting and tentative; the science and artistry of marketing research continues, unfazed by those who would try to catalog it. Fortunately for us, the *Journal of Marketing Research* is designed as a continuous agent for initiating, monitoring, and recording the variety of methods and techniques subsumed under the label of marketing research. *JMR* began and continues to be the beacon to the future of marketing research.

To all of us – editor, reviewer, author, or reader – *JMR* has played a major role in advancing the art and science of marketing research. A fitting tribute to the end of this article is to salute those distinguished *JMR* editors (see Table 11-7) for their intellect, devotion to duty, and innate belief in the field of marketing research. When it comes to marketing research methodology, *JMR* is, indeed, the very "Best of Show."

NOTES

[1] Originally appeared in the *Journal of Marketing Research* 40, (February 2003), 1-9.

REFERENCES

Kamakura, W. A. (2001), "From the Editor," *Journal of Marketing Research*, 38 (February), 1-2.

Myers, J., Massy, W. F., and Greyser, S. (1980), *Marketing Research and Knowledge Development,* Englewood Cliffs, NJ: Prentice-Hall, Inc.

Sheth, J. N., ed. (1977), *Multivariate Methods for Market and Survey Research,* Chicago: American Marketing Association.

Chapter 12

Personal Reflections and Tributes from the May 2002 Conference Celebrating Paul Green's Career

In May 2002, mentors, colleagues and students, friends and family gathered together to celebrate Paul Green's four decades of contributions to marketing research. In addition to the formal assessments of the field in other chapters of this book, the event inspired a wide variety of other tributes – from personal reflections to poetry to song. On the following pages, we offer a cross-section of the reflections and creative work celebrating the life and work of Paul Green. We begin with personal reflections from his long career and end with poetry and song, inspired by his work and life.

Welcome and Opening Comments
David Schmittlein
Deputy Dean, The Wharton School, University of Pennsylvania
Former Chairman, Marketing Department

On behalf of the Wharton School, Dean Patrick Harker, and myself, I would like to welcome those of you who have traveled to be with us to recognize Paul Green's many contributions.

Today's academic program included some of the best and most productive researchers in marketing. They provided an illustration of the way that research in marketing has advanced, and continues to evolve. Paul Green's influence on this evolution came through in many ways in those sessions. Some of the speakers, of course, acknowledged a direct debt to his scholarly work. Others experienced Paul as a collaborator and a mentor, or benefited from Paul's great generosity of spirit. And still other speakers illustrated how the rich vein of inquiry Paul opened up for the field in the 1960s and 1970s has been a lifeblood for the academic discipline of marketing.

Peter Drucker has said that business has only two basic functions – marketing and innovation. Paul Green has clearly been marketing's signature contributor to the intersection between the two. Indeed, this point seems so self-evident in his work, and so well made through the sessions today, that I would be foolish to try to expound further on it this evening.

Rather, I would like to be foolish enough to spend a few minutes trying to do justice to Paul's contribution to the Wharton School. I would also like to offer a couple of personal observations, if I may.

It is my understanding that when Paul completed his doctorate he had the opportunity to teach in either the Statistics Department or the Marketing Department at Wharton. He is reported to have chosen marketing out of a desire to work with the legendary Wroe Alderson, and also due to a sense of some extraordinary research opportunities that marketing provided. Certainly the Marketing Department at Wharton was never more fortunate than in this decision. In the early to mid 1960s, Paul joined with Wroe to initiate a stream of management sciences research at Wharton. When Ron Frank joined the Marketing Department in the early 1960s, Paul and Ron together took on the task to create a world-class set of faculty that were trained in the basic disciplines of economics, psychology, sociology, operations research and statistics, and that were also dedicated to changing the face of marketing practice. This recruiting drive led, over the next several years, to the hiring of (among others) Jerry Wind, Tom Robertson, Len Lodish, and Scott Armstrong.

During the 1970s Paul's research output, collaboration with others in the department (notably Ron Frank and Jerry Wind), and sponsorship of doctoral students led the Marketing Department to the first rank of research institutions in marketing.

This would be enough for one stellar career. But Paul Green continued his research through this past twenty years, and has seen it grow in impact in the wider marketing and management practitioner population. He has not only received nearly every award for research in marketing, but one of the leading awards in the field is named in his honor. The department and the Wharton School owe Paul a debt that it can never repay. It can, however, attempt to say "thank you."

I said that I would like to offer a couple of personal observations. While they have thoughts and emotions attached to them, they appear for me as finely drawn mental images. In doing this I want to acknowledge that there are others who have spoken – or will yet speak – who know Paul better than I.

- The first mental image is a typically animated, noisy – not to say contentious – department faculty meeting, especially one involving faculty recruiting. Paul raises his hand and offers a gentle observation or question, and the room suddenly exhibits pin-drop silence. It is a unique measure of respect for the speaker, unasked-for and freely given by the faculty. Paul often could have had 51 percent of the decision-authority from his colleagues if he asked for it. His preference, rather, has been consensus-building, mutual respect, and a willingness to let us all grow as colleagues by making our collective decisions – and learning by the result.

- Another image is of Paul describing a current research project to me in casual hall conversation. This scene is one of contrast, Paul calmly logically smoothly articulating a point of algebra, or data manipulation, or probability models, me in near panic, holding on by my fingernails to the ideas that are flying by with the speed – and yes, the elegance – of Concorde. Scary, but exhilarating.

- I also recall a scene played out numerous times – my looking in my departmental mailbox and seeing *another* manuscript authored by Paul, placed there with a nice handwritten note: "Comments welcomed." A strong motivator to get my own manuscript finished – and placed in Paul's mailbox.

- Another scene is an annual review of my performance, in the department chair's office, with a couple of senior faculty. I had recently received tenure and there had been a lull in my productivity. Paul kindly indicated that he so enjoyed the short (tiny) working paper I had been able to produce that year and suggested certain additional ideas I might pursue in the area. I, was ashamed that I had put his gentleness to such a test, and vowed not to repeat the experience.

- Regressing further in time, I end with two memories from August 1979. I was a Ph.D. candidate at Columbia going out on the academic job market in marketing. The first (and later) memory is of many a marketing academic's most stressful experience – the AMA interviews. I had 28 interviews for a faculty position at the AMA Educators' conference, most of which (happily) I do not recall. But I will always carry the image of a certain hotel room in Minneapolis, with (from right to left) Neil Beckwith, Ron Frank, and over by the window, Paul Green. I recall, equally, being struck by the force of Paul's intellect and graced by the warmth of his humanity. Together, they made Wharton seem a pretty great place to be. Then, moving back about a week in time, I see vividly a university reception hall in Madison, Wisconsin. I had just arrived at the AMA doctoral consortium and was standing with a couple of newly met friends. We collectively expressed our anxiety that this consortium of faculty and topics seemed almost devoid of the kind of research we had been trained to do. This was certainly true of the probability models I had experienced in my incubation at Columbia. I did however share with these new friends my opinion that, whatever else one might say about the consortium, it was nice that the organizers had arranged for such a wonderful piano player to entertain us from the corner. I don't recall who said, "You don't know who that is? That's Paul Green."

> But I do recall thinking – "Well, if Paul is here, and this is indeed who Paul Green is, marketing may be OK after all."

I believe I can say with confidence that not one of these events was at all memorable for Paul. My point instead is that great scholars, and great people, make an outsize difference each day, in their smallest moments, in ways they cannot be expected to envision or manage. The Wharton and marketing communities have been incredibly fortunate that the source of so many such influences has been Paul Green.

For my twenty years at Wharton, Paul has, by his example, forced me and others to confront a simple question: *"How would you like to be remembered?"* While we may not live up to it, we have a great example in front of us.

It is my understanding that a speech at these kinds of occasions must contain a quote from Emerson, Thoreau, or Robert Frost. Not wanting to be derelict in that duty, I choose the latter, and his observation that "Education is the ability to listen to almost anything without losing your temper."

By this measure and of course many more, Paul Green is the best-educated person I know. We, all of us, remain fortunate to continue to have him with us.

A Fertile and Creative Mind
Morris Hamburg
Emeritus Professor, The Wharton School

As Jerry Wind stated in his introduction, I was Paul Green's doctoral dissertation advisor. It is heartwarming for me to be here today at this conference in recognition of Paul's remarkable impact on both academia and industry and in celebration of his 40th anniversary at the Wharton School. I deeply appreciate the opportunity to have been included in the program.

Paul was my first doctoral dissertation student. I would like to say a few words as to how that came about. During the 1959-1960 academic year, as a Wharton faculty member, I attended an Institute of Mathematics for Application to Business at the Harvard Business School sponsored by the Ford Foundation. A total of forty faculty members of business schools throughout the country, mostly from departments in the functional areas of business such as marketing, finance, and management had been selected to attend the institute. The general purpose of the Ford Foundation was to encourage and assist the introduction and spread of mathematical modeling in university business administration programs. Howard Raiffa, who was a professor at the Harvard Business School, was the Director of the Institute. Since Howard was a pioneer and enthusiast in Bayesian decision theory and analysis, which was at that time a quite new area of statistics, he gave us a spirited infusion of interest in that field, as well as a well reasoned critique of classical statistical methods.

Upon my return to my position as an associate professor of statistics at the Wharton School in 1960, Paul, who was then working at DuPont, asked me whether I would be willing to be his doctoral dissertation supervisor. He had already received his master's degree in the statistics department at Wharton and had completed all of the required course work for the Ph.D. degree. It turned out that he was already involved in some applications of Bayesian decision analysis to marketing problems at DuPont, and he indicated that he would like to continue and extend that work into his doctoral thesis. I was delighted at the prospect of working with him on these real-world applications, and furthermore, we had become friends during his graduate student days. Thus, we segued into a thesis entitled, "Some Intra-firm Applications of Bayesian Decision Theory to Problems in Business Planning."

Paul, as you might expect, did a superb job in writing the thesis. I will merely say that I believe we both enjoyed ourselves and learned a great deal as we worked our way through the modeling and applications in the dissertation.

There was one application that particularly intrigued me. DuPont, at that time, produced an industrial end-use fiber for which top management was considering a price decrease. The decision problem was quite complex. Three other firms produced this fiber at identical prices to DuPont, and product quality and service among all four producers were comparable. There were four interrelated market segments. Furthermore, there was a competitive fiber produced by six other firms in the four market segments.

Paul designed and carried out a complex Bayesian decision analysis of four pricing alternatives. Most of the data consisted of informed judgments by sales management personnel. One of the price decreases emerged from the analysis as the recommended best course of action. Top management chose not to introduce that price decrease nor any of the other price decreases studied. In Paul's reflections on the study recommendations, he noted that it was possible that top management may have implicitly considered another course of action, namely to defer a price decrease to some future time, which, of course, was not an alternative considered in the original problem formulation. If indeed that was the case, then, for example, the alternative of a price decrease one year later could have been explicitly examined as well. Perhaps, for top management, we have here an example of the adage, "T'would be trite to state the obvious, were it not for the universal neglect thereof."

After completion of his thesis, Paul had a phenomenally prolific run of publications in a variety of fields using Bayesian decision theory and analysis. His work was extremely widely cited, and he developed a well-deserved reputation as an outstanding researcher.

However, with his fertile and creative mind, Paul went on to make seminal contributions to the other areas of modeling and applications that are being discussed at this conference such as multivariate data analysis, multidimensional scaling and clustering, and conjoint and related analyses. Nevertheless, I believe that it is fair to say that Paul carried over, throughout the succeeding decades, concepts and techniques that he dealt with in his doctoral dissertation such as the multiplicity of goals in decision making under uncertainty, alternative concepts of optimization, the intellectual wrestling match that takes place in the application of normative theories to real-world problems, Von Neumann-Morgenstern utility functions, tradeoffs, and sensitivity analysis.

Now, with your permission, I would like to engage in a bit of name-dropping. My own doctoral dissertation supervisor was Simon Kuznets, the second American to have been awarded the Nobel Prize in Economics. He was a professor of statistics at Wharton when I wrote my thesis. Incidentally, Paul Green wrote his masters degree thesis under Simon Kuznets, also. Both Paul and I have Ph.D. degrees in economics with majors in statistics. In those days, there was a single Graduate Group in Economics in the Wharton School that awarded doctorate degrees in economics with majors in the departmental fields such as finance, marketing, etc., as well as statistics and economics. The doctoral candidates took a set of required courses in economics and also had other examination requirements in economics. Therefore, you can add the term "economist" to Paul's list of academic qualifications, that is, if he permits you to do so.

I had a telephone conversation with Simon Kuznets during the week before he was to leave for Sweden to receive the Nobel Prize. At the end of our conversation, in a lighthearted way, I said, "Bon voyage, Simon. I think that the Nobel Prize people should be congratulated for being clever enough to have selected you for the award." There was a moment of silence at the other end of the line. Then Simon replied quietly, in his Russian-accented English, "Vell, I von't tell dem dis."

Simon Kuznets had a delightful sense of humor. He also was a gentle, unassuming and modest man. I am mentioning these characteristics because they all describe Paul Green as well. Returning to the matter of the Nobel Prize, if there was such an award in the field of marketing research, I think you would agree that a prime candidate to be the first recipient of that prize would be Paul Green.

I would like to tell you an anecdotal story about a friend of mine, the late Fred Karush. Fred was a professor of microbiology in medicine at Penn's medical school. He was an outstanding scholar in his field, and I attended a ceremony in his honor for the unveiling of a portrait of him to be hung in the medical school. After a number of speeches that extolled Fred's virtues and accomplishments, it was his turn to speak. Fred strode to the podium and said, "You know, if my father was here today, he would be very proud of me. If my mother was here today, she not only would have been proud of me. She would have believed all of these outrageously generous things that were said about me today."

I will conclude my comments by saying that if Paul Green's father and mother were here today, they both certainly would be very proud of him. Also, they would be very well advised to believe all of the nice things that have been said about him.

Stimulating and Enriching Conversations

Raymond R. Burke
E.W. Kelley Professor of Business Administration
Kelley School of Business, Indiana University

When I joined the Wharton faculty, I had the good fortune to be assigned to an office next door to Paul Green. Fresh out of school from the University of Florida's Ph.D. program, my mind was focused on theoretical issues in consumer psychology. Given Paul's reputation in marketing research and modeling, I did not think we would have much to talk about. In fact, our conversations were some of the most stimulating and enriching experiences that I had during my years at Wharton. Paul valued interdisciplinary research, and his innovations in the field of marketing reflected a deep understanding of consumer behavior, psychometrics, and statistics. He was continually exploring ways in which the science of consumer psychology could be used to improve management decisions, including product design, pricing, advertising, promotion, and assortment planning. Paul also recognized the importance of working with practitioners on real-world problems, and developing software to make his analytic techniques broadly accessible. His work set an example for the Wharton faculty and profoundly affected my view of the discipline and future research.

Hindsight: A Thank You to Paul Green

Gordon A. Wyner
Executive Vice President – Strategy, Millward Brown, Inc.
Chairman of the Executive Committee, Marketing Science Institute

On the occasion of his retirement from Wharton I would again like to thank Paul Green for being a mentor to me. As a Ph.D. student in sociology at the University of Pennsylvania, I took Paul's graduate course in Measurement and Data Analysis which was a broad and deep introduction to quantitative methods in marketing for segmentation, positioning, and value proposition development. In retrospect (I took the course about 25 years ago), it's clear that this experience was incredibly worthwhile at the time and continues to be important to this day.

The Observed Data

Naturally the course had extensive coverage of conjoint analysis, along with perceptual mapping, clustering, regression analysis, and other multivariate techniques. The short story is that decades later I am still applying all these methods (and a few others) as a consultant, and they have been critical to my growth and development all along. I've used them in different ways in marketing and business strategy for clients as well as in strategy development within my company. They also helped me to contribute to the marketing field as an editorial board member for *JMR,* a Trustee of the Marketing Science Institute, occasional writer, and columnist for *Marketing Management* and *Marketing Research* magazines.

The methods have evolved somewhat over time. In the early days, high-speed data communication used to mean hauling boxes of IBM computer cards onto the subway. The big risk factors were that you would drop the deck of cards and lose the order, or that the card reader would jam halfway through a run and you'd have to stay there longer. I recall getting into a do-loop with a particularly large discriminant analysis that cost $400 of computer time. We don't usually have to worry about these kinds of costs anymore.

Today we have more sophisticated versions of older methods and some new methods. We implement methods more quickly and apply them in different business contexts, e.g., CRM, the Internet. Costs are lower, overall efficiency is greater, but there are greater risks of misapplications by people who use automated software but don't have a good understanding of the underlying methods.

However, the core ideas are still with us. Companies are still trying to figure out what to offer to which customers and who are the key competitors; quantitative methods continue to play important roles. Despite many challenges over the years, segmentation and tradeoff analyses are indispensable for identifying and sizing opportunities. Applications of the methods continue to create value for marketers and for their customers.

Drilling Down a Level

Beyond the key ideas and methods Paul went deeply into some of the underlying component elements. Foremost among them for me was *experimental design.*

Through other coursework in statistics, economics, and sociology I had learned some of the basics. Here I learned about fractional designs (in all their resolutions) and their links to model specification and estimation. I learned about alias patterns, modular arithmetic, and easy-to-use catalogues if all else failed.

The ability to select a subset of design combinations and to predict hundreds or thousands more was truly magical (which I have learned has both scientific and commercial value). Importantly experimental design has the unique ability to test out marketing stimuli that don't exist in the current environment, revealing potential value for marketers that can't be inferred from past behavior.

I still see the increasing digitization of business as fertile ground for real-world, real-time experimentation, over and above being a platform for questionnaire data collection. It surprises me that experimental design has not achieved greater adoption. It calls for applying existing methods in a new way, something I observed in Paul Green's work years ago.

Another key area explored in the class was *measurement* itself. While I haven't found a direct application of the intricacies of Coombsian data classification, I know it's important. At a basic level the distinctions between perceptual, evaluative, and preference measures and the mechanisms for generating them are very useful, and are not as widely understood as they should be. I became particularly intrigued by the "upgrading" of ordinal to interval data through algorithms like MONANOVA, another one of those magical properties.

I am certain that understanding measurement properties enabled me to move forward with useful client applications rather than become mired in debates about unmet assumptions. Meeting assumptions is often not a simple binary outcome, but a matter of degree, which usually can be informed and evaluated by some data analysis.

Coursework with Paul Green was always heavily laden with *geometric expressions* of the key concepts, which had several benefits for me. It gave me another way to learn the underlying models for many of the methods. When looking at equations and matrices didn't sink in, there was always the spatial representation.

The geometric view also gave me a feel for the linkages between many of the key concepts. I recall that conjoint and multi-dimensional scaling, can, with the help of psychophysics, be related.

Lastly, I became comfortable with the idea that there are many kinds of spaces (e.g., psychological, not just geographical) and you define what are the axes and what are the objects to suit the problem you are addressing. A certain agility is required to move easily between these different representations.

These are just a few of the things that resonated with me the most. There were still more topics like decision models for consumer behavior and of course Bayesian approaches. It seems like a lot of topics for a single course, but they were all covered.

Stepping Up a Level

Finally, I just want to mention a couple of themes that have been influential in my thinking and work over the years that in some way relate to what I learned from Paul Green. These are some of the "latent variables" of my education. While these were clearly generated by many different influences, two stand out as being seeded in that course I took in the mid 1970s.

One theme is *parsimony*, an important goal in any scientific work. Sure I learned about it in other courses, starting with an undergraduate philosophy of science class. What strikes me about the lessons learned in Paul's class is that we were always reducing the dimensionality of something.

Start broad, reduce redundancy, and represent the situation in fewer variables. Got variation? Get segments. Borrow parameters. Find the smallest set of predictors. While it may not have been intentional I experienced my first real close shave with Occam's razor. Solutions to real world problems depended upon somehow managing complexity.

Finally, I came away from his class with a better sense of the *connections* of a lot of apparently differing things. Theoretical and practical. Geometry and algebra. Axes and data points. Conjoint and MDS. Social science and marketing science. Academic and commercial.

I always felt that Paul put a lot of important things together for us and then left it for the student to make more of the connections. I suspected that he sometimes left out just enough details to make it difficult and challenging for us. If his goal was to stimulate curiosity, he succeeded.

Thoughts about Paul Green
Richard M. Johnson
Chairman, Sawtooth Software

Paul Green has had an enormous beneficial effect on the practice of marketing research. Being a practitioner, my method for measuring Paul's effect on our field involves recognizing how much the practice of market research has changed, in directions suggested and aided by Paul's contributions. So let me describe the field as I first saw it in the early 1960s.

It was common for surveys to ask about perceptions of products on many attributes. But practitioners seldom attempted to study relationships between attributes. If products were rated on, say, 30 characteristics, the results were usually treated as if the characteristics were independent of one another. This was, of course, before the development of computer resources that facilitated any multivariate techniques.

Also, and perhaps more striking, the data analysis was almost always done at the aggregate level. Although we knew that different people wanted different things, we lacked the tools to study heterogeneity.

I believe the two biggest advances I have seen since the early '60s are: (1) moving from univariate to multivariate descriptions of products and other objects of interest, and (2) increased recognition of heterogeneity in consumer preferences.

The '60s and '70s were wonderfully productive in terms of our ability to perceive subtleties and complexities of markets. I suppose one must have personally experienced those years to grasp fully the magnitude of the change. In particular, the syntheses of information provided by perceptual maps have contributed greatly to our insights about markets. Paul, with his students and colleagues, played a critical role in educating us about new approaches made possible with techniques developed at Bell Labs and elsewhere. And the benefits of perceptual maps sometimes came in unexpected ways.

Let me tell you one story illustrating the impact of perceptual mapping. My friend John Fiedler is a practitioner who has made uncommonly productive use of perceptual mapping. One day in the mid-'80s, he was taking a tour of a General Motors plant, conducted by representatives of both management and the union. John, who had seen the insides of many manufacturing plants, thought this one seemed particularly advanced, appearing clean, bright, and full of modern automation gear. At the end of the line was a shiny new car, and beside it, on an easel, was what John recognized as a perceptual map. It showed relative positions in perceptual space of the car being produced, as well as the positions of many of its competitors, most of which were Japanese.

John couldn't resist asking "What's that?" The shop steward stepped forward with an explanation something like the following: "That's called a perceptual map. It shows how people perceive our product, compared to others. We're over here, and our main competitors are over there. The Japanese are giving us fits lately, with products that are perceived to be of higher quality. Our job is to produce cars of such high quality that our position moves from where we are now over to here, with the Japanese products."

I don't know whether Paul was personally involved in developing that particular perceptual map, but I am certain that his influence contributed greatly to the advancement of our art which gave rise to it.

The other major trend I've noted is our increasing ability to recognize and accommodate heterogeneity in preference. In the early 1960s, we knew that people differed in their preferences, but we lacked the techniques to account for heterogeneity.

Although sophisticated marketers offered competing brands in the same category, the analysis of preference data took little account of heterogeneity of preference in the consuming public. Potential new products often had to pass the test of being preferred to the category leader by a majority of consumers. This, of course, produced a strong tendency for new products to be similar to one another, near the center of the distribution of consumer preferences.

Strictly aggregate analysis made it nearly impossible to aim products at distinct segments. However, in the late '60s and early '70s analytic methods permitting market segmentation burst upon the scene. The increasing availability of computer resources, together with methodological developments, made it possible to divide consumers into more or less homogeneous segments. Paul was busy investigating cluster analysis methods. This was one of the most exciting marketing research frontiers, and it is no surprise that Paul was active in furthering methodological knowledge.

But I think one of Paul's most valuable characteristics has been a wide-ranging awareness of things going on in related fields. It was he (with colleagues, of course) who noticed a difficult article by Luce and Tukey in a somewhat obscure journal in another field, and recognized its applicability to marketing research. By introducing conjoint analysis to the marketing research community, Paul provided the first practical way of accounting for heterogeneity at the level of the individual customer. The impact of this development has been so great as to defy quantification. Individual-level conjoint analysis has become a standard tool of practitioners for meeting many research objectives.

Most recently, hierarchical Bayes methods have provided a way to obtain yet more precise estimates of individual customers' values, and it is noteworthy that Paul was a co-author (with Lenk, DeSarbo, and Young) of a path-breaking article on that topic.

During the past 40 years we've progressed from strictly aggregate analysis of preferences, through analysis at the level of market segments, to the possibility of studying preferences at the individual level. Paul has been deeply involved at each of those stages.

As a practitioner myself, I've been impressed that his work has been clearly enough reported to be understandable by practitioners, and sufficiently practical to be really useful.

The Warmest Memory: Tribute to Paul Green
Howard Moskowitz
Moskowitz Jacobs, Inc.

Arlene (Gandler) and I were getting married at the Harvard Club. We invited Paul, who was gracious enough to join the festivities. In Paul's usual debonair and sweet fashion, he found himself instantly attracted to a piano. And of course, during the course of the pre-ceremony festivities Paul insisted on playing. He insisted because the piano was there, the people were there, and Paul was there. Need I say more? Well, as the guests arrived to the club, a number wanted to find out how much to tip that "handsome, suave" piano player. To my chagrin I found it was Paul. No surprise there. However, what did come as a surprise was that enough folks thought he was playing a gig, and for tips, that I had to run to three or four of them and tell them that Paul, in fact, was a guest. I remember one lady, who having realized that Paul was a guest, was somewhat saddened by the fact that she might have to endure a wedding ceremony rather than hearing this distinguished professor play his piano.

Nonetheless, Arlene and I were duly married, and Paul did play a little later (for about a minute or two). I understand that he looks for gigs now and then. I wonder whether he is waiting for any of his other colleagues to marry. Hmm... sounds like a good source of income if you ask me.

Parenthetically, having observed Paul at conferences, this could be a wonderful career for him. I would be delighted to recommend him to customers.

Why Editors Love Paul E. Green

Vijay Mahajan
University of Texas at Austin
Indian School of Business, Hyderabad, India

Ten Reasons to Love Paul E. Green

10. He is likely to say "yes" when asked to serve on your editorial board.
9. The best way to get him to publish an article in your journal is to put him on your editorial board.
8. Don't let it bother you that Paul may be the most over qualified person to serve on the board.
7. If you want to put one person from the Wharton School on the editorial board, you do not need to go beyond Paul Green.
6. The best way to attract young researchers to publish in your journal is to put Paul on the editorial board.
5. Among all your editorial board members, Paul is likely to write the most cited article for your journal.
4. You can always count on Paul for a timely review. He is also likely to write more reviews than any other editorial member.
3. He is very loyal and you can count on his commitment forever.
2. He is likely to write an article that is appreciated by both academics and practitioners.
1. You can honor your journal by naming an award after Paul and influence the thinking of young researchers.

Illustrative Achievements from Paul Green's Career

1. Highest cited Wharton faculty member, 1988–1993, Lipincott Library Study, University of Pennsylvania.
2. Presenter at 27 Annual Doctoral Consortia for Marketing Ph.D. Students, American Marketing Association, 1964-2001.
3. Green and Srinivasan (1978), "Conjoint Analysis in Consumer Research: Issues and Outlook," *Journal of Consumer Research;* most cited paper in the *Journal of Consumer Research.*
4. From 1991-2001, Paul Green reviewed 79 articles for the *Journal of Marketing Research.* The average board member reviewed 47 articles during the same time period. Paul's average review time was 25 days compared to 43 days for all the other board members.
5. Paul Green appeared for the first time as a board member in the February 1965 issue of *JMR* (first issue was February 1964). He is the only board member from that time who continues to serve on the board today.

Reflections on Being Paul Green's First Doctoral Student
Lester Neidell
University of Tulsa

I arrived on the Penn campus in August 1965, with a fresh S.M. from MIT's Sloan School. I was not really committed to the Ph.D. program or to a university career. I was at Penn because my appointment as an MIT Fellow in South America vanished when rebels kidnapped and killed the head of the Cali Development Bank where I was to work for two years. Somehow, two or three years on the Penn campus just didn't seem to be as intriguing as two years in Colombia, South America. But I had not yet met Paul Green.

I really had very little knowledge of what a Ph.D. program entailed, and determined that I would spend no more than two years at Penn. . . . I believe that not only was I Paul Green's first doctoral student, but also the first to complete the Ph.D. with Paul as the principal advisor.

Reflecting on my short career at Penn I realize that in my haste I missed a golden opportunity to be more than a Ph.D. student – that Paul offered me the prospect to be a colleague as well. Perhaps I was one of only a few of Paul's students who did not co-author an article with him.

I think Paul's forte was, and is, his quiet strength, buttressed by a voracious appetite for knowledge, and a deep loyalty to his students and colleagues. Paul's quiet questioning invariably left students a little puzzled, but never with a feeling that they were completely inept. Despite any private misgivings he might communicate to a doctoral student, his public stance was an unswerving allegiance to the student's efforts.

Others more eloquent than I have lauded Paul's contributions to the profession. But Paul's students know that they were, and are, the most fortunate.

* * * * *

The following remarks and recollections were contributed via videotape from several colleagues who were unable to attend the conference in person.

Conducting Business with Honor
Patrick Harker
Dean, The Wharton School

Paul, I'm sorry I couldn't be here tonight. I wanted to add my congratulations and thanks for all you've done for the Wharton School. Through the years, through your tenure, we've risen not only in the public perception of the school, but more importantly, in terms of our academic output – the scholarship that we've created. You've been a major part of that rise through the years. Now, I wanted to thank you again for all you've done, on behalf of all the deans that you've served under, or I should say that have served you – because ultimately deans come and go, but the faculty endure. And so your lasting contributions to the school, through both your conjoint analysis and all the major advances you've made in marketing, but also in terms of the spirit of the school – what you've brought to the school in terms of being a gentleman and teaching students how to conduct business with honor – will never be forgotten. Thanks again for everything, and good luck.

A Striking Contribution to a Profession
Ron Frank
President, Singapore Management University

Paul, this is a special time in your life, to say the least. If anyone has made more of a contribution to marketing in the last 40-50 years, I don't know who it would be – a direct contribution, through your publications, the impact on your fellow academics, and on the discipline, especially in the area of mathematical, psychology and related methodologies. I wonder how many hundreds of people have used that methodology because you've pioneered its development, its operationalization, its implementation? Maybe the most important thing you did was to legitimize it by the early applications that you were involved in throughout your career.

It's a striking contribution to a profession, but there's an indirect contribution also. I wonder how many hundreds and probably thousands of people, in firms throughout the world, have used various methods, applied them to marketing problems without even knowing what reference it is that led to the current methodology being in current use – without knowing that Paul Green stands behind that methodology as much as or more than most other professionals? So three cheers for one part of your life, namely the profession of public contributions.

But I know another part of your life, namely the part that we shared for 19 years at the Wharton School and I want to comment on that very briefly. I can recall in late 1964 that I wound up being interviewed by you and Wroe Alderson, and Wroe passed away shortly thereafter. I wound up coming to Wharton because of the two of you. And I can recall not only our early authorship, but I can recall [Reavis] Cox, Charlie Goodman, and [Orin] Burley, about one year after my arrival, turning over recruiting to the two of us. It's rare that the people in one generation in a discipline trust the next generation to continue to develop the department and the discipline. But that they did. And that led to a lot of interesting folks in Wharton's Marketing Department – Jerry [Wind], Len [Lodish], Dave [Reibstein], Scott [Armstrong], and [Tom] Robertson. Within about 4 to 5 years, what I'm really proud of is, they were no longer dependent on us. The department essentially hit critical mass. And that critical mass of quality has continued over the decades ... pushing the bar higher and higher. The department stands as a better department than it was then, and I am confident that it'll stand as a better department in the next 10-15 years as time goes on.

And in many ways I have you to thank for that as a colleague, because I don't think without your help – without the two of us working on it during that early period – that the transition would have been made anywhere near as effective. Marketing, in the context of Wharton, became the second standard department. The first to be hunkering down in that direction was finance. Not bad for a career, Paul ... not bad at all.

I can leave you with one piece of advice. Having retired once and gone back, I keep kidding people that the reason I've taken this particular job is that I want to retire the second time having enjoyed it thoroughly the first time. I wish you and everyone else the best.

"Paul Green's Sidekick"
Abba Krieger
The Wharton School

I'm sure I know virtually everyone in the audience, but I probably should begin by introducing myself. I am Abba Krieger: Paul Green's sidekick. I can't think of an event I would like to attend more than Paul's retirement conference. Particularly, since "retirement" is in quotes. But unfortunately, a Jewish holiday and the events scheduled, which precluded changing the date, made this impossible.

After these seemingly immaterial occurrences, it turns out to have more relevance than originally thought. After all, the distinguished participants don't have to be bored by what would've been a long-winded speech.

Ironically, Paul and I started out working together from a very innocent encounter. We were two of the faculty members on a committee to which students could appeal if their distinguished record in the MBA program warranted dismissal. Needless to say, Paul and I immediately gravitated to each other as we voted as a block to readmit every one of these students.

After one of these meetings, Paul asked me a question. That led to our first paper and, given his energy, we haven't stopped since. This was twenty years ago. The moral of the story is, I guess, one should not take committee assignments lightly.

Shortly thereafter, my wife and I had our third child. This meant that we needed to move to a larger home. Everyone knows how fussy bankers can be. Even though I had made the modest amount of consulting income, the bank was balking over OK'ing the mortgage. Paul sent in a letter to the bank certifying that the consulting income could be relied upon and the mortgage was granted. This led to our first consulting agreement, which I must sheepishly admit looks like this: Paul did the work and Abba shared in the profits. At least today I'm carrying a bit of a load.

Our relationship has been fabulous to me and this goes well beyond any financial gains. I've never met anyone who is so delighted in having a paper accepted or having a program running that makes an idea accessible. You would think that after almost 200 refereed papers and 15 or so books, the excitement would dim. All I can say is that I cannot think of another person who deserves all of that excitement over his wonderful academic successes. I learned a lot about research from Paul. I always favored the "cute" proof myself. Of course what is cute to me is probably trivial to many others. Paul always favors an idea that has impact. And so with Paul's creativity the idea would be born. This idea would be implemented with my computer skills. Since Paul is such a nice guy, he would humor and allow me to take my "itty-bitty" proof and put it into an appendix. There is no wonder that a great deal of what is now very good practice in marketing research is an outgrowth of Paul's contribution.

I have dubbed ourselves as the "odd couple." I single-handedly have slowed down Paul's creativity by adding clutter to his office. So Paul has now retaliated by making neat piles of my folders, in random order, on desktops and on bookcases. But, in fact, we are more similar than different. The disagreements in our relationship have only stemmed from his feeling that I'm doing too much of the work and wanting to compensate me somehow for it, and my knowledge and guilt that he really truly does most of the work. This looking out for each other is the hallmark of our relationship and the successes that we've had over the past twenty years. We call each other all the time. Our quip now is [to each other], "You're the boss." "No, you're the boss." Well Paul is truly the boss. But, in any case, I expect I will see him first thing on Monday morning ... so much for retirement.

Let me close with the obvious. Because even if you know Paul casually, I'm sure that you'll agree that he is the kindest, most humble gentleman you have ever met. Paul received numerous calls from marketing research professionals, faculty at Penn, and other universities and students around the globe. He spends a great deal of time patiently answering questions, meeting when feasible, and sending FedEx packages with reprints. I often think about what must be the reaction of the person at the other end of the line. It goes something like this, "I have just spoken to the Paul Green and boy is he nice." Well he is *the* Paul Green and he is the greatest.

Quiet and Humble
Steve Hoch
Chairman, Marketing Department, The Wharton School

I hope you've enjoyed the first day of the Paul Green fest. I wish I could join you, but I'm roasting my tail off in Hyderabad right now. Marcia, Michele, and David did all the hard work for organizing the conference. I was assigned three reasonably straightforward tasks. First, I had to choose the wine. Now, that's normally an easy thing for me to do, but admittedly it makes it a little bit tougher when you have to face the Pennsylvania Liquor Control Board. Second, I was supposed to keep Jerry Wind in line. Now, as most of you who know Jerry know, that's an impossible task. And third, and this is my most pleasurable task, I get to start off the roast of Paul Green.

When I came to Wharton seven years ago, I knew Paul only by his stellar reputation and because I learned how to do the Herpes Simplex Method using Paul's excellent book, *Analyzing Multivariate Data*. It was immediately clear to me that Paul was a great guy – quiet and humble.

. . . Now, before passing off the roasting duties to all of you, I would like to introduce a special guest. When Jerry and I were planning this conference, I said to myself, Wouldn't it be great if we could find Paul's freshman roommate here at Penn? Well, amazingly enough, I found him just right around here on campus. In fact he's sitting right over here [standing next to the statue of Benjamin Franklin, seated on a bench]. His name is "Frank Benjamin." Let's go over and see what he has to say. Hey Frank. How ya' doin'? Frank? [Knocks twice on statue] Frank? Hmm, I guess he's taking a nap. Well, maybe I ought to pass the roasting duties off to you guys. And we'll come back when Frank wakes up.

Paul, one last thing: You are the one, dude.

TRIBUTES, POEMS AND SONGS

A Tribute to Paul Green

For helping us build our intellectual identities
   at a time when they were most fluid.
For offering us a model of hard work, hard thinking,
   and intellectual honesty.
For helping us understand how research can be exciting and fun.
For your leadership, mentorship, and especially your friendship.

We praise you, we honor you, we thank you.

Your Ph.D. Students

Pradeep Bansal	*Marcia Flicker*	*Les Neidell*
Max Bosch	*Kris Helsen*	*Jackie Oler*
Frank J. Carmone	*Joel Huber*	*Ambar Rao*
Wayne DeSarbo	*Arun Jain*	*Robert Rothberg*
Susan Douglas	*John Keon*	*William Rudelius*
Chaim Eherman	*Jinho Kim*	*Joel Steck*
James Emshoff	*Vicki Morwitz*	

'Twas the Time Before Conjoint
(or Account of a Visit from Paul Green)
Cathy Schaffer
Associate Professor, Albion College

'Twas the time before conjoint, when all through the shop
The computers were whirring; they never do stop.
The disk drives were humming, the lamps were ablaze
But thoughts were not coming, the brain was a-daze.

The weary analyst down at this data he gazed
Staring down with blank looks, more than slightly amazed.
All judgment regressed, cognition grew bleary
How do I analyze this, where is the theory?

When out in the hall there arose such a clatter
The analyst ran to see what was the matter
Away down the hallway he flew like a flash
Forgetting his key in his curious dash.

He stood in the hallway and looked all about
When the door slammed behind him and he was locked out
Then suddenly there on the staircase appeared
A man many grad students surely revered.

He talked about trade-offs, attributes and utilities
Ideas that for years would generate fees
More rapid than racecars his ideas they did come
Novel and creative and useful, in sum.

Partworths and utilities and a self-explicated score!
This he would model, this and much more.
And as Green used all the knowledge he could muster
He said, "If all else fails, we can always cluster."

And so Green called in Krieger, saying to him
This is all great but we need a good acronym.
How about BUNDOS or SIMOPT or HIER?
Surely one of these will get us a buyer.

And so a new technique called conjoint was born
Whose use and application still has not worn
Many students have used this idea in their theses
Dissecting, improving and tweaking the pieces.

And what of this fellow, this man we call Green
A cheerful colleague in Steinberg Hall often seen.
A cheerful hello, and always a greeting
As Schmittlein would know, never late for a meeting.

He gave so much knowledge to the marketing field
And his love of his work he never concealed
He has never been accused of being conventional
Indeed this great man is multi-dimensional.

A father to three and a granddad to five
A couple of great-grandkids round out the tribe
A man who loves music, good movies and wine
One who is frequently tucked in bed by nine.

To many a mentor, a colleague but mostly a friend
And so to him all of our best wishes we send

Of the thoughts I express, many here would agree
Thank you for all you've done for us, good luck P.E.G.!!

A Tribute to Paul Green on the Occasion of His Completion of 40 Years at the Wharton School of the University Of Pennsylvania

Richard R. Batsell
Associate Professor, Rice University

Researchers come
From far and wide
To honor that Paul
Who is our pride.

Some come black,
And some come blue,
Having heard from a journal
Their latest review.

Some come red,
And some come white,
Some in the morning,
And some at night.

But all come Green,
With envy we do,
Of all he produced
That was honored too.

Statistics, sadistics
That was the start,
A steely beginning
To a lifetime part.

Over 6 per year,
For 45 straight,
And still growing
At this late date.

Co-authors abound,
Over sixty-three,
In this family academic
Just picture the tree.

Research sons,
And research daughters,
Branches galore
And the depth of still waters.

And the one most eager
Counting 48, not meager
Is Penn's own
Abba Krieger.

And the topics, they span
Across whole fields,
From advertising to optimizing
From pricing to yields.

To demonstrate the point
With proper tone,
I'll even reference that one
On Bile Duct Stones.

Positioning products
And designing them too,
Fractioning factorials,
And discriminating who.

Allocating effort
To make more sales.
How many levels?
How many scales?

Conjoined products,
And conjoined authors,
Multivariate connections,
And consulting coffers.

Similarity perceptions,
Preference analysis,
And never, not once,
Author's paralysis.

All these are part
Of his contribution.
It takes two whole days
To just list the attributions.

Would Bayes have predicted
He would do so much –
Even with priors,
On the insightful touch?

Recognition yes,
But an ending, no.
Revisions pending,
Publications yet to go.

So the dilemma becomes
How we properly thank
This research leader,
This impact tank.

Suddenly, at once
The answer is clear:
A conference to honor
This man we hold dear.

So we all gather and talk;
To each other nod,
And smartly salute,
This research God.

Paul Green in Song: A Visit to the Land of Conjoint Analysis
John Hauser
MIT Sloan School

Piano Man
Sing us a song, you're the piano man
Sing us a song tonight.
Well, we're all in the mood for a study
And you've got us feeling all right.
Paul (B. Joel) Green, Columbia Records, 1973

The Methods They Are a Changin'
Come academics, businessmen
Please heed my call
Don't stand in the doorway
Don't block up the hall
For he that gets referenced
Won't be he who has stalled.
There's now conjoint methods
And they are ragin'
It'll soon shake your windows

And rattle your walls
For the methods they are a-changin'
Paul (Bob Dylan) Green

Forever Young
May your heart always be joyful,
May your song always be sung,
May you stay forever young.
Bob Dylan

Thank You
Paul Green
The Wharton School

For me, this evening is an evening of "thank you's" – thank you's to the many people who have influenced my career and my life. As for my life, I've recently become a great grandfather, twice over! My family seems to be ever increasing.

Where should I begin? My gratitude to Jerry Wind, for starting this whole thing, is both wide and deep. Jerry and I go back to 1966, when he first came to Wharton to join Ron Frank, who had recently arrived, and me. Jerry and I have shared many adventures, from fishing in the waters of Acaba to getting temporarily lost in Paris while trying to find the HEC Conference Center. Jerry's energy and creativity keep all of us on our toes.

Thanks to Steve Hoch, our illustrious chairman, who somehow loosened the department's purse strings. (I hope that I won't become an indentured servant after this is all over.) Thanks also to our cheerful department staff who toiled mightily over names and addresses of invitees, transparency production, and a host of other details to make this event happen.

Thanks to my many mentors, from whom I've learned so much. Doug Carroll has taught me more about multidimensional scaling than I ever thought I could learn. He and I had several adventures together, including one in Paris when Doug had his pocket picked in the Tuileries Gardens, on the eve of Bastille Day. Disconsolate, we returned to our one-star hotel in the wee hours of the night, only to sleep through all of the morning parades that marked this major event.

For the past 20 years, I've worked with Abba Krieger. Abba is about the most versatile and creative scholar that I've ever met. He considers his ability to write new computer code on the fly as child's play – simply a minor, throwaway skill. His talents are as many as his kindnesses to others – a true mensch.

I've also learned much from my doctoral students – Vithala Rao, Arun Jain, Frank Carmone, Wayne DeSarbo, Joel Huber, Cathy Schaffer, Les Neidell, Pradeep Bansal, Jinho and Jonathan Kim, just to name some of these highly successful scholars.

I've been fortunate enough to have had over 60 co-authors, from both academia *and* industry. Marsh Greenberg, Dave Wachspress, Karen Patterson, Mila Montemayor, Jeff Savitz, Bruce Shandler, Terry Vavra, and Bob Zelnio are a small sampling from this long list of talented practitioners. Howard Moskowitz has cheerfully made presentations to Jerry's and my classes over the past decade.

I would be most remiss if I did not mention my long-time ski buddies *and* co-authors: Jerry Albaum and Scott Smith. They, along with Frank Carmone and I, have ploughed through a lot of snowdrifts and nacho dips along the way.

Ron Frank, Jay Minas, and Pat Robinson, friends since the early sixties, also deserve my thanks for their many kindnesses over a long period of time.

Nor will I ever forget my early mentors: Wroe Alderson, of course, Simon Kuznets, and Morris Hamburg. I'm especially proud of the fact that I was Morris's first Ph.D. student.

As I look back over the years – 12 in industry and 40 years in academia – I have been amply blessed with the goodwill of those with whom I've worked and played together.

To my departed wife, Betty, I owe a very special debt of gratitude. I miss her – not only for the lifelong joy that she brought to those around her, but also for her unconditional love of both husband and children. I would also like to thank Donna Peters for the friendship, love, and affection that she has brought into my life.

In sum, I'm sure I've left out people who should also be named. Blame it on my post senility. In any case, it's been a full life, these past 75 years. As an amateur pianist, it seemed fitting to close my remarks with reference to a beautiful ballad by the late Michel Legrand, entitled, "How Do You Keep the Music Playing?" The poignant lyrics of Alan and Marilyn Bergman end with:

> "If we can try every day
> to make it better as it grows,
> with an luck I suppose,
> the music *never* ends."

Nor should the scholarly output of the Marketing profession ever end. Given the high level of talent and drive of the teachers and researchers assembled here, I have no doubt about that *ever* happening. Thanks to all of you for helping me celebrate a certainly long – and, I hope, fruitful – career.

UNIVERSITY *of* PENNSYLVANIA

The President

May 17, 2002

Dr. Paul Green
Professor of Marketing
1480 SH-DH
University of Pennsylvania
Philadelphia, PA 19104-6371

Dear Paul:

Allow me to add my note of congratulations to the chorus of well deserved praise that you will hear from your colleagues and friends this evening. Mention the name of Paul Green in marketing and academic circles, and words like "giant," "legend," "exemplary educator," and "fabulous role model" come pouring out of the mouths of the thousands of faculty, students, and practitioners who have been inspired by your teaching, your writings, your utter dedication to your work, and your genius.

Classical music had Beethoven. Modern physics had Einstein. Baseball had Babe Ruth. And Modern Marketing Theory and Practice has Paul Green. You have pioneered the field of quantitative marketing analysis with landmark advances such as the development of conjoint analysis, a tool has led directly to the creation of the Courtyard by Marriott chain, EZPass, and countless other innovations.

Following Benjamin Franklin's advice to rise early, you are known as the scholar who literally turns Wharton on daily by showing up in your office at 6 a.m every morning as you continue to push the envelope on your groundbreaking research.

We are all delighted and thankful that your research at Wharton will continue unabated in your new office in Huntsman Hall. I am sure you will be the first to turn on the lights in Wharton's new home, but please wait until we have the certificate of occupancy!

Wharton and Penn have been a huge part of your life as a student, scholar, and practitioner. To the Penn community, you have been larger than life. We are proud to claim you as our own, and we look forward to the next big thing that you will bring to the world of marketing.

All the best,

Judith Rodin

100 College Hall • Philadelphia, PA 19104-6380 • Phone: 215-898-7221 • Fax: 215-898-9659 • Email: president@pobox.upenn.edu

A Tribute to 40 Years of Pioneering Research

The dinner to honor Paul Green brought together family, friends, students, and colleagues, including leading scholars in the field.

Friends, collaborators, and co-editors of this volume, Green and Wind share a laugh during the celebration.

Defining the Field of Marketing Research

During the conference, Green and other participants discussed progress and prospects for marketing research and modeling.

The conference concluded with a standing ovation.

Chapter 13

Continuing the Aldersonian Research Tradition

Yoram (Jerry) Wind
Paul E. Green
The Wharton School, University of Pennsylvania

Wroe Alderson was *the* leading figure in marketing theory from the early fifties up to his death in 1965, at the age of 68. He defined marketing thought and helped to launch and shape the careers of other leaders of theory and practice in the field, including Paul Green. Very few marketing educators are aware of Wroe's writings and his accomplishments as a deep thinker in marketing theory, as well as a pragmatic consultant who easily worked in both theory and marketing practice.

Today, however, there appears to be a welcome renaissance in Aldersonian ideas, spearheaded by a number of current marketing scholars, including Stephen Brown, Morris Holbrook, and Ben Wooliscroft. We welcome this newfound interest in his work and this recognition of debt that current marketing theory and practice owe to the Aldersonian tradition.

WROE ALDERSON: HIS LIFE AND WORK

Wroe Alderson's academic training was spread over three universities: George Washington, MIT, and the University of Pennsylvania. His publications include *Marketing Behavior and Executive Action*, *Theory in Marketing* (with Reavis Cox) and *Planning and Problem Solving in Marketing* (with Paul Green). He served as past president of the American Marketing Association and was highly active in The Institute of Management Sciences.

From the inception of his business career with the U.S. Department of Commerce, Wroe Alderson was deeply involved in the advancement of marketing science both in the business and academic communities. An eminent educator and consultant with truly interdisciplinary scope, he frequently contributed to the thought and literature of other fields. His wise counsel was sought by university presidents, corporate chief executives, and government leaders alike.

Among Wroe Alderson's many pursuits and accomplishments were: heading the internationally prominent marketing consulting firm of Alderson Associates; the establishment of the annual Marketing Theory Seminars; serving as a Trustee of the Marketing Science Institute; founding the Management Science Center at the University of Pennsylvania; and engineering the migration of the famed Operations Research group at Case Institute to Wharton in 1963. Alderson also received the prestigious Parlin Award in 1954.

AN INTRODUCTION TO SOME KEY ALDERSONIAN IDEAS

Alderson's landmark book, *Marketing Behavior and Executive Action,* published by Richard D. Irwin, provides a detailed review of his thoughts on the interface between marketing theory and executive decision making. We offer a brief overview of some of the ideas that we believe were central to this thinking and contributions to the field, including:

- *Heterogeneity of both supply and demand:* This notion was a precursor to the subsequent ideas of market segmentation and niche marketing. Increased product variety provides consumers with offerings nearer their ideal points. Firms can strive for differential advantage through product variety.
- *Organized behavior systems:* Firms are perceived as ecological systems that grow and adapt to change; each seeks its own niche (Alderson's functionalism).
- *Sorting functions:* The important role of providing marketing economies through intermediate sortings of goods; the associated principle of postponement was a precursor to the current use of just-in-time inventory control.
- *Inductive theorizing:* An approach that emphasized inductive theorizing from market place events, as a complementary viewpoint to neo-classical theories of firm behavior.

In order for the reader to get some measure of the man and his thoughts, excerpts from three sections of his 1957 book *Marketing Behavior and Executive Action* are reproduced here:

Part 1: Marketing and the Behavioral Sciences

The conception of an organized behavior system is the starting point for the present approach to marketing theory. Given only the elements of power and communication which characterize every group, the system may discharge certain primitive functions and exhibit survival value. All marketing activity is an aspect of the interaction among organized behavior systems related to each other in what may be described as an ecological network. Operating systems are a subclass of behavior systems, distinguished by inputs and outputs and the structuring of processes to achieve efficiency.

The functionalist approach is concerned with the functioning of systems, and the study of structure is essential to the analysis and interpretations of functions. Every phase of marketing can be understood as human behavior within the framework of some operating system. Survival and growth are implicit goals of every behavior system, including most particularly those that operate in the market place.

Part 2: The Theory of Market Behavior

The functionalist approach to competition emphasizes rivalry within and among behavior systems in the search for differential advantage. Negotiation is a major topic in the present view, accounting for what may be called the vertical relationships of behavior systems as compared to the horizontal relationships constituting competition. The treatment of consumer motivation takes the household as the fundamental unit and considers aspects of its structure and functions which determine the course of consumer buying. The discussion of exchange describes four aspects of sorting which produce economies in matching supply and demand. Price is discussed in terms of the uses and limitations of marginal analysis. The possibilities of creative marketing in stimulating demand are considered with respect to such processes as product innovation and advertising. The market transaction is analyzed to show how it has been modified to increase marketing efficiency.

Two general comments may be useful to the student in relating marketing theory to economic theory. Economics starts with certain assumptions as to market organization, while marketing starts further back with attempts to organize the market and to establish the processes of orderly marketing which economics takes for granted. Marketing as well as economics is concerned about efficiency.

Part 3: Executive Action in Marketing

The culmination of marketing theory is in demonstrating its value as a perspective for marketing practice. The management of a marketing operation is first considered in terms of positive control over resources to meet predetermined goals. The principles of management take account of the fact that every operating system is necessarily a structure of power and communication. Next, the element of uncertainty is introduced, together with various approaches to problem solving in reducing uncertainty. Problem solving as an operation employs insight, systematic calculation, and selective exploration. The discussion of market planning shows how planning can become a technical and scientific procedure which can be delegated to staff specialists. Finally, the marketing viewpoint is shown to offer a constructive approach to management policy as a whole and to the reconciliation of management goals and public policy.

ANNUAL MARKETING THEORY SEMINARS AND ALDERSON LECTURES

One of Wroe Alderson's major achievements was the inauguration of the annual Marketing Theory Seminars, held in alternate years at the University of Vermont and the University of Colorado. These seminars were designed to foster fruitful exchanges among marketing educators, business executives, and consultants. The seminars offered a spirited and fruitful exchange among the "grand old scholars" of that period, who had much to say about the theory and practice of marketing. Wroe, a major contributor to the discussions, had interest and expertise not only in marketing but in operations research and economics as well.

Wroe Alderson Distinguished Lecture	
1985-86	Charles Goodman
1986-87	V. "Seenu" Srinivasan
1987-88	Sidney J. Levy
1988-89	John R. Hauser
1989-90	Donald R. Lehmann
1990-91	John D.C. Little
1991-92	Robert C. Blattberg
1992-93	Louis W. Stern
1993-94	James R. Bettman
1994-95	Donald G. Morrison
1995-96	John U. Farley
1996-97	Harold H. Kassarjian
1997-98	Richard Staelin
1998-99	Alvin J. Silk
1999-00	Glen F. Urban
2000-01	Frank M. Bass
2001-02	Paul E. Green

In the spirit of these discussions, the Wharton School's Marketing Department established the annual Wroe Alderson Distinguished Lecturer Series in 1985. The event honors the out-standing career of Wroe Alderson – teacher, consultant, and author – and provides a platform for sharing the insights of leading thinkers in the field (see box).

THE ALDERSON TRADITION

Wroe Alderson's research philosophy embodied three basic mandates about doing research in marketing:

- Select problems that, where possible, further marketing theory.
- Select problems whose solutions advance the state of marketing practice.
- Where possible, select problems that have high impact and transfer value across applications.

While these comments are easy to state, they are often difficult to implement. Researchers frequently encounter client resistance to change and reluctance to publicize methodology and results. It is hoped that future efforts in exposing general research ideas to wider audiences (without compromising clients' needs for discretion) will be both possible and favorably looked upon.

Wroe Alderson was a multifaceted person, not only in addressing theoretical and practical challenges in marketing, but also in his broader creativity and interests, as illustrated in the following poem. He established a rich tradition of combining research and application, as well as a high standard for those who followed. In his well-known quote, Sir Isaac Newton said that "if I have seen further . . . it is by standing upon the shoulders of giants." Wroe Alderson was one of the giants of the early development of marketing theory upon whose shoulders rests much of the later progress in the field.

A Poem by Wroe Alderson

Haverford Meeting, October 9, 1960

We have just had a week of golden October days beside the Chesapeake, with Heaven waiting in every sunset.

The hoarse cry of the wild goose is like a brute reaction to beauty too bright to be borne. A world in flames, over land and water, re-enacts the ancient and tragic mystery of Death-in-Life and Life-in-Death.

The dogwood leaves are dying in a burst of battle red. Oak and maple strew the lane with the vivid hues of passion and the soft shades of memory. And soaring there on a high stark limb is the scarlet banner of ivy.

On the water, where life first found its home, life is still harvesting life: a fisherman out in the chilly dawn; the sails of the oystermen at noon; a belated woman crabber poling her skiff through the ripples along the shore. Underneath the surface the living still feeds on the living – or faces death in the stab of the heron or the swoop of the osprey.

A philosopher speaking for the pantheism of the East has said that life is perpetual perishing. What we see now shall never be seen again. What we love most, even now is slipping away. We weep for beauty vanishing but beauty is its heir. The flower fading on its stalk will cast its seed for flowers to scent tomorrow.

A poet once prayed to be released from too much love of living. Let us rather pray to love life freely and to spend it freely. Time is our sovereign currency but let us not grasp it with a miser's hand.

And let no puny man fancy himself an Atlas, bearing the world on his shoulders. The world will not fall apart without us because God holds it together. Individually we are held and jointly we endure within the magnificent fabric of his grand design. The notes are transient – the symphony eternal. Our faith in a loving and eternal God is faith in the abundance of life.

PART SEVEN: FUTURE CHALLENGES FOR MARKETING RESEARCH

Colleagues cannot talk about Paul Green's "retirement" without placing quotation marks around the word. It is clear that he is continuing to make his mark on the field of marketing research through research and publication, and by helping to lead thinking about the future challenges of the field. In this concluding chapter, co-editors Green and Wind discuss the diffusion of new ideas in marketing research and practice. The relationship between theory and application has long been a focus of Paul Green's work. Many of his studies arose from the application of approaches from statistics, mathematical psychology, and other disciplines to real-world management challenges. In the following chapter, Green and Wind explore the interactions between academic researchers and managers and opportunities to strengthen the connections between theory and practice.

Chapter 14

Reflections and Conclusions: The Link Between Advances in Marketing Research and Practice

Yoram (Jerry) Wind
Paul E. Green
The Wharton School, University of Pennsylvania

Methodological developments in marketing research would go for naught if the methodology and research techniques were not applied by practitioners (i.e., industry consultants, marketing research firms, and intra-company professionals) and adopted by management. As noted throughout this book, one of the hallmarks of work by pioneers such as Wroe Alderson has been an intense interest in both research and practice. While individuals have spanned these boundaries, there is still work to do in building bridges between research and practice. This will ensure that new ideas are disseminated quickly into the hands of those who can benefit most from them and also will help maintain the relevance of research advances in the field.

The *diffusion* process, by which new technical developments are tested and implemented in the real world, is critical for answering the questions:

- Does the new marketing model or technique actually work at the business enterprise level?
- If it does work, is it a significant improvement over existing techniques used for similar purposes?
- Does the new technique lend itself to "standardization," so that its success does not depend on its original developer?
- Can objective criteria be developed to permit accurate measurement of the new technique's value vis-à-vis current procedures?
- Is the new technique readily teachable to industry researchers?

In this chapter, we examine this diffusion process and the challenge of bridging the gap between academic research and management practice. We explore the roles of organizations and journals in bridging or reinforcing the divisions between the two sides and we consider opportunities for bringing both sides closer together to improve the R&D and practice of marketing research and the adoption of its findings.

THE DIFFUSION PROCESS

Practitioners led the way in the early development of marketing research. "Modern" marketing research appears to be a phenomenon of post-World War II. However, as Wright-Isak and Prensky (1993) have pointed out, such early practitioners as Archibald Crossley, Elmo Roper, A. C. Nielsen, and Clark Hooper were already active in the 1930s. Academic marketing research tended to lag industry-based sample survey developments by several years.

If we take 1950 as a reasonable starting point for "more modern" marketing research, all was still far from sanguine in academia, as noted by marketing professor J. Howard Westing (1977):

> So far as the present is concerned we marketing professors seem to be losing our mooring to economics.... It is very doubtful that today, after more than a decade of behavioral studies and theorizing, we know significantly more about consumer behavior than we did at the start.... Turning to refined statistical analysis and model building, ...it would appear that the "mountain has labored and brought forth a mouse."... Marketing professors can continue on their present course by trying to create an academic discipline of marketing. If they do, they will become pariahs in the community, because there is no basic body of thought, and marketing professors will be quite properly viewed as poachers and panderers.

While this is rather "over-the-top" prose, Westing had a point. A few years later, Myers, Massy, and Greyser (1980), hereafter called MMG, produced a study that demonstrated the growing gap between research and practice. MMG decided to examine the accuracy of Westing's remarks by asking respondents to indicate their current intensity of use of a set of 13 tools/techniques that might be part of a marketing practitioner's "tool kit." Table 14-1 lists the 13 tools/techniques and includes brief descriptions of each.

As shown in the table, the items ranged over such concepts as various kinds of segmentation, through data-collection methods, such as focus groups and experimentation, to complicated decision models and multivariate statistical techniques. Each technique exemplifies a type of marketing "knowledge" that might play some part in a professional researcher's or manager's tool kit.

Table 14-1. **Tools and Techniques of the Marketing Practitioner**
Source: Myers, Massy, and Greyser (1980)

Technique	Description Used
Time-series analysis	a. Time-series analysis – the statistical analysis of trends over time
Bayesian analysis	b. Bayesian decision theory – decision trees, personalized decision analysis
Focus groups	c. Focus groups
Demographic segmentation	d. Market segmentation 1. Demographic (including socioeconomic) characteristics of present and/or potential consumers
User segmentation	2. Usage of product/brands by present and/or potential consumers
Psychographics	e. Psychographics – life-style analysis, attitude/interest/opinion studies
Multidimensional scaling	f. Multidimensional scaling – perceptual mapping
Cluster analysis	g. Cluster analysis
Factor analysis	h. Factor analysis
Conjoint analysis	i. Conjoint analysis and discrete choice
Formal experiments	j. Formal experiments using test and control areas and/or groups to test new products or elements of the marketing mix
	k. Marketing models – computer simulations to help answer "what if" questions in formulating marketing strategy
Response models	1. Models to relate marketing expenditure inputs to markets share and/or sales response
Computer simulation	2. Computer simulations of alternative marketing mixes

Data collection involved a mail questionnaire sent to a sample of the American Marketing Association (AMA) membership. The AMA's membership roster was used as the sampling frame, and members were classified into three groups: marketing managers, research managers, and commercial research suppliers. A random sampling procedure was followed in selecting respondents from each group. A total of 4,292 questionnaires were sent out and 1,271 usable replies were received.[1]

Table 14-2 shows the results for (a) "used frequently" and (b) "used at least once," for the three respondent groups – entries are percentages:

- Operating Managers (Oper Mgrs)
- Research Managers (Res Mgrs)
- Research Suppliers (Res Spplrs)

Table 14-2. Use and Trial: 13 Techniques Used and/or Tried
Source: Myers, Massy, and Greyser (1980)

Technique	Used Frequently ("Use")			Used Sometime ("Trial")		
	Oper Mgrs	Res Mgrs	Res Spplrs	Oper Mgrs	Res Mgrs	Res Spplrs
Demographic segmentation	54.9	64.1	72.0	91.2	95.7	98.3
Usage segmentation	52.0	59.9	68.6	91.6	91.3	94.6
Time-series analysis	43.4	45.2	27.8	81.6	87.2	69.9
Focus groups	35.4	51.1	62.3	76.6	85.9	95.6
Formal experiments	24.6	36.6	45.9	71.9	73.2	87.7
Psychographics	12.7	22.3	37.9	71.1	78.1	88.1
Response models	10.6	10.6	7.0	50.0	52.5	35.6
Computer simulation	10.1	8.7	6.5	45.5	47.6	35.6
Cluster analysis	5.2	7.7	16.5	53.6	62.2	76.3
Conjoint analysis	4.8	3.8	11.7	32.6	43.8	55.5
Multidimensional scaling	4.3	7.0	15.7	38.2	53.9	65.7
Bayesian analysis	4.2	10.5	2.2	59.8	50.4	45.3
Factor analysis	3.8	12.4	23.6	56.5	70.4	85.2
Means	20.5	25.5	30.6	63.1	68.6	71.8
Standard deviations	19.4	22.8	24.5	19.3	18.1	22.6

As MMG note, research managers' and/or research suppliers' responses to the "frequently used" question tend to be higher than those of line managers. The authors conclude:

1. Overall, segmentation, time-series analysis, and focus groups (the older, more established techniques) are the most widely used. More recent and complex techniques, such as cluster analysis, MDS, conjoint analysis, Bayesian decision theory, and computer simulation, are less commonly used.
2. Trial usage of techniques tends to be highest among consumer-goods manufacturers and lowest among retail firms.

MMG report that a similar study, launched by Georgia State University, shows similar results. Not surprisingly, both study teams noted that simpler techniques were adopted more quickly and used more frequently than the more complex methods.

In terms of frequency of use, research suppliers tended to lead in the use of segmentation, focus groups, experimentation, psychographics, cluster analysis, conjoint analysis, MDS, and factor analysis. These techniques all require specialization, either in terms of statistics or behavioral science (e.g., focus groups). In short, the (outside) research supplier plays an important role in information diffusion. The adoption sequence extends from technique developer (e.g., academic) to research consultant/supplier, to corporate research manager, to operating manager.

Tools Change, But the Gap Remains

While the techniques from 1980 (summarized in Table 14-1) are still used today, many new ones have been developed in recent decades. As reflected in the discussions in the previous chapters of the book, enormous developments have been made in the field. The tutorials and presentations made to the AMA's Advanced Research Techniques (A/R/T) Forum offer an illustration of some of these developments. A sample of the A/R/T Forum tutorials, shown in Table 14-3, indicates the range of the new approaches that were considered important for practitioners. The primary focus of the Forum is on a range of specific methods and their applications. Among the topics, for example: consumer evaluation of really new services, a presentation by Paul Green on the TrafficPulse study, the effect of removing "fence-sitting" options on consumer attitude and preference measurements, using a dual-response framework in choice modeling, capturing heterogeneity by allowing respondents to eliminate unacceptable attribute levels, fusing data of different sources, advances in data mining and stochastic gradient boostings.

Table 14-3. **Examples of Topics Covered in A/R/T Forum Tutorials (1998-2002)**

Applied probability models
Choice experiments
Bayesian models
Choice modeling
Data mining
Latent cluster and segmentation models
Cart decision trees
Web mining
Hierarchical Bayes
Segmentations with mixture models
Multivariate adaptive regression splines
Choice modeling with Gibbs sampling
Measuring and modeling brand loyalty

Although much has changed in the range and sophistication of these models, one thing probably has not changed. The findings of MMG and other studies still appear to hold today. The gap remains between research and practice.

As one indication of how this divide is perpetuated, the AMA itself holds separate conferences for academic and industry participants. Through this structure, the two sides are kept apart, yet, as the discussion of diffusion suggests, many advances in methodology come at the intersection of research and practice. In the future, we need to find ways to encourage more collaboration.

BRIDGING THE GAP

Figure 14-1 illustrates a typical diffusion process for new marketing research ideas. Most new methods and techniques are initiated by academics who are primarily interested in their publication in academic journals. Marketing research suppliers and industry consultants (whose groups may contain academics as well) respond to the new developments and, through their vested interests, move the technology along, typically in the form of consulting engagements. As indicated by the dotted lines, feedback then flows back to the researchers, helping to refine the research and suggest new directions and management challenges to address.

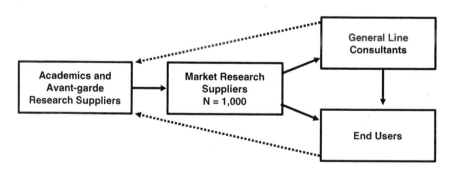

Figure 14-1. **Typical Diffusion Process for New Models and Methods in Marketing Research**

Hence, it behooves industry consultants and research suppliers to keep abreast of new developments and be flexible enough to incorporate those innovations into their own consulting practices. In so doing, their efforts can provide pragmatic "tests" of how the techniques work in practice, what their pitfalls may be, and how deficiencies can be rectified. Applications-oriented journals, such as *Marketing Research* also provide an avenue for practitioner feedback and help "close the loop" between innovation and adoption.

There are a variety of strategies that researchers and practitioners are taking, or could take, to bridge this gap. This process, however, is often accompanied by changes in the original methodology of either a corrective or extended nature. Obviously, some new academic ideas do not hold up in practice, necessitating correction or, possibly, abandonment. There is a need for continuous interaction and feedback loops between idea and application.

Keeping Up with Research

William Neal (1998), founder and chief officer of Sophisticated Data Research, a major consulting firm in marketing research, has written extensively on the subject of information diffusion. Neal points out how important the marketing research methodologist has become in "spreading the word" regarding new models and techniques. He views the research methodologist as one with training in statistics, psychometrics, micro-economics, *and* marketing. He stresses the role of communicator and the ability to explain complex concepts to managers in relatively simple terms.

Neal also emphasizes the role that the availability of inexpensive and easy-to-use software (much of which was originally supplied free from Bell Laboratories) plays in the early adoption of new techniques. Neal then focuses on three avenues practitioners can use to keep up with the growing field of marketing research: Subscribe to and *read* the academic journals; follow what is happening among leading-edge academics; and keep adding to one's skills by attending advanced seminars in new methodology, such as the AMA's A/R/T Forum and the Management Sciences (INFORMS) conferences.

The American Marketing Association provides a wide variety of training programs to help practitioners keep up with new developments in research methodology. Perhaps the most visible is the A/R/T Forum, mentioned above, held once a year, which offers attendees new techniques, presented by top academics and industry consultants. In addition to plenary sessions, the Forum offers seminars and discussion sessions as well as poster presentations. Ample time is provided for audience participation, both formally and casually. The A/R/T Forum is now going into its fourteenth highly successful year. Another outstanding annual meeting is the Sawtooth Software Conference, which also emphasizes new methodology and research applications.

In 1980, the AMA launched its first Marketing Research Conference. It is now in its 23rd year. The AMA also runs annual Applied Research Methods Conferences that emphasize tutorial learning. Some 4,000 industry researchers have attended at least one of these tutorials since the program began.

In addition to the AMA, a number of other organizations also promote marketing research in specific areas. For example, the Advertising Research Foundation (ARF) has helped disseminate advertising research, and other organizations have contributed to sales management, direct marketing and other specialized marketing domains.

In sum, the AMA, other professional organizations, and private companies such as Sawtooth Software, provide ongoing opportunities for corporate analysts to sharpen their skills and keep up with recent developments in marketing research.

Trends that Stimulate the Development and Diffusion of Marketing Research

Five recent trends have occurred that further the continued development of marketing research and modeling.

1. Marketing research firms, through mergers and acquisitions, are becoming larger and larger. Traditionally, the top 50 marketing research firms have dominated the field; if anything, the concentration is increasing. Moreover, research suppliers are rapidly becoming global in their operations.

2. General management consulting firms are adding marketing research capabilities, either by acquiring marketing research affiliates or forming strategic alliances with them. Mercer Consulting, for example, has a large and diversified group of marketing research professionals. McKinsey has close ties with a number of full-service marketing research firms.

3. Many of the research techniques with demonstrated performance, such as conjoint analysis and experimental choice analysis, are being accepted and appreciated by higher levels in end-user companies – including executives in corporate board rooms and strategic planning groups.

4. We have seen the increased use of CRM, the proliferation of direct marketing, and the increased importance of data base marketing, which includes appropriate analytics.

5. The current economic downturn increases the pressure for cost cutting, increased efficiency and effectiveness of marketing and marketing research, the focus on the ROI of marketing and the increased interest in optimal resource allocation among marketing tools, brands, segments, countries and businesses.

Taken in concert, these trends bode well for users of sophisticated research tools that can handle strategy-based problems. In addition, newer tools for data mining and targeted customer marketing have received increased attention in this age of computers and the Internet.

Recognizing Articles that Contribute to Marketing Practice

The practical focus of academic research can be reinforced through recognition. For example, the Paul E. Green Award is presented for the article in the *Journal of Marketing Research* of the preceding year that demonstrates the most potential to contribute significantly to the practice of marketing research or the practice of marketing. Table 14-4 list recipients of the award and illustrates the applied focus of their topics. As a further emphasis on practice, the award is presented at the AMA's A/R/T Forum.

Table 14-4. Winners of the *Journal of Marketing Research*'s Paul E. Green Award

---

2002: William R. Dillon, Amna Kirmani, Thomas J. Madden, and Soumen Mukherjee, "Understanding What's in a Brand Rating: A Model for Assessing Brand and Attribute Effects and Their Relationship to Brand Equity," November 2001.

2001: Carrie M. Heilman, Douglas Bowman, and Gordon P. Wright, "The Evolution of Brand Preferences and Choice Behaviors of Consumers New to a Market," May 2000.

2000: Marnik Dekimpe and Dominique Hanssens, "Sustained Spending and Persistent Response: A New look at Long-Term Marketing Profitability," November 1999.

1999: Gregory S. Carpenter, Venkatesh Shankar, and Lakshman Krishnamurthi, "Late Mover Advantage: How Innovative Late Entrants Outsell Pioneers," February 1998.

1998: Carl F. Mela, Sunil Gupta, and Donald R. Lehmann, "The Long-Term Impact of Promotion and Advertising on Consumer Brand Choice," May 1997.

1997: Peter S. Fader and Bruce G. S. Hardie, "Modeling Consumer Choice Among SKUs," November 1996.

1996: Leonard M. Lodish, Magid Abraham, Stuart Kalmenson, Jeanne Livelsberger, Beth Lubetkin, Bruce Richardson, and Mary Ellen Stevens,: "How T.V. Advertising Works: A Meta-Analysis of 389 Real World Split Cable T.V. Advertising Experiments," May 1996.

THE ROLE OF PROFESSIONAL JOURNALS IN DIFFUSION

As William Neal noted, professional journals have a central role to play in putting new ideas into practice. The heart of any applied research-oriented discipline contains two essential components:

- The availability of media for disseminating information (typically, technical journals, conference proceedings, industry tutorials, etc.), and
- Feedback on the extent to which corporate researchers and consulting groups have found the information to be useful in solving real business problems.

As emphasized earlier, this feedback loop is essential to evaluating how worthwhile new methods and techniques are and the directions in which they can be improved.

The field of marketing research and related disciplines currently are the focus of a wide assortment of journals, including:

- *Journal of Marketing Research*
- *Journal of Marketing*
- *Journal of Consumer Research*
- *Marketing Science*
- *Marketing Research* (for practitioners)
- *Journal of Advertising Research*
- *Decision Sciences*
- *Management Science*
- *Marketing Letters*
- *International Journal of Research in Marketing*

As we look back across the 40 years of research in marketing, the *Journal of Marketing Research* (*JMR*) continues to be the flag bearer for research excellence, as discussed in Chapter 11. Historically, the American Marketing Association was composed of educators *and* practitioners. Its mandate, as described by William R. Davidson, President of AMA in 1964, was to seek articles of the following types:

- Presentations of new techniques for solving marketing problems, "new" in the sense of not having been previously used to solve *marketing* problems,
- Demonstrations of different ways in which known techniques may be used to solve marketing research problems,
- Clarifications of marketing theories or of methodology initially thought too difficult to understand,
- Contributions to marketing knowledge based on the use of experimental methods or other analytic techniques, and
- Reviews of developments and concepts in related fields that may be applicable to marketing research (Davidson 1964).

While the much older *Journal of Marketing* (*JM*) had earlier published a wide array of articles (including some involving marketing research), under the editorship of Stewart Britt, *JM*'s contents took a marked turn toward more general articles on marketing management, marketing education, and social significance. Hence the time seemed to be right for a *new* marketing journal – one that emphasized research techniques and methods useful for research professionals employed in consulting or corporate enterprises, as well as academics.

Under Bob Ferber's editorship, in 1964 an editorial board of nine members was recruited – three academics, five professional marketing researchers, and one corporate director of marketing research. *JMR*'s mission appeared to be very clear at that time: to publish developments in new models, techniques, and methods to advance *both* the state of the art and the state of practice in marketing research.

Subsequently, *JMR* was followed, a decade later in 1974, by the *Journal of Consumer Research (JCR)*, whose audience was made up of scholars primarily interested in the consumer (rather than the marketing manager). *JCR* focused on such questions as:

- How can consumers make better informed purchase decisions?
- How can research be used to improve consumer information regarding competing brands?
- How can governmental bodies be better informed regarding product quality and pricing decisions?
- How can truth in advertising and promotion be better regulated to protect consumer interests?

Ron Frank was the first editor of *JCR*, which was sponsored by ten professional organizations, clearly recognizing the interdisciplinary perspective of consumer research and behavior. Under his stewardship, the journal (and the Association of Consumer Research) was off to an excellent start. In addition, *JCR*'s audience and article contributors were sufficiently dissimilar to *JMR*'s audience and contributors that their domains of interest (business managers versus consumers) were demarcated.

In contrast, *Marketing Science* came on the scene almost two decades after *JMR*. The first *Marketing Science* board consisted of Don Morrison, editor, and three area editors: Seenu Srinivasan, Subrata Sen, and Jerry Wind. Its review board consisted of 32 members, 29 of whom were academics.

An Academic Focus

If there is one constant to today's admixture of marketing journals, it is the strong tendency for review boards and *ad hoc* reviewers to be drawn from the academic sector:

- In *JMR*, November 2002, 94 review board members were listed; all were academics.
- Between July 1, 2001 and June 30, 2002, *JMR* utilized over 150 *ad hoc* reviewers; only one was listed as a non-academic.
- In the first issue of *Marketing Science* (Winter 1982), there were three area editors and 32 reviewers listed; only three of the 32 were not from academia.
- In the Winter 2002 issue of *Marketing Science*, there were 14 area editors and 55 reviewers; only three of the reviewers were non-academics.

Good reasons for this situation can easily be found. Non-academics are rarely rewarded for their efforts as either senior author or coauthor. Indeed, instances have occurred where company employees have been dissuaded or even rebuked for requesting time off to write journal articles. This, of course, is in marked contrast to the cachet attached to preparing articles that both academics and research consultants enjoy.

Still, articles *do* get published by combinations of academic consultants and industry practitioners, even if it is the consultant who carries the brunt of the writing. As noted earlier, consultants also provide a useful bridge between academics and end-user firms through their help in explaining the more technical points of new methods and techniques.

Potential Journal "Wars": Boon or Bane?

Is there room for still more journals that publish marketing research articles? As shown earlier, there are at least eight journals that publish marketing articles on a regular basis. In addition, specialty journals (that at least have "marketing" in their titles) abound. The Haworth Press alone lists 19 journals with "marketing" somewhere in the title. Not to be outdone, the International Press lists 21.

Looking at closer competition among the primary journals, it would seem that *JCR* contributors have carved out a niche that is relatively immune to "encroachment." *JCR* appeals to a variety of tastes ranging from carefully-designed experiments (with ANOVA) to further-out forays into consumer post-modernism and other such venturesome market niches.

In contrast, *Marketing Science* would appear to be a stronger competitor to *JMR* than either *JCR* or *JM*. Papers on marketing science methods appear to be significantly increasing. Also, while *JMR* still rules when it comes to methodological techniques (e.g., hierarchical Bayes), it is not clear as to how the two journals, *Marketing Science* and *JMR,* will fare in the future.

The New Guy

As if the *JMR* vs. *Marketing Science* competition isn't enough, there's a new "kid on the block" about to enter the fray. The incipient journal is *Quantitative Marketing and Economics*. Its editors are Rajiv Lal and Peter Rossi. As the editors state: "*QME* will focus on the intersection of Marketing, Economics, and Statistics, with an emphasis on the analysis of important problems of relevance to marketing." Its aims and scope are as follows:

> *Quantitative Marketing and Economics* publishes research in the intersection of Marketing, Economics, and Statistics. Our focus is on important applied problems of relevance to marketing using a quantitative approach. We define marketing broadly as the interface between firms, competitors, and consumers. This includes but is not limited to consumer preferences, consumer demand and decision-making, strategic interaction of firms, pricing, promotion, targeting, product design/positioning, and channel issues. We embrace a wide variety of research methods including applied economic theory, econometrics, and statistical methods. Empirical research using primary, secondary, or experimental data is also encouraged.

QME will be published quarterly by Kluwer Academic Press. Over 30 highly respected scholars have been selected for its review board. Publication of *QME* starts in early 2003 and it will be available in both hard copy and online. All journal correspondence, including submissions, will be electronic.

If *QME* makes good on its agenda, there is every reason to believe that it will invade the territory heretofore occupied by *JMR* and *Marketing Science*. It will be interesting to see how three top-rated journals, devoted to quantitative marketing, will fare in years to come.

For those who see this "triadic" competition as upsetting, only time will tell how the journal marketplace will settle down. For the more hardy souls who welcome hard-fought competition, it's more a case of "Let the games begin!" Proof of the pudding ultimately lies in how well the diffusion process works and how *practitioner* adoption is facilitated by the new entry.

FUTURE APPLICATIONS OF RESEARCH AND MODELING APPROACHES

The interplay between theory and practice is also helping to draw together different approaches to marketing research and focus them on specific marketing decisions. The different approaches to marketing research discussed in this book – including Bayesian approaches, multivariate analysis, multidimensional scaling and clustering, and conjoint analysis – have been developed as independent streams, each with its own evolution. Individual researchers and practitioners often specialize in one approach, which has deepened the sophistication of these tools. As shown in Table 14-5, each of these tools is used to address specific types of marketing decisions.

Table 14-5. **Applications of Key Research and Modeling Approaches**

Marketing Decisions	Approaches					
	Bayesian	Multi-variate Analysis	MDS & Clustering	Conjoint Analysis	Decision Support Models	Multi Methods
Understanding Customers		X	X	X		X
Marketing Strategy		X	X	X		X
Market Segmentation		X	X	X	X	X
Positioning			X	X	X	X
New Product	X			X	X	X
Pricing	X	X		X	X	X
Distribution	X	X		X	X	X
Adv. & Communication	X	X		X		X
Competitive Strategies		X		X		X
Customer Satisfaction				X		X
Relationship Marketing				X		X
Business Strategy				X		X

As evident in practice and in much of Paul Green's applied work, we expect to see much greater focus on multi-method approaches. As marketing challenges become more complex and marketing researchers become more sophisticated, there is tremendous power in combining different approaches to address a broader range of decisions. Instead of focusing on the methods – picking up a hammer so that every problem looks like a nail – the focus is shifting more toward the marketing decisions that need to be made. Researchers and practitioners can then select the tools that are best suited to addressing those specific decisions.

This use of multiple methods to address real-world marketing decisions is part of the tradition established by Wroe Alderson and Paul Green. Through four decades of marketing research, we have created a powerful set of sophisticated approaches to marketing challenges. These have slowly moved into practice through publication in journals and direct applications to corporate challenges. Now we have an opportunity to draw these together and creatively combine them to develop innovative research designs that incorporate the best approaches and tailor them to the particular marketing challenge to be addressed. While each of the streams of marketing research will continue to be refined, this central ground of multi-methods is one of the rich areas for future study and practice.

In examining the diffusion process of methodologies, we cannot ignore developments in related fields. For example, while developments in areas such as Total Quality Management (TQM) – with its emphasis on customer satisfaction – data mining initiatives, and Customer Relationship Management (CRM), did not originate as marketing research initiatives, they do contribute to the development and diffusion of marketing research methodologies.

This discussion highlights another divide that must be bridged for marketing research to achieve its greatest impact: cutting across different disciplines and functions in the organization. We need to consider expanding the scope of our applications of the tools and approaches of marketing research. Marketing has often been left out of key initiatives such as TQM or data mining, which have been spearheaded by operations and IT. Marketing research approaches have the potential to contribute to these types of strategic initiatives if researchers can think more broadly about applications. Even initiatives such as Customer Relationship Management (CRM) that have involved marketing often have broader applications. For example, CRM approaches are now being extended by Siebel to Employee Relationship Management (ERM) and Partner Relationship Management (PRM). Similarly, marketing research tools and approaches that are applied to external customers can also be used effectively with internal "customers" and other stakeholders. This suggests that if we expand our thinking beyond the narrow confines of strictly functional marketing challenges, we can find many other ways to use these valuable and sophisticated tools to address other strategic issues in our enterprises.

CLOSING THE GAP

How can researchers and practitioners work more closely together? We need to move away from the model of letting an academic researcher or research institution do the research and merely hoping that a marketing research firm will pick it up and start applying it. In the tradition of Wroe Alderson and Paul Green, we need to think about applications at the same time we are designing research projects. There are a variety of ways that we can increase the real-world orientation of research, including:

- Addressing the increased concern of management about the ROI of marketing expenditures,

- Assuring that the research designs and methods used address important management issues and concerns and lend themselves to the needed integration of research and modeling; the two should not be viewed as separate domains,
- Ensuring that the methods developed capture the latest developments in related disciplines such as statistics, mathematical psychology, decision processes, computer science, econometrics,
- Assuring that the new methods developed offer a better solution than the currently used approaches. This requires that Ph.D students and other researchers familiarize themselves with current practice and not only with the published articles in the field,
- Appraising the value of the new approaches to practitioners,
- To the extent possible, validating the newer research approaches on relevant samples. (Research based on Marketing 101 students can go only so far.)

Increasing real-world orientation would make our research more relevant to practitioners and put the results into their hands more quickly. On the research side, closer ties with practitioners can also provide robust data sets and offer a rich set of research problems for researchers to tackle in the years ahead. This is not to say that research should be limited to the questions raised by practitioners or that managers should be involved in every future research project. It means that we need to increase the awareness of both researchers and practitioners of one another so that they can most effectively work together to advance the theory and practice of the field.

NOTES

[1] Academics were also sampled. Here we focus only on industry practitioners and research suppliers.

REFERENCES

Davidson, W. R. (1964), "Introducing the Journal of Marketing Research," *Journal of Marketing Research*, 1 (February), 9.

Green, P. E., Johnson, R. M., and Neal, W. D. (2002), "The *Journal of Marketing Research*: Its initiation, growth, and knowledge dissemination," *Journal of Marketing Research*, 40 (February), 1-9.

Myers, J. G., Massy, W. F., and Greyser, S. A. (1980), *Marketing Research and Knowledge Development*, Englewood Cliffs, NJ: Prentice-Hall, Inc.

Neal, W. D. (1998), "The marketing research methodologist," *Marketing Research*, 10 (1), Spring, 21-25.

Westing, J. H. (1988), "Marketing educators must switch to helping real world meet real world problems," *Marketing News,* 11, July 29, American Marketing Association.

Wright-Isak, C., and Prensky, D. (1993), "Early marketing research: Science and application," *Marketing Research*, 5 (4), Fall, 16-23.

Strategies for Bridging Research and Practice: Lessons from Paul Green
Comments by U. N. Umesh, *Washington State University, Vancouver*

How can researchers increase the value of their work for practitioners? In the long run, the value of research will be judged by the eventual usage of the research to solve important practical problems that have high benefit to society or to solve simple everyday problems but on a very widespread basis. What characteristics make research more useful to practitioners? Two strategies used extensively by Paul Green in his work help to increase the value of research for managers:

- **Focus on real-world problems.** The key to Paul Green's contribution to the practice of marketing research is that the business problems come first and the techniques follow, based on the need to achieve the best solution. Because of his focus on rigorous solutions to practical problems, Green's work is widely disseminated both in the marketing research literature *and* in books on marketing management for practitioners.
- **Completeness.** The highly educated manager should be able to apply all the steps in a practical application by simply reading the article or research paper. This completeness is a hallmark of Green's publications. As Bradlow, Lenk, Allenby, and Rossi note in Chapter 1, "The completeness of the work – that is, the fact that his research describes *all* the necessary BDT [Bayesian Decision Theory] steps from start to finish – provides the roadmap that practitioners require ...." A casual review of marketing journals in recent years suggests that articles often allocate extensive space to background material or past research at the expense of focusing on the "completeness" of applying the technique. Given the limited amount of journal space and the vast amount of past research that the current researcher can and needs to refer to, this type of emphasis is understandable. Perhaps an outlet should be developed where complete step-by-step applications are presented, so the technique can be used pervasively in the real world.

If these lessons from Green's work are kept in mind by researchers, they will increase the likelihood that their work will be used by managers. This will help ensure that more of the breakthroughs and advances in thinking about marketing research actually make it into practice.

APPENDIX

Paul E. Green – Curriculum Vitae

700 Jon M. Huntsman Hall
3730 Walnut Street
University of Pennsylvania
Philadelphia, PA 19104-6371

University Rank
Professor Emeritus of Marketing, Wharton School, and S. S. Kresge Professor Emeritus of Marketing, University of Pennsylvania

Education
A.B. (1950), A.M. (1953), Ph.D. (1961), all from the University of Pennsylvania; Undergraduate Major –Mathematics/Economics; Graduate Major – Statistics

Industry Experience
1958-1962   Market Planning Consultant, E. I. DuPont De Nemours & Co., Wilmington, Delaware
1955-1958   Supervisor of Operations Research Group and Senior Market Analyst, Lukens Steel Co.
1953-1954   Commercial Research Analyst, Lukens Steel Co., Coatesville, PA
1950-1953   Statistician, Sun Oil Company, Philadelphia, PA

Teaching Experience
1997-   Professor of Marketing and S. S. Kresge Professor Emeritus, Wharton School, University of Pennsylvania
1971-1996   S. S. Kresge Professor of Marketing, Wharton School, University of Pennsylvania
1965-1971   Professor of Marketing, Wharton School, University of Pennsylvania
1962-1965   Associate Professor of Marketing and Deputy Director, Management Science Center, Wharton School, University of Pennsylvania

319

1961-1962   Guest lecturer in Marketing, Wharton School, University of Pennsylvania

1959-1960   Guest lecturer in Statistics, University of Delaware, Evening Division

1954-1955   Instructor in Statistics, Wharton School, University of Pennsylvania

Professional Societies

American Marketing Association

The Institute of Management Sciences

American Statistical Association (Fellow)

Psychometric Society

Association for Consumer Research (Fellow)

American Institute of Decision Sciences (Fellow)

Society for Multivariate Experimental Psychology

Academy of Marketing Science (Senior Fellow)

Outside Professional Duties

Associate Editor, *Decision Sciences*, 1990-1998

Editorial Board, *Journal of Classification*, 1984-2002

Editorial Board, *Marketing Science*, 1985-1994

Editorial Board, *Journal of Marketing Research*, 1965-2002

Editorial Board, *Journal of Consumer Research*, 1973-1987

Editorial Board, *Journal of Business Research*, 1973-1975

Editorial Board, *Journal of Marketing,* 1978-1997

Editorial Board, *Journal of the Market Research Society (London)*, 1981- 2002

Editorial Board, *Journal of the Academy of Marketing Science*, 1991-1997

Editorial Board, *International Journal of Research in Marketing*, 1985-86

Advisory Board, Academy of Marketing Science, 1988-1990

Occasional Reviewer: *Management Science, International Journal of Research in Marketing, Journal of Consumer Research, Psychometrika, Multivariate Behavioral Research*

Executive Council - Philadelphia Chapter, American Marketing Association, 1965-1967, 1968-1969

Referee - *Journal of the Operations Research Society, Management Science*, 1967-1969, 1970-1971, 1973-1974; *Psychometrika*, 1975-1979, 1980-1981, 1981-1982; *Decision Sciences*, 1971-1981; *Academy of Marketing Science*, 1985-1986; *IJRM*, 1986-1988

Educational Advisory Committee on Pharmaceutical Marketing - American Marketing Association, 1967-1968

Parlin Award Committee - Philadelphia Chapter, American Marketing Association, 1972-1979, 1982-1987

Marketing Series Co-Editor - Holt, Rinehart & Winston, Inc., 1967-1978

Vice President - Marketing Education Division, American Marketing Association, 1967-1968

Chairman - TIMS College on Marketing, 1970-1971

Advisory Council - Association for Consumer Behavior, 1970-1974

Board of Directors - Philadelphia Chapter, American Marketing Association, 1976-1977, 1977-1978

Census Advisory Committee, 1980-1983

Policy Board - Academy of Marketing Sciences, 1982-1985
Advisory Board - SEI Center for Advanced Studies in Management, 1989-1995

Awards/Honors

Alpha Kappa Psi Award (1963). Presented for the article, "Bayesian Decision Theory in Pricing Strategy," *Journal of Marketing*, January 1963

S. S. Kresge Professor of Marketing, Wharton School, University of Pennsylvania, 1971

Silver Medal Paper, J. Walter Thompson Award, "Advertisement Perception and Evaluation: An Application of Multidimensional Scaling," with F. J. Carmone, 1970 Competition

Honorable Mention, AMA Research Design Competition, 1971, for paper, "On the Measurement of Judgmental Responses to Multi-Attribute Stimuli"

First Prize, American Psychological Association (Division 23) Research Design Competition, 1972

Parlin Award for the Advancement of Science in Marketing, American Marketing Association, 1977

Named most cited marketing scholar over the 1972-75 period in an international study of professional journal citations (Robinson and Adler)

Beta Gamma Sigma Distinguished Lecturer, 1978

Paul D. Converse Award, 1978

Tenth Annual Albert Wesley Frey Distinguished Lecturer at the University of Pittsburgh, March 1978

Elected to Fellow of the American Statistical Association, 1980

Elected to the Attitude Research Hall of Fame, 1981

Elected to Fellow of the American Institute for Decision Sciences, 1981

Elected to Senior Fellow of the Academy of Marketing Science, 1991

Elected to Fellow of the Association of Consumer Research, 1990

Elected to the Society of Multivariate Experimental Psychology, 1982

Alpha Kappa Psi Award (1981). Presented for the article, "A General Approach to Optimal Product Design via Conjoint Analysis," *Journal of Marketing*, October 1981 (coauthors: J.D. Carroll and S.M. Goldberg)

Honorable Mention, *Journal of Retailing*, best paper award for 1983-1984

Kellwood Distinguished Lecturer, Washington University, November 1984

Special Award for "Contributions to Multidimensional Scaling," presented by the Marketing Science Institute, November 1986

Finalist, O'Dell Award, *Journal of Marketing Research*, 1982

Finalist, O'Dell Award, *Journal of Marketing Research*, 1987

Finalist, Franz Edelman Award (Marketing Science), 1988

Winner, O'Dell Award, *Journal of Marketing Research*, 1989

Keynote Speaker, Ninth Annual Consortium for Marketing Faculty, Michigan State University, June 1989

Winner of Best Paper in the Marketing Research Track, AMA Educators' Meeting, August 1989

Presenter at 22 Annual Doctoral Consortia for Marketing Ph.D. Students (from 1964 to 1994)

Winner of Best Paper in the *Journal of the Academy of Marketing Science*, 1989

Ranked first in Marketing in national study of the top 32 US business schools in 1990. Criteria: (a) publications, (b) journal citations, and (c) peer ratings

Ranked first in citation analysis (1965-1986) of *Journal of Marketing, Journal of Marketing Research*, and *Journal of Consumer Research*

Recognized with seven entries (highest number) in L. M. Robinson and R. D. Adler's *Marketing Megaworks: The Top 150 Books and Articles*, Praeger 1987

Winner of the 1991 Marketing Educator of the Year award, American Marketing Association, and Richard D. Irwin Publishing Company

Winner of the 1992 Outstanding Marketing Educator Award, Academy of Marketing Science

Most cited paper in the *Journal of Consumer Research*: "Conjoint Analysis in Consumer Research: Issues and Outlook," with V. Srinivasan (1978)

Alpha Kappa Psi Award (1991). Presented for the article, "Segmenting Markets with Conjoint Analysis," *Journal of Marketing*, October 1991 (coauthor: Abba M. Krieger)

Most frequently cited Wharton faculty member, based on the Social Science Citation Index entries, from 1988 to September 1993, the time period of the University of Pennsylvania's Lippincott Library study

ACR December 1990 Newsletter: Named most active reviewer of marketing journal submissions during 1979-1982; named one of the top five during 1985-1988

ACR December 1993 Newsletter: Highest cited scholar with regard to *JCR, JM*, and *JMR* combined, over the period 1969-1988

Doctorial Consortium presenter, 1992, 1993, 1994, 1995, 1996, 1997, 1998, 2001

Winner of Best Paper Prize, with Jonathan Kim, in the 1993 Academy of Marketing Science Annual Conference, May 1993

"The Paul Green Award" established in 1996 by the AMA's *Journal of Marketing Research*, for the *JMR* paper in the previous year that "shows or demonstrates the most potential to contribute significantly to the practice of marketing research and research in marketing"

Lifetime Achievement in Marketing Research Award, American Marketing Association, 1996 (first winner)

Finalist, J.D.C. Little Award, *Marketing Science,* with P. Lenk, W. DeSarbo, and M. Young

List of "Best Researchers in Marketing in 1997," article in AMS, 1997

Top marketing researcher in *JCR + JM+ JMR* based on 1969-1980 citations

Wei Lun Distinguished Professor, public lecture, "Marketing Science or Marketing Engineering?" May 1998, Hong King University

Selected in a worldwide survey as one of the "Ten Most Distinguished Authors in Marketing." Tribute by de Géreaud Cliquet appears in the chapter, "Paul E. Green: "L'Analyse de données en Marketing," Alain Jolbert (ed.), EMS, France, 2000

The article, "Benefit Bundle Analysis," with Y. Wind and A. K. Jain, was selected by the *Journal of Advertising Research* as one of its top classics in advertising research, *JAR* "classics" issue, Winter 2000

Featured Academic, Marketing Science Institute Website, April 2001

Keynote Speaker, "Marketing Research Methodology: Past, Present, and Future," Fortieth Anniversary of the Marketing Science Institute, April 2001

Student Award: "The Paul Green Knowledge Creation Award," awarded to Jason S. Breemen, 2nd-year MBA, The Wharton School, April 2001

2002 Wroe Alderson Distinguished Lecturer, The Wharton School

Books

Alderson, W. and P. E. Green (1964), *Planning and Problem Solving in Marketing*. Homewood, IL: Richard D. Irwin.

Green, P. E. and D. S. Tull (1966), *Research for Marketing Decisions*. Englewood Cliffs, NJ: Prentice-Hall, Inc. Second edition, 1970; Third edition, 1975; Fourth edition, 1978; Fifth edition 1988.

Green, P. E., P. T. FitzRoy, and P. J. Robinson (1967), *Experiments on the Value of Information in Information in Simulated Marketing Environments*. Boston, MA: Allyn and Bacon.

Green, P. E. and R. E. Frank (1967), *A Manager's Guide to Marketing Research: Survey of Recent Developments*. New York: John Wiley & Sons, Inc.

Frank, R. E. and P. E. Green (1967), *Quantitative Methods in Marketing Analysis*, Prentice-Hall, Inc.

Green, P. E. and F. J. Carmone (1970), *Multidimensional Scaling and Related Techniques in Marketing Analysis*. Boston, MA: Allyn and Bacon.

Green, P. E. and V. R. Rao (1972), *Applied Multidimensional Scaling*. New York: Holt, Rinehart & Winston.

Green, P. E. and Y. Wind (1973), *Multi-Attribute Decisions in Marketing*. New York: Holt, Rinehart & Winston.

Green, P. E. and M. Christopher, eds. (1973), *Brand Positioning*. London: EJM Publisher.

Green, P. E., with contributions by J. D. Carroll (1976), *Mathematical Tools for Applied Multivariate Analysis*. San Diego, CA: Academic Press.

Green, P. E., with contributions by J. D. Carroll (1978), *Analyzing Multivariate Data*. Hinsdale, IL: Dryden Press.

Green, P. E., P. K. Kedia, and R. S. Nikhil (1985), *Electronic Questionnaire Design and Analysis with CAPPA*. Palo Alto, CA: The Scientific Press.

Green, P. E., F. J. Carmone, and S. Smith (1989), *Multidimensional Scaling: Concepts and Applications*, Boston: Allyn and Bacon, 1989.

Carroll, J. D., A. Chaturvedi, and P. E. Green (1998), *Mathematical Tools for Applied Multivariate Analysis*, revised edition. San Diego, CA: Academic Press.

Lattin, J., J. D. Carroll, and P. E. Green (2002), *Analyzing Multivariate Data*. Pacific Grove, CA: Brooks/Cole – Thomson Learning.

Monographs with Computer Software

Green, P. E. and A. M. Krieger (1985), *Conjoint Analysis and Buyer Choice Simulation with HYCON*.

Green, P. E. and A. M. Krieger (1986), *Product Positioning and Preference Analysis with METRIMAP*.

Green, P. E. and A. M. Krieger (1986), *Conjoint Analysis and Computer Simulation with HYSIM*.

Green, P. E. and C. M. Schaffer (1987), *Advertising and Concept Testing with ADVAL*.

Green, P. E., A. M. Krieger, and C. M. Schaffer (1987), *Optimal Product Line Design and Positioning with OPTPRO*.

Green, P. E. and A. M. Krieger (1996), *User's Guide to CONJOINT DISPLAY*.

Green, P. E. and A. M. Krieger (1999), *User's Guide to SIMOPT*.

Green, P. E. and A. M. Krieger (1999), *User's Guide to VOICE*.

Green, P. E. and A. M. Krieger (1999), *User's Guide to BUNDOPT*.

Green, P. E. and A. M. Krieger (1999), *User's Guide to HIERMAPS*.

Book Chapters

Green, P. E. (1963), "The Computer's Place in Business Planning: A Bayesian Approach," in *Marketing and The Computer*, W. Alderson and S. Shapiro (eds.). Englewood Cliffs, NJ: Prentice-Hall.

Green, P. E. (1964), "Decision Theory in Market Planning and Research," in *Models, Measurement and Marketing*, Market Research Council (eds.). Englewood Cliffs, NJ: Prentice-Hall.

Green, P. E. (1964), "Uncertainty, Information and Marketing Decisions," in *Theory in Marketing*, R. Cox, W. Alderson, and S. Shapiro (eds.). Homewood, IL: Richard D. Irwin.

Two chapters in *The Nature and Sources of Marketing Theory*, Marketing Science Institute, McGraw-Hill, 1965.

Three chapters in *Promotional Decision Making: Practice and Theory*, Marketing Science Institute, McGraw-Hill, 1965.

Green, P. E. (1966), "Consumer Use of Information," in *On Knowing the Consumer*, J. W. Newman (ed.). New York: John Wiley & Sons.

Green, P. E. (1967), "A Behavioral Experiment in the Economics of Information," in *The Psychology of Management Decision*, George Fisk (ed.). New York: John Wiley.

Green, P. E., P. T. FitzRoy, and P. J. Robinson (1967), "Experimental Gaming in the Economics of Information," in *Applications of the Sciences in Marketing*, F. Bass, C. King, and E. Pessemier (eds.). New York: John Wiley & Sons.

Green, P. E. and H. Sieber (1967), "Discriminant Techniques in Adoption Patterns for a New Product," in *Sales Analysis: Some Applications of Quantitative Techniques*, P. J. Robinson and C. L. Hinkle (eds.). Boston, MA: Allyn & Bacon.

Green, P. E. (1968), "Decision Theory Applied to Pricing Problems," in *Pricing Theories, Practices and Policies*, A. Phillips (ed.). Philadelphia: Univ. of Pennsylvania Press.

Green, P. E., R. E. Frank, and P. J. Robinson (1968), "A Behavioral Experiment in Risk Taking and Information Seeking," in *Explorations in Consumer Behavior*, M. Sommers and J. Kernan (eds.). Austin, TX: University of Texas Press.

Green, P. E., M. H. Halbert, and P. J. Robinson (1968), "Perception and Preference Mapping in the Analysis of Marketing Behavior," in *Attitude Research on the Rocks*, I. Crespi (ed.). Chicago: American Marketing Association.

Green, P. E. (1970), "Decision Theory and Related Techniques in New Product Introduction," in *Handbook of Marketing Management*, V. Buell (ed.). New York: McGraw-Hill.

Green, P. E. and M. Greenberg (1970), "Ordinal Methods in Multidimensional Scaling," in *Handbook of Marketing Research*, R. Ferber (ed.). New York: McGraw-Hill.

Green, P. E. (1971), "Effects of Task on Similarities Judgments," *Attitude Research Reaches New Heights*, C. King (ed.). Chicago: American Marketing Association.

Green, P. E. (1971), "Nonmetric Methods in Multivariate Data Analysis," in *Essays in Marketing Theory*, G. Fisk (ed.). Boston, MA: Allyn and Bacon.

Green, P. E. and F. J. Carmone (1972), "Marketing Research Applications of Nonmetric Scaling Methods," in *Multidimensional Scaling*, A. K. Romney, R. N. Shepard, and S. B. Nerlove (eds.). New York: Academic Press.

Green, P. E. (1973), "Multidimensional Scaling and Conjoint Measurement in the Study of Choice Among Multiattribute Alternatives," in *Studies in Multiple Criterion Decision Making*. Columbia, SC: University of South Carolina Press.

Green, P. E. and Y. Wind (1973), "Some Conceptual, Measurement and Analytical Problems in Life Style Research," in *Life Style and Psychographics*, W. D. Wells (ed.). Chicago: American Marketing Association.

Green, P. E. and J. McMennamin (1974), "Market Research Analysis," in *Marketing Handbook*, S. H. Britt (ed.). Chicago: Dartnell Corp., 501-514.

Green, P. E. and V. R. Rao (1975), "Nonmetric Approaches to Multivariate Analysis in Marketing," in *Multivariate Procedures in Marketing*, J. N. Sheth (ed.). Chicago: American Marketing Association, 237-254.

Green, P. E., J. D. Carroll, and F. J. Carmone (1977), "Some New Types of Fractional Factorial Designs for Marketing Experiments," in *Research for Marketing*, J. N. Sheth (ed.). Greenwich, CN: JAI Press.

Green, P. E., Y. Wind, and M. Greenberg (1977), "Design Considerations in Attitude Measurement," in *Moving Ahead with Attitude Research*, Y. Wind and M. Greenberg (eds.). Chicago: American Marketing Association, 9-18.

Green, P. E. and J. D. Carroll (1981), "New Computer Tools for Product Strategy," in *New Product Forecasting: Models and Applications*, Y. Wind, V. Mahajan, and R. Cardozo (eds.). Lexington, MA: Lexington Books, 109-154.

Green, P. E., J. D. Carroll, and S. M. Goldberg (1981), "A General Approach to Product Design Optimization via Conjoint Analysis," in *Product Policy: Concepts, Methods, and Strategies*, Y. Wind (ed.). Reading, MA: Addison-Wesley.

Green, P. E. and Y. Wind (1983), "Statistics in Marketing," in *Encyclopedia of the Statistical Sciences*. New York: McGraw-Hill.

Green, P. E., F. J. Carmone, and C. M. Schaffer (1988), "An Individual Importance Weights Model for Conjoint Analysis," in *Data, Expert Knowledge and Decisions*, W. Gaul and M. Schader (eds.). New York: Springer-Verlag.

Green, P. E., A. M. Krieger, and C. M. Shaffer (1988), "Dominated Options in Conjoint Modeling: Is Their Occurrence Recognized?" in *Data, Expert Knowledge and Decisions*, W. Gaul and M. Schader (eds.). New York: Springer-Verlag.

Green, P. E. and A. M. Krieger (1989), "A Hybrid Conjoint Model for Price-Demand Estimation," in *New-Product Development and Testing*, W. Henry, M. Menasco, and H. Takada (eds.). Lexington, MA: Heath.

Green, P. E. and A. M. Krieger (1991), "Conjoint Analysis: Methods and Applications," in *Handbook of Marketing Research*, M. J. Houston (ed.). New York: McGraw Hill.

Wind, Y., V. R. Rao, and Green, P. E. (1991), "Behavioral Methods," in *Handbook of Consumer Theory and Research*, T. S. Robertson and H. Kassarjian (eds.). Englewood Cliffs, NJ: Prentice-Hall.

Green, P. E. and A. M. Krieger (1993), "Conjoint Analysis with Product Positioning Applications," in *Handbook of Operations Research Series*, Vol. 5, J. Eliashberg and G. L. Lilien (eds.). New York: North-Holland, 467-515.

Green, P. E., J. McMennamin, and S. Amirani (1993), "Market Position Analysis," in *Marketing Handbook*, 3rd edition, S. Levy, G. Frerichs, and H. Gordon (eds.). Chicago: Dartnell, 553-569.

Green, P. E. and A.M. Krieger (1998), "Using Conjoint Analysis to View Competitive Interaction Through Customers' Eyes," in *Wharton on Dynamic Competition,* G. Day and D. Reibstein (eds.). New York: Wiley.

Green, P. E., J. Wind, and V. R. Rao (1998), "Conjoint Analysis: Methods and Applications," in *Handbook of Technology Management,* R. Duff (ed.). Boca Raton, FL: CRC Press, 1998.

Reviews, Editorials, and Invited Papers

Review: Green, P. E. (1964), "*Marketing Executive and Buying Behavior*, by John A. Howard," *Journal of Marketing Research*, January.

Review: Green, P. E. (1965), "*Models of Markets,* by Alfred R. Oxenfeldt (ed.)," *Journal of Marketing Research*, February.

Review: Green, P. E. (1966), "*Optimality and Human Judgments,* by Shelly and Bryan (eds.)," *Journal of Marketing Research*, February.

Review: Green, P. E. (1966), "*Value and Decision Theory*, by P. Fishburn," *Journal of Marketing Research*, February.

Review: Green, P. E. (1967), "*A Theory of Data* by C. H. Coombs," *Journal of Marketing Research*, November.

Invited Editorial: Green, P. E. (1968), "Where is the Research Generalist?" *Journal of Marketing Research*, November.

Review: Green, P. E. (1972), "A Course in the Geometry of *n* Dimensions," *Journal of Marketing Research*, February.

Review: Green, P. E. (1972), "Linear Algebra," *Journal of Marketing Research*, August.

Review: Green, P. E. (1987), "Conjoint Analyzer," *Journal of Marketing Research*, August.

Review: Green, P. E. (1990), "Analyzing Complex Survey Data," *Journal of Marketing Research*, November, 502-503.

Review: Green, P. E. (1992), "Statistical Principles in Experimental Design," *Journal of Marketing Research*, August, 378-379.

Review: Green, P. E. (1992), "CONSURV: Conjoint Analysis Software," *Journal of Marketing Research*, August, 387-390.

Review: Green, P. E. (1992), "MCA+: Correspondence Analysis," *Journal of Marketing Research*, November, 278-241.

Review: Green, P. E. (1992), "CORANA: Correspondence Analysis," *Journal of Marketing Research*, November.

Review: Green, P. E. (1995), "Elements of Dual Scaling: An Introduction to Practical Data Analysis," *Journal of Marketing Research*, August, 382-383.

Invited Paper: Carroll, J. D. and P. E. Green (1995), "Psychometric Methods in Marketing Research: Part I, Conjoint Analysis," *Journal of Marketing Research*, November.

Invited Paper: Carroll, J. D. and P. E. Green (1997), "Psychometric Methods in Marketing Research: Part II, Multidimensional Scaling," *Journal of Marketing Research*, May.

Invited Paper: Green, P. E., R. M. Johnson, and W. D. Neal (2003), "*The Journal of Marketing Research*: Its Initiation, Growth, and Knowledge Dissemination," *Journal of Marketing Research*, February.

Articles and Proceedings

Green, P. E. and L. L. Haines (1957), "Operations Research for Managers," *ASQC Middle Atlantic Conference Transactions*, February.

Green, P. E. and L. L. Haines (1957), "Statistical Procedures in Standards Auditing," *The Journal of Industrial Engineering*, September-October. (Reprinted in one book.)

Green, P. E. and L. L. Haines (1957), "Industrial Statistics Help Solve Steel Plant Managerial Problems," *Iron and Steel Engineer*, October.

Green, P. E. and S. R. Calhoun (1958), "An Environmental Framework for Break-Even Analysis for Planning," *N.A.A. Bulletin*, March.

Green, P. E. and S. R. Calhoun (1958), "Making Money with Mathematics in Purchasing," *Purchasing*, 3 (March).

Green, P. E. and S. R. Calhoun (1958), "Simulation: Versatile Aid to Decision Making," with S. R. Calhoun, *Advanced Management*, April.

Green, P. E. (1958), "Other Staff Groups Can Use Statistics Too," *Industrial Quality Control*, May.

Green, P. E. and S. R. Calhoun (1959), "Solving Your Plant Problems by Simulation," with S. R. Calhoun, *Factory*, February.

Green, P. E. (1960), "Applications of Monte Carlo Simulation in a Steel Company," *ASQC Metropolitan Conference Transactions*, February.

Green, P. E. (1962), "Decision Theory and Chemical Marketing," *Industrial and Engineering Chemistry*, 54 (September), 30-34.

Green, P. E. (1962), "Bayesian Statistics and Product Decisions," *Business Horizons*, 5 (Fall), 101-109. (Reprinted in three books.)

Green, P. E. (1962), "Decisions Involving High Risk," *Advanced Management*, October. (Reprinted in one book.)

Green, P. E. (1962), "Bayesian Decision Theory in Advertising," *Journal of Advertising Research*, December, 33-41 (Reprinted in four books.)

Green, P. E. (1963), "Bayesian Decision Theory in Pricing Strategy," *Journal of Marketing*, 27 (January), 5-14. (Reprinted in eight books.)

Green, P. E. (1963), "Risk Attitudes and Chemical Investment Decisions," *Chemical Engineering Progress*, January.

Green, P. E. (1963), "The Profit Maximization Hypothesis," *Growth and Profit Planner*, February.

Green, P. E. (1963), "The Role of Bayesian Statistics in Advertising and Marketing Management," *New Techniques for Decision Making in Advertising Management*, Association of National Advertisers, May.

Green, P. E. (1964), "Bayesian Classification Procedures in Analyzing Customer Characteristics," *Journal of Marketing Research*, 1 (May), 44-50.

Green, P. E., M. Halbert, and J. Minas (1964), "An Experiment in Information Processing," *Journal of Advertising Research*, September.

Green P. E. (1965), "The Future Role of Management Science in Pharmaceutical Marketing," *Proceedings of World Congress on Marketing*, New York, June.

Green, P. E., M. H. Halbert, and P. J. Robinson (1965), "An Experiment in Probability Estimation," *Journal of Marketing Research*, 2 (August), 266-273.

Green, P. E., M. H. Halbert, and P. J. Robinson (1965), "Experimental Gaming in Consumer Brand Choice Behavior," *The Business Quarterly*, September.

Green, P. E., M. H. Halbert, and P. J. Robinson (1966), "Canonical Correlation: An Exposition and Illustrative Application," *Journal of Marketing Research*, 3 (February), 32-39.

Green, P. E., W. S. Peters, and P. J. Robinson (1966), "A Behavioral Experiment in Decision Making Under Uncertainty," *Journal of Marketing Research*, 3 (February), 261-268.

Green, P. E. and D. S. Tull (1966), "Covariance Analysis in Marketing Experimentation," *Journal of Advertising Research*, 6 (June), 45-53.

Green, P. E., M. H. Halbert, and P. J. Robinson (1966), "A Behavioral Experiment in Sales Effort Allocation," *Journal of Marketing Research*, 3 (August), 261-288.

Green, P. E., P. J. Robinson, and P. T. FitzRoy (1966), "Advertising Expenditure Models: State of the Art and Prospects," *Business Horizons*, Fall.

Green, P. E. and R. E. Frank (1966), "Bayesian Statistics in Marketing Research," *Applied Statistics*, September.

Green, P. E. (1966), "The Role of Experimental Research in Marketing: Its Potential and Limitations," *Proceedings of the National Meeting of the American Marketing Association*, September.

Frank, R. E., P. E. Green, and H. Sieber (1967), "Household Correlates of Purchase Price for Grocery Products," *Journal of Marketing Research*, 4 (February), 54-58.

Green, P. E., R. E. Frank, and P. J. Robinson (1967), "Cluster Analysis in Test Market Selection," *Management Science*, 13 (April), B387-B400.

Green, P. E., I. Gross, and P. J. Robinson (1967), "A Behavioral Experiment in Two-Person Bargaining," *Journal of Marketing Research*, 4 (November), 374-380.

Green, P. E. and F. J. Carmone (1968), "The Performance Structure of the Computer Market: A Multivariate Approach," *Economics and Business Bulletin*, 21.

Green, P. E., F. J. Carmone, and P. J. Robinson (1968), "A Comparison of Confusions Data and Direct Similarities Judgments," *Proceedings of the Denver Conference of the American Marketing Association*, R. L. King (ed.), American Marketing Association.

Green, P. E., Y. Wind, and P. J. Robinson (1968), "The Determinants of Vendor Selection: The Evaluation Function Approach," *Journal of Purchasing*, 4.

Frank, R. E. and P. E. Green, (1968), "Numerical Taxonomy in Marketing Analysis," *Journal of Marketing Research*, 5 (February), 83-93.

Green, P. E. (1968), "On the Value of a Continuing Education," *Marketing News*, April.

Green, P. E., F. J. Carmone, and P. J. Robinson (1968), "Nonmetric Scaling Methods – An Exposition and Overview," *Wharton Quarterly*, 2 (Spring-Winter), 27-41.

Green, P. E., A. Maheshwari, and V. R. Rao (1969), "Dimensional Interpretation and Configuration Invariance in Multidimensional Scaling: An Empirical Study," *Multivariate Behavioral Research*, 6 (April), 159-180.

Green, P. E. and F. J. Carmone (1969), "Multidimensional Scaling: An Introduction and Comparison of Nonmetric Unfolding Techniques," *Journal of Marketing Research*, 6 (August), 330-341.

Green, P. E. and V. R. Rao (1969), "A Note on Proximity Measures and Cluster Analysis," *Journal of Marketing Research*, 6 (August), 359-364.

Green, P. E., C. Hinkle and P. J. Robinson (1969), "Cluster Analysis in Industrial Marketing," *Journal of Purchasing*, August.

Green, P. E. and V. R. Rao (1969), "Configuration Invariance in Nonmetric Scaling: An Empirical Study," *Proceedings of the Cincinnati Educators Meeting of the American Marketing Association*, August.

Green, P. E., F. J. Carmone and L. B. Fox (1969), "Television Program Similarities: An Application of Subjective Clustering," *Journal of the Market Research Society*, 11 (Fall), 70-90.

Green, P. E. and A. K. Maheshwari (1969), "Common Stock Perception and Preference: An Application of Multidimensional Scaling," *Journal of Business*, 42 (October), 439-457.

Green, P. E., A. K. Maheshwari and V. R. Rao (1969), "Self Concept and Brand Preference: An Empirical Application of Multidimensional Scaling," *Journal of the Market Research Society*, 11 (October), 343-360.

Green, P. E. (1970), "Measurement and Data Analysis," *Journal of Marketing*, 34 (January), 15-17.

Green, P. E. and A. K. Maheshwari (1970), "A Note on the Multidimensional Scaling of Conditional Proximity Data," *Journal of Marketing Research*, 7 (February), 106-110.

Green, P. E. and V. R. Rao (1970), "Ratings Scales and Information Recovery – How Many Scales and Response Categories to Use?" *Journal of Marketing*, 34 (July), 33-39.

Green, P. E. and F. J. Carmone (1970), "Marketing Research Applications of Nonmetric Scaling Methods," *Operational Research Quarterly*, September.

Green, P. E. and F. J. Carmone (1970), "Marketing Research Applications of Nonmetric Scaling Methods," *First Symposium on Nonmetric Multidimensional Scaling*, University of California, Irvine.

Green, P. E. and F. J. Carmone (1971), "Stimulus Context and Task Effects on Individuals' Similarities Judgments," *Proceedings of the 3rd Annual Attitude Research Conference*.

Green, P. E. and V. R. Rao (1971), "Multidimensional Scaling and Individual Differences," *Journal of Marketing Research*, 8 (February), 71-77.

Green, P. E., V. R. Rao, and D. E. Armani (1971), "Graphology and Marketing Research," *Journal of Marketing*, April.

Green, P. E. and V. R. Rao (1971), "Conjoint Measurement for Quantifying Judgmental Data," *Journal of Marketing Research*, 8 (August), 355-363.

Green, P. E. and F. J. Carmone (1971), "The Effect of Task on Intra-Individual Differences in Similarities Judgments," *Multivariate Behavioral Research*, 6 (October), 433-450.

Green, P. E. and V. R. Rao (1971), "A Rejoinder to 'How Many Rating Scales and How Many Categories Shall We Use in Consumer Research – A Comment,'" *Journal of Marketing*, 35 (October), 61-62.

Green, P. E. and V. R. Rao (1972), "Configuration Synthesis in Multidimensional Scaling," *Journal of Marketing Research*, 9 (February), 65-68.

Green, P. E., Y. Wind, and A. K. Jain (1972), "Benefit Bundle Analysis," *Journal of Advertising Research*, 12 (April), 31-36.

Green, P. E., F. J. Carmone, and Y. Wind (1972), "Subjective Evaluation Models and Conjoint Measurement," *Behavioral Science*, 17 (May), 288-299.

Green, P. E., Y. Wind, and A. K. Jain (1972), "A Note on the Measurement of Social-Psychological Belief Systems," *Journal of Marketing Research*, 9 (May), 204-208.

Green, P. E. and A. K. Jain (1972), "A Note on the Robustness of INDSCAL to Departures from Linearity," *Proceedings of the AMA National Conference,* August.

Green, P. E. (1972), "Multi-Attribute Decisions in Marketing Behavior," *Wharton Quarterly*, September.

Green, P. E., Y. Wind and A. K. Jain (1972), "Preference Measurement of Item Collections," *Journal of Marketing Research*, 9 (November), 371-377.

Green, P. E. and Y. Wind (1972), "On the Measurement of Judgmental Responses to Multiattribute Marketing Stimuli, *Research Design Competition*, American Psychological Association.

Green, P. E. and Y. Wind (1973), "Recent Approaches to the Modeling of Individual's Subjective Evaluations," *Proceedings of the Madrid Conference on Attitude Research,* February.

Green, P. E., Y. Wind and A. K. Jain (1973), "Analyzing Free Response Data in Marketing Research," *Journal of Marketing Research*, 10 (February), 45-52.

Green, P. E., F. J. Carmone, and Y. Wind (1973), "Consumer Evaluation of Discount Cards," *Journal of Retailing*, 49 (Spring), 10-22.

Green, P. E. (1973), "Measurement of Judgmental Responses to Multiattribute Marketing Stimuli," *Sensory Evaluation of Appearance*, ASTM STP 545: American Society for Testing and Materials, September, 139-153.

Green, P. E., Y. Wind, and A. K. Jain (1973), "Higher Order Factor Analysis in the Classification of Psychographic Variables," *Journal of the Market Research Society*, October.

Green, P. E. (1973), "On the Analysis of Interactions in Marketing Research Data," *Journal of Marketing Research*, 10 (November), 410-420.

Green, P. E. (1973), "On the Design of Multiattribute Choice Experiments Involving Large Numbers of Factors and Factor Levels," *Proceedings of the Association for Consumer Research*, November.

Green, P. E. (1973), "Multivariate Procedures in the Study of Attitudes and Status Impressions," *Social Science Research*, December.

Green, P. E. (1974), "A Model of Product-Features Associations," *Journal of Business Research*, 2 (April), 107-118.

Green, P. E. and F. J. Carmone (1974), "Evaluation of Multiattribute Alternatives: Additive Versus Configural Utility Measurement," *Decision Sciences*, April.

Green, P. E. (1974), "On the Design of Choice Experiments Involving Multifactor Alternatives," *Journal of Consumer Research*, 1 (September), 61-68.

Green, P. E. and M. DeVita (1974), "A Complementary Model of Consumer Utility for Item Collections," *Journal of Consumer Research*, 1 (December), 56-67.

Green, P. E. (1975), "Marketing Applications of MDS: Assessment and Outlook," *Journal of Marketing*, 39 (January), 24-31.

Green, P. E. (1975), "On the Robustness of Multidimensional Scaling Techniques," *Journal of Marketing Research*, 12 (February), 73-81.

Green, P. E. and Y. Wind (1975), "New Ways to Measure Consumer Judgments," *Harvard Business Review*, 53 (July-August), 107-117.

Green, P. E., Y. Wind and H. J. Claycamp (1975), "Brand Feature Congruence Mapping," *Journal of Marketing Research*, 12 (August), 306-313.

Green, P. E. (1975), "MDS Applications in Marketing: The Art of the States," *U.S.-Japan Seminar in Theory, Methods, and Applications of Multidimensional Scaling and Related Techniques,* University of California at San Diego, August.

Green, P. E. (1975), "The Robustness of Linear Models under Correlated Attribute Conditions," *Proceedings of the AMA Educator's Conference,* August.

Green, P. E. and M. DeVita (1975), "An Interaction Model of Consumer Utility," *Journal of Consumer Research*, 2 (September), 146-153.

Green, P. E., J. D. Carroll, and F. J. Carmone (1976), "Superordinate Factorial Designs in the Analysis of Consumer Judgments," *Journal of Business Research*, 4, 281-295.

Green, P. E., F. J. Carmone, and D. P. Wachspress (1976), "Consumer Segmentation Via Latent Class Analysis," *Journal of Consumer Research*, 3 (December), 170-174.

Green, P. E., F. J. Carmone, and D. P. Wachspress (1977), "On the Analysis of Qualitative Data in Marketing Research," *Journal of Marketing Research*, 14 (February), 52-59.

Green, P. E. (1977), "A New Approach to Market Segmentation," *Business Horizons*, 20 (February) 61-73.

Green, P. E. and F. J. Carmone (1977), "Segment Congruence Analysis: A Method for Analyzing Associations Among Alternative Bases of Market Segmentation," *Journal of Consumer Research*, 3 (March), 217-222.

Green, P. E. (1978), "An AID/Logit Procedure for Analyzing Large Multiway Contingency Tables," *Journal of Marketing Research*, 15 (February), 132-136.

Green, P. E. and F. J. Carmone (1978), "Some Methodological Alternatives to the Analysis of Life Style Data," *Review of Economics in Business*.

Green, P. E., F. J. Carmone, and A. K. Jain (1978), "The Robustness of Conjoint Analysis: Some Monte Carlo Results," *Journal of Marketing Research*, 15 (May), 300-303.

Green, P. E. and W. S. DeSarbo (1978), "Additive Decomposition of Perceptions Data Via Conjoint Analysis," *Journal of Consumer Research*, 5 (June), 58-65.

Green, P. E. (1978), "Marketing Research in the 1980's," *The Executive*, June.

Green, P. E., J. D. Carroll and W. S. DeSarbo (1978), "A New Measure of Predictor Variable Importance in Multiple Regression," *Journal of Marketing Research*, 15 (August), 356-360.

Green, P. E., J. D. Carroll, and W. S. DeSarbo (1978), "An Extended Application of the d2 Measure of Predictor Variable Importance," *Proceedings of the Educators Conference of the American Marketing Association,* August.

Green, P. E. and M. DeVita (1978), "Some Multivariate Aspects of Brand Image Measurement," *Proceedings of the Educators Conference of the American Marketing Association,* August.

Green, P. E. and V. Srinivasan (1978), "Conjoint Analysis in Consumer Research: Issues and Outlook," *Journal of Consumer Research*, 5 (September), 103-123.

Green, P. E., V. R. Rao, and W. S. DeSarbo (1978), "Incorporating Group-Level Similarity Judgments in Conjoint Analysis," *Journal of Consumer Research*, 5 (December), 187-193.

Carroll, J. D., P. E. Green, and W. S. DeSarbo (1979), "Optimizing the Allocation of a Fixed Resource: A Simple Model and its Experimental Test," *Journal of Marketing*, 43 (January), 51-57.

Green, P. E. (1979), "The Future Marketing Researcher," *Proceedings of the American Marketing Association,* June.

Green, P. E. and W. S. DeSarbo (1979), "Componential Segmentation in the Analysis of Consumer Tradeoffs," *Journal of Marketing*, 43 (Fall), 83-91.

Green, P. E., J. D. Carroll, and W. S. DeSarbo (1980), "Reply to 'A Comment on a New Measure of Predictor Variable Importance in Multiple Regression,'" *Journal of Marketing Research*, 17 (February), 116-118.

Green, P. E. and W. S. DeSarbo (1980), "Two Models for Representing Unrestricted Choice Data," *Proceedings of the 1980 Meeting for the Association for Consumer Research.*

Green, P. E., W. S. DeSarbo, and P. K. Kedia (1980), "On the Insensitivity of Brand Choice Simulations to Attribute Importance Weights," *Decision Sciences*, 11 (July), 439-450.

Carmone, F. J. and P.E. Green (1981), "Model Misspecification in Multiattribute Parameter Estimation," *Journal of Marketing Research*, 18 (February), 87-93.

Green, P. E., S. M. Goldberg, and M. Montemayor (1981), "A Hybrid Utility Estimation Model for Conjoint Analysis," *Journal of Marketing*, 45 (Winter), 33-41.

Green, P. E., J. D. Carroll, and W. S. DeSarbo (1981), "Estimating Choice Probabilities in Multiattribute Decision Making," *Journal of Consumer Research*, 8 (June) 76-84.

Green, P. E., J. D. Carroll, and S. M. Goldberg (1981), "A General Approach to Product Design Optimization via Conjoint Analysis," *Journal of Marketing*, 45 (Summer), 17-37.

Green, P. E., W. S. DeSarbo, and P. K. Kedia (1981), "Reply: On the Sensitivity of Brand Choice Simulations to Attribute Importance, Weights," *Decision Sciences*, July.

Harshman, R. A., P. E. Green, and Y. Wind (1982), "A Model for the Analysis of Asymmetric Data in Marketing Research," *Marketing Science*, 1 (Spring), 205-242.

Mahajan, V., Green, P. E., and S. M. Goldberg (1982), "A Conjoint Model for Measuring Self and Cross Price-Demand Relationships," *Journal of Marketing Research*, 19 (August), 334-342.

Green, P. E., S. M. Goldberg, and J. B. Wiley (1982), "A Cross Validation Test of Hybrid Conjoint Models," *Proceedings of the Association for Consumer Research*, San Francisco.

Green, P. E., V. Mahajan, S. M. Goldberg, and P. K. Kedia (1983), "A Decision Support System for Developing Retail Promotional Strategy," *Journal of Retailing*, 59 (Fall), 116-143.

Green, P. E. and C. M. Schaffer (1983), "Ad Copy Testing: Diagnostic Procedures for Summarizing Perceptual and Executional Impact," *Journal of Advertising Research*, 23 (October-November), 73-80.

Green, P. E. and S. M. Goldberg (1983), "Hybrid Conjoint Models Based on Canonical Correlation Procedures," *Proceedings of the 1983 Winter Educators Conference of the American Marketing Association.*

Goldberg, S. M., P. E. Green, and Y. Wind (1984), "Conjoint Analysis of Price Premiums for Hotel Amenities," *Journal of Business*, January.

Green, P. E., and C. M. Schaffer (1984), "A Simple Method for Analyzing Consumer Preferences for Product Benefits," *Journal of the Market Research Society*, 26 (January), 51-61.

Green, P. E., F. J. Carmone, and P. Vankudre (1984), "Bootstrapped Confidence Intervals for Conjoint-Based Choice Simulators," *Proceedings of the 1984 Winter Educators Conference of the American Marketing Association,* February.

DeSarbo, W. S., J. D. Carroll, L. A. Clark, and P. E. Green (1984), "Synthesized Clustering: A Method for Amalgamating Alternative Clustering Bases with Differential Weighting of Variables," *Psychometrika*, 49 (March), 57-78.

Green, P. E. (1984), "Hybrid Models for Conjoint Analysis: An Expository Review," *Journal of Marketing Research*, 21 (May), 155-169.

DeSarbo, W. S. and P. E. Green (1984), "Choice-Constrained Conjoint Analysis," *Decision Sciences*, 15, 297-323.

Green, P. E. and A. Krieger (1985), "Models and Heuristics in Product Line Optimization," *Marketing Science*, 4 (Spring), 1-19.

Green, P. E. and A. M. Krieger (1985), "Buyer Similarity Measures in Conjoint Analysis: Some Alternative Proposals," *Journal of Classification*, Spring.

Green, P. E., A. M. Krieger, and C. M. Schaffer (1985), "Quick and Simple Benefit Segmentation," *Journal of Advertising Research*, 25 (June-July), 9-15.

DeSarbo, W. S., P. E. Green, and J. D. Carroll (1986), "An Alternating Least-Squares Procedure for Estimating Missing Preference Data in Product Concept Testing," *Decision Sciences*, 17 (Spring), 163-185.

Green, P. E. and A. M. Krieger (1986), "The Minimal Rank Correlation, Subject to Order Restrictions," *Journal of Classification*, Spring.

Carroll, J. D., P. E. Green, and C. M. Schaffer (1986), "Interpoint Distance Comparisons in Correspondence Analysis," *Journal of Marketing Research*, 23 (August), 271-280.

Green, P. E. and A. M. Krieger (1987), "A Consumer-Based Methodology for Designing Product Line Extensions," *Journal of Product Innovation Management*, 4.

Green, P. E., A. M. Krieger, and J. D. Carroll (1987), "Conjoint Analysis and Multidimensional Scaling: A Complementary Approach," *Journal of Advertising Research*, 27 (October/November).

Carroll, J. D., P. E. Green, and C. M. Schaffer (1987), "Comparing Interpoint Distances in Correspondence Analysis: A Clarification," *Journal of Marketing Research*, 24 (November), 445-450.

Green, P. E. and J. D. Carroll (1988), "A Simple Procedure for Finding a Composite of Several Multidimensional Scaling Solutions," *Journal of the Academy of Marketing Science*, 16 (Spring), 25-35.

Green, P. E. and A. M. Krieger (1988), "Choice Rules and Sensitivity Analysis in Conjoint Simulations," *Journal of the Academy of Marketing Science*, 16 (Spring), 114-127.

Green, P. E. and J. D. Carroll (1988), "An INDSCAL Approach to Multiple Correspondence Analysis," *Journal of Marketing Research*, 25 (May), 193-203.

Green, P. E., C. M. Schaffer, and K. M. Patterson (1988), "A Reduced-Space Approach to the Clustering of Categorical Data in Market Segmentation," *Journal of the Market Research Society*, 30 (July), 267-288.

Green, P. E., A. M. Krieger, and P. Bansal (1988), "Completely Unacceptable Levels in Conjoint Analysis: A Cautionary Tale," *Journal of Marketing Research*, 25 (August) 293-300.

Green, P. E., K. Helsen, and B. Shandler (1988), "Conjoint Internal Validity Under Alternative Profile Presentations," *Journal of Consumer Research*, 15 (December), 392-397.

Wind, Y., P. E. Green, M. Scarbrough, and D. K. Shifflet (1989), "*Courtyard by Marriott*: Designing a Hotel Facility with Consumer-Based Marketing Models," *Interfaces*, 19 (1).

Green, P. E. and A.M. Krieger (1989), "Recent Contributions to Optimal Product Positioning and Buyer Segmentation," *European Journal of Operational Research*, 41 (2), 127-141.

Green, P. E., A. M. Krieger, and R. N. Zelnio (1989), "A Componential Segmentation Model with Optimal Design Features," *Decision Sciences*, 20 (2), 221-238.

Green, P. E., K. Helsen and B. Shandler (1989), "Correlated Price in Conjoint Analysis: An Empirical Comparison of Part-Worth Estimation Models," *Proceedings of the 1989 Educators' Conference*, American Marketing Association, August.

Green, P. E. and K. Helsen (1989), "Cross-Validation Assessment of Alternatives to Individual-Level Conjoint Analysis – A Case Study," *Journal of Marketing Research*, 26 (August), 346-350.

Carroll, J. D., P. E. Green, and C. M. Schaffer (1989), "Reply to Greenacre's Commentary on the Carroll-Green-Schaffer Scaling of Two-Way Correspondence Analysis Solutions," *Journal of Marketing Research*, 26 (August), 287-306.

Green, P. E., J. D. Carroll, and J. Kim (1989), "Preference Mapping of Conjoint-Based Profiles: An INDSCAL Approach," *The Academy of Marketing Science*, 17 (4), 273-281.

Green, P. E., F. J. Carmone, and J. Kim (1990), "A Preliminary Study of Optimal Variable Weighting in K-Means Clustering," *Journal of Classification*, 7 (2), 271-285.

Green, P. E., J. Kim, and B. Shandler (1990), "Predictive Accuracy of Classification and Regression Trees (CART) Versus Conjoint Analysis," *1990 Proceedings of Academy of Marketing Science*, 8 (April), 366-370.

Green, P. E. and A. M. Krieger (1990), "A Hybrid Conjoint Model for Price-Demand Estimation," *European Journal of Operational Research*, 44 (October), 28-38.

Green, P. E. and V. Srinivasan (1990), "Conjoint Analysis in Marketing: New Developments with Implications for Research and Practice," *Journal of Marketing*, October.

Green, P. E. and C. M. Schaffer (1990), "Importance Weight Effects on Self-Explicated Preference Models: Some Empirical Findings," *Advances in Consumer Research*, Fall, 476-482.

Green, P. E., A, M. Krieger, and M. K. Agarwal (1991), "Adaptive Conjoint Analysis: Some Caveats and Suggestions," *Journal of Marketing Research*, 28 (May), 215-222.

Agarwal, M. K. and Green, P. E. (1991), "Adaptive Conjoint Analysis Versus Self-Explicated Models: Some Empirical Results," *International Journal of Research in Marketing*, 8 (June), 141-146.

Green, P. E., C. M. Schaffer, and K. M. Patterson (1991), "A Validation Study of Sawtooth Software's Adaptive Conjoint Analysis," *Proceedings of the 1991 Sawtooth Conference*, Ketchum, ID.

Green, P. E. and Abba M. Krieger (1991), "Modeling Competitive Pricing and Market Share: Anatomy of a Decision Support System," *European Journal of Operational Research*, July.

Green, P. E. (1991), "Musings on Method in Consumer Research," Fellows Award Speech, *Advances in Consumer Research*, Fall.

Green, P. E. and A. M. Krieger (1991), "Product Design Strategies for Target-Market Positioning," *Journal of Product Innovation Management*, 8 (Fall), 189-202.

Green, P. E. and A. M. Krieger (1991), "Segmenting Markets with Conjoint Analysis," *Journal of Marketing*, 55 (October), 20-31. Winner of the 1991 Alpha Kappa Psi award.

Helsen, K. and Green, P. E. (1991), "A Computational Study of Replicated Clustering with an Application to Market Segmentation," *Decision Sciences*, 22 (November/December), 1124-1141.

Krieger, A. M. and P. E. Green (1991), "Designing Pareto Optimal Stimuli for Multiattribute Choice Experiments," *Marketing Letters*, 2 (4), 337-348.

Green, P. E. and J. Kim (1991), "Beyond the Quadrant Chart: Designing Effective Benefit Bundle Strategies," *Journal of Advertising Research*, 31 (December), 56-63.

Green, P. E (1992), "Citation Classic: Methodology in Consumer Research," *Current Topics*, 8 (April).

Green, P. E. and A. M. Krieger (1992), "An Application of a Product Positioning Model to Pharmaceutical Products," *Marketing Science*, 11 (Spring), 117-132.

Green, P. E. and A. M. Krieger (1992), "Product Line Price Optimization with Conjoint Analysis," *Proceedings of the Academy of Marketing Science*, April.

Green, P. E. and A. M. Krieger (1992), "Modeling Competitive Pricing and Market Share: Anatomy of a Decision Support System," *European Journal of Operational Research*, 60 (July), 31-44.

Green, P. E. and A. M. Krieger, and C. M. Shaffer (1992), "Some Methodological and Empirical Findings Regarding Self-Explicated Preference Models," *Proceedings of the Summer Marketing Educators' Conference*, August, Chicago: 433-439.

Green, P. E. (1992), "Paradigms, Paradiddles, and Parafoils," Editorial, *Journal of the Academy of Marketing Science*, 20 (Fall), 377-378.

Green, P. E. and A. M. Krieger (1993), "A Simple Approach to Target Market Advertising Strategy," *Journal of the Market Research Society*, 35 (2), 161-170.

Green, P. E. and A. M. Krieger (1993), "Generalized Measures of Association for Ranked Data," *Journal of Classification*, 10 (June), 93-114.

Kim, J. S. and P. E. Green (1993), "Replicated Weights Determination in the SYNCLUS Optimal Variable Weights Clustering Program," *Proceedings of the Academy of Marketing Science Annual Meeting*, 122-129.

Green, P. E., A. M. Krieger, and C. M. Schaffer (1993), "A Hybrid Conjoint Model with Individual-level Interaction Estimation," *Advances in Consumer Research*, 20 (October), 1-6.

Green, P. E., A. M. Krieger, and C. M. Schaffer (1993), "A Cross Validation Test of Four Models for Quantifying Multiattribute Preferences," *Marketing Letters*, 4 (4), 368-380.

Green, P. E., A. M. Krieger, and C. M. Schaffer (1993), "An Empirical Test of Optimal Respondent Weighting in Conjoint Analysis," *Journal of the Academy of Marketing Science*, 21 (4), 345-351.

Green, P. E. and A. M. Krieger (1994), "A Hybrid Conjoint Model with Iterative Response Scale Adjustment," *Proceedings of the Academy of Marketing Science*, 17 (June), 273-279.

Chaturvedi, A. and P. E. Green (1995), "Software Review: SPSS for Windows, CHAID 6.0," *Journal of Marketing Research*, 32 (May), 245-254.

Green, P. E. and A. M. Krieger (1995), "Alternative Approaches to Cluster-based Market Segmentation," *Journal of the Market Research Society*, 37 (3), 221-239.

Green, P. E. and A. M. Krieger (1995), "Attribute Importance Weights Modification in Assessing a Brand's Competitive Potential," *Marketing Science*, 14 (3), 253-270.

Green, P. E. and J. Savitz (1995), "Applying Conjoint Analysis to Product Assortment and Pricing in Retailing Research," *Pricing Strategy and Practice*, 2 (3), 4-19.

Carroll, J. D. and P. E. Green (1995), "Psychometric Methods in Marketing Research: Part I: Conjoint Analysis," *Journal of Marketing Research*, 32, (November), 385-391.

Green, P. E. and A. M. Krieger (1996), "Individualized Hybrid Models for Conjoint Analysis," *Management Science*, 42 (June), 850-867.

Krieger, A. M. and P. E. Green (1996), "Modifying Cluster-based Segments to Enhance Agreement with an Exogenous Performance Variable," *Journal of Marketing Research*, 33 (August), 351-363.

Krieger, A. M. and P. E. Green (1996), "Linear Composites in Multiattribute Judgment and Choice: Extensions of Wilks' Results to Zero and Negatively Correlated Attributes," *British Journal of Mathematical and Statistical Psychology,* 49, 107-126.

Lenk, P. J., W. S. DeSarbo, P. E. Green, and M. R. Young (1996), "Hierarchical Bayes Conjoint Analysis: Recovery of Partworth Heterogeneity from Incomplete Designs in Conjoint Analysis," *Marketing Science,* 15 (2), 173-191.

Schaffer, C. M. and P. E. Green (1996), "An Empirical Comparison of Variable Standardization Methods in Cluster Analysis," *Multivariate Behavioral Research,* 31 (2), 149-167.

Carroll, J. D. and P. E. Green (1997), "Psychometric Methods in Marketing Research: Part II, Multidimensional Scaling," *Journal of Marketing Research,* 34 (May), 193-204.

Shea, J. A., P. E. Green, et al. (1997), "What Predicts Gastroenternologists' and Surgeons' Diagnosis and Management of Bile Duct Stones?" *Gastrointestinal Endoscopy,* 46 (July), 40-47.

Chaturvedi, A., J. D. Carroll, P. E. Green, and J. A. Rotondo (1997), "A Feature Based Approach to Market Segmentation via Overlapping K-Centroids Clustering," *Journal of Marketing Research,* 34 (August), 370-377.

Green, P. E., A. M. Krieger, and T. Vavra (1997), "Evaluating New Products," *Marketing Research,* Winter, 12-21.

Schaffer, C. M. and P. E. Green (1998), "Cluster-Based Market Segmentation: Some Further Comparisons of Alternative Approaches," *Journal of Marketing Research Society,* 40 (April), 155-163.

Krieger, A. M., P. E. Green, and U. N. Umesh (1998), "Effect of Level of Dis-aggregation on Conjoint Cross Validations: Some Comparative Findings," *Decision Sciences,* 29 (Fall), 1049-1060.

Green, P. E. and A.M. Krieger (1998), "Slicing and Dicing the Market," *London Financial Time,* September, 185-189.

Green, P. E. and C.M. Schaffer (1999), "Cluster-Based Market Segmentation: Some Further Comparisons of Alternative Approaches," *Journal of Marketing Research Society,* 40 (April), 155-163.

Vavra, T., P. E. Green, and Abba Krieger (1999), "Evaluating EZ-Pass: Using Conjoint Analysis to Assess Consumer Response to a New Tollway Technology," *Marketing Research,* Summer, 5-16.

Green, P. E. and A. M. Krieger (1999), "Evaluating Demand for Innovative Products," *London Financial Times,* September, 55-59.

Krieger, A.M. and P. E. Green (1999), "A Cautionary Note on Using Internal Cross Validation to Select the Number of Clusters," *Psychometrika,* 64 (September), 341-353.

Krieger, A.M. and P. E. Green (1999), "A Generalized Rand-Index Method for Consensus Clustering of Separate Partitions of the Same Data Base," *Journal of Classification,* 16, 63-89.

Krieger, A.M. and P. E. Green (2000), "Market Segmentation Involving Mixtures of Quantitative and Qualitative Variables," *Journal of Segmentation in Marketing,* 4 (1), 85-106.

Schaffer, C. M., P. E. Green, and F. J. Carmone (2000), "An Empirical Assessment of Univariate Screening Procedures in Cluster Analysis," *Journal of Segmentation in Marketing*, 4 (1), 107-125.

Green, P. E. Y. Wind, A. M. Krieger, and P. Saatsoglou (2000), "Linking Soft Data Collection Techniques with Strategic Market Modeling: A Case Application," *Marketing Research*, 12 (Spring), 17-25.

Krieger, A. M. and P. E. Green (2000), "TURF Revisited: Enhancements to Total Unduplicated Reach and Frequency Analysis," *Marketing Research*, 12 (Winter), 30-36.

Chaturvedi, A., P. E. Green, and J. D. Carroll (2001), "Market Segmentation Using Categorical Data," *Journal of Classification*.

Green, P. E., A. M. Krieger, and Y. Wind (2001), "Thirty Years of Conjoint Analysis: Reflections and Prospects," *Interfaces*, 31 (May-June), S56-S73.

Green, P. E. (2001), "The Vagaries of Becoming (and Remaining) a Marketing Research Methodologist," *Journal of Marketing*, 64 (July), 104-108.

Krieger, A. M. and P. E. Green (2002), "A Decision Support Model for Selecting Product/Service Benefit Positionings," *European Journal of Operational Research*, 142, 187-202.

Green, P. E. and A.M. Krieger (2002), "What's Right with Conjoint Analysis?" *Marketing Research*, Spring, 24-27.

Wind, Y., A.M. Krieger, and P. E. Green (2002), "Marketing Research in the Courtroom: A Case Study that Shows How Analytical Methods Can Be Applied to the Law," *Marketing Research,* Spring, 28-33.

Green, P. E., R. M. Johnson, and W. D. Neal (2003), "The *Journal of Marketing Research*: Its Initiation, Growth, and Knowledge Dissemination," *Journal of Marketing Research*, 40 (February), 1-9.

Krieger, A. M., P. E. Green, L. Lodish, J. D'Arcangelo, C. Rothey, and P. Thirty (2003), "Consumer Evaluation of 'Really New' Services: The TRAFFICPULSE System," *Journal of Marketing Services*, 17, April.

Illustrative List of Conjoint Analysis Applications
by Paul Green and Colleagues

Consumer Nondurables
- Bar soaps
- Hair shampoos
- Carpet cleaners
- Synthetic-fiber garments
- Gasoline pricing
- Panty hose
- Lawn chemicals
- Facial tissues
- Food and beverages

Financial Services
- Bank services
- Auto insurance policies
- Health insurance policies
- Credit card features
- Consumer discount cards
- Travel and entertainment packages
- Financial planning

Consumer Durables
- Automotive styling
- Automobile and truck tires
- Pickup truck design
- Car batteries
- Apartment design
- Toasters
- Commercial lawn mowing

Other Services
- Car rental agencies
- Telephone services and pricing
- Employment agencies
- Information retrieval services
- Employee benefits packages

Health Care/Pharmaceuticals
- Ethical drugs
- Diagnostic equipment
- Health maintenance organizations

Industrial Goods
- Copying machines
- Printing equipment
- Facsimile transmission
- Data transmission
- Portable computer terminals
- Diagnostic x-ray equipment
- Computers

Transportation
- Domestic airlines
- Transcontinental airlines
- Passenger train operations
- Freight train operations
- E-Z Pass
- TrafficPulse

Business Strategy
- McKinsey
- Booz-Allen
- A. D. Little
- BCG
- Bain
- Andersen Consulting

Brand Equity
- Shell-Texaco merger

Quality Function deployment
- Xerox copiers

Customer Satisfaction
- IBM
- Chrysler
- FedEx
- UPS

Index